BRETTLES OF

A history of a famous Derbyshire hosiery company and brand

Rod Hawgood and Gary Spendlove

Mayoral procession passing Mansion House, London.

BRETTLES OF BELPER

A history of a famous Derbyshire hosiery company and brand

Rod Hawgood and Gary Spendlove

ACKNOWLEDGEMENTS

First a confession: I never worked for Brettles. In fact, before I moved to Belper in 2006, it was just a name to me. Then I met Gary Spendlove, who had worked his way up through the ranks of George Brettle & Co. and now owned the brand – and he educated me. For the past year I have researched the history of the company, and am amazed how involved I have become. I now feel as though I was at least a 'fly on the wall' at every stage of its history, that each sports day or celebration event described is a good memory, and that every Works Manager's death was a personal loss.

I owe thanks to a number of people. First of all, on primary research, a big thank you to the staff of Belper North Mill Museum, especially to Natascha Wintersinger and Ray Marjoram, who have given me access to a large number of very relevant historical pictures and artefacts, and to renowned media photographer Nick Lockett for his services. Thanks to local historian Mary Smedley for her advice on the first chapter, helping to weed out some unconfirmed 'facts'. Thanks to the staff of Belper Library, of Derbyshire Records Office, and of the St John's Chapel Heritage Centre, having spent many hours at these worthy establishments, poring over books, documents and pictures.

I appreciate the earlier written accounts of various periods of Brettles' history, in particular, Negley Harte's exhaustive history of the original partnership and the first century of George Brettle & Co. For readers who would like a more detailed account than mine, especially of the financial progress and crises of the company, I would unhesitatingly direct them to Harte's book, 'A History of George Brettle & Co. 1801 - 1964', compiled in 1973. I have also been glad of the story of 'Ward Brettle & Ward' written by William Ward and John Finney in 1823, for the much later summary history compiled in-house for the bicentennial 'Brettles Supplement' of the Belper News in 1986, and for the older articles in the *Derby Mercury*, *Derby Evening Telegraph*, *Derbyshire Advertiser*, *Hosiery Times* and *Womens Wear News*. For the most part these have corroborated and confirmed each other; where they have differed, it has been an interesting challenge to reconcile them.

I wish to thank those employees of Brettles, past and present, too many to mention here, who have taken the time to tell me their stories and memories of past years. As I have carefully woven these together, I hope the result forms a worthy tribute to these important chapters of Belper's history; and of their own. Finally, a very special tribute to my friend and colleague Gary Spendlove, who has made all this possible – both the presence of the Brettles brand in Belper today, and also this book, which was his brainchild. He has been my inspiration and enabler in the writing of it.

Rod Hawgood

CONTENTS

INTRODUCTION

Welcome to the history of George Brettle & Co. I decided to compile this book primarily because the Brettles brand of Belper has a place in history as one of the world's largest hosiery manufacturers. The company were also one of the UK's largest employers, employing well over one thousand people in the late 19th century. Of course, in our age of multi-nationals and international business, a company of this size would not be considered as significant as it was a hundred years ago. But it is worth stating that a company like Brettles would still create many thousands of hours of employment for associated and co-operating business, for example with packaging, labelling, marketing, photography, transport, etc. You could add to this the many processes of garment manufacture undertaken away from the site, such as spinning, weaving, knitting, dyeing, printing, assembly, etc. All of these processes still come together for distribution from our Belper head office.

The earliest records of the Brettle family and its association with textiles appear in the eighteenth century. There was an association with the Wards' factory in Belper until George Brettle founded his own highly successful business. It is not easy to estimate the wealth of George Brettle but his net income would have been between two and three million pounds a year as a modern-day equivalent figure. As with most businesses, the fortunes of the company fluctuated, but a 'golden period' in the 1930s helped the then chairman Harry Twyford become Alderman, Sheriff then Lord Mayor of London just before World War II. There is clear documentation that Sir Harry entertained many members of the British monarchy and royalty from other countries. A wide mixture of international VIPs were also hosted by the Brettles Chairman, even including members of the German Nazi Party!

After the 1940 destruction of the London headquarters in the Blitz, the focus of operations was the factory built by Brettle at Chapel Street, Belper, which continued until the move to Alfreton in 1987. A major change to the business occurred in 1964 when the company became part of the Courtaulds empire. Various management strategies ensured the continuation of the brand, predominantly through the distribution network of what was still called 'the London side'. A tripling of the company's turnover in the 1980s and 90s was again seen to be a strong period for the company under the management of Chief Executive Gwyn Stevenson.

Following a failed management buy-out bid in 1997, the business was sold to Leicester-based underwear manufacturer Chilprufe. This could have been the end of the Brettles story, but the later demise of Chilprufe allowed the Slenderella management to purchase the Brettle and associated brands from the administrator and realise a lifelong ambition to own the brand and return it to its historic home in Belper.

The Brettles name is a registered trademark and the brand enjoys continuing growth as part of the Slenderella group. It is sold to consumers via many retail outlets, mail order companies and internet businesses, and exported to a number of countries around the world.

At the start of my career, in a meeting between myself and Tony Gray, the then Managing Director, Tony impressed me with a phrase, saying 'We are custodians of the brand.' So I am pleased and proud to say that the Brettles brand is again secure in committed private ownership and in a strong position to expand onwards into the twenty-first century. I hope you enjoy the story.

Gary Spendlove

1. THE ORIGINS OF BRETTLES

The name 'Brettles' has been well known everywhere for socks, stockings, knitted goods and textiles, but nowhere more than in its home town of Belper in the Derwent Valley of Derbyshire, where the business has grown and matured for over 200 years. From tiny beginnings in the early nineteenth century, it survived more than its fair share of difficulties to become the biggest local employer, comparing very favourably with other companies in manufacturing capacity and output, numbers of looms and of hands employed. From Belper, its products went far and wide. In recent times under its present management the Brettles range has been updated and has gone on to achieve record exports. The history of Brettles is therefore an important part of the history of Belper.

Earliest Origins

The fascinating story goes back at least three hundred years. For by the early eighteenth century, the English hosiery industry was concentrated in the three East Midlands counties of Derbyshire, Nottinghamshire and Leicestershire. It had been in the Nottinghamshire village of Calverton that in 1589 the 'stocking frame' was invented by William Lee, a young clergyman not long returned from Cambridge to his own village. It was one of the most complicated pieces of technology known to the pre-industrial world, with over two thousand separate parts, but it became the crucial piece of machinery in the European hosiery industry for the next three centuries.

London, as the political, commercial and fashion centre of the country, was the main market for high-quality luxury knitted silk goods, and it was natural that most of the early frames were established there. It was in London that the Worshipful Company of Framework Knitters was formed in 1657 to control the new trade, but by the 1690s that company was fighting a losing battle to maintain its privileges against the rising hosiery industry of the East Midlands. By the 1720s, more of the country's 8,000 stocking frames were in the East Midlands than in the London area,[1] the main competitive advantages being the supply of cheap labour, along with lower rents, fuel and food prices, combined with proximity to the supply of wool. Then the first pair of cotton stockings made in England were produced in Nottingham, from imported Indian yarn.[2]

Within the East Midlands, Leicester came to specialise in wool, Nottingham in cotton, and Derby in silk. To supply silk to this growing industry, Thomas Lombe built his silk-throwing factory in Derby in 1718. And Derby was the birthplace of the most important development of Lee's stocking frame forty years later.

Seven miles north of Derby, Belper had until the mid eighteenth century been a village of little consequence, regarded as 'low in population as it was backward in civility . . . the insignificant residence of a few uncivilised nailers',[3] a poorly paid and typically family occupation. In 1741 there was estimated to be just 532 people living there, in 113 houses. But the development of textiles in Belper owes its origins to three families – the Strutts, the Arkwrights and the Wards.

Strutt and Arkwright

Jedediah Strutt, the son of a small farmer, was born in July 1726 at Blackwell, near Alfreton. His mother came from Hazelwood near Belper. Jedediah's mechanical and creative abilities surfaced early when he built a working windmill, and his father apprenticed him at 14 to a wheelwright called Ralph Massey at Findern, just south of Derby, where he lodged with the Woollat family. In this family he met his future wife Elizabeth and her brother William, who later became his business partner in the framework knitting trade. Strutt finished his apprenticeship in 1747, and was briefly a journeyman wheelwright in Leicester, before returning to Blackwell to take over a farm left to him by his uncle.

However, Strutt's mechanical interests were directed towards the framework knitting industry. In the long, low garret of his farmhouse, he produced an attachment to the machine invented by William Lee over 150 years earlier to knit a firm rib for hosiery (previously only done by hand). In about 1758 the family moved to Derby, where Strutt and William Woollat went into business in hosiery. That year, Strutt's 'Derby Rib Machine' was finished, and patented for seven years.

Strutt and Woollat imported raw silk via London and spun it in their new silk mill at Derby. The thread was distributed to small frame shops and outworkers' cottages by the 'Middlemen', and the finished products were sent back to London. They then diversified into yarn, which was cheaper and more durable. In the course of his trading, Strutt was in regular touch with the development in Nottingham of a steady market in cotton hosiery, using cotton yarn from Lancashire and went into partnership with Samuel Need of Nottingham.

In 1768 Strutt entered into partnership with Richard Arkwright,[4] who had just come from Lancashire to Nottingham, the growing centre for cotton hosiery, bringing his ideas for revolutionising the process of spinning the raw material. With the help of Strutt and Samuel Need, Arkwright patented the Water Frame. Following this, again with Strutt's backing, by 1771 he had built his famous water-powered cotton-spinning mill at Cromford, just south of Matlock, marking the beginning of the Industrial Revolution.

Above: View of Round Mill (built 1809) with Mule Room (1820), Reeling Mill (1807) at centre and Junction Mill (1810) right, from West Mill. (Photographer A N Smith 1959) Courtesy of Belper Historical Society.

Strutt now focused his attention on Belper, seven miles downstream from Cromford. Inspired by Arkwright, but frustrated by the quality of yarn available for his hosiery business, Strutt did the same there. Between 1776 and 1778, he built his first large cotton mill at Belper. He followed this with a second between 1784 and 1786 (North Mill) and a third between 1793 and 1795 (West Mill). And Strutt did more for Belper than build the mills: he provided a good deal of workers' housing, in streets opposite North Mill named 'Long Row', 'Short Row' and 'The Clusters'. He also built the Unitarian chapel in 1788. Strutt lived in Belper himself during the 1780s, then built a small mansion at Milford near his latest mill, just south of Belper.

Belper Bridge, North Mill & chimney (built 1852), about 1900. Courtesy of Belper Historical Society.

Bridge Foot, West Mill and the 1897 Jubilee Clock tower. Courtesy of Belper Historical Socity.

East Mill, Round Mill, The Gangway and offices, from West Mill. (Photographer A N Smith 1959). Courtesy of Belper Historical Society.

West Mill with Junction & other buildings since demolished (Photographer A N Smith 1962). Courtesy of Ray Marjoram and Belper Historical Society Collection.

From Belper to America

The textile revolution spread throughout the British Isles to Europe, and went much further, thanks to another son of Belper, one of Strutt's managers. Samuel Slater was born in 1768, in Blackbrook near Belper, the fifth son of William Slater. The family were Methodists, and Thomas Slater held services in their kitchen from 1767. They were involved when John Wesley visited Belper in 1782 and 1786 and preached in the Market Place. The Central Methodist Church was built in 1807, and 'John Slater' built a chapel at Blackbrook in 1816.

Samuel Slater started a six-year apprenticeship with Strutt in 1782, at age 14, working in his Belper Mill, during which he found a way to wind more cotton onto a bobbin. Strutt was pleased with him and trained him to oversee the making of cotton frames, and later to help manage the construction of his new factory at Milford. Slater also helped Strutt in arranging the purchase of land and of water rights for this project.

However, Slater came across a newspaper from Philadelphia, USA in which he read of the generous bounties offered in the States to encourage manufacture. In 1789 he went to London and bought his passage to New York, a voyage that took 66 days. He found the American textile industry very much in its infancy, with water power unknown and cotton spinning still done by treadmill and donkey wheel, giving an uneven and lumpy yarn. His landlord was a blacksmith, and it was advantageous that Slater had experience of manufacturing machine parts. In great demand due to his experience, in January 1790 he started as a Manager for Moses Brown, a Quaker, with his company Almy & Brown at

Pawtucket, where he built a mill on the Arkwright model, which was claimed to be the first factory in America. This involved using some trade secrets learned from Strutt, and consequently he became known in Belper as 'Slater the Traitor' and took delight in sending a sample of his products to Strutt! In 1791 he married Hannah Wilkinson, daughter of his landlord, and in 1798 he entered a new partnership with his in-laws as Samuel Slater & Co., and also started a Sunday School for the children of the workers. How interesting that over two hundred years later, the towns of Belper and Pawtucket USA are twinned – any rivalry that may have once existed long since replaced by this expression of the 'special relationship' between the two countries

Samuel Slater and his factory in America (Photographer: Nick Lockett).

From Village to Town

Back in the Derwent Valley, the building of mills continued apace. During the last quarter of the eighteenth century a string of textile mills were built along the Derwent between Matlock and Derby. These inevitably changed the predominant employment from agricultural to industrial and increased the valley's population. Strutt lived at Milford in his closing years; he died in 1797 and was buried in the chapel at Belper which he had built just nine years earlier.

Strutt's sons, William, George and Joseph Strutt, continued the family business as 'W.G. & J. Strutt', and their cotton-spinning mills were the centre of the community. William had been with his father in the business for many years and now pioneered the much-needed fireproof mills as a response to the frequent fires. His first was built at Derby in 1793. In 1803 Belper's wood-framed North Mill burnt down, but William rebuilt it the following year to his revolutionary design, being iron-framed throughout, one of the first such buildings.[5] William's designs were also used in Derby buildings, such as the Infirmary built in 1810, which employed a heating system used in North Mill. He designed the St Mary's Bridge and other bridges, including one at Milford for access to the mills.

The coming of the mills had transformed Belper into a factory town. The first census, in 1801, recorded a population that had grown more than eightfold from 532 to 4,500 in just 60 years. By then it was considered to be 'one of the most flourishing places in Derbyshire', its population exceeding any town in the county except Derby itself. It then reached 5,778 by 1811, 7,235 by 1821, and slowed to 7,890 in 1831. A second spurt brought it to 9,885 in 1841, then it slowed to 10,082 by 1851, at which point it plateaued and stabilised for the next century.

Meanwhile the Strutts continued to invest in Belper philanthropically, building the town's first school (and one in Derby), which employed teachers and 'pupil teachers'. They later contributed in a large way to the cost of the new Anglican church of St Peter built between 1822 and 1824, replacing the small St John's Chapel, which is now a heritage centre. Church growth accompanied population growth in Belper, with the Central Methodist Church already established, Christ Church built in 1850 near the mills, the Congregational Church in 1872 and the Baptist Church in 1894, as well as smaller churches on the outskirts such as Pottery Methodist Church.

The Wards

Focussing in on hosiery, the Brettles story begins with John Ward senior, who in the second half of the eighteenth century carried on a hosiery business in Belper. It is unclear when this began, but in a letter to a prospective customer in 1812 his son stated, 'Our house is upon an establishment of 50 years' standing. We therefore do not spring up as new adventurers, in soliciting your orders' – which suggests it went back at least to 1762. In another letter two years later, he referred to men at Windley who up to 25 years earlier had been 'working to' his father, therefore in the 1780s.[6]

John Ward's mother had been a Strutt of Newton, near Blackwell in Derbyshire, and his sister Elizabeth married John Strutt, possibly the brother of the famous Jedediah Strutt.[7] So the two families were related before the latter became a successful Derby hosier, and before his partnership with Arkwright and the building of the spinning mill in 1776 that was to

Above: 'Kilburn Cheveners on Danesbury Rise, 'Denby Bottles', 1920' and **left**: 'Group of Cheveners, Mrs E.A. Gamble of Ripley (born 1905) on right, 1913'.

so utterly transform the community of Belper. Such family connections were important in business life, and significantly, a 'Mr. Ward' helped Arkwright with the building of the original Cromford Mill.[8]

It was very relevant to the Wards business that there were already many independent home-based handloom workers around Belper, and it was also a centre of 'chevening' (called 'clocking' by the London guilds), which was the embroidery onto stocking sides of a simple standard design resembling a lamp post with two branching legs. 'Clocked' stockings are over four hundred years old, for Queen Elizabeth I is reputed to have worn similar pairs of embroidered hose. This was a cottage industry, which was developed to produce a range of beautiful intricate designs embroidered onto stockings and socks. The source of the word 'chevening' is uncertain; one explanation is that it came from France, brought over by the French silk workers. Another attractive explanation is that it comes from the Chevin Ridge on the edge of Belper. Certainly, an old word that used to be used in Belper was 'chevir', meaning 'bring to a head'. The operation of 'clocking' or chevening involved bringing a thread of embroidery up the leg of a stocking to its head, using a blunted needle. The cheveners joined the seam of the stocking by hand in its undyed, unfinished state.[9]

The marriage register shows that on 16th April 1759, John Ward had married Susannah Bradley, the daughter of Benjamin Bradley, a well-to-do yeoman farmer of Belper.[10] This marriage produced seven children, the oldest being John junior, who was involved in the business by the early 1790s, since he was to write in 1812 that he had been making fashioned drawers 'for more than twenty years',[11] and by 1799 the firm was known as 'Ward & Son', a partnership business.[12] The Wards were big customers of the Strutts. Ledgers show that in 1799, the Wards were buying yarn worth some £20 per month from the cotton-spinning North Mill, and in the following year these yarn purchases increased substantially to average £60 per month.[13]

By 1801, John senior had retired, and his place was taken in the partnership business by James Carter Sharp of Duffield (just south of Belper). As 'Ward Sharp and Co.' they opened a warehouse in the City of London at 6 Cateaton Street.[14] There, a William Bacon was employed to sell their hosiery products to the retailers. Previously they would have sold to one of the larger hosiers, the wholesale or merchant hosiers who acted as middlemen between the producer and the retailer. Now, Ward and Sharp were able to deal with retailers direct, and could claim, as they did to a London retail customer in January 1802, that they 'charged you the same prices as we sell to the wholesale warehouses in town (who serve the retail shopkeepers). We therefore judge it is a thing impossible for them to sell you the same qualities at the same prices.'[15]

Following this important move into wholesale and into the London market, the firm seems to have initially undergone a considerable expansion. In 1802 their purchases of yarn from the Strutts totalled £1,475, an average of over £120 per month, twice as much as in 1800.

However, it would seem that this spurt was not maintained, and that problems arose at the London end. Customer complaints were received in 1802; John Ward claimed that 'complaints are both novel and unpleasant to us'. But when James Sharp went to London in 1803 to survey the affairs at that end, he was deeply dissatisfied. Indeed, in the words of John Ward's brother William, he was 'incensed at the manner in which they had been conducted' and the effects on the business, so much so that he 'determined upon withdrawing himself from the partnership'.[16]

John's brother William Ward was at this time employed in another London hosiery warehouse at 1 Milk Street, near Cateaton Street, which was owned by Thomas Smith and Sons. He knew of the problems and also that his brother John was 'individually insolvent' and that he was 'under arrest at the suit of Mr. Arkwright for about £700 or £800, in whose favour judgement was suffered to go by default for a debt contracted . . . previously to his partnership with Mr. Sharp'.[17] William therefore became alarmed for the consequences for John and for the family if the business had to be wound up abruptly, and he began to seriously consider 'whether any possible means could be found of saving his brother from approaching destruction'.[18] In seeking to offer a rescue deal, his thoughts turned to George Brettle, who like himself, was living in the house of Thomas Smith and Sons in London, and whom he regarded as of 'integrity and perseverance'.

Enter George Brettle

Nothing is known of the earlier years of George Brettle. Stories prevalent later in the firm were that he had been a Belper framework knitter, or that he began making stockings at Ilkeston in 1782, and that he rode to London in 1787 to sell his stockings, but these dates are discounted by the one known fact that he was born on 1st January 1778 (so he would have been a child prodigy!). There is therefore no firm evidence of any previous time spent living or working in Belper.

An article in the *Derby Evening Telegraph* of 5th March 1954 records that George Brettle's father Edward had been in business in Cateaton Street (now Gresham Street) as 'E. Brettle and Co. – haberdashers and merchants', and established the brand 'House of Brettle' in 1786, probably never dreaming that its bicentennial anniversary would be celebrated at Belper in 1986.

George Brettle served his seven-year apprenticeship with Thomas Smith and Sons in Milk Street, living with the other apprentices in the domestic quarters attached to the Smiths' warehouse. By this means he became a neighbour and colleague of William Ward – and the rest, as they say, is history.

2. GEORGE BRETTLE AND THE WARDS

In 1803 a crucial meeting took place – William Ward introduced George Brettle to his brother John as 'the means of rescuing John from his fearful situation'. As a result, on 21st July 1803 the new partnership of 'Ward Brettle & Ward' was formed by Brettle and the Wards to take over the business, assets and liabilities of Ward Sharp & Co. It was found that net assets totalled £3,067, of which £567 was to be credited to John Ward and £2,500 to James Sharp, who, however, allowed his capital to remain in the new partnership, in exchange for annual interest of 5 per cent and an allowance of £150 for seven years, after which time the sum was to be repaid in full. There was not even any cash in hand, just some stocking frames, a quantity of unsold stock and some book debts. Neither George Brettle nor William Ward brought any capital to the partnership, only a knowledge of the trade and the capacity to work hard, though they had the use of the Wards' Belper warehouse in Derby Road and the leased warehouse at Cateaton Street, London from the old Ward Sharp & Co.

On top of this uninspiring collection of assets, the bills accepted by Ward Sharp & Co. were daily becoming due, and there was also the problem of William Bacon, the warehouse manager, who had earlier been promised continued employment under such terms as could have constituted partnership in the eyes of the law. Indeed, shortly afterwards a bill was drawn by John Ward upon 'Ward, Brettle & Ward & Co.' and in explanation John Ward stated that the '& Co.' was intended for Bacon, John having promised that he would appear to the world as a partner![1]

In the view of William and George, Bacon was 'a man of broken fortunes and totally without credit', in more ways than one. They sacked him, and consequently one of the first things the new firm had to face was a bill in Chancery filed against them by Bacon. The beginnings of Ward, Brettle and Ward were far from auspicious.

The new partnership was surrounded by what William Ward called 'difficulties of the most appalling and distressing description', including the legacy debts, new bills arriving every week and the nightmare of litigation. Reflecting on the period, George Brettle wrote: 'I know and have experienced the racks and torments of embarrassed finances', and later he described it as 'the most anxious and painful course that men ever passed through'.[2]

Amazing Growth

Despite this, the dominant theme of the 30 years after 1803 was expansion, whether measured by the number of frames, of people employed, the range of goods produced or dealt in, by turnover, profit or assets – all told the same story.[3] In the first decade of the nineteenth century, each new frame cost from £25 to £50 depending on size, and a second-hand one £10. But partnership assets were £3,067 in 1803, £4,160 in 1805 and grew to £8,544 by late 1807.

The business became a valued employer in Belper. In late 1808, John Ward informed a customer that they had 'seven to eight hundred workmen constantly at work'. More were taken on in each of the following years, including 1812 when trade was briefly depressed. In November 1812 John Ward could claim that 'we have in our employ for several years upwards of one thousand workmen, consequently we make a great variety of sorts, we believe more than any other house in the trade'.

Pre-Factory Production

It should be explained that right up to about 1850, hosiery production was mainly a domestic industry. Most of the knitting machines owned by Brettles, as by the other hosiers, remained hand frames worked in the operatives' dwelling houses or in small workshops attached to them. In 1823, there were only 33 frames at the Belper warehouse. The remainder were in workshops up to 25 miles away from Belper. Ward Brettle & Ward frames could be found as far north as Wessington, Alfreton and Sutton-in-Ashfield, and as far east as Heanor and the suburbs of Nottingham, the places from whence stockingers later gave evidence to an 1844 inquiry. These domestic workshops contained between two and six frames, and sometimes up to ten.[4] Another special group of outworkers employed around Belper were the 'cheveners', who embroidered designs onto stockings and socks.

Journeymen, travelling on horseback, were employed to deliver the yarn from the Belper warehouse to these workshops each week, then to bring the almost-completed stockings back for linking and seaming. Then the finished goods were taken by coach and horses, or by pack-horses, mainly to the London warehouse, apart from some to customers in the Midlands and North.[5]

Marjorie Blount records that for the first two decades of the nineteenth century, many stockings were brought into Belper in bulk by carrier's cart from Nottingham to the warehouse, then collected and distributed by 'chevening mistresses' to the local women on their books. Often women would not receive their work until three in the afternoon, and it would be required for despatch early the next morning. One could often see rows of women, 'sitting in their doorways of their homes in order to catch the last of the light, with starched white aprons crackling and their bobbin-stands humming as they spun and threaded the silk', then often sitting at their table late into the night, with a lamp pulled close, intent and absorbed in her work. Every Saturday morning the mistresses could be seen 'carrying neat white bags, notebook in hand, going to collect their money'.[6]

Factory production, such as characterised the late eighteenth century, was unknown in the hosiery business at that time. The term 'manufactory' was sometimes used, and this incorporated both the warehouse and the multiplicity of small domestic workshops which were either outbuildings to or on the top floor of the framework knitters cottages.

The rapid advance in the number of framework knitters employed was matched by extensions to the firm's warehouse space. In 1812 the Belper premises were referred to as having been 'lately enlarged', and in 1809 or 1810 new larger London warehouse premises were taken at 119 Wood Street, replacing Cateaton Street, which was to remain the London address for the next 130 years. Wood Street formed part of that area north-east of St Paul's Cathedral which was the 'heart of London' for textile interests. There were many other hosiery houses, textile warehouses and a variety of dealers in goods such as lace, silk and ribbons. It was in nearby Gutter Lane in 1828 that Samuel Courtauld & Co. took their first London premises, the forerunners of the Courtaulds empire that would one day acquire the Brettles business – but that was still well over a century ahead.

In London, unlike Belper, a large number were employed within the warehouse, and discipline was strict. There was in fact even a 'scold's bridle' for use as a punitive measure for over-talkative women'! There was an article about it entitled 'Old Time Bridle' in the *Yarns* magazine of 1929, though it was already viewed as a curiosity that was last used 'many years ago'.[7]

Products

It would also be useful at this point to review the extent of the partnership's product range. The term 'hosiery' defined products made from yarn, whether silk, cotton or woollen, by the process of knitting. Usually wool or worsted was used in the Leicester area, cotton in the Nottingham area, and silk in the Derby area. The main hosiery products were stockings (called 'hose' in the trade) and socks (called 'half-hose', 'socks' being the term reserved for children's socks). The leading products of the Belper establishment were cotton stockings of various sorts – plain and ribbed, white, black and coloured, coarse and fine. They also made or dealt in pantaloons, drawers, gloves and caps.

In the first quarter of the nineteenth century, the number of drapers greatly increased. Drapers dealt primarily in pieces of cloth – whether woollen, cotton or linen – for the home production of clothing and bedding. They also kept a certain amount of ready-made clothing, hats, gloves and various hosiery, besides a multiplicity of threads, tapes, ribbons and trimmings that went by the name of haberdashery. It was to cater directly for this growing breed of trader that the wholesaling side of the partnership had been established. In addition to their own products, to supply their 'extensive connection among the retail linen drapers', the partnership also dealt in haberdashery and in various woollen piece-goods, sourced from the Manchester area and made from Yorkshire wool.

Over the first twenty years, many Ward Brettle & Ward customers outside London and the Home Counties were served direct from Belper, especially those in the Midlands and Yorkshire. The regular coach service between Birmingham and Sheffield passed through Belper, and was used to transport smaller quantities to both places. Goods were also sent by the wagons of Pickfords and other carriers to Liverpool, including some for shipment to Dublin. But from the mid 1820s it became normal to take all products to the London warehouse and then dispatch them from there. For example, a new Birmingham customer in 1822 had his order sent via London, 'from which place', it was explained, 'we shall prefer executing your orders, as we can do it more expeditiously and equally as advantageous to you in price as if sent from our manufactory, being in the habit of forwarding three or four times every week our goods as they come to hand to our London warehouse'.[8]

Wards factory, relatively recent, possibly by Fred Robson, courtesy of Belper Historical Society.

Wards workroom, Derby Road, about 1914, photographer unknown.

Above and opposite page: Wards workrooms, postcards by H Burkinshaw before 1919
Courtesy of Ray Marjoram and Belper Historical Society Collection.

'Trouble at Mill'

All, however, was not well between the partners – George Brettle and William Ward, the London partners, fell out with John Ward, the Belper partner. A dispute arose in 1823 over the way in which John was dealing with the Derbyshire stocking makers and over some building alterations. The Belper warehouse was mainly owned by John Ward, rent being paid by the partnership after 1803 for its use. John was building a new 'Trim Shop' there, a place in which the finishing processes were to be undertaken on the knitted goods, and was charging this work to the partnership. In Brettle's view this cost should have been met by John Ward as owner, or, if not, then arrangements should have been made for the others to share in the value of such buildings in the event of dissolution of the partnership. George wrote to him on 17th July 1823 that these alterations were 'simply to please your fancy' and that the business should not be charged, and also alleging irregularities in John's conduct of his end of the business, in that he had taken some £150 'out of the trade cash for his own use and not posted it to his debit'. John did not reply to this letter, and George wrote again on 28th July. This elicited an offer to 'stop the new erections' and a plea of unfair treatment. Then, on 9th August, John Ward offered to withdraw from the partnership.

A period of recrimination was then unleashed. In early September, John Ward wrote to George Brettle, superciliously in the third person:

> JW after twenty years acquaintance hopes he may presume to say that it would give him great pleasure to see GB in the same spirit he was in ten years ago. The increase of riches has certainly brought with it an undue increase of avarice, not only perceptible to JW but he has heard it noticed by customers.

Four days later, George Brettle responded in the same vein:

> In regard to GB's avarice, he thinks he may fairly shake hands with his worthy friend JW on that score. He has however the satisfaction to think that he has never indulged that passion at the expense of another mans labour.[9]

William Ward hurried to Belper to attempt a reconciliation, but John would have none of it. William, entirely in agreement with George Brettle, reluctantly recorded that they had both always felt that 'no reliance whatever could be placed on the co-operation of John Ward'. The firm's difficulties in its early years were in his view 'greatly aggravated by the total indifference which John Ward at all times displayed, even on the most trying occasions. Not only so but he even increased these distresses by making purchases of land and houses at the time when the necessities of the firm were the most severely pressing'.

The dispute was exacerbated by John Ward's insistence that Benjamin Bradley Ward, the youngest of the three Ward brothers, should replace him as partner. Benjamin had some years previously been unsuccessful in his own business, having managed in two years to lose not only £700 of his own money but the £1,000 business capital that 'Ward, Brettle & Ward' had lent him. He had then been employed by the partnership 'by way of asylum for him' and upon the express assurance to George Brettle that it should be 'at a modest salary'.

But William Ward stated that 'Benjamin Ward is by no means a person who would be the object of our free choice. We do not consider him by any means competent to the management of our concern, and he would consequently be a dead weight on us by perpetuation of a tax on our industry.'[10] Thus both Brettle and William Ward now categorically refused to have him as a partner, objecting to such 'dictation' by John Ward and feeling that they could run the firm by themselves. But as a sop they agreed to raise his salary to £400.

John Ward left the partnership on 18th September 1823, gave up his claim that Benjamin should succeed him, and allowed the remaining two partners the continued use of the Belper warehouse. He left his £31,506 share of the business almost entirely in the hands of the other two partners, with agreed terms that it be repaid at the end of ten years, and that in the meantime he would be paid 5 per cent annual interest, a concession that George Brettle felt was 'a terrible tax upon our future industry'. John retired to Cheltenham 'to attend to the restoration of his injured health'.

It may seem surprising that a family that had supported each other so loyally at their own cost − rescuing first John then Benjamin Ward − should fall out so badly, and more so that one of them, William, should side with a family outsider in preference to his own brothers. But no doubt he had good reasons. 'Contracts of partnership,' wrote Brettle, 'like those of marriage, must spontaneously flow from the feelings and the will.' Referring to William, he wrote: 'That our partnership should have endured so long and with so much harmony is a thing almost without parallel in the commercial world.' It might have been expected at this stage that the business name would have been simplified to 'Brettle and Ward', but this did not happen; it continued as 'Ward Brettle & Ward', perhaps at William Ward's request to leave the road open for another sibling to join in the future.

Left: Rear of Brook Cottage adjacent to Wards factory, where John then Benjamin Ward lived, showing the mill chimneys.

Below: Early picture of Brook Cottage, with the Smith family, 1800-1810. (Courtesy of Ray Marjoram and Belper Historical Society).

Growth and Prestige

Despite the payments to John Ward, business growth accelerated under the management of the two remaining partners. They turned a £14.6k net loss in 1822 into a £7k (9.2%) net profit the following year, which grew to 17.3 per cent and to a peak of nearly £22k net profit in 1827.

Products by now went all over the British Isles, and to mainland Europe and even America. And in addition to the main range of hosiery, the firm also produced silk stockings, which in those days were exclusive to the nobility and to royalty. They made silk stockings for King George III, silk stockings and socks for George IV, the stockings worn by Queen Victoria on her Coronation day, and cotton stockings made for Queen Marie of Spain. Similarly with quality underwear, they made the vest that Lord Nelson was wearing when he met his death at Trafalgar, which is still preserved at Greenwich.

In 1824 the firm owned 269 stocking frames in Belper.[11] But in 1829 Stephen Glover, a local commercial investigator, noted that the growth of the business had made the business 'the most extensive hosiers in the kingdom'. In addition to large quantities of ordinary hosiery, they produced '2000 dozen pairs of silk hose weekly and little less than one hundred thousand dozens yearly'. He later wrote: 'Messrs Ward Brettle & Ward of Belper are esteemed to be the most extensive manufacturers of hosiery goods in the world. They employ about 400 silk stocking frames . . . besides 2,500 cotton hose frames.'[12]

Luxury at Brixton

From owning next to nothing at the beginning of the nineteenth century, the partners made themselves wealthy men. In 1803 they had been collectively net debtors to the extent of nearly £2,000. By 1823, when John Ward left the firm, his share was worth over £31,000, and ten years later the shares of George Brettle and William Ward were worth £117,839 and £115,992 respectively. The annual salaries they had originally allowed themselves from the business were £91 and £105 respectively. By 1820, George's salary had already grown to £900, at a time when the threshold of the middle classes was put at £250 per year, from which it was possible to employ at least one servant. By the end of the decade George was receiving £1,400 per annum, and William similarly, enabling them to become 'gentlemen' in the upper reaches of the expanding middle class – and such was the life that they grew to lead, if one can judge by the houses they bought for themselves.

In about 1817 George Brettle established himself at Raleigh Lodge, a substantial residence with fifteen acres of land on Brixton Hill in Surrey, on what was then the southern edge of London. Here he could enjoy what at the time was called the 'remarkably pure' air of Brixton,

where many 'elegant seats and villas' were just beginning to be built, while being less than five miles from the firm's warehouse in Wood Street.[13] At about the same time he married a wife, Mary, who bore him two daughters, then three sons between 1819 and 1822.

Likewise, in the early 1820s William Ward became a resident of Cornwall Terrace, one of the grandiose Corinthian edifices newly erected by James and Decimus Burton to complete Nash's splendid plans for Regent's Park. Less than three miles from the Wood Street warehouse, William could enjoy the illusion of living in a magnificent mansion in a landscaped rural park. *The Gentleman's Magazine* referred to him as 'William Ward Esq. of Cornwall Terrace, Regent's Park and Wood Street, Cheapside, a very eminent wholesale hosier.'[14]

Left: Picture of Mrs. Mary Brettle (Courtesy of Ray Marjoram and Belper Historical Society Collection).

Death of the Partners

But monetary wealth and material luxury are only for this life; death comes to hovels and palaces alike. In his palatial house at Regent's Park, on 29th August 1833, William Ward died at the age of 58. His death activated an agreement he had reached with Brettle in 1827, which provided that neither the business nor the surviving partner should suffer in the event of the death of either of them. Ward's share was valued at the time of his death as £123,083/4/1d, and Brettle agreed to pay this to Anne Ward, William's widow, over ten years, with annual interest of 5 per cent. Even for someone in Brettle's position, payments on such a scale could not be easily made.

And so it was that George Brettle became the sole remaining partner. William had no children. Benjamin Ward, who had remained as the Belper factory manager, then made a fresh bid to become a partner in place of William, which was again refused. Realising that a serious rift was now likely, in February 1834 George purchased a piece of land known as 'The Croft' almost opposite the Belper warehouse, which had been owned by John Slater, a Shottle farmer. Then, to give a clear message, he changed the name of the concern to 'George Brettle & Co.' and wrote to all suppliers and customers accordingly on 7th August 1834. Later that month, Benjamin Ward issued a disingenuous contradictory circular, saying that his brother had died intestate, and that the manufacture of hosiery would be carried out at the same address as it had for many years, 'the last ten of which has been under my own immediate superintendence'. George Brettle responded with a corrective saying that for the last ten years he and William Ward were the only partners and that business would in future be conducted under the name of George Brettle & Co.[15]

From this point, production at the old premises became a breakaway rival concern. John Ward resurrected his business acquaintance with James Carter Sharp, his original partner of 1802, with his brother Benjamin and one 'Sturt', and the separate firm that they started became 'Ward Sturt & Sharp', producing in the original 'Ward Brettle & Ward' factory in Belper and using Leak Smith & Jones as their main selling agents, then renting their own London premises in Wood Street.

The loss of the Belper warehouse must have been a big blow to George Brettle. Many goods supplied by the business were not their own produce, so sourcing these would not have been affected, but with their own manufacturing resources at Belper and only the London warehouse remaining, maintaining quality and continuity of stock must have been a nightmare. George could have taken this opportunity to manufacture elsewhere in the country, but chose to continue doing so in Belper for commercial and economic reasons. A known and experienced workforce was crucial.

It should be remembered that at this time hosiery production was still mainly a domestic industry. At the time of the parting of the ways, most of the knitting machines remained hand frames worked in the operatives homes in the area around Belper.[16] So the loss of a warehouse did not mean the loss of the productive assets.

Many of the pre-1834 frames had belonged to the partnership and therefore now belonged to George Brettle. For these, all that had to be altered was the arrangement for the delivery of yarn and the collection and destination of finished goods, so the damage to George Brettle's manufacturing capacity would have been limited. But most of the frames belonged to individual stockingers or bagmen; these workers with their own frames would have had a choice as to who they worked for.[17] Many may have thought it less risky to produce for the existing Belper mill (the Wards), and daily life for these stockingers would have continued unchanged. We do not know how many transferred allegiance – no doubt incentives would have been offered by both sides, but unfortunately there appears to be no record of this.

Clearly, Brettle's new building at 'The Croft' had to be erected very quickly. The first stone was laid in May 1834 and it was completed by June 1835. New staff would have been recruited, or old staff re-employed. And so, after a ten months' gap, Brettles had a Belper base once again, and anyone travelling from Derby through Belper would have passed between the two rival concerns, together no doubt employing a large percentage of Belper residents. It is interesting that both in Belper and in London, as is often the case with rival banks today, the two had adjacent premises.

Then disaster struck – after just four months' production at the new factory, George Brettle suddenly died on 18th October 1835. Like William Ward at his time of death, he was only 58, and now the business was totally denuded of top management, with no partners left, and also a new cashflow problem. Only two payments had been made to Anne Ward, and under the terms of the agreement, the whole balance now became due in six months. How could the business survive such a plight?

But survive it did, for George Brettle had provided for just such a situation, and his family were also committed to the continuation of the business. In the will made four months before his death, George had stipulated that a £20,000 share be left to his wife and £10,000 to each of his daughters, and the remainder of his estate and management of his business be left in the hands of three friends, 'upon trust to carry out my trade and business of a wholesale hosier and manufacturer of hosiery now carried on in Wood Street, Cheapside and at Belper . . .'.[18] The three trustees were to be John Samson of Broad Street, Cheapside, Thomas Stokes, a wholesale hosier of Leicester, and Benjamin Hardwick, a solicitor of Cateaton Street. They were intended to operate the business until Brettle's youngest son attained the age of 21, enabling all sons to become partners.

But early in 1836, soon after the will had been proved, John Samson and Thomas Stokes both renounced the powers and rights that Brettle had conferred on them, leaving Benjamin Hardwick as the sole trustee. He somehow managed the business, while continuing to practise as a solicitor in the partnership of Hardwick and Davidson close to the Wood Street premises. The three Brettle sons were employed in the business, but under the terms of their father's will they were not allowed to undertake any decision-making or management in those years.

So it was not a good situation. Both partners dead, no full-time top management, a partly 'new' workforce at Belper whose loyalty and reliability had yet to be tested, and an immediate big debt to William Ward's widow. That the business survived the 1830s is nothing short of a miracle.

One person who seems to have given some continuity was Thomas Wilson Elstob, who had worked for the firm since 1827. For some years he had been manager of the 'counting house department' and had been George Brettle's 'confidential clerk'.[19] It would appear that he then played a crucial role in the management of the Belper manufactory during the period of Benjamin Hardwick's trusteeship. Trusted by the Brettle family, who expressed their 'utmost confidence in his integrity', he was destined to become a partner alongside the Brettles' sons.

3. UNDER THE BRETTLE BROTHERS

The year before his death, George Brettle had renamed his firm 'George Brettle & Co.', signifying a final break with the Ward family. His son George Henry must have been very happy about this name, and would eventually become the sole owner. But that was some years ahead – all was now in place for the three sons to become equal partners. After eight years of management by trusteeship, in 1843 George Brettle's three sons succeeded to their partnerships. Edward was 24, George Henry was 23 and Alfred was 21, and they

Above: Brettles Fire Engine, manufactured 1840.

made Thomas Elstob into the fourth partner without obliging him to provide any capital.[1]

The firm that the Brettle brothers inherited in 1843 was a prosperous one, though in output it had not yet made up the ground lost to the Wards business nine years earlier. Back in 1829 they were said to have employed 400 silk frames and 2,500 cotton frames, so 2,900 in total.[2] In 1844, Brettles had 'about 300 to 500' silk frames and only 'about 2,000' cotton frames, so at least 500 cotton frames fewer than before.[3] Meanwhile, the Wards firm had grown to a peak of about 4,000 frames, though only about half of these were owned, the rest belonging to individual stocking-makers or 'bagmen'. That firm was described by the Parliamentary Commissioner in 1844 as 'the most extensive manufacturers of hosiery in the kingdom'.[4]

By this time, it does seem that the two Belper companies were about the largest of their kind in the country. For comparison, in 1844 the well-known hosier Samuel Fox of Derby employed 700 frames.[5] One Nottingham hosier claimed to be 'perhaps as large a frame-holder as any individual in the country' when he employed 700 frames.[6] In 1841, William Felkin referred to the largest house in the trade as employing 3,000 frames, the second 2,000, a third and fourth about 1,800 each and a fifth employing 1,500.[7] Almost certainly the two biggest were the Wards and Brettles of Belper, followed by the two leading Nottingham firms, Hurst Sons & Ashwell, who employed 2,000 frames in 1844, and I. & R. Morley, who employed 2,700 frames in 1854.[8]

The domestic system of production suited both 'man and master', and the number employed was very much greater than the number of frames. 'The principal part of the framework knitters' family', stated one Belper stockinger in 1844, 'are employed in their business.'[9] Thomas Whittaker McCallum, the manager of Wards' cotton department, indicated that the 4,000 frames they employed created employment not only for 4,000 framework knitters, but also for about 2,000 seamers, 800 winders, 100 frame-smiths, needle-makers and sinker-makers, 100 dyers and bleachers, 300 embroiderers or cheveners, and 200 minders, trimmers and makers up – a total of some 3,500 in addition to the knitters themselves.[10]

Furthermore, size and quality apparently went hand in hand. Benjamin Morley of Nottingham stated in 1844 that the two Belper companies and his own 'make the best goods'. Referring to a market trend towards cheaper products, he complained that the threat to top-quality lines 'bears more upon ourselves and the two Belper houses than all the rest put together'.[11]

The Life of the Brothers

Like their father before them, the three brothers established themselves as 'gentlemen', whose lives were not restricted by the need to be over-involved in the day-to-day business of dealing in hosiery.

Of the three brothers, Alfred seems to have been considered the 'black sheep' of the family, and lived a stylish but unstable life. He was apparently married five days after his 21st birthday in 1843, but his wife died after two years. By 1852 he was living at Combe Hay House, a fine mansion in a wooded valley in Somerset, a few miles south of Bath. In 1855 he moved to an address off Park Lane in London, and the following summer to a residence in the Champs Elysées in Paris. There, in somewhat mysterious circumstances, he died in October 1856, aged only 34. It was officially stated that he died of epilepsy, but it appears that in reality his death was the result of falling out of his carriage after drinking too much champagne at the Chantilly races. He left most of his money to a 'Mrs Sophie Cunningham' and her children. A report of Chancery proceedings of 1864 refers to her as Alfred Brettle's daughter, but it seems very unlikely for a man of 34 to have a married daughter, let alone one with three children.[12] An air of mystery surrounds his life and death. Be that as it may, Edward and George Henry Brettle had to repay his share, which was valued at £57,447, and did so at the rate of £3,829 per annum from 1857, plus 4 per cent interest on the outstanding sum.

Edward Brettle, the eldest brother, remained a bachelor. He lived for a time in Regent Street, before taking the lease of an elegant flat in the Albany, off Piccadilly, in 1850. His account book shows that he took a large salary from the business and his expenditure levels were very high from the start – £1,909 in 1844, £1,765 in 1845, £3,593 in 1846, then never less than £3,000 in the ensuing years up to 1860. He paid regular subscriptions to the City of London Club, the Royal Yacht Club, the Society of Arts, the Surrey Reform Registration Society, and contributed £200 to the Patriotic Fund at the beginning of the Crimean War. By his forties, he had a grand country residence and a substantial estate at Henley Park in Surrey, between Aldershot and Guildford.[13] But he died on 20th May 1867 aged 47, as the *Derby Mercury* said, 'after a lingering illness of cancer in the throat'.[14]

Meanwhile, Thomas Elstob had played an increasingly important part in the running of the firm. This was reflected in his salary, which was £800 in 1844 then increased by £100 each year, except in 1847 when it jumped by £300. By 1853 he was receiving £1,800 and a sixteenth share of profits. It seems likely that he played the most important management role until his death in October 1866.

Poverty alongside Riches

The high salaries of top management contrasted sharply with the wages of the workers. In 1844 the typical wage of the framework knitters employed by Brettles – on their manager's own estimation – was between seven and fifteen shillings a week.[15] At most, therefore, the best workmen could earn up to £37 per year. Nor was this confined to Brettles. One Belper stockinger, after careful comparison of earnings, estimated that in 1844 the average earnings of the framework knitters in the town, clear of deductions, was 7/2d per week – less than £20 per annum.[16]

Nor was this just a Belper problem. The poverty of framework knitters and their families throughout the country was notorious in the early nineteenth century. Several Parliamentary enquiries were held to investigate the problems of the hosiery industry, of which the most exhaustive was undertaken in 1844–5, in the course of which the Belper companies were visited. William Wallis, who was the manager of the cotton department of George Brettle & Co. at the time, produced some figures for the Commissioner to show the year-by-year costs of making pairs of stockings and that both prices and wages were closely related to costs.[17] From these figures it appears that wages fell rapidly between between 1811 and 1819, recovered slightly in the early 1820s, fell again between 1825 and 1829, then stabilised in the 1830s and early 1840s. 'There has been no alteration, to my knowledge', stated Wallis in 1844, 'within the last twelve years.'[18]

On top of this, the stocking workers with 'company frames' had to pay 'frame rents' for the use of these, which was a running sore. Brettles' rates had long been fixed: they charged their workmen between 10d and a shilling a week according to the size or gauge of the frame. The managers regarded a fixed rent as fairer than charging a percentage on the work actually done, since that would, as Wallis put it, 'charge the hardworking man more than the idle one'.[19] But what appears to have been overlooked by management is that these frame rents were forming an increasing burden on the stockingers when their earnings were falling or the cost of living rising.

John Webster Hancock, manager of the Brettles silk department, was a fierce defender of the system of frame-renting. He was a man of strong individual opinions, and he did not hesitate to inflict them at length on the Commissioner on his 1844 visit to Belper. Hancock showed himself as having no great sympathies with the workers. He stated:

> There is sadly too much 'pretty prattle' to the working classes nowadays. It grows fulsome and they will get no good by it in the end. Their faults are many, and many of them are faults which they themselves could mend. I am no worshipper of the working classes. I have seen too much of them . . . Flatter them with fine words, tell them of great rights which are unjustly denied them, and which they could wield to perfection if they had them, and no men could be more attentive. You are an oracle; they will follow you through any political moonshine. But try to do them some good in their everyday business, and you are met on every side by knavery and tricks . . . The right of capital to gag and rob is not more universally acted upon than the right of poverty to cheat. Make it a rule to allow men their rent during sickness, and some rogues would scarcely ever be well. Our machinery would be worked for other people, and the workmen would pocket the rent. Every night's poaching, every drunken bout, every row and spree would be at our expense.[20]

Not a desirable boss, perhaps! But he was also scathing of capitalism:

> 'The main source of the evils facing the trade is the competitive system. All business now is war. We have left off in Europe, at least, the musket and the bayonet, and have taken to a sort of thuggery in the streets. Look where you will, they are all at it, stifling one another.'[21]

It would be interesting to know what the Brettle brothers thought of their Belper manager's outspoken views. Interestingly, the 1845 report said that Brettles employed two thousand hand frames on cotton hosiery, spread over the neighbouring villages for twenty miles around, in shops of between two to ten frames.

The poverty of hand-frame workers was a long-standing problem that Brettles inherited rather than created. An interesting 'talk on Belper' in 1901 (author unknown, but stored in St John's Chapel) states:

> In olden times, the old hand frame could be heard in this town and in the villages and hamlets around, with its well-known 'z-z-z-gigglle-a-gog-gog'. Wherever you hear that music, you could hear poverty. One man who had done it all his life told me, 'Stockinin is the poorest trade in the world. Many a thousand men has worked at it all their lives, never get above six or seven shillins a wick. Some as done rather better at the best sorts o work. But its bin a poor job for me, aw can assure yo. Need to pay for frame rent, for standing room, cost of needles, and light and life itself.'

The Royal Commission had started a long process, which would lead eventually to frame rents being abolished throughout the UK, but this prospect of lost revenue motivated management to recover it in other ways, to 'rein in' the frames for greater control, and to look for ways to centralise production and gain the economies of scale. As is so often the case in capitalist progress, a small victory gained for the workers, in this case home-based handloom workers, would be offset by the loss of their independence and autonomy in the long term.

New Fashions

Certainly the competition amongst hosiery manufacturers was intense, and market pressures from the late 1830s had forced them to trim costs – including labour – to the bone. Changes in fashion can be crucial for the textile trades. Up to 1837, as Hancock stated, 'middle class ladies including the wives and daughters of the better class of shopkeepers, manufacturers and professional men, were large consumers of silk stockings'. Thereafter, the demand fell off sharply, and depression rapidly struck the framework knitters. In the early 1840s Brettles were forced to set many of them to the making of woollen and thread gloves.[22]

Chevening had experienced a revival as the simple Regency style went out of fashion and the more elaborate wardrobes of the Victorians came into vogue. It had become the fashion to wear embroidered lisle, cashmere, cotton or silk stockings beneath the voluminous petticoats of the time. Indeed, the stockings worn by Queen Victoria on her Coronation day came from Brettles, and the firm subsequently added increasingly to its range of patterns and designs offered.

But the finest quality of silk stockings came to be less in demand with both ladies and gentlemen. The former were taking to long dresses, and the latter to trousers and boots. As Victorian practice succeeded Regency style, ladies were not showing off as much leg, and did not feel the need for the top-quality and more expensive stockings, which were now seen as impractical.

The new thinking was set out in 1844 by John Withers Taylor, the manager of Ward Sturt & Sharp's silk department:

> The moment a lady got a pair of good stockings on, if it was a dusty day they would not be seen for the dust covering them, and if it was a wet day they would be all over mud so that there would be no inducement for any lady to put on a pair of well-fashioned stockings. The gentlemen, on the other side, have taken to wearing boots

almost universally, and they want nothing under the boot of a fine kind. It does not matter to them how the stocking is made, if it will wear as well. All these things have a tendency to drive the manufacture into a lower grade altogether, for an article that is purely invisible in the wearing.[23]

Left: 'Lisle Stockings' and **below** 'Prices of Socks, 1856' (Photographer : Nick Lockett).

GEORGE BRETTLE & CO.,
119, WOOD STREET, LONDON.

MANUFACTORY, BELPER, DERBYSHIRE.

1856 to March 1857

PRICES OF SOCKS.

COTTON	1	2	3	4	5	6	7	8	9	10	WORSTED	1	2	3	4	5	6	7	8	9	10
F. White		0 10	1 4	1 10	2 4	2 10	3 4	3 10	4 4	4 10	Wt., Blk., Slate, Sorted & Grey		2 2	2 8	3 2	3 8	4 2	4 8	5 2	5 8	6 2
Fine		1 0	1 6	2 0	2 6	3 0	3 6	4 0	4 6	5 0	Best Wt.,Bk.,Slate,Sorted&Grey		2 8	3 2	3 8	4 2	4 8	5 2	5 8	6 2	6 8
Best Fine		1 6	2 0	2 6	3 0	3 6	4 0	4 6	5 0	5 6	Scarlet		2 4	2 10	3 4	3 10	4 4	4 10	5 4	5 10	6 4
Super		1 11	2 5	2 11	3 5	3 11	4 5	4 11	5 5	5 11	Best Scarlet		2 10	3 4	3 10	4 4	4 10	5 4	5 10	6 4	6 10
Fine Bleached		1 1	1 7	2 1	2 7	3 1	3 7	4 1	4 7	5 1	Best 3 Threads Sorted		4 3	4 9	5 3	5 9	6 3	6 9	7 3	7 9	8 3
Super ditto																					

George Brettle II

The death of Elstob in 1866 and Edward Brettle the following year left George Henry Brettle as the only remaining partner and now in sole charge of the firm which already bore his name. Whilst continuing to take an active interest in the business, like his brothers he too had set himself up with a country seat. From about 1864 he had lived at Mongewell House in Oxfordshire, on the Thames just a mile downstream from Wallingford. Surrounded by 'extensive and well-arranged grounds' of some eighty acres, the house was formerly the southern seat of the Bishop of Durham.[24]

At that time, the firm consisted of five departments, each dealing in quite a range of goods:

- **Hosiery** – cotton hose and half-hose, silk and spun, lisle thread plain and lace, Balbriggan hose, socks, woollen and merino hose, shirts and pants, underclothing.

- **Fancy Hosiery** – knitted polkas, gaiters, boots, caps, hair nets, etc.

- **Gloves** – kid, silk, lisle, thread, cashmere, mitts, etc.

- **Haberdashery** – fringes, trimmings, braces, purses, umbrellas, carpet bags, shirts, neck ties.

- **Flannels** – real and imitation Welsh, Lancashire and Saxony, blankets and serges, carpets, rugs.

The majority of these items were bought in, so the commercial side of the firm in London continued to be considerably greater than the manufacturing side at Belper.[25]

George's takeover of the ownership and top management of the firm was not the easiest of times, and before the end of the year, recognising his responsibilities but feeling unable to commit to lone management, he brought four of the firm's senior employees into the partnership. These were William Smithyman Bean, Parmenas Martin Burgess, George Dickson and Frederic William Sharp. Bean had been in the firm since 1829, Sharp since 1835, Dickson since 1838 and Burgess since 1840.

Above: View of Brettles Mill and surroundings. Postcard Picture taken by Mrs Stone, Nether Heage, 1900s.

Towards Mass Production

The main company achievement of this period was the late progression to full factory production. The domestic system had hung on as it suited both sides of the industry, for it enabled convenient family involvement, maximised use of the frames and output, and had the advantages of today's remote and flexible working. That apart, management had long believed that it was or would be very difficult to harness steam power or water power for centralised hosiery production. 'One great argument against our introducing the factory system', said one of the Wards managers in 1844, 'is that we cannot find any means of employing steam power.'[26] For Brettles, John W. Hancock had gone further: 'Stockings cannot be made by power, and I believe they never will be.'[27]

But the need to attain the economies of scale would find its own solution. The first successful factory producing hosiery had been erected in 1851 by the Nottingham firm of Hine & Mundella. Opening in the same year that the Great Exhibition at Crystal Palace was focusing attention on industrial progress, it excited much attention.[28] But most hosiers decided to 'wait and see'.

The breakthrough nationally came in the 1860s through William Cotton, the best-known name of those involved in the mechanisation of hosiery, who then invented the most satisfactory form of rotary frame, the original 'Cotton's Patent'. The rights to this were bought by Hine & Mundella, who extended their factory accordingly in 1866, and later also by Morleys of Nottingham.

But already, small moves towards factory production had been started in some places, including Belper. Here the way was led by Wards, who had introduced steam power into their dyeing and bleaching works by 1846. Their 'extensive' finishing establishment was situated opposite their warehouse on the Derby Road, immediately to the south of Brettles' warehouse, and there they employed a 40 hp steam engine.[29] Brettles products at that time were still being sent to specialist dyers and bleachers in Nottinghamshire. In 1849 the Wards warehouse was destroyed by fire, but it was rebuilt the following year, and with it a factory containing 30 ordinary hosiery frames, 36 circular machines and six or eight described as 'very wide ones that go by steam power'.[30]

Brettles appear to have started their first real factory at about the same time. John Ross, manager of the firm much later, in the 1930s, did his own research and concluded that 'about 1850, accommodation was provided for both hand-frames and power rotary frames in factory premises'.[31] It is not possible to trace his sources, but in 1873 it was discovered that 'the Factory' (which was described as 'fire-proof') and 'the Factory Frames' were not covered by insurance as was the warehouse. In 1874 there was reference to 'the Factory' having been 'kept going constantly' during the previous two years.[32] So, at the latest, it was up and running by 1872.

The outside hand looms were brought into the factory. In the early days of no gas or electricity, night work and anything 'after dusk' was a problem. Brettles' solution was to hang a glass bowl of water, coloured light blue, beside a machine, and then put a lighted candle behind it. The bowl refracted the light right along the machine, giving a glow which resembled daylight.[33]

But the coming of electricity enabled the scaling up of production and of exports. Related to this, in 1870, Charles Cotton, brother to the better-known William Cotton, and who was also a hosiery machine builder, invented an improved rotary knitting machine.[34] Brettles became interested in this. On 3rd May 1871 Isaac Hanson, by now the Belper manager, wrote to the partners in London about it:

> In regard to the new Patent Frame, Parker and I saw it yesterday and have an idea of its making as valuable a machine as Morleys & Mundella's patent . . . In some points it is superior . . . There are several Nottingham people after it, but the man agrees to hold it open for GB & Co. until Tuesday next. He wants to come and install it in our shop at £2 per week, would be finished in about a month, and would then sell it to us for £80, and would sell the patent for £250 . . .

This was agreed, and Brettles bought the patent in order 'for them to either build, work or vend the said machine'.[35] They then developed the improved methods it brought to the production of fashioned wool, mercerised lisle and pure silk stockings. Sales and customers grew and the firm made a serious start with exporting. All this appears to have been achieved during the years of George Henry Brettle's leadership and that of his four chosen co-partners.

But just four years after this team was fielded, it was left captainless. George Henry Brettle became seriously ill late in 1871, and on 29th January 1872 he died, aged just 52. One of his partners wrote of 'his shattered constitution' that 'in trying to remedy the evils of one disease it affected another, and so the poor man died of dropsy and diseased liver'. He was buried in a simple grave in the grounds of the old Norman church at Mongewell, where his brother Edward was also buried. But both brothers' names (though not Alfred) appear under that of their father on his monument in St Peter's Church at Belper, close to the altar. Constructed by Sir Richard Westmacott, and described by Pevsner as 'of the best workmanship', it portrays a languishing Grecian female.[36]

Thus the business had survived and grown under George Brettle's sons, but had been overtaken by some others. Within a decade of George Brettle's death in 1835, the claim to be 'the most extensive hosiers in the kingdom' could no longer be made, as the Wards expanded their manufacturing capacity and outstripped them for the next sixty years. Also, by mid century the claim to be the largest firm of merchant hosiers had been lost to I. & R. Morley, whose London warehouse was rebuilt on a grand scale in 1850.[37] But survive they did – and survive well.

Opposite: Brettles Memorial, St Peter's Church, to George Henry Brettle and Edward Brettle (Photographer: Nick Lockett).

IN MEMORY OF
GEORGE BRETTLE. ESQUIRE
OF RALEIGH LODGE. BRIXTON HILL:
BORN 1ST JANUARY 1778. DIED 18TH OCTOBER 1835.

ALSO OF **EDWARD**. ELDEST SON OF THE ABOVE:
DIED 20TH MAY 1867. AGED 48 YEARS.

ALSO OF **GEORGE HENRY BRETTLE. ESQRE**
OF MONGEWELL HOUSE:
SECOND SON OF THE ABOVE DIED 29TH JANY 1872
IN HIS 52ND YEAR.

4. THE COMING OF THE TWYFORDS

Like both his brothers, George Henry Brettle left no sons, and so there was a good deal of concern about the future of the firm. However, as George Dickson, one of the four remaining partners, wrote to a customer in March 1872, 'It was Mr Brettle's dying wish that dear old Wood Street should be protected . . . I am happy to tell you that arrangements are being made that the business will be continuing as before, as the widow has been left sole executor . . .' Apart from a few personal bequests to servants, George Brettle left all his property to his wife, Helen.[1]

In June 1872 Helen signed a new partnership agreement with her husband's junior partners, Bean, Burgess, Dickson and Sharp. She was to have 'paramount control' of the business, while its management was to be undertaken by the others, with George Dickson as 'the financial partner' having 'the principal and chief management'. The partners were to have a larger share in the firm's profits than they had previously: each was to receive a sixth of the profits, and Helen Brettle the remaining third. George Dickson said the partners thought the new agreement 'a very fair and liberal paper'. It was arranged to have 'a mahogany box' in which to send the accounts to Mrs Brettle for her periodic perusal, and this arrangement continued throughout the rest of her life.

In April 1873, fifteen months after she had been widowed, Helen Brettle found a new husband. She married a Colonel Henry Robert Twyford. He had been an officer in the army, a Captain in the 36th Regiment of Foot Soldiers, and from 1864 a Lieutenant Colonel in the 2nd Administrative Battalion of the Hampshire Rifle Volunteers.[2] The Twyfords lived at Trotton, a village in Sussex between Midhurst and the Hampshire border, where they were lords of the manor.[3]

When Helen Brettle became Mrs Twyford, it was agreed that she would carry on the business of George Brettle & Co. as 'femme sole', independently of her husband. She sold Mongewell House in Oxfordshire, and they set up home together at Bournemouth.

Weathering the Great Depression

The 1870s were the decade which came to be perceived as the 'Great Depression' compared with the previous Victorian prosperity. It was a tough time for the business, and for the hosiery trade as a whole, and this was reflected in George Dickson's reports from Wood Street to Helen Twyford. In April 1874 he wrote that trade was 'very far from satisfactory', and later that year that 'business is very indifferent and backward, that is, people will put off their purchases to the very latest time'.

After a slight improvement in 1875 and 1876, he wrote in 1877 that trade was 'very bad indeed', and noted that in terms of payments the firm was receiving 'numerous applications for accommodation' from its customers, and that he had 'never felt nor known such internal anxiety regarding business'.

Helen Twyford expressed her disappointment at that year's accounts:

> The expenses sweep away the bulk of the profits, I might almost say the whole. Belper again allowed to languish, its production getting lower year by year whilst we buy from other manufacturers what we are capable of producing ourselves. Unless some very great change in the result of our trading takes place, there is no inducement to me to continue the house as far as I am concerned.

Solemn words, but no immediate solution was at hand. In 1879 again, Dickson said trade was simply 'deplorable'.[4]

Dickson recognised that part of the problem was German competition. From the 1860s the textile area of Chemnitz had been quick to adopt the latest technology and machinery.[5] And in 1876 Dickson was especially concerned to hear that the German manufacturers had lowered their wages by 10 per cent, making them lower even than those in England and their prices consequently more competitive.

Besides this, there were internal problems in the company. Frame rents had been finally abolished by Act of Parliament in 1874, but discontent over rates of pay continued, and in 1876 the firm had to face its first major strike of factory employees. However, damage was mitigated by the large stocks and slowness of trade. 'I know it is painful for you and us to see the factory steam-power still,' wrote Dickson to Isaac Hanson, the Belper manager, 'but it could not occur at a time more suitable for us.' Were it not for the strike, he pointed out, the factory would only 'be working for the uncertainty of next year's trade'.[6] The firm were saved the expense of paying wages at a time when more output was not needed. It was well timed; in terms of production, it was expedient to stand still.

The firm received expressions of sympathy from other manufacturers, and Wards offered their help, placing their machinery and premises at Brettles' disposal. Caught in the same slump themselves and with spare capacity, they could no doubt well afford to do so! However, it does suggest that whatever acrimony there may have been between the two Belper firms was now a thing of the past.

Soon after, George Brettle & Co. lost three of its partners. In May 1877 William Smithyman Bean died, after 46 years with the firm. In the same year Frederic William Sharp retired, having reached his personal goal of having accumulated capital of £20,000. Then in October 1879 Parmenas Martin Burgess resigned, after 39 years with the firm, leaving George Dickson as the only working partner. The following year, Helen Twyford brought two more senior employees into the partnership. They were Isaac Hanson, Belper factory manager since 1864, and John Scott, cotton department manager in London. At the same time, in a new will she left the business to her husband, expressing her 'wish and intention . . . that my said husband carry on the same for his own benefit after my decease'.[7]

At the end of 1880 George Dickson compiled comparative figures for the previous forty years. These have not survived, but remarkably, despite the problems described, he said in summary that the sales for 1871–80 showed a total increase of £155,837 over those for 1861–70, and of £312,203 over those for 1841–50. Furthermore, early in the depression the firm had invested in its future. In 1874, improvements to the factory buildings and to the steam engine had been undertaken, and new frames put in. A new access road was made at the back of the factory 'for the purpose of carrying coals, timber and boilers or other heavy machinery'.

Colonel Twyford's Takeover

In the general election of 1880, Colonel Twyford stood as the Conservative candidate for Newport on the Isle of Wight, and was only narrowly defeated.[8] In 1881 Helen Twyford's health began to fail and, despite periods of convalescence at Brighton and Hastings, she died in November 1882. Her nominal control of her first husband's firm had lasted ten years.

Though a retired soldier with no experience of hosiery or any other trade, Colonel

Twyford shouldered his new responsibilities and met with his wife's junior partners on 24th November 1882, just 22 days after her death. Two days later, George Dickson, who in recent years had effectively become the head of the business, suddenly died. In the new articles of partnership that took effect from December 1883, he was replaced by John Scott in 'the general supervision of the London business', and, as a third junior partner, in came John Henry Mallard, manager of the worsted department. Twyford himself was to have 'paramount control', but 'shall be at liberty to absence himself therefrom or employ himself therein at his own will and pleasure'.[9]

In 1883, a year after his first wife's death, Twyford married Lady Duke, née Jane Amelia Bennett, widow of Sir James Duke, first baronet, who had died in 1873.[10] The new couple had houses in London at Queen's Gate, South Kensington, later in Cadogan Square, and also at Hove.

The main commercial change taking place in the last quarter of the nineteenth century was that an increasing proportion of the firm's output took the form of knitted underwear rather than stockings. Also, whilst many established customers continued to visit the Wood Street premises to place their orders (where a wine room was maintained for their entertainment), another feature of the period was the rise of the commercial traveller. This change was necessitated by the increasing number of customers outside the London market, and was facilitated by the growing rail network during the second half of the century. It went hand-in-hand with changes in the nature of the customer base, with the evolution of many retail drapers into department stores. Peter Robinson, Swan & Edgar, Debenham & Freebody, Marshall & Snelgrove, Shoolbreds, Whiteleys and Barkers were all well-known names of the time, who were supplied by George Brettle & Co.

Isaac Hanson continued as partner and as Belper factory manager, and also became a JP and a leading figure in many community activities. He lived at Chevin Mount, the house he had built for himself overlooking the factory on a hill on the other side of the Derwent, until his death in 1911.

Right: 'Chevin Mount, Manager Isaac Hanson's house on Chevin ridge.' (Courtesy of Ray Marjoram and Belper Historical Society).

Cosy Consolidation

All indicators are that the 1880s and 90s were better years for Brettles than the 1870s had been. The closing years of the nineteenth century, and indeed the first decade of the twentieth century, saw the business strong and profitable, but not marked by innovation or dramatic growth. Rather it took pride in having become a long-established respected business, valued by all who dealt with it, maintaining time-honoured practices, but perhaps resting rather complacently on its laurels. Further real growth and innovation awaited the arrival of another Twyford, and, ironically, the First World War.

There is ample testimony from employees and customers alike to their fondness for 'dear old Wood Street', as George Brettle had called it. One customer who visited regularly from 1866 described it as 'one of the most charming warehouses in the city'.[11] For the live-in employees, there was a camaraderie that grew in the bedrooms (generally with four beds) and the common rooms above the warehouse and offices. There had been established since 1850 a library, a debating society, the 'Oberon' cricket and football clubs (see Chapter 8).[12] Over these years, many spoke of their enjoyment of the 'larking and ragging', the talking after lights-out, the sports matches, the club dinners and suppers, the trips to Gilbert & Sullivan operettas and other attractions.

One letter that shows how well the employees were looked after was written by a newly-employed youngster to his aunt:

> I got paid today as they always pay monthly . . . The food is jolly good, the dinner from the joint, served just like it is in a restaurant at 2/6 per luncheon. The meat is carved off and brought to us by a waiter. We can have hot meat which is roasted, or we can have cold meat, ham, beef, tongue or lamb, with salad or pickles or mint sauce. The waiter then hands us a dish of potatoes to help ourselves from, then the greens, then brings us mustard, salt, pickles, salad or whatever we want, then bread, and finally pours us out a glass of water or ale or stout, whichever we prefer. You should see the fellows shift the beer, pints of it, and they can have as much as they like, as we can with everything. We can have two or three helpings of meat if we like. Sometimes we have fruit or custard, and afterwards cheese . . .[13]

Working a Hand frame, Silk Hosiery, June 1923.

Old Neddy Smith working his hand frame.

There is evidence of considerable employee loyalty at both London and Belper. The best example of this is Edward 'Old Neddy' Smith of Belper, who spent 87 years working for Brettles! He had begun work on his father's hand-loom at the age of ten in 1827, and continued to knit on it for the rest of his life. His early adulthood was spent very much under the shadow of his dominant father, who received the wages and passed nothing on to his son until the age of 28, when Ned was granted just one shilling a week because he was caught stealing his father's tobacco. The old man thrashed him for this, to which Ned is reported to have said: 'Make it a good 'un, it's the last you'll ever gie me, it'll be your turn next.' Soon after this he at last became a Brettles wage earner in his own right. Well over sixty years later, at the age of 96, he was indignant at being offered retirement with a generous pension, and retorted: 'If they couldna find me more work, I'll get another job.' He continued working until three weeks before his death at the age of 97 in January 1914. It was said that he had never seen the sea, and not even been to Derby until he was in his nineties.[14]

The early years of the new century saw the loss of all of the 'junior' partners. In 1901 Isaac Hanson retired after his long reign over the Belper factory. Scott died on the last day of 1903 and Mallard in August 1904. Thereafter, Henry Robert Twyford was the sole partner in the business until his death in 1913. His second wife had died in 1900. He retained an active part in management, and whilst spending more time at London, he maintained a house at Belper, 'Sunny Bank', and spent some time there every summer. In Derbyshire he was known as 'a very generous subscriber to local institutions and charities, besides being a staunch supporter of the Conservative cause'.[15]

Sunny Bank House, Twyford's second home in Belper.

St Peter's Church Belper.

DULCE ET DECORUM EST PRO PATRIÂ MORI.

IN MEMORY OF
ERNEST HENRY SAMUEL TWYFORD,
A MAJOR IN THE ROYAL SCOTS (LOTHIAN REGIMENT),
AND FORMERLY OF THE CAMERONIANS (SCOTTISH RIFLES),
WHO WAS KILLED IN ACTION AT BADFONTEIN, IN THE TRANSVAAL,
ON 13TH APRIL, 1901, IN THE 38TH YEAR OF HIS AGE.
HE WAS THE ELDEST SON OF CAPT. ENNIS RICHARD HENRY TWYFORD,
OF THE MADRAS STAFF CORPS,
AND NEPHEW OF LIEUT. COLONEL HENRY ROBERT TWYFORD,
(LATE AUXILIARY FORCES),
OF SUNNY BANK, IN THIS PLACE.

Twyford Memorial, St. Peters Church, to Ernest Henry Twyford (1863–1901) son of Ennis Richard Henry Twyford, brother of Henry Robert Twyford, killed in Boer War. (Photographer : Nick Lockett)

5. FROM PARTNERSHIP TO COMPANY

Old Colonel Twyford died in April 1913, leaving no children by either of his marriages, just a stepson by his second, Sir James Duke, second baronet, who was never concerned in the firm. He left the business equally to his nephews Lionel Thomas Campbell Twyford and Harry Edward Augustus Twyford, the sons of his late brothers.[1]

The following month, the report of the firm's accountants, Josolyne Miles & Co., drew attention to a number of faults in the way the firm's business was conducted. They commented on the unnecessarily high stock levels, the slow turnover of stock, the heavy travelling expenses of travellers, the relatively high salaries of some, and the inadequate system of accounts.[2] These pressing issues were addressed by the two Twyfords; for example, they decided to pay the travellers by a combination of salary and commission, thus introducing a 'productivity' incentive. Other changes followed, some of them small, but together indicating that progress was afoot. In late June it was decided to replace the three horse vans with a one-ton motor van. In October the North London 'horse brougham' was replaced by a motor car. The firm was being dragged into the twentieth century.

In January 1914 the business was incorporated as a private limited company, George Brettle & Co. Ltd, which of course required it to produce proper annual accounts. Lionel Twyford, as the elder brother, became Chairman of the new company, but almost immediately was recalled to the active list as a Brigadier General, and then sent to war. So Harry was the active director from the start.

The same month, at Belper, 'Old Neddy' Smith died, the last surviving man to remember George Brettle senior. A link with the past was broken; it was the end of an era, and the start of a new one.

In March 1915 Alfred Murrell Gibson became the third director. He had served the firm since joining it in 1889 at the age of 17, first in the underwear department, then as West End representative from 1906. He was promoted to Buyer in 1913, to General Manager in 1914, and to Director in 1915.

The Fortunes of War

After war broke out in 1914, a number of workers signed up and joined the armed forces, including two who were later to become directors. H.O. Randall was already in the London Rifle Brigade Territorials and was quickly mobilised; he served with them and later with the RAMC in Egypt and Palestine. W.H. Inch served with the Kensington Battalion of the London Rifles and in the Machine Gun Corps, saw active service in France, where he was wounded, and later became a Second Lieutenant in the Kings Royal Rifles.[3]

However, company investment continued. In 1915 a new type of machinery was introduced into the factory besides the established 'Cotton's patents' – circular web machines, which cut underwear, and ribbed knitting and seamless hose began to be used. The factory was producing underwear and stockings in cotton, silk and wool, besides a quantity of knickers, ties and gloves.

The First World War was a good period for Brettles. From a modest £38,090 in 1914, their sales multiplied nearly five times to £176,062 in 1918. Army orders for underwear and stockings constituted a high proportion of this increase in production. But there was another factor. In 1915, the warehouse of Ward Sturt & Sharp in London was bombed by a Zeppelin and seriously damaged by fire, which in retrospect marked the beginning of the end for that partnership business. From this point on, their Belper building was used only as a warehouse, to accommodate the stocks from London. Their manufacturing ceased and was transferred over the road to Brettles, who then became Wards' main supplier. Brettles could not have possibly known that there would be another world war in a little over twenty years' time, in which they would suffer the same setback in the Blitz, but survive it.

After the War

At the end of the war it was decided to build an extension to the factory. To this end in 1919 a further field behind the factory was purchased from G.H. Strutt, and the extension built and equipped with new plant. In the same year, William Miller Bowness was appointed manager of the Belper factory. Most of his experience had been outside the company: he had worked his way up through a Mansfield hosiery factory, had been a traveller and had worked for a London shipping house. One of his first actions as Manager was to introduce double shift working. The increased production was creating a bottleneck in the finishing stages, so he also rented a large building in Wirksworth, north-west of Belper, to provide extra accommodation and labour for linking, seaming and other such operations. Output crossed the £200,000 line in 1919 and reached £264,391 in 1920, a striking difference from the £38,090 of just six years earlier.

Above: Brettles Seaming Room, Wirksworth, probably 1930s and below Mr. Rayford, Head of the Counting House (later Company Secretary) at his desk, 1910.

In 1920, soon after his return from war, Lionel Twyford died, and Harry succeeded to the Chairmanship of the company; he was to oversee its growth and to remain in charge of it right through until its acquisition by Courtaulds in 1964. Also in 1920, Frank John Rayson was made a director. Rayson had joined the firm in 1875 and risen to be Chief Clerk, and, after 1905, 'Head of the Counting House'. Since the company had been formed in 1915, he had been its Secretary.

In 1925, Harry Twyford's son Richard was brought onto the board. Born in 1900, Dick Twyford had spent his earliest years in his mother's native Australia, then moving to Penang and to New Zealand. After coming to the UK, he spent some time with a firm of machine makers in Nottingham before joining the Wood Street staff in 1923, becoming Manager of the Claims department.[4]

In the firm's manufacturing processes, working on a large scale had become the norm. Mary Smedley records that the last local independent home-based framework knitter had finished working his own frame at Bargate in 1913.[5] The employed hand-loom workers and their looms had been brought in-house some years previously, and had no doubt found the transition difficult. But by this time most of them had retired and their looms had been scrapped. A small number of hand frames were kept at the factory up to the mid 1930s to meet the occasional special orders, such as swimsuits for oriental royalty and their harems, and very high-quality hose for the super-rich. One of the last special orders to be produced this way was some silk half-hose for Primo Carnera, the giant Italian heavyweight boxer. Otherwise it was mass production by powered machinery. The same changes had taken place throughout the textile industries, and Brettles was by no means the last to complete them.

Through Boom and Slump

During the inter-war period, the old staple industries were hard hit, especially as the bottom was falling out of the export market. Meanwhile some newer industries that were orientated to home demand for consumer goods had a high growth rate. While historically belonging to the first of these categories, apart from small slumps in the early 1920s and 30s the overall experience of the hosiery industry was one of growth. Whilst the general cotton and woollen industries declined, numbers employed in hosiery as a whole rose from under 100,000 in the early 1920s to more than 133,000 in the late 1930s. Total production of stockings increased from 25,400,000 dozens in 1924 to 35,981,000 in 1937, and of underwear from 6,514,000 dozens to 12,789,000.[6]

Brettles shared in the prosperity of the hosiery industry. Record profits were made between 1917 and 1919, and a high proportion of these were ploughed back into the firm – £95,966 in 1917, £142,672 in 1918, and £141,119 in 1919. At the height of the firm's fortunes, there were proposals for it to acquire John Smedley Ltd, an old-established high-quality hosiery manufacturer at Lee Bridge, north-east of Belper. Draft heads of agreement were drawn up, but, for reasons unknown, these proposals were not pursued. However, it is interesting that a few years later Brettles were selling some Smedley lines: 'Star Seat' ladies' knickers and 'Jay Finish' silk and wool trunk drawers.

Over the inter-war period as a whole, Brettles' output of manufactured goods rose. Back in 1914, production at Belper had provided only a seventeenth of the total goods sold by the firm in London. By 1921 it accounted for almost a fifth of total sales, and by the late 1920s about a quarter, a level that was maintained throughout the 1930s.

But it was not all progress. The boom of 1917–19 was followed by a short slump, which turned a high profit of £141,119 into a loss of £103,836 in 1920, and a smaller loss of £15,472 in 1921, whilst sales fell from a peak of one and three quarter million in 1920 to just a little over a million the following year. The firm was forced to borrow from the National Provincial Bank, who were asked to provide an overdraft facility of £120,000 in March 1920, increased to £165,000 in August. In 1922, debentures worth £35,000 were reissued to nominees of the bank as security for their loans.[7]

Overall productivity increases were considered necessary to rectify the situation. Thus in 1923 it was decided to require all London departments to make a gross profit of 16 per cent per annum. Some failed to do so, and as a consequence Haberdashery (the smallest department) was closed down in 1924 and the Bandanna department in 1927. At this time the largest departments were the Lisle (accounting for a quarter of sales) and Silk departments, and these were able to meet their targets. The firm's tough measures in response to the slump appear to have proved successful.

The Lisle department accounted for a sixth of sales in 1920 and about a quarter from 1927. The main products in this category were the various ladies' fully fashioned stockings, made at Belper out of fine mercerised cotton, and sold under the names of 'Silkestia' and 'Lustrinia' in a range of colours, from black to flesh and from purple and lilac to sky blue. 'Silkestia' were plain and unpatterned; 'Lustrinia' had a small design on the side known as 'self clox'. The department also handled a growing quantity of artificial silk hose such as 'Gleam'.

Big Factory Photo Session, June 1923

Manufacturing

Finishing department, Fashioned Underwear, June 1923.

Circular Web machines, June 1923.

Stocking Frame making, June 1923.

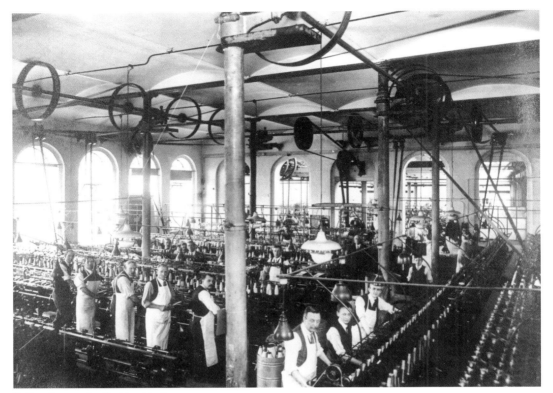

Cotton Frames for Fashion Hosiery.

Seaming Hose, June 1923.

Ribbed Underwear, making up, June 1923.

Ribbed Underwear department, June 1923.

Packing into boxes, June 1923.

The 'Pairing' process, June 1923.

'Boarding' – stretching hosiery of preformed shades, June 1923.

Corner of Winding Room, June 1923.

Services

Brettles Textile Laboratory.

Printing Department.

Mechanics Shop.

General Office, June 1923.

Factory Garage, cars & drivers, 1920s.

Direct Current Generators, June 1923.

Canteen and Parties

Canteen Kitchens, 1920s.

Brettles Childrens Christmas Party, 1929.

Brettles Childrens Christmas Party, 1929.

Framework Knitters Christmas meal, 17th December 1932.

Machine Builders

In 1928, the firm began making its own machines, which was most unusual for a hosiery manufacturer. The complex machines capable of knitting several garments at once, which the industry used in the 1920s, were normally built by specialist engineering firms, the most important being that established by William Cotton in the 1870s. W.M. Bowness, the Belper manager, travelled to the United States and Germany on the firm's behalf to investigate best-practice technology, and concluded that German machines were unsuitable and that British firms would take over a year to supply. He decided that the development would be done in-house and that he would directly supervise it. The mechanics' shop was consequently extended and the firm's engineer, Ron Sheppard, was set to designing and building the machines. By the end of 1928, the long 39-gauge full-fashioned machine, with variable speed motor and specially designed control gear, was ready to knit sixteen garments at once.

In the same year, large additions were made to the factory buildings; a new extension, costing £14,000, covered 36,000 square feet and contained over twenty of the latest full-fashion machines. On 21st December 1928 there was a grand party held to celebrate the opening of the factory extension, attended by over a thousand employees and guests. The highlight of the evening was the starting up by Mrs Twyford of the first machine for making fully fashioned hose that had been built on the premises by Brettles' own workers. This landmark occasion led Bowness to proclaim that the event was 'the greatest day in the history of the company'. Harry Twyford claimed that productivity per worker had risen 73 per cent since 1913 and that if duties on raw silk imports were removed he would immediately give orders for another extension and find employment for 300 to 400 more.[8]

Several more machines were in the process of construction at the time. In fact, Bowness suggested there was no reason why the firm might not start making machines for other manufacturers, and for a time 'machine builders' was added to its letterhead. Five more machines were built over the next few years, but only for Brettles' own use. In 1932 Bowness brought in a German technical expert, Fritz Friedrich, to help with this work, and he was provided with a house in Derbyshire. But it was found that he had little idea of how to erect a hosiery machine, and after two years he was dismissed.

First fully-fashioned machine built by Brettles, December 1928.

Drawing of 119 Wood Street and Belper Mill, showing directors, managers & salesmen, 1929
(Photographer: Nick Lockett).

North side of Brettles Factory, Chapel Street, Belper, 1920s/30s.

Exit Ward Sturt & Sharp

In 1930, the once rival firm of Ward Sturt & Sharp ceased trading, perhaps an early victim of the 1930s recession. Its turnover in the 1920s had languished between £353,000 and £460,000, in 1929 they had made a net loss, and, facing a greater loss in 1930, the remaining partners, H. Leader Sturt and Wilfred L. Sturt, placed the firm in the hands of its creditors for its assets to be realised. Though there remained a £38,687 surplus of assets over liabilities, the firm was liquidated.[9]

And so it was that, nearly a century after George Brettle had been forced to give up the use of Wards' warehouse, his company had the opportunity to purchase it back. In the event they decided not to purchase the warehouse itself, but for the low price of £2,950 they did buy the Ward property on their own side of the Derby Road. On the site was the Dye House that Wards had built some years before, and this enabled Brettles to start their own dyeing, which had previously been done by outside dyers (they invested £15,000 in this over the next three years). Also included on the acquired site was the old framesmiths' shop which they had long rented from Wards; the sock department and most of the circular machinery were moved there, and it later became the 'Belnit' factory.

The main Wards building was acquired by Dalton & Co. and used as an oil refinery for some years. The 'Wards warehouse' building still stands today, as does the adjacent Brook Cottage, which was home to John Ward then to Benjamin Ward. Though empty and somewhat the worse for wear, it is now a listed structure.

It appears that many of Wards' employees were taken on. At the end of 1928 Brettles had been employing 800 people in Belper, but by the end of 1930 it was over a thousand. The firm was now easily the largest employer in Belper. At the height of its prosperity, it commenced publication of a magazine entitled *Yarns*, proudly subtitled 'The Magazine of the House of Brettle', with a shield marked 'B' and the Latin motto 'Labor Omnia Vincit': 'Hard Work Conquers All'. Thirteen issues were produced between 1929 and 1932, when publication ended as there was less good news to tell.

Right: Cleaning Wards Boiler following purchase, October 1933 – showing W. Spendlove, R. Blount, A. Parkin and others.

Below: Brettles Dye House.

View from Dyeworks Chimney top, about 1930.

Traction engine pulling Boiler, 30 tons, 30 ft. long, 8 ft.6 inch diameter.

Boiler arriving from Dukinfield, end view.

Roof top view from Brettles facing north.

New Factory Boilers in situ, Brettles Mill, Belper.

Through the Recession

It is clear that the company did suffer briefly from the recession of the early 1930s. One classic symptom of this was a freeze on recruitment. Whilst other firms around made redundancies, so that the numbers of unemployed grew, the worst that Brettles staff had to face was a resort to short-time working and consequent pay cut, which naturally brought some discontent. The message went out to staff that they were 'lucky to still have a job'. In the last 1932 issue of *Yarns*, one anonymous manager inserted a poem entitled 'Get On or Get Out':

> There's many a man can do your job
> As good or better than you.
> There's many a man to take your place
> And be glad of the offer too!
>
> If you want your job, get on with your job.
> If not, it's up to you
> To quit it now and so make room
> For a man more keen to do.
>
> Get on with your job or get out of your job,
> Which are you going to do?
> We can't waste time on slackers now,
> So choose – it's up to you.
>
> It's up to you to make of your job
> The best success you can.
> If you can't do that, it's up to you
> To give it to those who can!

At least they had that choice, unlike today, when most workers in such circumstances apparently have no choice at all! The same magazine carried a letter from 'Chairman Mr Alderman Twyford' saying:

> I am afraid many have been disappointed with 1932 who had hoped to have seen a revival of trade and better times. However, we must look forward, with our hearts full of hope that 1933 may be the turning point, and that trade will improve and with it bring prosperity to all of us.[10]

But his hopes for 1933 were premature, as it was another year or two before the firm would turn the corner.

It might be assumed from the foregoing that the company had been making heavy losses, but this was not the case. In fact the firm suffered much less in the 1930s slump than it had in that of the early 1920s. The rate of profit had fallen from 10 per cent in 1930 to 5 per cent, after which it rallied. Perhaps the London perception, and Harry's comments, had more to do with the state of the wholesale side.

In fact the internal accounts indicate that whilst the London side of the company was still making small losses until 1939, the Belper side was making decent profits again from 1934:[11]

Year:	1934	1935	1936	1937	1938
London	(2,214)	(2,930)	(87)	(2,047)	(3,679)
Belper	15,635	15,004	13,940	18,628	20,610

Perhaps this was a factor in an emergency management decision that would be made in 1941. Be that as it may, it is a familiar feature that, in times of recession, companies gain briefly from competitors who go out of business as some of their customers are picked up, which can mask the effect of the underlying economic circumstances. No doubt Brettles did this and it must have helped them ride the recession.

Left: Belper Carnival Hosiery Queen 1936: Brettles employee D. Sheldon.

Out with the Old

In August 1936, Deputy Factory Manager John Ross poignantly noted in his scrapbook: 'Wallis Walker and William Haslam pensioned off. These two men are the last of our hand-frame workers. So ends an old industry.' And after 1936, the only outworkers mentioned in the firm's books were cheveners, who embroidered designs onto stockings and socks, a local specialist occupation. Smedley records that there were still cheveners operating in Belper until the mid 1980s.[12]

On the London side, the early 1930s had seen the end of 'living in' at 119 Wood Street; the cosy paternalism enjoyed by generations of apprentices was over. The space was needed, and it became cheaper to pay employees to find digs than to keep up an elaborate domestic economy.

However, under Harry Twyford's direction, the firm had increased the other provisions made for its growing number of employees. The self-help Oberon Insurance Society – the 'Coffin Club' – founded in 1920, was replaced in 1928 by the introduction of life insurance and a pension for all employees from the age of 65 that was widely regarded as a model scheme.[13] Harry claimed that 'Brettles was the first firm in the textile trade to have a staff pension insurance scheme.' In 1933, as a new year gift to its workers, and probably as a compensation for the privations, the firm increased the cover by 25 per cent while leaving the employee's contribution unchanged.

PENSION AND BENEFIT SCHEME
for Employees of
GEORGE BRETTLE & CO. LTD.

Employees' Annual Earnings.	Amount of Annual Pension (payable monthly for life) from age 65.	Amount of Death Benefit.	Weekly Cost to Employee.
A. £150 and under	£1 for each year of service	£100	1/-
B. £151 to £250	£2 for each year of service	£200	2/-
C. £251 to £400	£3 for each year of service	£300	3/-
D. £401 to £500	£4 for each year of service	£400	4/-
E. Over £500	£5 for each year of service	£500	5/-

Above: Brettles Pension Scheme leaflet (Photographer : Nick Lockett).

Meanwhile, Harry Twyford himself, whose main residence was in London, achieved social and civic prominence there. In 1929–30 he had acted as President of the appeal for the General Porters Benevolent Association, which had raised a record total.[14] In 1930 he was elected to the City's council, and a few months later, to the aldermanic bench as the representative for the ward of Cripplegate, and also served as a city magistrate. In 1934 he was elected Sheriff of the City, and in 1937 became Lord Mayor of London. To celebrate the occasion, all Belper employees of Brettles were invited to a dinner at the Drill Hall in Derby, and almost a thousand were present. Finally, in 1938 he was made a Knight of the British Empire (KBE), thus becoming 'Sir Harry'.

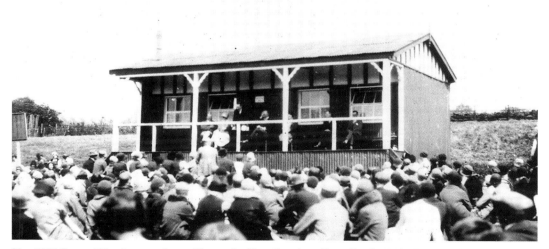

May 1929 General Election meeting at Oberon Pavilion. Speakers: Harry Twyford, Mr. Bowness & Mr. Wragg.

Above: Lord Mayor's Day 1888, the Procession passing the Mansion House depicted on 1937 Christmas card from Sir Harry & Lady Twyford.

Left: Sir Harry Twyford, Lord Mayor of London in his regalia.

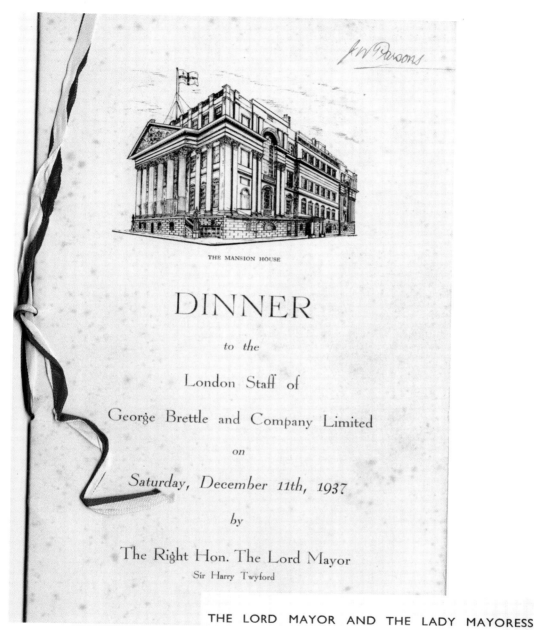

THE MANSION HOUSE

DINNER

to the

London Staff of

George Brettle and Company Limited

on

Saturday, December 11th, 1937

by

The Right Hon. The Lord Mayor

Sir Harry Twyford

THE LORD MAYOR AND THE LADY MAYORESS

request the honour of the Company of

J. W. Parsons Esq

at Dinner on Saturday, December 11th

at six-thirty for seven o'clock

THE MANSION HOUSE
LONDON

R.S.V.P.
to H. RANDALL,
119, Wood Street

Morning Dress

Above: Mansion House Dinner Menu, Programme & List of Guests, 11th December 1937.

Right: Lord Mayor & Lady Mayoress Twyford dinner invitation to JW. Parsons.

67

Canteen, Womens Room, June 1923.

Banquet given by Sir Harry Twyford, November 1937.

Sir Harry & Lady Twyford and Mr & Mrs Richard Twyford.

Sir Harry Twyford, Lord Mayor of London, Guildhall, 9th November 1937. Neville Chamberlain to the Mayors right hand.

Brettles Museum in Belper 1980s, showing the Browse Shield.

COLONIAL & FOREIGN AGENTS.

		Representing :—
Gollin & Co. Pty. Ltd.	17 Mincing Lane, E.C.	AUSTRALIA & NEW ZEALAND
„ „ „	Pioneer House, York Street, Sydney	AUSTRALIA
„ „ „	6 North Terrace, Adelaide	AUSTRALIA
„ „ „	234/6 Flinders Lane, Melbourne	AUSTRALIA
„ „ „	King Street, Perth	AUSTRALIA
„ „ „	P.O. Box 913, 18 Victoria Street, Wellington	NEW ZEALAND
J. Y. Foster & Co.	P.O. Box 1436, Cape Times Building, 17 Church Street, Cape Town	SOUTH AFRICA
„ „	P.O. Box 5655, 9 President Buildings, Von Brandis Street, Johannesburg	
Edgar B. Walters Organisation	Bartholdi Building, 23rd Street and Broadway	NEW YORK.
S. E. Spence	242 St. James Street, Montreal	CANADA
Hilton & Inman	109 Wool Exchange, E.C.	INDIA
Michael Setton, Sons & Co.	P.O. Box 84, Cairo	EGYPT
	P.O. Box 519, Alexandria	
Joseph Dichy & Co.	P.O. Box 207, Beirut	SYRIA
Grigio Hermanos	Casilla 748, Buenos Aires	ARGENTINE
	Calle Mercedes 811, Montevideo	URUGUAY
Kolbjorn S. Hansen	Fredensborgveien 4, Oslo	NORWAY
A. Lucas	Vesterbrogade 5B, Copenhagen	DENMARK
Victor Hjorts	Brunkebergstorg 15, Stockholm	SWEDEN
Haardt & Lombardi	Via Spiga 22, Milan	ITALY
A. Lopez	Paz, 19 & 21, Madrid	SPAIN
W. H. Davis	39 Rue Lafayette, Paris	FRANCE
A. Nooteboom	19/21 Rosengracht, Amsterdam	HOLLAND
	13 Rue Madelaine, Brussels	BELGIUM
J. E. Pace & Co.	225 Strada Sent' Ursola, Valletta	MALTA

List of Colonial and Foreign Agents in 1914.

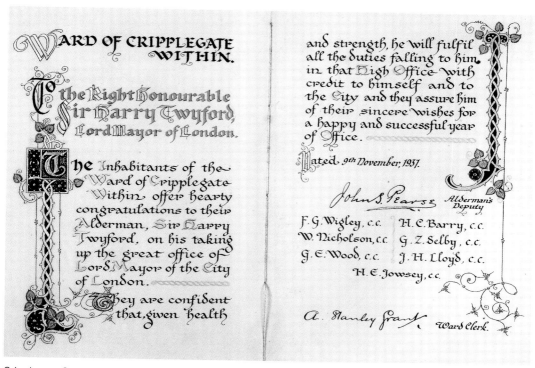

Cripplegate Complimentary letter to Harry Twyford, Lord Mayor of London, 1937 (Photographer: Nick Locket).

Left: Sir Harry Twyfords Medals (Photographer: Nick Locket).

Mansion House Visitors Book Signatures

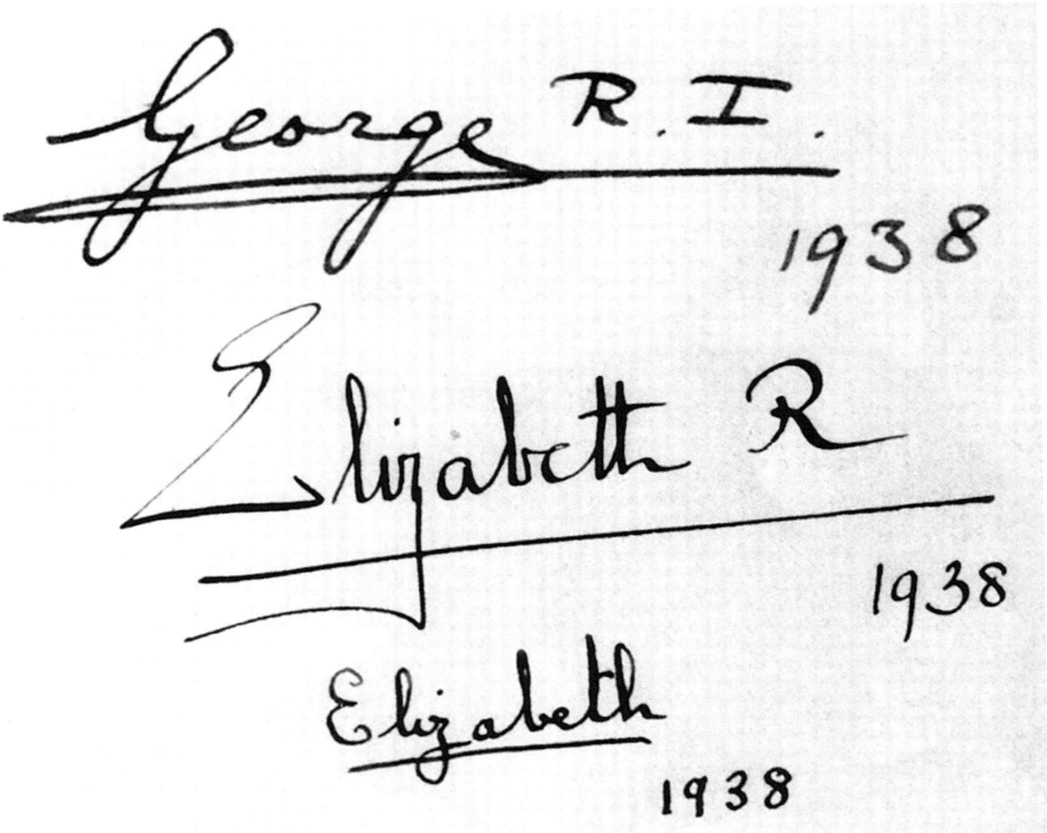

George R. I.

1938

Elizabeth R

1938

Elizabeth

1938

Signatures: King George & Queen Elizabeth 1938.

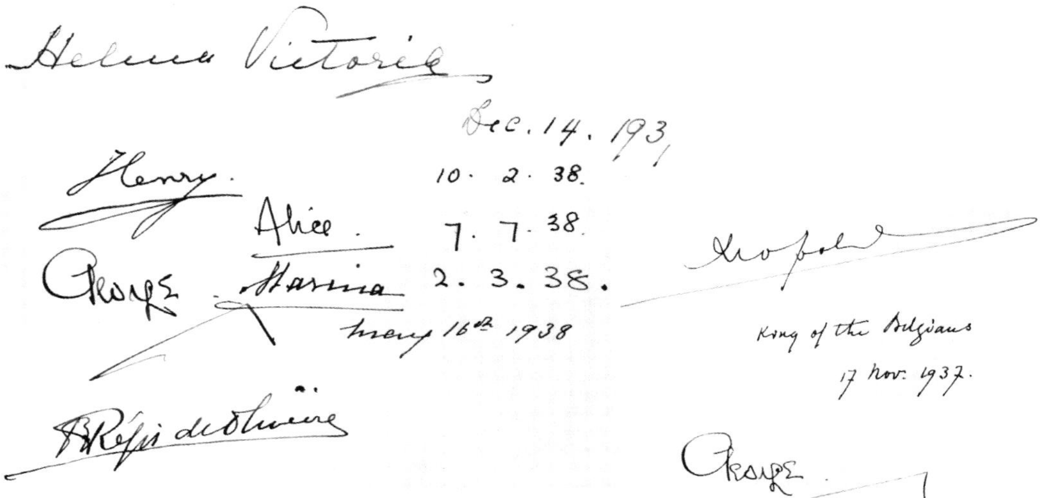

Helena Victoria

Dec. 14. 193/

Henry.

10. 2. 38.

Alice.

7. 7. 38.

George.

Marina

2. 3. 38.

mary 16th 1938

Leopold

King of the Belgians

17 nov. 1937.

George.

Royalty Signatures, Mansion House visitors book.

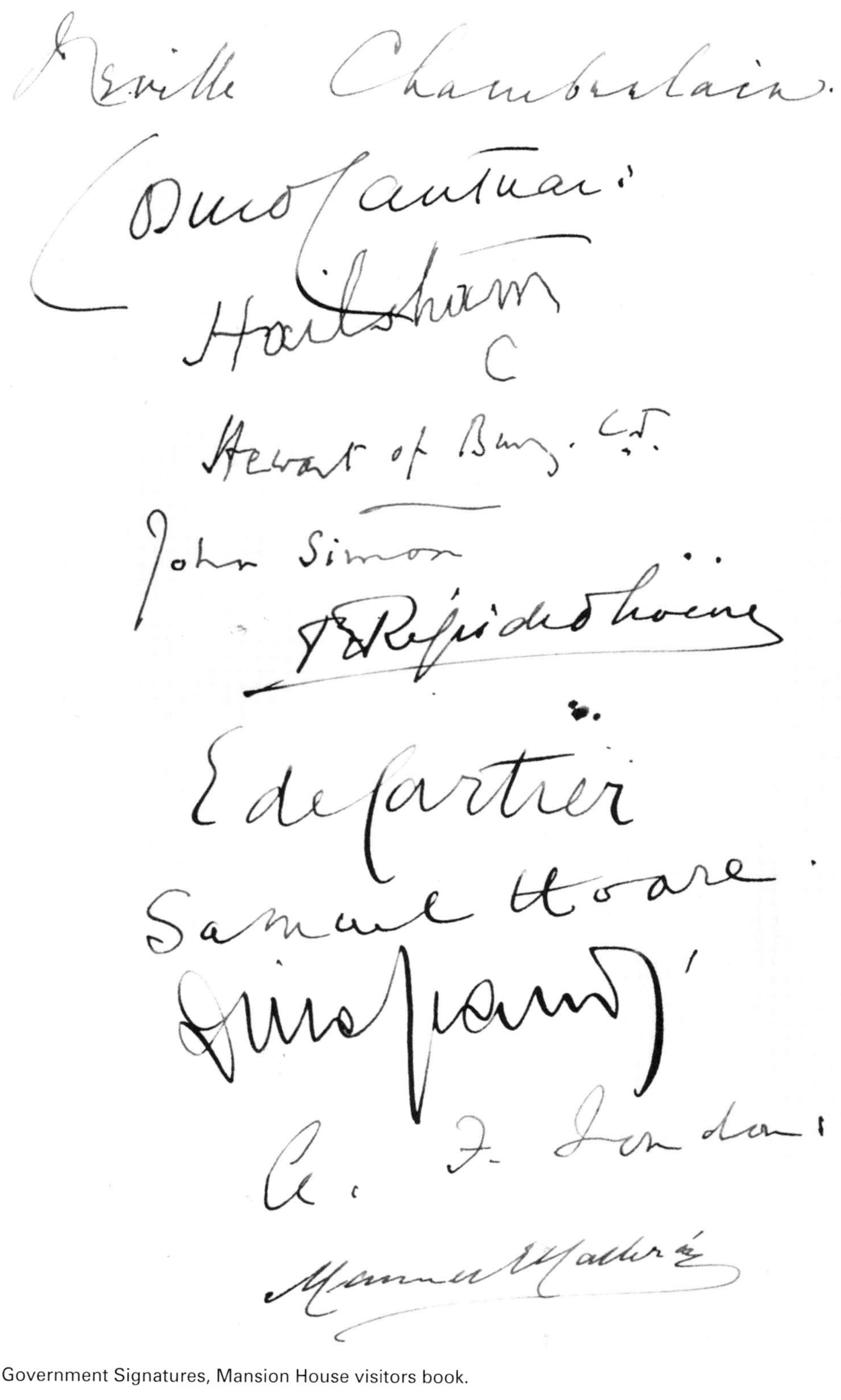

Neville Chamberlain.

Cosmo Cantuar:

Hailsham
C

Stewart of Bury. C.J.

John Simon

[illegible signature]

E de Cartier

Samuel Hoare.

[illegible signature]

A. F. London:

[illegible signature]

Government Signatures, Mansion House visitors book.

Going Public

In 1936, to raise more capital, Brettles changed from being a private to a partly public company. Its nominal capital was increased from £250,000 to £305,000, and the amount issued was increased from £202,000 to £301,874 by capitalising £99,274 of the undistributed profits. A new category of preference shares was created; these were sold at par to the British & Allied Investments Corporation and made available for dealing on the Stock Exchange. Thus, for the first time, a substantial amount of outside capital entered the firm. When the firm thus 'went public', the announcement in *The Times* described it as 'self-contained and believed to be equipped as one of the most up-to-date factories in the United Kingdom'.[15] The term 'self-contained' referred to the firm's machine-building activity, which continued until 1938. All in all, there was little resemblance between the firm on the eve of the First World War and that on the eve of the Second.

The Late 30s

Also around this time, there were several director changes. In 1933 F.J. Rayson retired as Director and Secretary after fifty-nine years of service, leaving Gibson and Dick Twyford the only directors for four years, under Sir Harry Twyford. Then, in 1937, Alfred Page was appointed to the Board. Page was a chartered accountant, for forty-seven years a member of Brettles' solicitors, Josolyne Miles, Page & Co. Since 1924 he had been special financial adviser to Brettles, a role which had clearly been appreciated. In 1938 Henry Osmont Randall was also made a Director. A native of Jersey, he had joined the firm as an apprentice in 1907, living above the Wood Street warehouse. He had worked in the Silk and Ladies Underwear departments, becoming Despatch Manager in 1926, and succeeding Rayson as Company Secretary in 1934.[16]

Of more impact on Belper, in 1937 the Factory Manager W.H. Bowness died; the entire factory was closed on the day of his funeral. He was succeeded by his deputy, John Ross, who had spent all his working life at Brettles. Starting at age 16 in 1900, he had become manager of the circular machine department during the First World War, then, in 1920, Deputy Manager of the factory under Bowness.

In the late 1930s there began to be a feeling that the styles of stockings being produced by the company were no longer up-to-date or smart enough. This case was made by Charles Doerr and Ivor Boyes, both then travellers for the Fancy Goods department, and much later to both become directors in the 1960s. As a consequence, it was decided to employ a designer named Alfred Weihs to develop the product lines, especially the fashionable varieties of knitted outerwear. Weihs was contracted to spend regular periods in Paris studying the latest fashions, as well as in Belper looking at the factory. But the designer was found to be 'very excitable and nervy', and after two valuable workers had resigned because of him it was decided to end his appointment. By then, the prospect of renewed European war had put paid to this development.

Second World War

The outbreak of war had a negative effect on the firm in various ways. First, with compulsory conscription, many male employees were called up into the armed forces, and most of their places had to be filled by women. A number of families faced financial difficulties with their menfolk away, and the firm paid allowances to them. Patriotic appeals led the company to invest in substantial quantities of government stock. Chairman Twyford visited the Belper factory in War Weapons Week and 'inspected the troops' in Belper Market Place. A more controversial incident was the sacking in 1940 of an employee who was a conscientious objector.

But the major effect of the war was the double bombing that destroyed the company's London premises of 130 years. Fortunately, the counting house and some other departments had been evacuated to Belper early in 1940. The first bomb fell on 119 Wood Street on the night of 10th November 1940, causing serious damage and destroying £61,891 worth of stock. The second fell on the night of 29th December, destroying the remaining £9,578 worth of stock and the building itself.

From a historian's point of view, the worst loss of the bombing was the destruction of virtually all the firm's financial records for the second half of the nineteenth century and the early years of the twentieth, making for an incomplete account of the firm's growth during those decades.

The famous Browse Shield (see Chapter 8) was saved from the ruins of Wood Street, and thence attained an even greater significance and reverence in Brettles minds, highly coveted and valued by those to whom this trophy was awarded from year to year. Today it resides in Belper North Mill Museum.

The firm took a temporary office in the Textile Exchange Buildings, and later in Regent Street. However, the whole commercial and warehouse side of the business was now moved to Belper at the beginning of 1941, as were all the employees except a skeleton office staff. This would have involved something of a squeeze physically, and five departments were closed down – Fancy Goods, 'Manchester Goods', Gloves, and Ladies and Gents Outfitting – departments that were heavily dependent on other suppliers rather than on what was produced at the Belper factory.

The war brought no boost to sales as the previous war had. Rather, following the Belper consolidation and closure of some departments, sales fell from just over £1.2m in 1940 to £753,164 in 1941, and reached their lowest point in 1942, at £620,293. The level of production fell too, due partly to the exodus of men and partly to the drop-off in demand. Both began to pick up in the last two years of the war, and were set to accelerate with the coming of peace.

Rather belatedly, in August 1944, the firm started a 'Contact' newsletter for its members serving in the forces, the first issue carrying a reassuring message by Harry Twyford, expressing appreciation for their brave efforts to 'maintain the empire' and the hope that their return home and to 'normal contact with the company' would not be long delayed. The newsletter listed two employee deaths, two missing, two wounded, one decorated 'DSM', one mentioned in despatches', and six prisoners-of-war – four in German hands and two in Japanese hands. The remaining pages were filled with letters from servicemen.

The second issue, issued in December 1944, listed four promotions, three of them to Major, and four discharged on medical grounds. Life was not put on hold for all – it also reported two marriages and one engagement. The 'Home News' section reported that the 'Comforts Fund' had benefitted over the previous two years from the proceeds of two 'Oberon Concert Parties' arranged by Mr E.H. Meredith; also that the Cricket XI had kept going, with the empty places being filled by employees in their fifties who had escaped call-up. Despite this they had done well, playing 18 matches, of which they had won eight, drawn six and lost only four (more on this in Chapter 8).[17]

Number 3 must have been an interesting newsletter, coming out in 1945 around the time of victory, but unfortunately it has not survived. It was of course some time after this before most of the troops were discharged, and the last issue, number 4, came out in February 1946. It reported three army promotions, two marriages, three births, and one death in Japanese hands on 28th October 1944. By mid 1946 most of the serving employees had returned, and the 'Contact' newsletter was discontinued.

North view of Factory in snow, 27th January 1940.

Sir Harry Twyford inspecting troops, War Weapons Week, March 1941.

War Weapons Week, Belper Market Place, March 1941.

Brettles Christmas Party, 1940s.

6. THE POST-WAR PERIOD

There had been a few management changes during the early 1940s. In 1941 Alfred Page had died and A.M. Gibson had retired from directorship, whereupon Ernest Edward Hall had been made a director. Hall had been employed by the firm since he joined as an apprentice in 1896, had been trained by John Scott and in 1914 had become buyer for the Lisle department. He had then sat on the board for five years alongside H.O. Randall and Harry Twyford before retiring in 1946.

Thereupon Hall's seat as director was offered to W.H. Inch, another long-serving employee. Inch had joined in 1908 as an apprentice at Wood Street, transferred to the counting house in 1910, becoming its manager in 1933, and had moved to Belper with the others in 1941.

Following the destruction of 119 Wood Street by bombing, the London activities had been relocated to Belper in 1941, but a complete separation was maintained between this and the manufacturing side (the factory). The wholesale side, including the warehouse, was still referred to as the 'London side'. Staff were very aware of an elitism shown by and accorded to the latter, such that even staff in the 'Counting House' which served the 'London side' felt superior to those in the Wages office which served the factory! This demarcation persisted for over twenty years.

Trade was beginning to pick up as the war ended. The number of commercial visitors to the firm rose from 444 in 1944 and 665 in 1945 to 765 in 1946 and nearly a thousand in 1947. Sales that year were over £930,000, and in 1948 reached the pre-war level of £1.2 million. The rate of profit, which had remained between 7 and 8 per cent from 1940 to 46, reached 9 per cent in 1947 and 11 per cent in 1948.

There were, however, problems on the supply side – continuing shortages of yarn and of fuel, and the virtual impossibility of obtaining new machinery to gradually replace the ageing equipment. Both British and American machines were in very short supply, and it became advantageous for firms to 'club together' in their purchase and use of new machines.[1] Brettles' response this time was not to build their own machines as they had done before the war; the sort needed in the late 1940s were much bigger and more sophisticated. Rather, in 1946 they began a rather strange association with a much smaller firm, the Charnos Hosiery Company, owned by Charles Noskwith. In exchange for a deal on machine purchases, Brettles provided two loans to Charnos for new factory premises at Ilkeston, east of Belper, and agreed to buy a large proportion of their output.

In 1947 two of the very latest fine-gauge 30-at-once hosiery machines made in Pennsylvania were obtained for £10,000 each. They were ordered by Charnos but then purchased from that firm by Brettles, who from then on continued to replace and add to their stock of machinery. Output then grew some more, and by 1949 it exceeded the production level in the boom years of the 1920s, and continued to increase to three-quarters of a million pounds in 1951, whilst actual sales reached two million pounds. Where was it all going? Certainly, exports were growing, and there were now sales agents in 14 countries – in Australia, New Zealand, Egypt, India, Burma, South Africa and Canada, as well as in France, Belgium, Holland, Denmark, Norway, Sweden and Italy.

Another major problem in the late 1940s was the shortage of labour. Even at the end of 1946, it was proving difficult to get sufficient linkers and seamers to process the work of the knitters. In 1948 management investigated some premises near Chesterfield as a possible place to tap a new source of female labour, and later that year they even considered looking to Tyneside for 'finishing labour'. In 1949 a large house was purchased as a hostel for 20 to 30 'German refugee girls'.

A 1947 essay on Belper (author unknown, but held at St John's Chapel) states:

> The principal industry at Belper is not cotton but hosiery, there being many firms in the town producing a multiplicity of goods, including underwear and outerwear. Of these, the most important is Messrs George Brettle & Co. Ltd . . . It now stands in its own grounds of 23 acres, of which 7.5 acres are built on, and employs some eight hundred workers. The raw materials from which they manufacture are silk, previously from Macclesfield [now from Strutts?], cotton from Lancashire, wool from Yorkshire, rayon from Coventry, Birmingham, Liverpool and Aintree, and nylon from Courtaulds at Coventry.

Relationship Problems

In the late 1940s some personality clashes arose between managers. In 1946, Dick Twyford had returned from military service as a major. He was made Director in charge of the production side and instructed to work closely with John Ross, the Factory Manager, without interfering with the latter's duties. That proved to be difficult! In November 1946, on the eve of a trip overseas, Sir Harry made an appeal for 'unity and friendly relations' while he was away, which was recorded in the Directors' minute book. But the minutes record that, after management discussions, some decisions could not be agreed and were deferred until Harry's return.

Factory unity under Dick Twyford proved impossible, and within a year John Ross took early retirement. He was succeeded as Factory Manager by Walter Bennett, a newcomer to the firm, who had been the Technical Manager for R. Rowley & Co. Ltd, hosiery manufacturers at Leicester, and a lecturer at Loughborough Technical College. Bennett held the gold medal of the Worshipful Company of Framework Knitters and the silver medal of the City and Guilds of the London Institute. Harte comments that a good deal of the factory's subsequent success in the 1950s was due to Bennett's technical and managerial abilities, just as it had been to those of Bowness in the 1920s.[2]

Ross's retirement did not bring unity, however. Dick Twyford was still a factor, and some kind of unpleasantness arose between Bennett and E.H. Meredith, the Sock department buyer. Sir Harry attempted to restore peace by offering both of them seats on the board. He was, however, deeply displeased by whatever had happened, and stated that if anything similar were to happen again 'he would place his shares on the market and the company would lose its present private control'.

But Sir Harry also had reasons of his own for wishing to do so. In January 1948, In view of his advancing age and the prospect of heavy death duties, he changed the company's articles and the firm became a fully public company, with the sale of 300,000 ordinary shares with a nominal value of five shillings each. By the end of the year there were over two thousand shareholders. In 1950 more finance was raised when the share capital was increased to £405,000 by the creation of 400,000 new shares. A final capitalisation of £100,750 was made in 1954.

In May 1951 Sir Harry announced that he was pleased by the better feelings among the directors, and asked them to approve Dick Twyford's appointment as Deputy Chairman, which they duly did.

Womens Wear News of that year included a Brettles page in its 'Personality Parade' series, with a large photograph of 'Major H.R. Twyford, Deputy Chairman and Joint Managing Director' alongside that of 'Sir Harry Twyford KBE, Chairman and Joint Managing Director' and smaller pictures of five other directors. It states:

> The business was converted into a private family company in 1914 and a Public Company in 1936. Most of the Directors have spent practically all their business lives in the service of the Company – Mr. H.O. Randall (Secretary) since 1907, Mr. W.H. Inch (Counting House Manager) from 1908, Mr. E.H. Meredith (Buyer) since 1911, Sir Harry Twyford 1913 and Major H.R. Twyford 1919.[3]

But three years later there was another personality crisis involving Dick Twyford, and this time he resigned. In March 1954 he was given leave of absence until he reached the age of 55 in the September, when the firm was able to give him a pension.

The Shop Floor

By now the company had a large factory workforce, each of whom were provided with a Brettles 'Employees Handbook'. This interesting booklet describes the business carried on by the company as 'the manufacture of ladies' and girls' fashioned stockings, children's socks and underwear for men, women and children'. It claims that 'since the end of the war, considerable extension and replacement of plant and machinery as well as modernisation of buildings has been carried out at considerable cost, so that all machinery is up-to-date, and the working conditions throughout the business brought as near to perfection as possible'.

So what were these working conditions? It states that 'the normal working hours for factory operatives and staff' were 8am to 5.55pm, whilst 'office and clerical staff' started at 8.30am and finished at 5pm. All staff shared the same lunch hour of 12.25 to 1.25pm and it would appear that this was unpaid, though they were allowed a ten-minute paid break mid morning and mid afternoon. These hours of work were said to be 'determined by and based upon the joint agreement between the National Union of Hosiery Workers and the National Hosiery Manufacturers Federation'.

The booklet is less specific about pay, but states that 'most of the processes in the Factory and Dyeworks are on a piece-rate basis' and that 'these rates are regulated by the National Joint Industrial Council'. One employee issued with the handbook was N. Chamberlain, who wrote on the first page that he had started work in 1928 at just eight shillings a week, back in those non-union days. What progress they must have seen.

The booklet describes the 'Ticketograph' system then 'in operation for all processes up to dyeing and finishing of hose and children's socks, and for underwear from the cutting stage onwards . . . A ticketograph ticket is made out for each ten dozen lot of children's socks, each five dozen lot of ladies' hose and one dozen of underwear'. Employees were responsible for ensuring that every 'lot' had a ticket when the work was given out to them and when it was returned as completed. This then fed into the make-up of wages which were 'computed by the Factory Counting House Staff'.[4]

Above: Factory front, 1950s and **below** Factory North Corner, 1950s.

The Counting House

In September of 1951, Syd Clarke, one of the sources for this book, who had been in the RAF, joined the company and was employed in the Belper Counting House with a Mr Ernest Staings who had worked there for most of his life, both of them working under W.H. Inch.

Syd spent much of his time between Mondays and Thursdays working out the wages for the factory production and office staff, helped by eight female staff, and all worked out manually. On Fridays, Ernest and Syd went by taxi to the National Provincial (later Nat West) Bank – always at the same time! – to pick up the cash, then returned to 'bag' it for each department and make up the individual envelopes, and everything had to be balanced to the exact old penny. Then each member of the Counting House had a department to pay out. Syd recalls that there were ten departments to pay: Hosiery Knitters (men), Seaming Room (ladies), Footers and Heelers (ladies), Menders ('rough' and 'finished'), Hosiery Finishing, Socks department (knitted and finished), Underwear, Dye House (dying and preboarding), Circular or Web Knitting (men) and Office Weekly. The few monthly salaries were paid into bank accounts at the end of the month. Syd also helped Ernest Staings with the Purchase Ledger (mainly of yarn for knitting, from British Nylon Spinners), the Petty Cash and Cash Book and the Nominal Ledger of Assets, and they produced a complete year-end Profit and Loss Account.

By the early 50s there was again a small London showroom at 48 Conduit Street in Mayfair, next to the Westbury Hotel. Confusingly, the wholesale activities at Belper were still referred to as 'the London side', and Syd Clarke recalls that:

> Goods knitted for the London side were invoiced out to the warehouse and credited in the Belper or Factory side, which had to be balanced monthly, and a cheque was actually sent from the London side to the Counting House and paid into the bank! The two were treated as separate companies all year, until the year end when they were 'amalgamated' in the accounts.[5]

Another of Syd's memories from the early 1950s was the monthly sales of 15 & 30 denier nylon stockings held in the former Wards building, at 7/6d a pair. For most people, these had been almost impossible to obtain during the war years, and now they were in great demand, with queues stretching round the car park.

Director Changes in the 1950s

Following Dick Twyford's retirement, two new directors were appointed at the beginning of 1955, neither of them full-time and both brought in from outside the firm. F.M. Welsford had been a solicitor at the Biddle, Thorne, Welsford & Barnes partnership, and R.B. Wynne had been the company's bank manager at the National Provincial Bank! Wynne became Deputy Chairman after Dick Twyford's departure and later became Managing Director after Sir Harry's resignation of that post in 1960.

There were several director retirements in these years, starting with E.H. Meredith in 1954. Then W.H. Inch and H.O. Randall, the Company Secretary, both with over fifty years' service, retired at the same time in January 1959. W.H. Inch was succeeded as Counting House Manager by C. Haskell, who had joined the firm's Counting House in 1926 and been appointed Chief Cashier in 1951.

But H.O. Randall's responsibilities were split. He was succeeded as Company Secretary by Mr. P.A. Nash, who had joined the Counting House in 1928 and been Assistant Credit Manager since 1951. Meanwhile C.G. Gosling was appointed to succeed him as Warehouse Manager and Staff Manager. He had joined the firm in 1925 and been a traveller in Kent and in North and East London, and had been appointed Sales Manager in 1949. Gosling's position as Sales Manager was taken by Charles J. Doerr, who had joined the firm in 1927 and served in the Entering Room and then the Lisle department until 1946, before becoming a traveller in South Yorkshire and Lincolnshire.[6] Later, in 1961, a third part-time director was brought in – W.B. Ross Collins, a partner in the insurance brokers Sedgewick Collins & Co.

During the 1950s, the shareholders were well looked after in terms of dividends. Between 1948 and 1949, annual dividends of 7.5 per cent had been paid. Following increased profitability, this rose to 12.5 per cent in 1950, to 15 per cent in 1953 and to a peak of 20 per cent in 1956. Thereafter, profits began to fall, and dividends returned to 15 per cent in 1957, then to 10 per cent in the following two years.[7]

Circular or Rotary Knitting Machines.

Circular or Rotary Knitting Machines.

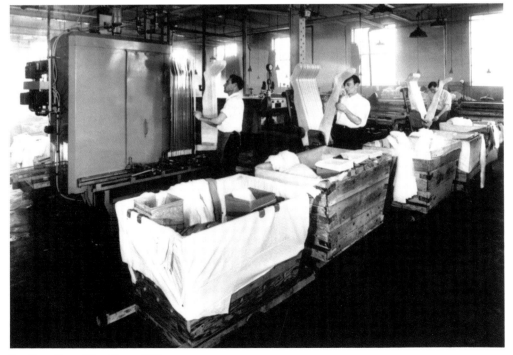

Pre-Boarding of Stockings, 1950s.

Arthur Smith, Fully fashioned Knitting, 1950s.

Brettles men at Summer School (1952 – 1957)

Bill Aldread being welcomed to Worcester college Oxford 1952.

1952 Summer School (Sandy Taylor on left, Bill Aldred on right).

1953, Worcestor College, Oxford (From Left: T. Brown, P. Nash, S. Gibson, G. Poole).

1957, Worcester College, Oxford (Left to Right: D. Wingfield, T. Brown, J. Parker).

Reprinted from the "Derbyshire Advertiser," January 16th, 1959

BELPER DIRECTORS RETIRE

Two directors of George Brettle and Co. Ltd , Belper, whose total service with the firm is over a hundred years, are to retire from active service on Monday.

They are Mr. H. O. Randall, a director, secretary and warehouse manager of 295, Duffield-road, Allestree, and Mr. W. H. Inch, director and counting house manager, of 395, Duffield-road, Allestree.

Both Mr. Randall and Mr. Inch started with the firm as apprentices, when it had premises in London. Like all the other apprentices of their day, they lived above the firm's warehouse.

Mr. Randall joined the firm in 1907. A native of Jersey, he served in the silk and ladies' underwear departments. In 1926 he was appointed dis-patch manager, in 1933 he became secretary and in 1938 was made a director.

He served with the R.A.M.C. and London Rifle Brigade in the 1914-18 war in Egypt and Palestine.

Mr. Inch joined the firm in 1908 and two years later went into the counting house. He became manager of the counting house in 1933 and in 1946 was made a director.

A native of Wisbech Mr. Inch served with the Kensington Battalion (London Regiment) and in the Machine Gun Corps during the 1914-18 war. He saw active service in France where he was wounded. Later he became a Second Lieutenant in the K.R.R.

The London premises of Messrs Brettle was destroyed during the 1939-45 war and the staff were moved to Belper.

Mr. C. G. Gossling, who was appointed director last year is to succeed Mr Randall as warehouse manager and staff manager.

Mr. Gossling joined the firm in 1925 and was a traveller in the Kent district and in East and North London. He was appointed sales manager in 1949.

Mr. C. Haskell has been appointed Counting House Manager to succeed Mr. Inch. Mr. Haskell joined the firm in 1926 and in 1951 was appointed chief cashier.

Mr. C. J. Doerr will take over as sales manager from Mr. Gossling After joining the firm in 1927, he served in various departments and then became a traveller in South Yorks and Lincolnshire.

Mr. P. A. Nash, who joined the firm in 1928, has been appointed secretary. In 1951 he was made assistant credit manager.

Belper Directors Retire, January 1959 (Standing: C. Haskell, C.J. Doerr, P.A. Nash. Sitting: W.H. Inch, H.O. Randall, C.G. Gosling).

Life on the Shop Floor

The ordinary workers were mostly unconcerned with such things, and the camaraderie of daily life in the factory continued the same. It is well described by a poem from this period called 'Flimsy Girl':

Nowt but a slip of a thing, swapped school for Brettles.
'You'll be on the flimsies' they said, and in my head
Were wings, a sort of ballet flapping perhaps – but instead
I was left in a room with a sheaf of thin paper, alone.

I went bonkers, so I left there for the dyeworks
And onto the half hose. We sat, long poles between our legs
To turn the socks, then stack according to their tags.
The girls were alright, but after a day, did my knees ache.

Young we were, and scornful of the older ones' 'tut, tut, tut'.
We'd just chatter, turn up the latest hits on the radio.
'Oh Carol' it sang, don't think of your work tomorrow,
Get home, doll up for a night of jiving at the Regal or Troc.

Morning after town, there'd be a roar and 'Jump on' from this lad,
So I did, 'cause if you were late, they'd dock your money off.
Then at work, we'd chew the fat, us girls, and have a laugh,
But then go quiet; we wouldn't want to see our Mr Winkler cross.

Between my childhood and settling down as wife and mother
Were those sticky nights of teddy boys and brothel creepers,
High heel shoes, the dancing frocks, that 'Oh Carol' from the speakers,
The piecework days of turning socks, packing, checking jumpers.[8]

Exit Strategy

Slowly, Sir Harry began to shed his responsibilities. In 1960, at the age of 90, he gave up being Managing Director but continued as Chairman. There were management concerns about the succession. After all, four times previously owners of the firm had died without a natural successor within the firm – in 1835, 1871, 1882 and 1913 – and the first three of these occasions were each accompanied by an upheaval in the firm's affairs. (On the fourth, Harry Twyford had taken over.)

It must have been a disappointment to the grand old man that his hopes for Dick Twyford to succeed him had come to nothing, and from this point it appears that he tried to sell the company. In 1961 there were negotiations with a possible buyer of the firm's issued ordinary shares. The offer was ten shillings per share, which totalled a little over £600,000 when the firm's net assets were valued in its own books at over £824,000. Sir Harry refused to sell for less than eleven shillings per share, and the offer was rejected – a mistake, in retrospect.

The lowest profits came in 1963; a small 5 per cent dividend was still paid, but financed out of reserves.[9] In March 1963, at the age of 93, Sir Harry resigned as Chairman but remained a member of the Board, and R.B. Wynne became the new Chairman. Taking account of recent poor performance, another buyer offered 7/6d per share. Harry now seemed resigned to selling at a low price, and advised the directors accordingly, but they rejected the offer in November.

In early December Wynne suggested an offer be invited from Courtaulds, which duly happened. Courtaulds offered one of their ordinary £1 stock units for ten of Brettles' ordinary shares, and five of their 6 per cent preference shares for six of Brettles' 5 per cent preference shares. The total value of the offer was £465,000, when Brettles was valued in its own books at £780,000. By Christmas it was decided to accept their terms. Courtaulds had got a bargain, and the new year would bring a new era.

Sold to Courtaulds

The first few weeks of 1964 saw Brettles beginning to undergo changes comparable to those which took place after 1913 under Harry Twyford. By the end of January, Twyford, Welsford and Collins had retired as directors – Sir Harry after serving for fifty years. He retired to Sidmouth, and ensured the respected memory he left behind in Belper by leaving £200 to each of some 200 pensioners of the firm. After just over three years of retirement, he died at Sidmouth in 1967.

In early 1964 three Courtaulds men were appointed to take the places of those who had retired: T.P. Jennison, G.H. Tarrant and C.W. Powell. Wynne retired as Managing Director in May and as Chairman in September, and was replaced in these capacities by Powell and Jennison respectively. There were, however, still some directorships from old Brettles men: J.L. Bush (Merchandise) and C.G. Gosling (Administration) continued, Charles Doerr (Sales) was appointed, and later Ivor Boyes. Doerr and Boyes had both started their careers as travellers for the Fancy Goods department, and became directors under Courtaulds management.

7. THE COURTAULDS YEARS

Thus 1964 was the first year of Brettles under Courtaulds, no doubt an uncertain time for managers and staff alike. For the short term, T.P. Jennison and George Tarrant were appointed as Directors early in the year, and R.B. Wynne retired as Managing Director in May and as Chairman in September. Courtaulds established Brettles' new management team of Charles Powell as Managing Director, J.L. Bush as Merchandise Director, Jack Price as Financial Director and C.J. Doerr as Sales Director. Powell, a long-term Courtaulds executive who had been based at their Coventry headquarters, came to combine the offices of Chairman and Managing Director as Wynne had done earlier. As MD he reported to the Courtaulds Hosiery divisional director, who in turn reported to the main management board, within which Lord Kearton and Sir Christopher Hogg held the top jobs.

The immediate experience of staff was a tightening up of discipline. For example, up to this time, at 11am and again at 4pm every day, in their 'quarter-hour coffee break', some of the Buyers left the main building and headed over the road to the Lion Hotel. This was of course outside normal licensing hours, but clearly the hotel bar was an attraction, and beyond this we can only speculate! After the takeover, however, these trips to the Lion were promptly stopped.

The acquisition of Brettles was just a beginning. It was soon decided that Brettles should become the main hosiery production unit of the Courtaulds group. Courtaulds apparently intended to control the hosiery market, for in 1965 it acquired four other similar though smaller companies – Hartwood Hosiery (who supplied Littlewoods and Woolworths), F.W. Sellers (who supplied Boots and Woolworths), Tor Hosiery of Matlock, and Play Girl Nylons, which all became part of Brettles.

All this required changes. First, non-hosiery activities had to be shed to other companies within the group. Syd Clarke of the Counting House recalls:

> They took over and they only wanted the Knitted and Dyehouse departments, so I was joined up with the Company Accountant on the London side (warehouse) to help join the two together, helped by the incoming financial people of Courtaulds, mainly from Spondon (East Derby). Mr. J.A. Price was my new boss. Others in my office from Belper after 1964 were accountants Bob Foster (transferred from Spondon) and Peter Curl, who was new.

Secondly, there had to be a reorganisation of production. During the previous hundred years, small extra buildings and extensions had been continually added with little thought to overall planning. This resulted in an elegant but sprawling collection of buildings with a range of disconnected activities being undertaken. Therefore a work study graph of the time traced the movement of goods during production as a zig-zag line, which told its own story of to-and-fro backtracking. The challenge now was to replace this with a continuous semi-circular line representing a logical and efficient flow of production from yarn store to despatch. This was no mean task and required radical changes.

In March 1966 Oswald Hibbert moved from Blount and Co., another Courtaulds subsidiary, to succeed Walter Bennett as the Production Director. In a press statement he stated: 'Mass production is the only way to compete today. We are utilising every square inch of space, and the key to the whole thing is a vastly improved work flow. We have plans to go still further, and all improvements are being made with further expansion in mind.'[1]

By 1967 the Belper factory was only producing knitted stockings and tights, whilst other production had been moved to factories elsewhere. The sock and half-frame machines were moved to the factory of Messrs Meridian at Ilkeston. The machinery of the Underwear Knitting section was moved, some to Meridian at Nottingham and some to Foster, Clay & Ward at Middlesbrough – both Courtaulds subsidiaries. This cleared the decks for the much-needed improvement of workflow in stocking production at Belper. All single-feed machines were scrapped, and the new plant included 120 eight-feed Zodiacs, various twin-feed equipment, Marshall Arm conveyors and two Bentley reciprocated-heel machines. By these means, stocking production was increased by 150 per cent.

These changes were said to be brought about without any redundancies amongst the company's staff of 881. Management engendered a productivity-conscious climate, and sought to involve staff in the vision in various ways, including a monthly £10 prize and smaller prizes for ideas that would boost efficiency. Production meetings of all managers were held every two weeks. The main customer was now Marks and Spencer.

Manufacturing and Sales Divided

In 1967, the Brettles company was split into two divisions of Courtaulds. The factory side, whilst remaining George Brettle & Co. Ltd. for the time being, came under Courtaulds' Hosiery division along with Hartwood Hosiery, F.W. Sellers, Blount & Co. and Aristoc, whilst the warehouse and shop came under Courtaulds' Distributors division along with Cooke Watts, Tagge, Holts of Leeds and Samuel Farmer of Leicester, and took the name of 'Brettles Sales'. Whilst Brettles had narrowed its production range since the early 60s, however, Brettles Sales was able to diversify its product range.

By the early 1970s, the two halves had become new Courtaulds companies. George Brettle & Co. Ltd. had become Courtaulds Hosiery Ltd, with David Fry as Managing Director, one of the Fry family of chocolate fame. Meanwhile the wholesale side had become Courtaulds Distributors Ltd, trading as Brettles Sales, with Mr C. Gosling as Managing Director, thus indicating that the old name 'Brettles' was to be preserved only as a well-known trading name.

From this point, our story is mainly that of Brettles Sales. At first, Mr J.L. Bush was as Merchandise Director, then Ivor Boyes. In 1972 Boyes became Managing Director, and Tony Gray took his place as Merchandise Director. Tony had worked for Kayser Bondor, a major lingerie producer, and had joined Brettles in 1964 as a lingerie buyer, but had found the product range somewhat dated; for example it included 40 styles of pyjamas and a large selection of nightdresses, including winceyette, all long length! Tony had updated the range, and added housecoats, which was a great success and doubled turnover. In making these changes, Tony recalls that he forged a good working relationship with David Fry, the MD of Courtaulds Hosiery, whose interests included cricket and jazz.

Tony started a regular sales conference which brought together buyers and sales staff and at which new ranges were introduced. These were held first at Nottingham University, and later at the New Bath Hotel (Matlock Bath), the Peveril of the Peak Hotel (Dovedale), the Makeney Hall Hotel (Derby), Ashbourne Gateway Hotel, and further afield at Hinckley Island and Stratford-upon-Avon. Working with the Scotland sales representative, Tony led a first-ever sales and marketing drive to the Shetland and Orkney Isles which was very successful. Tony also remembers organising and going on trade missions to Nigeria (which brought £50k worth of sales), New Zealand, Japan, and one to Panama that was sponsored by the British Overseas Trade Board.

Internal Organisation

The names of the departments at this time show the widening of the product range. Each was headed by its own Buyer, also known as Merchandiser, for example George Wyatt for the Ladies Underwear & Woven department. Of seven Buyers known to have operated during the early 1970s, at least five had been commercial travellers for the company – Leo Collins (Children's Clothing), Doug Penton (Lingerie), Sandy Taylor (Casuals), Michael Hayman (Hosiery) and Graham Newton (Menswear). This perhaps indicates the promotion opportunities that existed and that the company rewarded experience and merit.

Beneath the Buyer of each department was a Supervisor or 'first man', then typists, porters, 'enterers' (who manually wrote out dockets) and 'order pullers' – such quaint terms remained.

The Despatch department (including the 'entering room') was managed by Denis Campbell and employed at least 16 workers. Here, goods from each department were assembled and matched to the delivery dockets, then packed and despatched. During the busy seasons of spring and autumn, the Despatch department often became inundated with boxed merchandise, chutes became overloaded, and 'wheelers' lined up waiting in train-like fashion.

Another key department was Accounts (still known as the 'Counting House'), within which Syd Clarke was the Accountant, Peter Knight the Credit Controller and Paul Naylor the Assistant. A fuller account of the departments follows in Chapter 9.

The Lighter Side

Work life was not all serious. Former employees remember that occasionally, when pressure of work was not so great, you could pull a 'wheeler' out from under a bench and find some worker in there, either sleeping or put there for a joke if they were a new starter. The chutes that came from the departments on the higher floors were not only used to send goods down to Despatch, but sometimes a new recruit or trainee would be sent down the chute, on the pretext that this was normal! Other well-known pranks were to send newcomers to get 'fixture stretchers' (fixtures were shelves) or 'long weights', or to tell them to send water-softening tablets out with the swimwear!

There were no longer separate men's and women's canteens as in the early years, but there were separate staff and management canteens. The canteen was used for a variety of social events, including dances and discos. It would seem that the company also catered for the spiritual needs of its workers, and Syd Clarke remembers that the Methodist minister acted as a chaplain and visited a different department each day, and used to say grace at the annual staff Christmas dinner.

The festive season was celebrated well. Christmas lunches were held in the canteen, and were served to the staff by management. Michael Hayman and Leo Collins were well known for serving in fancy dress. Festivities often continued in the local pubs. Also, many employees invited their colleagues to their birthday and other parties; the pubs and clubs of Derby were popular venues. This writer was passed two wedding photographs of the period, both consisting mainly of Brettles staff, no doubt colleagues of the bride or groom (or both). The company also supported its own football, cricket, table tennis, darts, dominoes and other sports teams, which mostly still bore the historic Oberon name (see Chapter 8).

New Staff and Director Changes

On 30th July 1973 something happened that probably seemed quite unimportant at the time. Gary Spendlove started work at Brettles, in the Despatch office, which had up to forty staff. None could have guessed then that this young man would one day be the means of the Brettles brand's survival. Gary became a trainee sales representative under Edward Gosling (son of C.G. Gosling, the former MD). He recalls a large sales force, including six reps for Greater London alone and thirty for the rest of the country, and a busy Export department. Hilary Shanahan, the agent for Eire, won the highest export orders, and Chris Petken the North London rep had the highest UK sales figures.

In 1975 Ivor Boyes retired and Tony Gray replaced him as Managing Director of Brettles – the second time he had been promoted into Ivor Boyes' shoes. Tony was replaced as Merchandise Director by Graham Newton, who had been Menswear Merchandiser. In September Gary Spendlove became the sales rep for the Midlands area, then in December 1976, as part of a swap, he moved and became the rep for Central and Southern Scotland.

Long Service Awards, New Bath Hotel, Matlock, 1975, includes Glen Hartshorn 58 years old, 43 years with Brettles, *Courtaulds News* August / September 1986.

Courtaulds Presentations outside the Belper canteen, 1979.

Sales to the Middle East

In 1975, the first comprehensive trade mission to the Arabian Gulf took place between 18th October and 13th November, promoting the forthcoming Spring & Summer 1976 range. It was a joint effort by 'the six member companies of the Courtaulds Wholesale Division', comprising Brettles Sales, Bradbury Greatorex, Batho Taylor & Ogden, Samuel Farmer, I. & R. Morley and M. Duke & Sons. Together, representatives went to Kuwait, Abu Dhabi, Dubai, Sharjah, Doha, Qatar, Oman, Bahrain and Saudi Arabia – a gruelling 36-day tour indeed. It cost £3,900 and brought firm orders totalling £127,509, a good start. The report, compiled just four days later by T. Hollingworth, L.H. Collins and W.O. Thorpe, stated:

> Sales achieved on any sales visit to this area will inevitably vary according to the order of visiting customers in relation to our UK competitors. Because of the number of different states to be visited, we might be first in one state, but will follow competitors like Martin Emprex and Cumberland Fashions in the next. To achieve any continuity of success, regular visits must be made to the area twice a year.[2]

In other words, the prosperity of the region was such that it was not necessarily price sensitive, and orders were likely to be placed with first comers. In any case, the report proved persuasive, and further group missions followed twice yearly.

A second trade mission to the same countries took place in 1976, between 27th February and 19th March. This time, while costing only slightly more, at £4,040, it took credit for a massive £305,237 of orders. The report five days later, again by Hollingworth, Collins and Thorpe, added that the contacts made on the first visit had 'led to many direct visits to our various showrooms and orders placed'. Courtaulds sales agents in the area were Messrs Spinneys, and it was at their showrooms that the products were displayed. However, the leaders of the trade mission were not completely happy with the support offered by Spinneys on the mission itself. The report complained that they were not once met off a plane and were only once given transport; this was to be corrected in the future. The report recommended that on large missions in future the representatives would divide into two teams, combining someone from each company, and each team would visit half the region – seemingly a more efficient and less exhausting method, which was subsequently followed.[3]

Later that same year, a smaller tour was made between 30th September and 22nd October, just to Saudi Arabia, Yemen and Libya. The tour cost £3,296 but only generated sales of £144,119. It would seem that the company were a little slow to adjust to cultural variations when engaging in Middle East sales, and the report, by N.A. Henderson and W.O. Thorpe, rather amusingly concludes: 'We feel that certain items can be excluded from future missions: Ladies' swimwear, Ladies' tennis dresses and skirts – no response at all. Ladies' nightwear – a smaller range to be carried'(!).[4]

Slump and Response

In 1979/80 the company saw a slump in UK business, and Courtaulds' top management required staff cuts. Tony Gray as Managing Director had made a point of getting to know all his staff and he used to do a shopfloor walkabout twice a day. He was now required to make a third of them redundant, which he remembers as a very painful experience. There were 38 redundancies, whilst several of the smaller departments were merged or closed.

In an effort to boost trade over the next two years, key departments launched new brand names – St Trop (swimwear), Gina Minetti (leisurewear), Niteline (nightwear) and Top Drawer (underwear) – all of which were successful. The Sales Managers co-ordinated the launch of their new ranges.

It would seem that the Courtaulds group also sought to improve efficiency further by centralising and combining the export activities of more of its companies, in joint missions. So on 19th May 1980, an Export Meeting was held at 'Courtaulds Distributors in Birmingham', to which were also invited 'Mr K. Senior, Export Manager of Brettles, and Mr D. Kellard, Sales Director of Morleys'. The meeting considered the relative success of various product lines, and concluded childrenswear and ladies' dresses had made a 'successful contribution' to the recent trips, but lines that required improvement were Brettles nightwear and Dukes skirts, and that there was a shortage of boyswear.[5] The autumn of that year saw a combined mission between 16th and 24th September to North Yemen, Bahrain, Saudi Arabia, Jordan and Egypt.

Courtaulds Hosiery (the manufacturing side) had abandoned the 'George Brettle & Co.' name in the early 70s. Outside Courtaulds, however, the name had been well respected, while that of 'Brettles Sales' meant nothing to the public. So by 1980, the old company name was reborn; Brettles Sales, as the sales and distribution arm, became the new George Brettle and Co. Ltd!

During the early 1980s, some Brettles staff were moved to other Courtaulds subsidiaries, and especially to Blount & Co. on Spencer Road or to Aristoc at Langley Mill.

The Stevenson Years

In 1981 by mutual agreement there were several director changes. Tony Gray chose to revert to the position of Merchandise Director, to specialise in his main strength. Gwyn Stevenson, who had worked for Courtaulds for 25 years, was brought in as Managing Director – and found himself locked in when wages were delivered on his first day! Gwyn had started his career in the lace industry in Nottingham and trained in lace manufacture at the Nottingham College of Art, then in Textiles and Management at Trent Polytechnic. He had joined Courtaulds in 1962 as Factory Manager, then Computer Project Manager, and progressed quickly to Administration Director, when he was involved in management training. He later became Managing Director of Holts of Leeds, then of S. & J. Watts of Manchester, whose offices are now the Britannia Hotel (both subsidiaries).

Also in 1981, a new showroom, designed by Derek Wingfield, was opened to attract buyers to visit and select their ranges. Derek had worked for years as the Lingerie department 'first man', Assistant Buyer then Menswear Merchandise Manager. The new showroom included a company museum, and both visitors and new staff found this very informative. Derek also played a major part in the growth of the factory shop on the A6.

Gwyn was a keen promoter of exports and extended Brettles sales to the Far East – Japan, Hong Kong and Taiwan. In particular he spearheaded the selling of woollen garments to department stores in Ginza, Tokyo, the most prestigious shopping centre in Japan. In 1987 he led a sales visit to Shanghai and Shenzhen in China. Gwyn was impressed by the efficiency and low cost of some Chinese producers despite the poor surrounding infrastructure, but was taken aback to find the army influencing their production decisions, a feature of the communist control economy.

Gwyn was also active in advancing European sales, and took exhibition space at the Salon de la Lingerie in Paris and elsewhere. Convinced that the reason many British companies struggled with exports was language barriers, he learned French, German, Italian and Danish and a smattering of Japanese. His belief in British exports went beyond Brettles, and in 1985 he became Chairman of the Intimate Apparel Committee of the British Knitting and Clothing Export Council.[6]

A list of the sales to various countries in 1984 has survived. The company exported to 31 countries that year, and some of the figures are particularly impressive. At the top of the scale, they exported £95k to Ireland, £85k to Saudi Arabia, £63k to Kuwait and £48k to Bahrain. It must be remembered that today's equivalent figures would be three or four times greater.

London Activities

Around this time, the permanently staffed London showroom at 48 Conduit Street, which had been managed by Sidney Foster, moved to 10 St George Street, still in Mayfair, under the management of Patricia Brooke. Patricia became somewhat famous, as Sarah Ferguson, the future Duchess of York, worked next door in number 11. Consequently Pat, at the front of the showroom, found herself filmed on national news for days on end, and wore a bright red jumper in order to stand out on television!

The showroom was well supported by retailers and became very important to the company. The main seasonal collections were launched there, as well as special promotion events. Carole Hunt, who was based in Alfreton, was always involved in and gave energy to the

London events. Carole's daughter Erica, a professional dancer, also worked as a Brettles showroom model for major sales events. There were also area shows in major UK cities and towns, including Belfast, Glasgow, Newcastle, Leeds, Cardiff, Bournemouth and Norwich.

The showroom in St George Street was just round the corner from Courtaulds' London headquarters in Hanover Square. The lease on this prestigious building cost £56,000 per annum, though this burden was reduced by sub-letting the ground floor to Sotheby's auctioneers. Gwyn Stevenson and Gary Spendlove were regular visitors to both buildings, and have vivid memories of one major sales event at Courtaulds headquarters, when a piece of scaffolding fell from a crane through the glass roof of their meeting room, causing injury to several colleagues from flying glass. One customer, Jan Tyrrell from Frillies of Horley, was quite badly injured whilst eating lunch.

Wood Street Showroom pictures

Showrooms at 48 Conduit Street W1, based in London's Mayfair.

1985/6 Events

The years 1985 and 1986 saw more structural and management changes. In 1985 George Brettle & Co, became part of the 'Brands Group', also embracing Cooke and Watts. John Simpson was appointed as Sales Director, and the following year Mike Moulds joined the company as Financial Director. Graham Newton was then the Warehouse Director.

In the winter of 1985/6, severe icy weather over the Christmas holidays caused the sprinkler system to freeze and consequently burst. Employees returning to work after the holidays found the building flooded. Structural damage and loss of damaged stock was considerable, and many departments had to be relocated while extensive repairs were carried out. Syd Clarke recalls:

> After the Christmas hols I arrived with the security man at 7am, and noticed the north side of the main building was covered in thick ice, like a frozen waterfall. When we entered at the rear of the building we could hear the rush of water pouring out of the sprinklers inside, but as the water hit the outside it froze solid! We didn't dare to switch any electrics on, as we might have had an explosion. So after getting in touch with our 'top brass' and the fire brigade, we retired with the post to a safer and dryer part of the building. We reported to higher staff members, some of whom soon arrived including Gwyn Stevenson the Managing Director and other directors to help sort out a real mess.

The bicentennial year of the brand was celebrated in 1986, as it was 200 years since the term 'House of Brettle' had been coined by George Brettle's father, then trading as E. Brettle & Co. in London (although of course the true predecessor to George Brettle & Co. Ltd was the partnership of Ward Brettle & Ward, which was formed in 1803).

A dinner dance was held at the Swallow Hotel in South Normanton for all employees to celebrate the occasion, at which a commemorative mug was presented to all. An impressive cake was made modelled after the Belper factory, complete with bushes and trees, all edible! The *Belper News* produced a special 12-page 'Brettles Supplement', including congratulations from firms all over the East Midlands and a potted history which has been a useful source of information.[7]

BiCentenial Celebration with Factory Cake.

Bicentenary *Belper News* Brettles Supplement, 1986.

Move To Alfreton

However, the following year, 1987, after 184 years in Belper, Brettles had to leave their home town. Courtaulds decided to sell the site, which raised £750,000, and relocated the company to modern leased premises at Alfreton, eight miles to the north-east. The employees were not happy about it, but most were willing to travel. The Duke of Devonshire officially opened the 'new' Brettles building. At the same time the company was computerised, and as a result was able to streamline its operations. Despatch, packing and total staff were fewer in number than in the Belper days.

The original Belper factory shop, sited in Brettles yard, had been for employees only and was mainly an outlet for hosiery seconds. Under the management of Joy Southern and Blanche Lambert, the offer of merchandise at the shop had increased and so had turnover. In the early 1980s, the shop had been taken over by the Wholesale division (Brettles Sales), moved onto the main A6 and opened to the public, which had greatly assisted the growth of retail business. When the main business moved to Alfreton, the shop relocated to the Derbel building opposite the main Brettles building, and manager Blanche Lambert retired. Under the management of Derek Wingfield and the merchandising skills of Mary Pugh, the shop continued to be an important part of the business.

M Moulds,
G Newton, J S Taylor,
G Stevenson,
D S Wingfield,
R A Gray at Meadow
Lane Alfreton.

Duke of Devonshire visits
Brettles to open new Building,
Alfreton (also showing Gwyn
Stevenson), 1987.

Above: Outside Brettles Offices, Meadow Lane, Alfreton, late 1980s (Mike Moulds, Graham Newton, Gwyn Stevenson, Tony Gray, GS).

Left: Front of Brettles Warehouse, Meadow Lane/Salcombe Road, Alfreton, late 1980s.

Right: inside Brettles Warehouse, Meadow Lane/Salcombe Road, Alfreton, late 1980s.

Brettles Christmas Parties, 1970s.

Gwyn Stevenson presenting an original watercolour picture to Sandy Taylor.

Brettles Letterheads

GEORGE BRETTLE & CO.,
119, WOOD STREET, LONDON.

MANUFACTORY, BELPER, DERBYSHIRE.

1869 letterhead.

TELEGRAMS: "BRETTLE.BELPER"

BRANDED GOODS:
"BELNIT" RIBBED UNDERWEAR
"OBERON" HOSIERY & UNDERWEAR.
"LUSTRINIA" "SILKESTIA" "GLEAM"
"GLOSOSE" AND "SUNDENE"

TELEPHONE: 70 BELPER.

GEORGE BRETTLE & CO. LTD.

MANUFACTURERS OF
HOSIERY & UNDERWEAR

BELPER, DERBYSHIRE
18th December 1937.

1937 letterhead.

Brettles

Meadow Lane Alfreton Derby DE5 7EZ
(0773) 520400 Fax: (0773) 836439 Telex: 94011434 PW 413 Ext: 124

1989 letterhead (Photographer : Nick Locket).

Increased Sales and Exports

The company continued to expand, and very prestigious stores became important customers, including Harrods, House of Fraser, Fenwicks, Fortnum and Mason, Owen Owen, Beatties and Beales, all of whom were stocking a variety of Brettles merchandise. The use of the Wolsey brand, with its royal warrants of Her Majesty the Queen and the Queen Mother, also added to the quality image of the business and opened more doors with specialist retailers and new export markets.

Export growth also continued, with merchandise being shipped to over forty countries worldwide. Gwyn Stevenson and John Simpson won substantial orders from various Middle and Far East countries. The Middle East potential expanded, with demand from the UAE (Abu Dhabi and Dubai), Bahrain, Kuwait, Libya, Oman, Qatar and Saudi Arabia. Brettles merchandise was available in many top stores in most of the oil-rich Arabic countries, and these customers bought the quality 100 per cent cotton items. Trading in these markets was profitable, but less consistent due to fluctuating oil prices, the generally volatile situation and various conflicts in this area in the 1980s and 90s. Branded high-quality underwear also found favour in the lucrative Japanese and Taiwanese markets.

In fact, by the end of the 80s the company had sales agents in 45 countries, over three times as many as forty years earlier. The newer countries to which they exported included the USA, West Germany, Greece, Finland, Iceland, Lebanon, Syria, Jordan, Cyprus, Malawi, Malaya, Bahamas, Iraq and the Falkland, Faroe, Canary and Pacific Islands as well as past and present British territories such as Gibraltar, the Channel Islands, Hong Kong and Singapore. The company also developed trade in the nearer-to-home European markets, with many new customers.

Left: Severely damaged Beirut customer's retail outlet, 1982.

Right: GS and Mike Meredith, Kuwait Sheraton Hotel, 25th February 1983.

Left: GS with UK Ambassador and Business Attache, Kuwait. **Right:** Bev Cruikshank at Abu Dhabi Airport, 1987.

Left: GS at Emirates / Oman border, 1988.

In the UK, up to forty regional shows were organised each season, with the London and Belfast events usually producing the top figures. The permanent London showroom on George Street, still managed by Patricia Brooke, moved again to Margaret Street, adjacent to that of Courtaulds brands Aristoc and Gossard, and remained important to the export and large account business.

Meanwhile at Alfreton, the sales staff used the Haddon and Chatsworth showrooms to display their new collections to retail customers. These rooms were also used as meeting rooms for the staff. Conferences at various local hotels were a bi-annual event of the company calendar. The Makeney Hall Hotel in Milford was one of the most popular venues. These conferences were an opportunity for staff and agents to meet and discuss the new season's collections as well as sales performance.

A gradual decline in the numbers of the middle-market independent retailers allowed a reduction in the sales force. Despite this, the efforts of contract and key account managers Mike Meredith, Don McLeish and Chris Ham sustained and increased overall company turnover. The merchandise teams were constant in their innovative designs, which allowed them to keep pace with the ever more demanding customers. Tony Gray as Merchandise Director, Bob Ash as Lingerie Buyer and the team worked hard to ensure the company maintained its 'cutting edge' image.

Above: Maria Erith with Brettles Roadshow merchandise.

Right: GS with Robin Murcell, Sales Director of I. & R.Morley, and Mike Franklin, Sales Manager of Courtaulds Distributors, later Dukes Sales Manager.

Below: Dukes Sales Force and management team.

Above left: Derek Wingfield, Gwyn Stevenson & Sandy Taylor at Alfreton (by kind permission of Mervyn Spencer, Field Photographic of Heanor).

Above: Princess Anne with John Simpson, Gary Spendlove & Gwyn Stevenson.

Left: Princess Diana visits Belper and talks to Brettles staff.

Organisational and Management Changes

Meanwhile on the bigger canvas, the Courtaulds group split into two – Courtaulds PLC including cellulose and plastics, and Courtaulds Textiles, which of course included George Brettle & Co. There was no longer a Courtaulds Distributors Ltd. Brettles then acquired the Dukes Separates brand – an important acquisition. With it came some very experienced staff with strong backgrounds in sales and design. With Jill Regan as Merchandise Manager and Mike Franklin as Sales Manager, the Dukes team developed its new fashion range 'Imogen', which, with a very profitable scarf, glove and accessory business, quickly added over two million pounds to annual turnover.

In 1993 Gary Spendlove, after just 18 years with the company, was promoted to Sales Director to take the place of John Simpson, who had left to become Managing Director of Laura Ashley. The same year saw the retirement of Tony Gray, and his place was taken by Bob Ash, who was promoted from Merchandise Manager in the Lingerie department to Merchandise Director.

Three years later another old-timer retired – Syd Clarke the Accountant. Syd was the company's longest-serving employee, having joined in 1951, straight from the RAF, as a

Wages Clerk in the 'Counting House'. He had continued in Accounts and Finance for the next 45 years.

The Brands

It would be appropriate to mark the mid 90s by a brief resumé of the large number of brands owned and sold by the company. In alphabetical order, these were:

Bairnswear – a Courtaulds brand used only on a collection of school knitwear.

Brettles – the original brand, already described in the foregoing and earlier chapters of this book.

Dukes Separates – acquired by the company from the Birmingham-based Courtaulds distributor. Dukes contributed approximately 35 per cent of the company turnover in the 1990s.

Gina Minetti – invented by Brettles management and used to expand the casualwear offer in the 1980s and 90s.

Hussar – a brand invented in-house and used only on menswear.

Imogen – a fashion brand created by merchandiser Jill Regan and her team as part of the Dukes Seperates operation. Imogen was a collection of quality co-ordinates.

Kayser – renowned high-quality underslips and lingerie. Satin nightwear was very strong in the 70s and 80s.

Meridian – a brand used to supplement the men's and ladies' underwear department. Meridian also complemented the men's socks offer.

Morley – one of the oldest brands used in the business, formerly owned by I. & R. Morley of Heanor. The brand was used very successfully on a profitable scarf and gloves collection.

Niteline – using a telephone logo, Niteline was part of a vibrant young sleepwear collection in the 1970s and 80s.

St Trop – this brand enhanced the company swimwear collection and was used expansively to increase export turnover.

Vedonis – the warm underwear and cotton selection was a large part of the company's success in ladies' underwear. The brand still currently enjoys wide distribution in department stores and mail order catalogues.

Walker Reid – previously used with more mature ladies underwear, and re-launched in 2004 as a brand of exclusive high quality pure cotton nightwear.

Wolsey – the royal appointments of the Queen and Queen Mother were a great advantage on the high-quality underwear and knitwear. Paula Hamilton modelled a very exclusive collection using the Wolsey brand.

Brettles Brand

Elegance in white from
Imogen Collection.

1989 Brettles Lingerie/Nightwear
Summer range.

1989 Brettles Lingerie/Nightwear
Summer range.

1989 Brettles Summer range.

1991 St Trop Swimwear/Leisurewear Summer brochure.

1996 Brettles Lingerie/Nightwear Summer range.

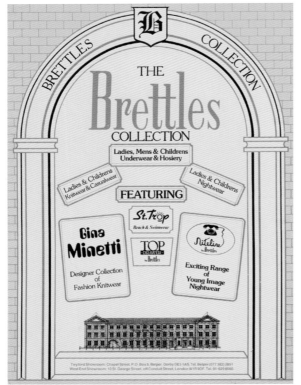

'The Brettles Collection' (Gina Minetti, St Trop, Top Drawer, Nightline).

Our collections are on permanent display at:

London
George Brettle & Co. Ltd., 10 St. George Street,
off Conduit Street, London W1R 9DF
Tel: 01–629 8560.
Contact Patricia Brooke for an appointment.

Alfreton
George Brettle & Co. Ltd., Meadow Lane,
Alfreton, Derby DE5 7EZ.
Tel: Alfreton (0773) 520400.
Telex: 94011434 BRET G. Fax: (0773) 836439.

Brettles trademark & addresses on brochure.

Patricia Brooke and Beachwear Collections at 10 St George Street W1.

Dynamic modelling of new
Wolsey underwear.

St Trop

Left: 1987 St Trop swimwear models.
Above: St Trop display stand at Swimwear Show, Olympia, 1990.

Imogen

Smart City-Girl look.

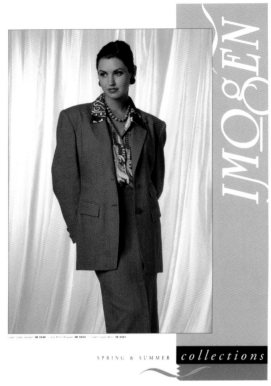

1996 Imogen Summer brochure.

Vedonis

Finesse Thermal Camisole, Vedonis brochure.

Wolsey Underwear
Modelled by top model Paula Hamilton

Wolsey Elegance in Pure Wool

Pure Cotton

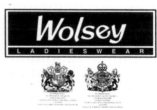

MEADOW LANE, ALFRETON, DERBY DE55 7EZ
TELEPHONE: 0773 520400 FAX: 0773 836439

LONDON SHOWROOM
13/14 MARGARET STREET, LONDON W1N 7LE

Wolsey brochure showing seal of
Royal Patronage.

From Courtaulds to Chilprufe

The 1996 accounts show Brettles with £711.7k net profit (16.5 per cent) on £4.3 million turnover, and Dukes at £169.8k net profit (8.5 per cent) on nearly £2 million sales. In any group, the net profit of an individual company depends on the way in which costs have been attributed, and on management charges, so it is perhaps more meaningful to note that the gross profits for the two brands were 34.5 per ent for Brettles and 29.4 per cent for Dukes. (Imogen sales had risen from £266k in 1992 to £962.6k in 1996, but no profit figure is given.) But by all available comparisons, Brettles was looking healthy.

By 1996, however, the Courtaulds group, like many others, was consolidating and concentrating on its core business, and discarding or selling off product lines now seen as peripheral to this. Courtaulds now identified hosiery as 'peripheral' and proposed to shed it.

In late 1996, six of the Brettles senior management team offered to purchase the company from Courtaulds Textiles and were expecting to commence trading as a privately owned independent business. But, unfortunately for the buyout team, at the eleventh hour a substantial offer was made by Leicester underwear manufacturer, Chilprufe Ltd, which was accepted by Courtaulds' main board of directors. The takeover was considered a move that would enable Chilprufe's collection of brands to potentially dominate the British knitted underwear market. Chilprufe already owned the White Swan trademark, so the acquisition made them a major player in the market sector.

Thus at the end of 1996 George Brettle & Co. became part of Chilprufe Ltd. Most of Brettles' staff were offered continued employment at the Meadow Lane site in Alfreton, some were moved to the Evington Valley Road factory in Leicester, while others were offered and took redundancy.

Many aspects of the Chilprufe experience were considered very positive by the former Brettles employees. These included a variety of import and export experiences, and included first visits to the Far East for some. The exposure to direct production (which few remembered) and the pressures of large-scale Far East manufacturing was again a new experience for many, although individuals recall being under considerable pressure when trying to keep the factories busy and also satisfy the demands of major accounts. But perhaps of greatest benefit were the relationships formed within the business that would prove mutually beneficial in the near future.

At first, the Brettles business continued to function as previously. After several management meetings, however, it became clear that the Brettles brand would not be part of any long-term Chilprufe strategy, and could possibly be phased out. It seemed that Chilprufe had no wish to expand the brand into the new millennium, and the name became less obvious in the marketplace. Some former Brettles management and staff, including Gary Spendlove, were not comfortable with the changing scenario and the new management style, and negotiated redundancy.

The Brettles Shop

Gary Spendlove ceased employment with Chilprufe on 31st October 1997. As part of Gary's redundancy package he acquired the George Brettle retail shop on Chapel Street in Belper, which came complete with staff members Mary Pugh, Sue Brindley, Mary Gould and Rachel Hall. This valuable asset, which was originally in the factory yard, had expanded and moved over the road into the building that had formerly been the manufacturing unit of Derbel Textiles. The extra floorspace had allowed a much wider selection of merchandise to be offered, which resulted in a substantial increase in turnover. Apparently a Llandudno coach company ran a regular trip to the Belper factory shop, as well as the new De Bradelei retail outlet which was situated in the former Brettles main three-storey building, and was also becoming very popular.

Although the Brettles Shop was in a poor condition in parts, it enabled Belper people to continue to buy Brettles produce, and also provided a secure and accessible building from which to start a new design, development and production company, Slenderella.

Meanwhile, back at Alfreton, the site closed at the end of 1999 and operations were moved to the Leicester site. The majority of staff now accepted redundancy, with just a few moving to Leicester. Just two years later, Chilprufe Ltd would go into receivership at the beginning of 2002, which could easily have been the end of the Brettles story. But it was not.

8. THE SPORTS AND SOCIAL CLUBS

Brettles had always provided for the social and recreational needs of its employees in various ways. Old ledgers indicate the purchase of sports equipment in the early years of the nineteenth century.

By 1850 they had established a library at 119 Wood Street, a debating society, a cricket club and a football club.1 Over the years many enjoyed the sports matches, the club dinners and suppers, the London trips to Gilbert & Sullivan operettas and other attractions. The earliest photographs are of the 'Oberon Cricket team' in 1858. Gary Spendlove writes (with tongue in cheek) that apparently the qualification for a plum job with Brettles was not a university degree or exceptional clerical ability, but a good 'right arm spin' or the skill to see off the pace attacks.

The origins of the term 'Oberon' are a little uncertain, but even in the late nineteenth century the firm was producing an 'Oberon' brand of ladies' and gents' underwear alongside

the Brettles brand. The exact date of the founding of Oberon Athletic Club is also difficult to determine, but at some point it seems the 'Brettles Sports & Social Club' became 'Oberon Athletic Club' or 'Association', an umbrella for the various clubs and teams. In 1900 it was recorded that C. Broughton, Manager of the Worsted department, donated £300 and R. Carvery, the Assistant Manager, £165 to the Oberon Athletic Club. But the fact that the 15th AGM was held in 1934

Above: Oberon second eleven Football team, 1908.

Left: Brettles Cricket team, 1910 (Front: Mr Pollett, Dick Martin ; Middle: Redfearn, Dover, McKenna, Sperrin, Claude Noakes ; Back: Randall, McCassidy, Abderson, Kirkbridge, Sampson, Kendall.

suggests that the club had been formed in 1919. On the other hand, the first edition of Yarns magazine in 1929 indicates that the score books of 'all Oberon Cricket matches since 1850' were extant.2

Prior to the First World War, it seems that the sports club went from strength to strength; the Brettles warehouse and factory were able to field three football and cricket teams, and had a full season's programme of fixtures, including shooting, tennis and crown green bowls. A notable pre-war Oberon athlete, W. Browse, was sadly killed in action at Ypres, and a solid silver memorial shield, standing an incredible 30 inches high, was presented to the club in his honour – the Browse Shield. For the next few decades this trophy was much coveted and was won by various individuals and teams. One of the last winners of the trophy was Ivor Boyes, who was to finish his career as Managing Director in 1975.

The Browse Shield, commemorating WH. Browse, killed in World War One (Photographer : Nick Lockett).

The 1920s saw major improvements in Oberon's sporting standards, resulting in the cricket club winning the City of London Championship. A highlight of the season was the visit of the Nottinghamshire county cricket team to London Oberon's Preston Road ground. This team included the great Harold Larwood. Both London and Belper also had football teams, and each year the firm staged a Twyford Challenge Cup match between the two, held alternately at both locations.

The 1929 match was played at Belper on 2nd March, with G.H. Ross acting as referee; the London team were especially strong that year, and beat Belper 9-2. 'Tea' was provided to both teams afterwards in the canteen, and the cup was presented by Mr Bowness, the Belper factory manager. In his speech he was 'pleased to note that the visiting team had on each occasion been successful, and that Belper hoped to maintain the tradition at Preston Road (the London ground) next season'.

The London team returned home and went on to play in the 'City of London TAASA Junior Championships' at Eltham a week later on 9th March 1929. Here they were even more successful, beating 'City Albion' 5-0. As a result they were promoted to the Senior League the following season. H.E. 'Monty' Montauban, the Honorary Secretary, wrote in Yarns that he 'felt confident they could find a cosy corner at 119 Wood Street for the Senior Trophy'.[3]

By 1929, when the first issue of Yarns magazine was published, the Athletic Club was well established, with football, cricket, tennis, bowls, swimming and athletics teams at London, all mirrored at Belper. The record of the club is not continuous, however: we have reports in Yarns between 1929 and 1932, AGM reports and accounts between 1934 and 1969, with some years missing.

Above: Brettles Tennis Club, 1920s and **right** Belper Oberons v Waingroves at Belper, 23rd March 1929. (Back row: N. Fryer, H.W. Hill, Edgar Tucker, Dick Martin, E.L. Davies, L.C. Boydon. Front row: A.M. Boby, Dover, G.B. Mason, Claude Noakes, M. Hunt, Parsonage.)

Sports in the 1930s

The Belper team was less successful than the London one in those early days. In January 1930 a *Yarns* article honestly reported:

> Belper club have not had a very successful season so far, and have only won one game. We are a very young side at present, but with perseverance, we shall give a better account of ourselves in future years. We enter the new year in a hopeful and confident manner.[4]

And in 1930 Belper Oberon's cricket fixtures included games against Belper Meadows, Ambergate, Cromford, Darley Dale and Wirksworth, all local teams with a long history.

In 1931 a new sports ground was opened at Raynes Park in Wimbledon for the London employees, with a newly built pavilion, replacing the former ground at Harrow.[5] At Belper, an extensive sports ground existed between the factory buildings and the River Derwent.

On 27th August 1932 the first Oberon Sports Day or 'Gala Day' was held at the club's new ground in Raynes Park. It was reported that the long jump was won by 'Brake' at a commendable 20' 4" and the high jump by 'Boyer' at an also impressive 5' 7". Whilst Belper staff were present, the participants in the event seem to have been mainly London staff: the 'Inter-Floor Relay Race' was won by 'the Ground Floor' (of 119 Wood Street). As well as the various races and contests, there was a fairground, 'light music was broadcast from a loudspeaker' and the report reads: 'The innovation of a microphone gave quite a modern touch to the proceedings, and was very effective in ensuring that races started on time.' At the end of the day, the prizes were given out by Mrs A.M. Gibson (wife of a manager), and there was a dance in the evening – a good time was had by all.[6] Also the annual London–Belper football match was held there for the first time.

From 1934 to 1969 there is a record of some annual general meetings and financial statements of the Oberon Athletic Club, which have been useful in tracing its progress. The patron up to 1964 was Sir Harry Twyford and the President was A.M. Gibson. The Honorary General Secretary was changed every three years or so – it was Mr A. Frapwell from 1933 to 1935, Mr R. Skidmore from 1936 to 1938 and Mr C.E. Gunn from 1939 to 1941 – whilst the Chairman and most officials were changed every year.

Sir Harry Twyford, the Company Chairman, contributed great enthusiasm to the club. He insisted that, for all fixtures, the club blazer and cap should be worn. Some of these still exist (though admittedly, by the 1980s, squad members usually arrived on match days in faded Levis and T-shirts!).

The Belper version of the constitution in the 1930s provided that membership was open to all employees of George Brettle, all wives, and, oddly, 'members of St Swithin's Church in Belper', which was 'subject to approval of St Swithin's Institute Committee'. Member subscriptions were 10 shillings; 'Outside' members' subscription was 15 shillings for gents, 12/6d for ladies.

Throughout the 1930s, the Belper AGMs were held in the canteen in late January each year, and the following are some of the reported highlights of those years. In 1934, it was recorded that the Cricket section won more matches than ever before, and the appointment of a second eleven was felt to be justified. Also in 1934, the Tennis section entered the fourth division of the Derby & District League, and did well the following year, only losing one match. Consequently, in 1936 they entered the third division, and again did well, finishing in third place.[7]

We may often complain about the English weather in our own times, but this was also a frequent problem at Belper in the 1930s. In October 1930, the report of the cricket season lamented: 'The clouds wept so piteously on every occasion we presented ourselves on the greensward, that in the end, the players gave up the ghost and longed for sunny skies. Not a single match was played here after the holidays, and only three away.'[8] A year later, the report reads: 'The annual cricket duel with London was held at Belper in uncertain weather. The ground was really unfit for the match, but there was no option but to carry on.'[9] And the following year, 1932: 'The ground was flooded at the start, with several feet of water' – surely an exaggeration![10] Again in 1937 the London cricket and tennis teams came up to Belper on Whit Saturday, but 'weather made play impossible'. The visit was not entirely wasted however: it is recorded that all attended an evening dance in the River Gardens Pavilion, and had a Peak District tour on Whit Sunday.[11]

The income of the Belper Athletic Club reached a peak of £124/1/3 in 1934. Only £10 of this came from employee 'member subscriptions', £35/4/6d from 'Other subscriptions', with £3 from 'Sale of grass'. A lower recorded income was £114/16/0 in 1936.

In 1936 the football section won the 'Belper Nursing Cup'. The following year the Belper Oberons won the Belper & District League Cup, and defeated the London Oberon team 7–2 at the annual friendly match.

In 1935, two members of the bowls section won the League Bowls Cup, presented by the *Derby Express*. In 1937 the bowls team played in the second division of the Belper & District Bowls League, and won the championship for the first time. By 1938 the bowls team were playing in the South Derbyshire Association League, and won half the matches they played that year.[12]

In 1938 the football team played in the Belper & District Amateur Football League and were 'runners up in three competitions'. This year they drew 5–5 in the away match with the London Oberons.[13]

On 27th November 1938 the club held its 19th AGM. The Executive Committee consisted of five ladies and ten gents. It was recorded that the Chairman was H.A. Widowson, the Honorary General Secretary was R. Skidmore and the Assistant Honorary Secretary was A.M. Fragwall. Member subscriptions that year totalled just £5. It was recorded that the Belper members had travelled to London at the end of the Coronation week to play the annual matches, including football, cricket, tennis, shooting, swimming and bowls.[14] In 1939 a new section, table tennis, commenced. Also that year for the first time there was income from whist drives.

Above: Oberon First XI Cricket team with Harry Twyford, 1931. Winners of the City of London Textile AASA Senior Cricket Championship.

Left: Brettles' Oberon sports ground at Raynes Park, opened 1931.

Left: Sportsground opening ceremony, Chairman Harry Twyford speaking, 25th July 1931, with Kynaston-Stud.

Below: Oberon Football Team, 1st Eleven, London, 1931–2.

Left: Aerial view showing sports ground & Strutts drive to Bridge Hill House, *Derby Times*, 26th March 1932.
Right: Brettles Sports Day, 1930s, shows gasometer at rear left, since demolished.

Above: Sir Harry Twyford playing first bowl on new Oberon crown green.

Left: Large group including Tennis players in front of dyehouse on the Oberon playing field.

Below: Sir Harry Twyford with cricket team, London, 1930s.

Brettles Cricket Club, 1930s.

Brettles Men's Tennis team, 1930s.

Disruption of the War

The records of some of the war years are unfortunately missing. However, following the destruction of 119 Wood Street by bombing, most staff (or their jobs) were relocated to Belper, and the London Oberon club effectively ceased, as did most sports activities. The London sports equipment was relocated to Belper. In 1941 the accounts included 'Carriage for moving London equipment: £13/10/0', and also showed a donation to Derbyshire County Cricket Club of 1 guinea.[15] Thereafter, such records as we have are accounts for the combined club, all the remaining London staff having relocated to Belper apart from London travellers and a few clerks.

During the war, the number of sections functioning competitively varied from year to year. In 1941 there was only cricket and table tennis; in 1945, only cricket and bowls, though there was some expenditure that year on a new table tennis table and football equipment. Cricket was the only sport played every year throughout the war, with several old cricketers coming back to help out. The eldest, William Ross, aged 59, had 'come out of retirement', but topped the batting averages. Others were 57, 55, 53, and two aged 49. Despite this the team had done well, playing 18 matches, of which they won eight, drew six and lost only four.[16]

Less sport meant less expenses, and in 1944 it was recorded that the club was 'building up a substantial balance which we shall no doubt require when the war is over'.[17] They certainly did, and henceforth would need additional fundraising activities to supplement the subscriptions.

After the War

After 1945, returning servicemen renewed their membership subscriptions and the full repertoire of activities was resumed in the late 40s as finance permitted. By 1947 the workforce was mostly complete again, and members' contributions totalled £60. There were various further fundraising activities, though proceeds and profits varied. In 1947, two dances were held at the Derby Assembly Rooms, which made a net profit of £27/13/10d. On 13th February 1948 another dance at the Assembly Rooms sold 265 tickets, with proceeds of £35/2/6d, but too many costs were incurred and the profit was only 17 shillings. Christmas draws raised profits of £28/9/6d in 1949 and £12/19/4 in 1950. Whist drives that year raised £8/11/6, but a Beetle drive fell flat, raising only a shilling – presumably no more were arranged. The total annual club income including subscriptions rose to £353/12/0 in 1951, and to a magnificent peak of £957/12/1d in 1968.

From the 1950s onwards, there were two distinct entities – Brettles Sports Club, which played on Saturdays, and Oberon Athletics Club, which played on Sundays. After 1950, most football was played on Sundays, and was thus an Oberon activity. The other regular activities throughout the 1950s were, for Oberon, cricket, hockey, tennis and bowls, while basketball was played between 1950 and 1953. The Sports Club played football, bowls, tennis and table tennis (1968 accounts).

As for Oberon Athletic Club officials in the 1950s, we know from a *Derbyshire Advertiser* article that Charles Doerr replaced H.G. Randall as Secretary of the club and that P.A. Nash replaced W. Inch as Treasurer. Randall and Inch both retired from the company in 1959.[18]

Brettles Sports Day, 1950s including E. Flinders, Ginny Allen, Dorothy Allsop, Sarah / Elsie Greatorex, Jim Bowler & wife' and right 'Shooting game, Derwent Street buildings to rear, 1950s'.

Sports under Courtaulds

After the Courtaulds takeover in 1964, the constitution and rules of the 'Oberon Sports & Social Club' were updated. Its objects were stated to be, firstly, the 'provision of opportunities for recreation, social intercourse, refreshment, the playing of games and sports for the benefit of its members'. And secondly, 'the provision and maintenance of a clubhouse in George Brettle & Co. Canteen'. The next clause, as rewritten, stated that 'every ordinary member shall be an employee of Courtaulds Hosiery Division (Spencer Road and Chapel Street Belper factories)'.[19] 'Spencer Road' was the Blounts factory, which was combined with the main Brettles factory, along with that of Aristoc of Langley Mill, under Courtaulds. The sports club activities mostly continued unchanged.

A receipt dated 24th September 1969, under the letterhead 'Brettles Sports Club' of Chapel Street, Belper was for eight cups for that autumn, some sponsored by individual directors past or present. There was a 'Brettles Challenge Cup' each for cricket, tennis and bowls and a 'Gibson Challenge Cup' for cricket and tennis (Men's Open). There were two more cups for bowls – a 'Bowness Bowls Cup' and a 'Sir Harry Twyford Cup' – and also a 'Randall Challenge Cup' for tennis (Men's Handicap). Consistent with this, the 1969 minutes state that the tennis and bowls teams won three trophies each, and the cricket team two trophies, all in solid silver – all in all a successful year.[20]

Memories of the 1970s

In the 1970s Oberon Football Club started playing in the Alfreton & District Sunday Football League in the fourth division, and played local teams such as Heanor Athletic for the Leaderflush Shield.

Gary Spendlove, who joined Brettles in July 1973, was involved in sports from the start. He reflects:

> Sport was always on the agenda at Brettles. Football, cricket, bowls, tennis, netball and hockey all had competitive teams. The local leagues featured the football and cricket sides. The football teams played Saturday and Sunday games, although they were organised by totally separate committees. The Sunday team usually used the Oberon name, which is still used by five-a-side teams in local leagues today. In the 1970s, many of the staff played in the matches, although to enhance the performance of the sides, quality, local players from outside the company were 'imported'. The cricket team in the 70s and 80s acquitted themselves well in the well-organised Works League, at times winning the league and the cup. The unwritten rule was for the cricket side to field nine employees, with two other players having to be related to current staff, usually wives or parents.

Interestingly, the grassland to the west of the company site used for sports also had an army assault course used by the Herbert Strutt School combined cadet forces. Strutt's School also used the Oberon ground for cricket, football and hockey matches. The Oberon playing field also contained a large bowling green, three tennis courts, and high jump and long jump training areas.

Social events were well attended, including an appearance by Gary Glitter in a large marquee on the Oberon field in the seventies. The canteen was a popular venue for dances, discos and concerts. Punk rock band 'Robin Banks and the Payrolls' performed at high volume to a mixed and somewhat deafened audience. Peter Oakley is remembered to have organised some excellent events, and kept a well-stocked bar. Former employees remember enjoying a splendid pint of beer after matches.

Gary recalls the inter-department six-a-side competitions, and that the Sports section played darts, dominoes and table tennis. Brettles Sports & Athletics played football on Saturdays, and Belper Oberon Football Club (which included 'outsiders') on Sundays. Brettles Sports also organised ladies' football matches. The cricket team was organised by Peter Oakley, and played in the Belper and District Works League against teams from Lubrizol, Stevensons, Dyers, Richard Johnson & Nephew and Denby Pottery. There were also matches arranged between other Courtaulds factories. After the matches at Belper, a buffet and bar were provided and there was plenty of socialising all round.

The next surviving document is a letter dated 1st November 1977 from Stewart Wrightson

(UK) Ltd, insurance brokers to Brettles Sports Club, confirming personal accident insurance for members playing football, cricket or in the 'Girls' Netball Team'. This was itemised and Football cover was by far the most expensive, costing £3.42 per member whilst the others each cost under a pound.

In 1982 Andy Conkleton, an established player, became Oberon Football Club Manager, and a series of successes followed. That year they won the Kimberley Shield for the Division Four Championship, and were duly promoted to the third division. In 1983/4 they took third place in that division, and the following year they did even better and were promoted again. In 1985/6 they came third in the second division; the next year they did still better and were runners-up. Finally, in 1988/9 they entered Division One and again immediately achieved third place.

A small cluster of documents from the end of the eighties include a letter dated 8th June 1988 from Brian Clough to Gary Spendlove, responding to an invitation to attend the club's end-of-season dinner in July (unfortunately Brian was unable to oblige on that occasion). Belper Oberon's 1989/90 accounts show income of £421.22 from subscriptions, £43 from raffles and £89 from 'blackouts'. A special menu indicates that a Belper Oberon Football Club dinner was held at the Talbot Hotel in Belper on 20th July 1990, with main course choices of steak, scampi or chicken.

There are several insurance documents from around this period, showing how members were provided for. There is a Renewal Receipt from the Excess Insurance Company dated 15th January 1980 for £49.88. A 1981 renewal quotation letter from broker Stewart Wrightson London Ltd, quaintly handwritten, shows a Death Capital Benefit of £1,000 for football and cricket players and a Temporary Total Disablement Benefit of £10 per week. A similar letter ten years later, dated 27th September 1991, shows significant benefit increases – Death Benefit or Permanent Total Disablement £3,000; loss of one limb or eye also £3,000; Temporary Total Disablement £30 per week for up to 104 weeks.

By 1990, Gary Spendlove was the Chairman of Belper Oberon Football Club. A copy remains of Gary's message to members as Club Chairman. This was also the occasion of Andy Conkleton resigning as Manager after eight years, though agreeing to continue as a committee member. He had earned the thanks of the whole club. The message also indicates the fundraising activities that were going on at the time. These included sponsored walks, car rallies, raffles, a raft race, and the selling of 'blackouts'. The football team were then in the Alfreton Sunday League first division. Sunday home games kicked off at 2.15pm in Eyes Meadow, Duffield. Training nights started at 6.30pm at Belper Sports Centre.

In the late summer of 1996, as the company was changing hands, a cricket match was played on Belper Meadows between the Brettles and Chilprufe teams, at which David Wall of Chilprufe was considered to be 'man of the match'.

It is nostalgic to reflect back, but the heyday of the sports and social club may have been the 1920s and 1930s, when the company invested large sums of money in the Belper and London sports grounds. The Preston road sports pavilion alone would have cost around one million pounds in today's terms. It is also important to remember that the sports club were very strong after the Second World War, with most staff making a small financial contribution from their wages.

The Oberon or Brettles sports and social clubs do not exist today as they did in previous times, but the present company sponsors some local sporting and secular events, and staff take part in charity quiz events and organise the occasional dinner or luncheon, though physical sports are not usually on the agenda. The company does, however, currently operate a cricket coaching programme with schools and youth groups. The Oberon name continues to be used by local five-a-side football teams in the well-organised Belper leagues, although no current staff members are involved. The league is organised by former Oberon team manager Andrew Conkleton and goalkeeper Mark Green.

Above: Belper Oberon v Polygon (Alfreton), 19th October 1975 (Back row: Brian Cornfield, Will Gascoyne, Chris Bacon, David Earnshaw, Duncan Bennett, Malcolm Knapp, Karl Schmit. Front row: Peter Nightingale (Manager), Steve Gascoyne, Nigel Oldrini (Captain), Mick Phillips, Gary Spendlove.

Right: Miss Brettle early 1970s.

9. PERSONAL MEMORIES

The history covered in Chapter 7 spans over thirty years, taking us well into the period remembered by many former employees, and is dotted with many personal recollections. This chapter combines the more extensive memories of some former directors and others with long careers. The first of these comes from Gary Spendlove, owner of the current Brettles business and Slenderella. He joined the old Brettles company straight from school on 30th July 1973, and has extensive memories of that period.

Above: Front of Brettles Factory in the 70s, Chapel Street, Belper.

Left: Side of Brettles Factory in the 70s, Chapel Street, Belper.

Working in the Despatch Department

Like many school leavers and teenagers, I started work feeling well educated and quite worldly wise. My first day at Brettles despatch department changed all that. There were so many colourful characters with wonderful stories. Tales about the war, working 'down pit', moving the London side from London (what was that all about?), sports and social clubs. Plus many personal yarns of triumph and tragedy, so it was no small wonder that I was hooked on the Brettles story from day one. As my employment progressed I became aware of vague quotations about various kings and queens, the Lord Mayor of London, Nazi politicians, ambassadors, political leaders, and even about supplying Admiral Lord Nelson's underwear – in fact more, incredible history than you could seriously comprehend, and totally beyond the experience of a Belper lad. But on reflection, all those stories were based on serious fact, and were only 'the tip of the iceberg'.

My first position as a trainee sales rep was in the Despatch Department, which occupied the part of the factory which is now the De Bradelei factory shop. The Despatch Department consisted of four sections: A–E, F–N, O–Z and 'Town', which was for the London area customers. The various retail customers were allocated to the section by the initials of their town. So, for example, a customer at Bridgnorth would be in the A–E section, whilst Harrods, or Pearsons of Enfield, or Fairheads of Ilford would be in the Town section.

As well as the four sections, there was the Despatch Office with Denis Campbell as the manager. Well respected as a perfect gentleman and renowned for his polite efficiency, Dennis, along with his assistant, John Haggerty, ran a tight ship. A subsection of the Despatch area was the Packers, most of whom were splendid characters with incredible stories to tell of old Belper, World War Two, life in the coal industry or, as they used to say, 'down t'pit'. The 'Adrema', 'Flimsy room' and loading bay were the other areas. Being sent to the Flimsy room to ask for a 'long weight' (or 'wait', as it transpired) on one's first day conjured up a nervous time, especially when one of the female staff slid the door behind me and asked my requirements – I have always been a little claustrophobic in confined spaces. Smoking was only permitted in the toilets, so tea breaks saw a towering inferno of tobacco smoke erupting from the gents' toilets, where each smoker had his own cubicle to sit down!

I was perhaps sold the job by the then Personnel Manager, George Morley. George was a former football league referee and very much 'old school', considered by staff to be a stern disciplinarian. Although small of stature, he carried an impressive authority, ensuring no staff extended tea breaks when they heard the click–click of his steel-tipped brogues on the stone floors. In fact some of the ex-military staff were seen to stand to attention in his presence.

Shopfloor Memories of the 70s

There were many others in Belper who started work with Brettles at around the same time as Gary or earlier, and I have managed to speak to a number of them, each with their particular memories.

Geoffrey Futter joined Brettles in 1965, soon after the Courtaulds takeover, staying for seven years. He worked first on the Ladies' Underwear sales side, putting orders together. Geoff remembers that, in the Factory, the original long knitting frames had been replaced by tall Zodiac frames made in Italy. People he remembers well from those days are George Wyatt, a buyer, Norman Jepson, the reception doorman, John Nind in Yarns, Arthur Hill in the Knitting department and Jim Workman in the Dye House. Later Geoffrey worked in the Wages Office with Sid Clarke.

Geoffrey remembers the complete separation between the manufacturing side (the Factory) and the wholesale side, which was still referred to as the 'London side', since this work had originally moved to Belper from London in 1940. He confirms the continued elitism and that staff in the 'Counting House' serving the London side still felt superior to those in the Wages Office serving the Factory!

Geoff also remembers the staff meeting that was held in 1971 to discuss the introduction of decimalisation, and recalls with some amusement asking what on earth 7/6d would be in new pence, and commenting how difficult it would be to multiply this by three, etc. Geoff left in 1972 to work for Denby Pottery as a financial manager, but after an absence of 38 years, he joined the present Brettles–Slenderella company in February 2010.

Ian Farrell also joined Brettles in the mid 1960s and worked in the Warehouse on ladies' casuals, sweaters and jumpers. His boss was Ivor Boyes, who was a Buyer but later went on to be a Director, then Managing Director. Ivor's deputy was Maurice Shanahan.

Ian remembers the wooden temporary canteen in 1971, used while a new canteen was being built by contractors Bowmer & Kirkland, which was opened the following year. The canteen was used not only for normal lunches but also for evening events for staff and outsiders of a dinner-cabaret kind. Most of the performers were local singers or tribute bands, but on one occasion Gary Glitter was the star! Because of the numbers expected this was held in a marquee, though the success of the event was marred when a glass was thrown and hit Glitter on the head. Rowdiness, it seems, is nothing new. Ian left Brettles in 1974 to work in the Police Stores in County Hall, Matlock.

Among those I spoke to were the two Palmer sisters, who both started with Brettles directly from school at age 15, seven years apart, and both served the standard six weeks in training school before being placed in their respective departments. **Edie Palmer** started in 1964, and was employed in putting elastic on tights, then on toe seaming. **Pat Palmer** started in August 1971, and worked in the Toe Seaming department with her sister. She recalls that there were 40 to 50 staff in the department, and the senior ones 'mothered' the newcomers such as herself. They each worked with a sewing machine and a suction tube, into which the stockings were drawn, enabling the worker to 'run through the seam'. Sometimes a joker would reverse someone's airflow so that stockings flew up into the air! Their 'boss' at this time was Alice Watson.

Company policy for filling new departments was to transfer staff on the basis of 'last in first out', so that the most experienced were normally left in place. So when a new 'Straightening Room' was started, Pat joined the new team there. The work involved stretching stockings over a glass leg, then flattening and stacking them into dozens. The products then went to the Dye House, then to Folding and Packing. Each department had its dedicated mechanic for repairing its own machinery.

The Palmers remember the winter of 1972 with its strikes and the 'three-day week' of power supply. The biggest problem, however, was when on occasions the power suddenly went off without warning, and the workers were pitched into darkness. Pat remembers having to descend a ladder in the dark and the chill of hearing cockroaches crunch under her feet!

Pat left in 1975 to work for Flanders. Edie by this time was employed in putting labels on pantaloons and vests, and in elasticating briefs that were intended for Marks & Spencer. From the mid 1980s, some staff began to be transferred to Blount & Co, another Courtaulds subsidiary on Spencer Road (the building is now a nursing home). Edie Palmer was moved there in 1986, but found it a rather harsh regime, with individual output targets being continually raised without any increase in pay, and she finally left in 1989.

Pat Thawley joined Brettles in 1968 and was posted to the 'Entering Room' (customer names A–E). She enjoyed this work and stayed in it for nearly twenty years. Among Pat's memories are the 'RM' (Ready Money) days, when staff were allowed to visit other departments and buy sample stock cheaply. The move to Alfreton in 1987 was no problem to Pat as she lived in nearby Heage. She was moved into the Lingerie department there, where she 'pulled the orders', including bulk orders for Makro. As a part of this she maintained a stock of labels for all the regular customers, and used 'Adrema' stamps for printing the labels. She worked partly in the warehouse, dealing with both incoming goods and outgoing orders.

Sue Brindley joined Brettles in 1972 and was moved several times to give her a breadth of experience. She started on telexing and copying, then moved to the internal Post Office where she worked with June Butler and Maj Walters. She then moved to the Entering Room (customer names O–Z), working with Wilf Watson and Joan Gibb, and it was here she met Pat Thawley, with whom she was to work closely in future years. The next move was into the factory shop, at around the time when this went from being a company shop for staff to being a public shop facing onto the street. Working in the shop saved Sue from moving with most of the workforce to Alfreton in 1987. Here she worked with Mary Pugh and Mary Gold. The shop sold a number of brands besides Brettles, including Marks and Spencer seconds, and was frequently visited by whole coachloads of customers.

Pat and Sue remember several colourful characters from Brettles' Belper days. One was George Hawkins, a spiritualist who claimed to see ghosts in the factory and also that there was a 'Brettles in the sky' consisting of deceased employees. Another was George Morley, the Personnel Manager, who behaved as though he was everyone's line manager and was somewhat feared. Most of the factory jobs involved continuous standing; as there were no seats, staff sometimes took a couple of minutes to sit on their bench when opportunity allowed. If George then passed by, he would shout 'Get off that bench', which was instantaneously obeyed with a shudder.

The Departments in the 1970s and 80s

Gary Spendlove now describes the Belper departments in the 70s and 80s, which were oddly numbered from 71. Possibly the earlier numbers had been departments in London up to 1940, or perhaps there was a more subtle presentational reason!

Each of the six departments in the 1970s was managed by a Merchandiser or Buyer, who had often been an area sales representative, so the Department Merchandiser's position was seen as a definite career progression. Although the Brettles collections were generally of classic design, the merchandisers were very much 'on the ball' with cutting edge fabrics and designs. New brands such as Gina Minetti, St Trop swimwear and Niteline lingerie were all internal innovations, adding considerable intrinsic value to the company.

Department 71 was **Menswear**, where Graham Newton as Buyer developed fine collections of knitwear and underwear. The men's sock department, also known as Half-Hose, had a reputation for excellent quality. Some items were even sold with their own darning wool ball – remember the darning mushroom? A major customer was the Central Electricity Generating Board or CEGB. They would purchase considerable quantities of heavyweight 'sea boot hose', which were also sold to deep sea fishermen. The high-quality men's warm underwear enjoyed a wide distribution throughout the UK. The 'first man' in Menswear was the very able William 'Bill' Aldred. The staff there occasionally enjoyed an impromptu game of cricket, the 'pitch' located in the second aisle of the main walkway! Long-serving member of staff Glen Hartshorne excelled at his version of department spin bowling.

Department 72, Hosiery, was originally the cornerstone of the Brettles business. The company had historically produced silk hosiery for King George III and Queen Victoria. Also, specialist hosiery was previously made for various celebrities and sports stars, including size 16 socks for World Heavyweight boxing champion Primo Carnera. Examples of such items are on display at the Belper North Mill Museum.

Pure cotton hosiery contributed substantially to the hosiery offering. Syldene and Belsheen hose were sold to major retailers. Some of these items were retailing at over £12 a pair – quite a luxury when a pint of beer was selling for two shillings (or ten pence today).

The superfine 'Cheri' fully fashioned stocking enjoyed a renaissance in the mid 1970s, the pointed heel adding a sexy image. A collection of fishnet and Italian lace hosiery also gave the company a cutting edge over much of the competition. Lisle stockings were also dyed white and supplied for stage and film productions of *Mutiny on the Bounty* and *Les Miserables*. The colourful and energetic Mike Hayman was the hosiery buyer, with the ever efficient John Abbot as first man. Mike had previously been a traveller for the company in North Wales, as had his father.

Department 73 was the **Children's department**. Brettles childrenswear also had a reputation for top quality, with the famous blue and white boxes visible in many quality retail outlets. Pure cotton socks were a major part of the department's turnover. Arcadian, Charter and Dualwear were sub-brands in the sock department. The pure cotton and pure wool underwear also contributed to a highly successful business. The Merchandiser, Leo Collins, had been a cornerstone of the sales force, and added his skill to the buying team. Leo also contributed greatly to the company export turnover in the 1970s, especially with visits to the Middle East. Specialist items such as baby nests were exported in volume to the Arab countries and North Africa. The department's 'first man' was the very experienced Trevor Brown, again a long-serving member of the management team. Prince Charles was known to have worn Brettles socks as a boy, adding to the company's Royal connection.

Department 74 was the **Lingerie department**, and had a reputation for innovation with style, fabrics and colours. The 1970s and 80s saw many developments in yarns and satin polyesters, viscose and nylon, including 'tricoloop', featured in the twice-yearly collections. Packaging also played a major part in the image of the business. In fact some staff joked that the black and gold dressing gown boxes were more valuable than the item they contained! The Brettles slip or underskirt collections were in great demand. 'Anti-stat' nylon was a major seller, along with the polyester and Celanese items. Tony Gray was the Merchandiser in the

1960s and early 70s, and was very innovative with the nightwear and dressing gown collections, which included luxury satin-lined quilts, pyroseen and botany wool dressing gowns. After his promotion to Merchandise Director, he was succeeded as Merchandiser by another excellent former traveller, Doug Penton, who was later succeeded by Don Whewell. Department 'first man' was Derek Wingfield, who became Menswear Merchandise Manager following the promotion of Graham Newton to a directorship. As part of the Courtaulds Textiles Division, the Brettles team had access to many development facilities and the technology of a major international company, which along with the Courtaulds Chemical Division was listed in the *Financial Times* 100 top companies. Tom Alton followed Derek Wingfield as first man, upon promotion from the Woven Underwear Export Supervisor role.

Department 75 was **Woven Underwear**. Historically this department was a flagship for Brettles. The underwear had previously been made at Belper, but the strategy was to design, with the finished goods being made at other established factories like Hodgkinson & Gillibrand, Harrison & Hayes, Ellis's, Vedonis, Ratby Garments and others. The underwear offering was considered to be medium to high quality, with many natural fibres included. The addition of more unusual fabrics such as Orlon, Banlon Nylon and Courtelle all guaranteed a 'cutting edge' to this department and were an important part of the success under Buyer Michael Hayman. Mike had taken the reins after the retirement of long-serving Merchandiser George Wyatt, and again had been promoted from the sales force (and his father had also been a successful traveller with the firm). Mike's first man was the dedicated Derek 'Paddy' Powditch, who was always prepared to work overtime and go the extra mile for the company at peak times. Tom Alton worked very hard to look after the many export orders, while Jack Rooth, ex-submariner Derek Barnes, music-loving Steve Kerry, Trevor Spencer and Minnie Harrison were key members of a very colourful team. Sadly Mike Hayman died prematurely, which was considered a serious loss to the merchandise management team.

The Woven department also had a great team ethos, with 'all hands on deck' when large deliveries arrived. The arrival of the blue box from Vedonis of Hucknall on a Friday afternoon always gave the staff a thirst for their Friday night pint. It would involve putting many hundreds of one-dozen boxes from the van onto 'wheelers' then onto the goods lift for checking and fixturing. The order pickers would then pull the orders prior to despatch via the 'Entering Room'. Interlock underwear created a large part of the Vedonis collection, so moving this stock was physically demanding, due to the weight of the fabric. '2057D' and '7477D' were the top-selling Vedonis items, and the Brettles 'R1470' pure cotton group was the department's best seller. Other winners were the wool groups of Grace, Regal, R1605 and Supreme. The top customers for underwear at the time were the Binns group from Sunderland. The Portsea Island Co-op of Hampshire was another major customer.

But it wasn't all work and no play. It was common for some members of staff to play dominoes or cards in their lunchtime; three-card brag with its various connotations was a popular game. On occasions, World War III nearly erupted after one of the younger syndicate produced a 'run on the bounce' or a 'prile of threes'. There was deep pressure surrounding these games, with heated verbal exchanges; well, what do you expect when you are playing for a penny a life?

Gary remembers that in certain hard winters, and when there were power cuts, free soup in generous quantities was provided by the management. The department junior would be designated to do the canteen run for a large jug of pea and ham or minestrone soup.

Department 76 was the **Ladies' Casualwear** department, but also included school knitwear and swimwear. Although not the traditional Brettles image of hosiery and underwear, the ladies' fashions expanded through the 1970s and 80s, and 21-gauge fully fashioned knitwear sales formed a large part of the department turnover. The parent company yarns were used extensively with sales in Courtelle knitwear. Trevira also took a substantial market share. The additions of the 'Gina Minetti' brand along with the St Trop swimwear ensured the fastest growth area in the business.

The Casuals department was the most southerly of the Brettles buildings, being on the part of the site acquired from Wards. The porters in Casuals were considered the fittest in the company as all assets had to be taken across the car park in wheelers or trolleys. The department was adjacent to the company infirmary or sick room, complete with company nursing staff. Another former traveller, J.S. or 'Sandy' Taylor, was the Merchandiser during this period. Sandy was succeeded by Charles Andrew as the business moved to Alfreton. The long-serving first man was Maurice Shanahan, who was succeeded by Christopher Burrows.

The Melissa Bell swimwear collection caused a sensation in the 1990s and attracted considerable publicity in the national press. The collection was launched in the packed 'Hollywoods' nightclub at Romford, to a celebrity audience, and the company hired a luxury coach from Alfreton for the occasion. Melissa Bell played the character Lucy in the *Neighbours* TV series, and guests at the event included cast members of *EastEnders*, *Neighbours* and *Home and Away*!

Sales Representatives and Sales Areas in 1984

Area & Area No.	Sales Rep	Area & Area No.	Sales Rep
Northern Ireland (35)	L. Reid	West Midlands (4)	A. Unwin
Northern Scotland (37)	B. Spence	East Midlands (3)	G. Bailey
Central Scotland (30)	S. Burnett	East Anglia (11)	T. Purkiss
South Wales (29)	G. Bayley	Essex (42)	E. Daniels
Greater London (61)	P. O'Connell	Kent (10)	S. Perrin
Tyneside and South-East Scotland (5)			J. Haswell
Lancashire and Greater Manchester (7)			G. Spendlove
Yorkshire and Humberside (9)			J. Atkinson
Cumbria and South-West Scotland (20)			F. Blakey
North Wales and Merseyside (24)			R. Arrowsmith
Avon, Wiltshire and Berkshire (27)			A. Fitchett
Hampshire, IOW, Channel Islands (15)			A. Croucher
Cornwall, Devon, Somerset, Dorset (18)			K. Mortimer

Merchandising Memories

Tony Gray served Brettles for over 22 years from 1972, including 16 years as Merchandising Director and six years as Managing Director. The following are some of his memories from the 1980s.

Tony remembers leading several successful promotions that boosted wholesale sales. One of these was a 'National Knickers Week', with several special offers including a 'Baker's Dozen' offer of one free pair for every twelve pairs ordered, and a prize offered to retailers for the best window display, for which competition was fierce, and sales were significantly boosted.

Tony was very aware of the need to be fashion conscious in the range offered. He wrote a booklet for buyers and sales staff entitled 'Unravelling the Mystery of Underwear', in which he stated that 'Retail buyers tend to be very conservative in their buying habits where underwear is concerned. They will buy what they sold last year, but need to be persuaded to try new styles and new ideas.'

One of Tony's special strengths was networking and relationship building. He struck up productive working relationships with fellow directors, especially Gwyn Stevenson, the MD, with staff, with the Hosiery Workers Union representative (which served him well when 'talking down' a 25 per cent pay rise bid), and very importantly with suppliers. One of these was John Raven, whose company, Ratby Garments, was an underwear manufacturer and supplier to Brettles. They went on several joint trade missions to Germany and Holland together, with a team of ten buyers and sales reps.

Following the closure of a gloves manufacturer, Tony arranged for its whole stock, including leather gloves, to be purchased by Courtaulds and moved to their London showroom in Albemarle Street, thus increasing the range. He also added headscarves to the range, and after meeting various European manufacturers sourced these from Lake Como in Italy and from Czechoslovakia.

One of Tony's memorable successes was the purchase of 500 dozen Japanese printed squares at a price that enabled them to be sold back to Japan at a worthwhile profit! He was very successful at negotiating prices with Asda by means of a special 'contract range', and, most importantly, helped enable the overall profit margin to be gradually doubled from 16 per cent to 32 per cent during his term of office.

Another noteworthy incident that Tony remembers from this period was a surprise order from Marks and Spencer for one thousand dozen bedjackets. This supposedly arose from a conversation between the wives of the Chairmen of the two great undertakings (M&S and Courtaulds) at some event, when the question was asked: 'Why don't we sell your bedjackets in our stores?' This was not the usual method of M&S marketing, but illustrates the way that things often happen! Accordingly, Tony sourced the 12,000 bedjackets from a manufacturer in Leek and the deal was done.

Tony's assistant, Michael Base, was a very energetic contributor to the Underwear department's management team, and also played a major part in the development of Dukes and Morley scarves and gloves.

Staff Memories from the late 1980s and 90s

Amanda O'Leary started with Brettles in 1987, working for Bob Ash, who at the time was solely responsible for buying nightwear and lingerie, before being promoted to Merchandise Director, which involved overseeing the buying in all departments. Bob was highly experienced and respected in his field, and she gained a great wealth of knowledge from him on the buying side, although she already had years of experience in textile technology, design and fabric converting.

Amanda remembers that Bob was seen as quite a fearsome person, and was a slow starter in the mornings. 'He liked to come in and sit down with his pipe (smoking indoors was strictly forbidden), a cup of coffee (made by Amanda) and his paper. By 10am he would have had his second cuppa and was ready for work. Staff members would approach the office, cautiously peer round the door and wait for me to either beckon them in or discreetly signal for them to come back later.'

Amanda particularly remembers one occasion when Gary Spendlove returned to the office after a six-week trip to the Middle East. 'He came along to our department to proudly show Bob the orders which he had taken for nightwear and lingerie; they were considerable and not to be sneezed at. Gary had given away a little margin here and there to secure the orders, but Bob, having not been consulted first, was furious. He seized the orders, ripped them in half and threw them in the bin. Gary stormed out after making some comment that Bob was never grateful, or words to that effect. I had thought about taking cover under my desk, but decided to make Bob a calming cuppa instead. After puffing on his pipe and drinking his tea, Bob retrieved the orders from the bin, sellotaped them back together, then went to thank Gary for his efforts.' Perhaps lessons learned all round!

Amanda went from being 'the office girl' to Assistant Buyer, which enabled her to use more of her previous experience and knowledge in textiles. She started to accompany Bob on his buying trips to Istanbul (a place she has continued to visit for 25 years), Spain, and various parts of the UK.

Amanda's perception was that Bob's bark was worse than his bite, and this became apparent as the years went on and he began to mellow. He was winding down towards retirement, and with mutual respect their roles became reversed, to the point that he would come into the office in the morning, make Amanda's coffee, then after his morning ritual ask her what he could do to help!

Elaine Salmon joined Brettles in March 1987, just six weeks before the company was moved from Belper to Alfreton. She remembers that Hortons of Ripley were contracted to run a works bus from Belper to Alfreton, calling at Heage and Ripley, and this ran for over ten years. She saw how the move from the 'rabbit warren' of departments at Belper into 'open plan' at Alfreton brought about a shared sense of the big team, and that staff of different departments got to know each other better. The social side was strong. Elaine remembers the Christmas parties at the Palais and Ritz in Nottingham and the Pink Coconut in Derby, and one at Higham Farm in 1999. Other outings included cycling round Rutland Water, tenpin bowling and the toboggan run at Swadlincote.

Elaine worked in the Accounts department with Paul Naylor, with Peter Knight as Credit Controller. She remembers some quaint terms being used, such as 'Renders' meaning creditors to whom money was owed. Company computerisation only began with the move to Alfreton, the company using a bespoke package, also used by Coats Viyella. In those early days of computerisation, much of the work apart from initial data input was done externally by a computer bureau in Derby.

When Gary Spendlove became Sales Director in 1993, Elaine became his PA and was also involved in Export work, along with Toni Elliot and Elaine Boyman. Elaine had been PA to

John Simpson when she met her future husband Ernie Lovell on a course. Ernie was a senior Courtaulds Training Officer who worked at the Courtaulds Training Centre at Woodside in Warwickshire. Toni Elliot made a positive contribution to the company's expanding export business, and was climbing the ladder of the young promotables. Unfortunately she was tragically killed in a car accident; her funeral was attended by most employees, and she was sadly missed.

When Chilprufe took over in 1997, the new management moved Elaine into the main Sales office. Then, when Chris Ham replaced Gary as Sales Director later that year, she worked as his PA.

The former Hosiery dept, now Belper Orangery (MacDonalds).

The frontage of Brettles buildings today, from roundabout.
Both photographs courtesy of Ray Marjoram and Belper Historical Society Collection.

Sales Manager Visits to Ireland

Gary Spendlove was promoted to Sales Manager in 1989, which involved regular visits to many different areas. Here he recalls a trip that he always enjoyed making.

Part of the Sales Manager's function was to visit the area reps and area sales managers. The general strategy was to boost trade and develop direct management links with key retail accounts. One of my favourite visits was two or three days in Northern Ireland with our esteemed Irish agent Lawrence Reid. Laurie introduced me to many of the finest retailers and department stores in the province. On my visits I built a lasting picture of the deep divide between Republicans and Unionists, and between many Catholics and Protestants, although clearly a huge majority of people had a great desire for peace. Thanks to God that, with the hard work and determination of many politicians, church leaders and ordinary people, the peacemakers eventually won the day.

I always had a warm welcome from our retail friends, and the vivacious Maureen Pimbley of Anderson & McAuley was always a 'good call'. We were always delighted to 'scratch the pad' in Andy Macs. The warm humour of the staff of Wattersons of Omagh made this one of my favourite calls. The buyer Veda Short and her assistant Lillian always had a ready smile and wonderful wit. Sadly, Veda lost her life in the Omagh bomb massacre. The textile world and the world as a whole shared a very dark day at the sad loss of a wonderful lady.

It was always a pleasure to visit the Houstons stores. Mr Kennedy, with his sons Steven, John and Phillip were always the perfect Irish gentlemen. The courtesy of Paul Cuddy and his father in Magherafelt was also memorable. We always made time for a coffee, and it always felt like I was with friends. I also have good memories of Dunlop & Carson, Moores of Coleraine, the White House in Portrush, and Marshalls of Saintfield, and of finishing the day with Roberta at Menarys, which was always a pleasant way to end my visit.

A bracing walk with Laurie Reid on and around the Giant's Causeway stands out as a fond memory. The city walls of Londonderry are also very impressive and well worth a visit. The North of Ireland has so much potential for tourism; thank God the continuing peace in the twenty-first century allows many people to visit and enjoy the historic beauty of the province.

Following my two or three days in the north I would board the train for Dublin and go on to visit customers in the south. I always enjoyed this journey, usually via Dundalk and Drogheda, a chance to relax after the full days in the north with their early starts and late finishes, and an opportunity to grab an hour's sleep. Apart that is from one occasion when four rough-looking Irish lads took exception to my broad Derbyshire accent and proceeded to berate me for most of the Irish 'troubles' over the last three hundred years. In fairness, an amount of alcohol had been consumed but a very diplomatic guard and several transport police ensured my safe arrival in the capital of the Irish Republic.

Dublin – what an amazing city! But I have never known a place so unimpressed by celebrity. At different times I saw Damon Hill, Bob Geldof, Bono and other members of U2 as well as one or two boy band members, but not one of them was hounded by the paparazzi or even autograph hunters.

Our Brettles agents for the Irish Republic were a highly regarded father and son duo, Stan and Randal Ferguson. The company previously had a very popular agent in Mr Hilary Shanahan. Hilary's wife was the Buyer from the Roches Stores group. He had held company performance records for sales of nightwear and dressing gowns. When the Roches orders were hand-picked in the Lingerie department you would see quite a mountain of quality individually boxed items for this major export customer.

Stan and Randal had a difficult act to follow, but they were very successful with the high-class Dublin department stores, especially Clerys, whose Buyer Pat Hussey and her staff were strong supporters of the Brettles brand, and always an absolute pleasure to deal with.

On one of my earlier visits to Dublin, accommodation had been arranged for me at the renowned Burlington Hotel. Due to a 'faux pas' in the booking arrangement there were a number of problems with the hotel, resulting in a stern letter from Stan Ferguson to the hotel manager suggesting that the hotel 'make amends'. As a result of Stan's letter I was personally invited to return to the Burlington Hotel and offered VIP treatment. I was given their top suite for the duration of my visit, complete with separate bedrooms and circular jacuzzi bath, which incidentally you had to walk up some steps to; I was certainly given the 'royal treatment'. In fact I was told that Henry Kissinger had been a previous occupant of that suite, along with a number of celebrities. Sadly, though, this accommodation was somewhat out of my price range on subsequent visits! But it was a most acceptable experience on that occasion.

Travels Abroad

Being Sales Manager and later Sales Director involved considerable overseas travel. Coming from a mining family (my father and great grandfather both worked at the local Denby Drury Lowe Colliery) was no preparation for many years of international travel. My first ever flight in an aircraft was a holiday to Italy, aged twenty. A few years later I clearly recollect, on a morning flight between Jeddah and Riyadh, being the only passenger in the first-class cabin of a Saudia 747. My thoughts still went back to family holidays in a caravan in Skegness or a cosy guest house in Scarborough. How I loved those family times – but how life had changed.

Left: As the local mines closed, many Derbyshire miners entered the textile industry. Here is a scene from Denby Drury Lowe Colliery.

I had no inclination when I started in 1973 that the Brettles path would allow me to visit almost one hundred countries. It included exciting visits to China, walking on the Great Wall, visiting Tiananmen Square and the 'Forbidden City' and also meeting many native Chinese people who kindly permitted me to partake of their hospitality – although I declined second helpings on most occasions. Snake, scorpion and cat are delicacies from the Far East that I would refuse in future. A whole sheep's brain on a wet night in the Lebanon's Bekaa Valley was hard to consume, but a Lebanese mezza is quite delicious, especially when washed down with the local Arak.

My Middle East trips have many memories. On one of numerous visits to the island of Bahrain, I was delighted to note we had twelve customers in and around the capital of Manama. But I was also pleasantly surprised to call in at a local garage and see Silkolene oil and Swarfega for sale. So not only were Belper companies selling thermal underwear to the Arab states, we were also selling oil back to the Middle East!

More negatively, I have been invited to public executions, but have always declined as I consider them to be barbaric. It still shocks me that this method of retribution is practised in many countries.

A first-hand experience of conflict, in Lebanon and Kuwait, was quite traumatic, in particular as I met so many lovely people in these places. The Kuwait Sheraton was a favourite hotel with a great restaurant. The Marriott Hotel, which had been an ocean liner, was a great location for a game of tennis with my good friend Bev Cruickshank. It was a sad experience just after the Iraq invasion to see these beautiful hotels largely destroyed. I personally had a very close call after leaving the Intercontinental Hotel in Amman in Jordan. After checking out and flying directly back to the UK, I arrived home in Belper about 12 hours later to learn from national TV that the same hotel had been wrecked by a massive car bomb.

Along with the amazing architecture of our old European cities, I have been fortunate to visit many ancient places. Pompeii, Rome, Ephesus and Cairo hold many memories, although Petra in Jordan would be my favourite. Before I lapse into a travellers' guide, it is enough to say that joining the company in 1973 allowed a local boy a wide world of opportunity which continues to the present day.

10. BRETTLES WITH SLENDERELLA

Gary Spendlove was one of the six managers who had earlier made a bid to buy the company from the parent business, Courtaulds Textiles, in 1996. Unfortunately for the buyout team, the Courtaulds main board decided to accept a bid from a major Leicester underwear producer, Chilprufe Ltd. Although the takeover had potentially created a major European textile business, the new company was destined not to succeed but to enter administration early in the new millennium. Meanwhile Gary agreed a redundancy deal with Chilprufe in October 1997 which included the purchase of the Belper factory shop, from which base he soon saw other possibilities for the future.

The Slenderella Story

As a young sales rep in Scotland in the 1970s, Gary had also become very aware of the Slenderella nightware and lingerie collections. The brand enjoyed a wide distribution and was sold in many of Scotland's top stores, including Jenners of Edinburgh, R.W. Forsyth, Frasers, Alexander Wilkies, Turnbull and Wilson, Arnotts and Patrick Thompsons to name but a few. The Scottish agent for Slenderella was the highly regarded Ian Lindsay. The brand was then produced by S. Newman Ltd., mainly on Tyneside. It was considered that the company manufactured a prized dressing gown collection. The quilted items were luxurious and aimed at the middle- to high-class market sector. Slenderella enjoyed an excellent reputation, producing exclusive styles both for the company's own label and for contract markets, including major department stores.

From humble home-spun beginnings in the East End of London in the 1920s, Slenderella had grown to acquire its own factory. This was destroyed by bombs in 1942, and they moved to Middlesex. Two years later, as the demands of the Second World War increased, the factory was requisitioned by the Ministry of Aircraft Production. The decision was then made to move to a large production unit in South Shields. From there, Slenderella became a recognised national brand.

The complete Slenderella story is told in Andrew Miller's book *The Earl of Petticoat Lane*.[1] As with Brettles, there are fascinating connections to the Royal Family and other renowned celebrities. Hollywood legends Elizabeth Taylor and Hedy Lamarr were known to have worn the company's products. The company were delighted when Miss Taylor and the cast of the acclaimed film *Little Women* publicised their garments. Further international acclaim followed when the company helped create Miss Lamarr's wardrobe exclusively for the golden screen classic *Samson and Delilah*.

In 1997 Gary discovered that the Slenderella brand was available for acquisition, with an almost limitless potential for development. He held discussions with Michael Freedman, as Director of S. Newman Ltd. and owner of the brand, which were successful. The legalities for the purchase of the Slenderella brand were undertaken by Robinsons solicitors of Derby, and the new company, Slenderella Wholesale Ltd, was incorporated on 19th November 1997. The owners are recorded as Gary with his wife Gaynor as the Company Secretary. The first wholesale premises were a small room at the rear of the Belper retail shop on Chapel Street, on which Gary had taken the lease.

The first retail customer to place an order from the new firm was Edna Dale of Leek, and the first multiple order was placed by the Beatties group of Wolverhampton. In the first year of trading, the company received the *Lingerie Buyer* magazine award for the UK's best classic nightwear collection, sponsored by Dupont. For the next two years the brand achieved the runners-up trophy, but again won the coveted crystal pyramid in 2001. The company has also received industry and Chamber of Commerce awards.

From Chilprufe to Slenderella

Chilprufe had taken over the Brettles business and the associated brands at the end of 1996. All of the other historic brands created a very strong ladieswear offer for the new company. However, it is worth noting that at a 1997 sales meeting in Alfreton the Chilprufe sales team believed the new Slenderella company to be a strong competitor.

No records are available to state the reason for the final demise of Chilprufe, but poor cash flow, declining quality and a consequent downturn in demand were certainly contributing factors. Chilprufe was put into receivership early in 2002. This allowed a sale agreement for the Brettles brand to be achieved between Stuart David Maddison for Chilprufe Ltd (in receivership) and Slenderella Wholesale Ltd. The Slenderella management paid a modest five-figure sum for the brand rights of Brettles. As part of the same deal, the Walker Reid brand was also acquired. Both brands were assigned to Slenderella by the Patents Office on 12th June 2002, and this greatly strengthened the offer available from the young Belper company. The agreement included the purchase of a large quantity of finished merchandise. Gary Spendlove recalls the event as 'the best day's business I ever did'.

Thus was the Brettle brand rescued and brought it back to its historic home town of Belper.

Growth and Celebration

Meanwhile the Slenderella office and retail outlet had moved from Chapel Street to the old Co-op building on King Street, Belper. This new address allowed warehouse space for twelve thousand items of stock. However, the rapid growth of the company necessitated a further move, this time to the former premises of another historic Belper business, Flanders Ltd, owned by the Litchfield family. Sadly the move meant the closure of the retail shop for a time, leaving many long-standing customers disappointed.

At first, from July 2002, the company just leased and occupied the former Flanders warehouse in Queen Street, and created some office space there. Again, due to swift expansion and the need to store a large dressing gown collection, an approach was made to John and Roger Litchfield, acting for Coppice Property, to purchase the whole of the site. The amicable negotiations were completed, and the company again had the capacity to expand. By 2003, it was supplying over 700 customers in the UK.

The year 2003 was the recognised 200-year anniversary of the establishment of Brettles in Belper, and time for a major celebration. Over 300 friends, guests and former employees attended the event, and many artefacts and historic memorabilia were displayed at various venues in the town. A 'Miss Slenderella' competition was won by local girl Frankie Corbett. For the event a booklet containing the condensed history of Brettles was created. So an anniversary that could easily have never happened was celebrated in style.

Above: Some retired employees at bicentennial celebrations, 2003.

Left: 2003 Bicentennial Cake with Peter & Mary Oakley, Dena Bell & Joy Exton.

Geoff Melbourne with Brettles original oil painting, 2003.

Former Management and Staff on Chapel Street during the Brettles Reunion in 2003.

Group of past and present employees outside Brettles former export officel, 2003.

Left: Group of Employees at sponsored cricket match, Belper Sportsground, 2003.

Below: Gary receiving award, 2003 (by kind Permission of JMS Photography).

In 2007 the warehouse was purchased, along with the adjacent office block. This was a big financial commitment, for an expanding and ambitious company. The staff joined in with contractors to get the building into shape, with renovations and redecoration needed. Its opening coincided with Gary's fiftieth birthday, and the staff laid on a party in the new offices, with Blues Brothers music. There was a great sense of achievement and celebration.

The next big step forward was in May 2008, when by popular demand the new Brettles Retail Shop was opened in Days Lane at the side of the premises, run by Julie Wheelhouse, with customers travelling considerable distances to make their purchases.

Above: Miss Slenderella Frankie Corbett driving past Slenderella's second home, 2004.

Left: Local MP Patrick McLoughlin and Slenderella staff.

Below: GS and Amanda O'Leary with BBC newsreader Kate Adie.

Above: GS and open-air Snooker, Beijing, China. 2006.

Right: Shanghai Skyline from hotel, China. December 2008.

Below: GS and Amanda at Korean meal, Quindhao, China. December 2008.

Right: Ablutions outside Sultan Hammet
Great Mosque, Istanbul, May 2009.

Below: Harvindar Singh Sodhi, GS and
Amanda at the Taj Mahal, India, May 2010.

Left: Captaining the Chinese Olympic Yacht, Qingdhao Bay, China.

At the time of writing, all the Brettles product groups are continuing to grow and garments are purchased daily in many retail shops in the British Isles. Export growth continues, with overseas sales contributing more than 12 per cent of the annual turnover. The quality and value offered will ensure the brand trades successfully into the twenty-first century. The history is wonderful and the future is very exciting.

A Winning Team

The current Brettles-Slenderella team includes a number who worked for the old Brettles company.

Geoffrey Futter was the earliest of the present team to join the old company, in 1965, as described in Chapter 9. After an absence of 38 years, he joined the present company in February 2010. He recalls that on 'his first day back' he was helping to man a stand at the MODA exhibition at the NEC. Since then he has been employed in a very versatile way on a range of work, according to what is needed at the time.

Pat Thawley has spent the longest of all the team with Brettles. She joined the old company in 1968, working in the 'Entering Room' then in the Lingerie department and also in the warehouse.

Sue Brindley joined Brettles in 1972 and worked in the internal Post Office, in the Entering Room and in the factory shop. In 1997, when the present company took over the Belper shop, Gary invited Sue to stay there, which she did. In 2007 Pat also started, and they became joint warehouse managers.

Elaine Salmon joined Brettles in March 1987, just six weeks before the company moved to Alfreton. She worked in the Accounts department, then became Gary's PA when he was Sales Director from 1993. In January 2000 Elaine and others were moved to the Chilprufe headquarters in Leicester. As Elaine lived in Ripley, the long commute to Leicester was inconvenient, and she was glad of the chance to leave in November 2000 to rejoin colleagues at Slenderella as Accounts Administrator. As such she was also involved in data input, though the company then only had two PCs, both in the warehouse office. Elaine has worked on credit control, chasing debtors and making sales calls.

Amanda O'Leary also started with Brettles in 1987, having already had some years of textiles experience. She became an Assistant Merchandiser at Brettles, and is now a Manager at Slenderella, a role in which she travels abroad extensively.

One recent member (who actually retired at the end of 2010) was **Margaret Dunstan**, who worked for Chilprufe and their original parent company Coats Viyella from 1987, in the Sales office at Leicester. From 1997 she was based partly at Leicester and partly at Brettles Sales office at Alfreton, staying with Chilprufe until the end then working briefly for the Receivers. Margaret started with Slenderella on 27th January 2003 as Sales Office Administrator. She brought many contacts and opened new doors for the new company. After a year she was promoted to Sales Office Manager.

The team also includes some who were not part of the old Brettles but worked for other textile companies, including **Julie Horne**, who was a Quality Controller for Jaeger Knitwear. She joined Slenderella in 2003 as Merchandise Assistant with Amanda and doubles up as Health & Safety Officer. Julie's position involves marketing, photography and assisting the general manager in producing new collections, including various international visits. In the UK, she is also involved with mail order customers, produces photographic images for promotional material and liaises with a modelling agency.

On a very positive note, we have recently welcomed Michael Meredith back to the company after many years of working with different brands in the ladieswear business. Mike brings to the company a wealth of sales and marketing experience.

The Late Noughties

All the staff I spoke to perceive the 'late noughties' as years of overall growth, especially the period from 2008, even as other companies have languished. The company has 'kept its finger on the pulse' of supply and demand changes. On the supply side, it has changed its focus from UK and European to Far East sourcing, due to the dwindling of the UK supply chain, whilst Italy and Turkey, both previously big suppliers, were becoming more expensive. Two new Brettles ranges have been introduced in the past four years – 'Gaspé', a range of 'young and sexy' lingerie and microfibre underwear which is ideal for the smaller lingerie shops (in contrast to that supplied by Walker Reid for the large multiples); and 'Slenders' briefs, which compete well on price with Kayser slips. The company has a stable comprehensive lingerie catalogue of products that sell well from year to year, whilst nightwear and swimwear brochures are changed each season in line with fashions.

Up & Coming Model Hannah with International Model Caprice.

Right: Slenderella model with brands (Slenders, Brettles, Walker Reid, Vedonis) in the *Lingerie Buyer*, February 2006.

Far Right: Front cover of Slenderella promotional leaflet. 2008?

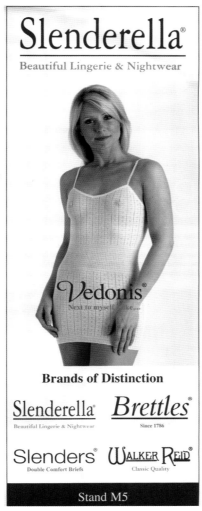

Un pizzico di insolenza per Slenderella

Slenderella, marchio leader in Gran Bretagna per il segmento lingerie da notte, propone per questa stagione un look completamente rinnovato con una linea bis giovane e fresca: Sassy Slenderella. Il disegno, un gatto nero che porta un collier d'argento, compare su un'ampia gamma di capi come pantaloni

Slenderella model with the companies first european magazine article 2001.

Best Business Award with newsreader Peter Sissons and Rolls Royce Chairman Sir Ralph Robins.

Town Criers, Mr and Mrs Arthur Bellaby, announcing the return of Brettles to Belper.

Former Management; Peter Knight, Paul Crosby, George Morley, Doug Penton, Peter Sinnock, Gwyn Stevenson with Gary Spendlove during a tour of Belper North Mill.

The Chapel Street factory shop, 1998.

Ward of Cripplegate Within.

The Inhabitants of the Ward of Cripplegate Within offer their sincere congratulations to their

Alderman, Harry Edward Augustus Twyford,

on his election to the ancient and honourable office of Sheriff of the City of London and trust that he may be blessed with health and strength to carry out his important duties.

They feel confident that he will at all times fulfil those duties with honour to himself and to the satisfaction of his fellow citizens and that his Shrievalty will add lustre to the great reputation of that high office.

It is the earnest wish of the inhabitants of the Ward that he may be spared to continue for many years the good work he has performed for the Corporation of the City of London as Alderman of the Ward.

Dated the 9th day of November 1934.

Hugh G. Taylor. *Deputy Alderman.*

G. Mart.   G. E. Wood.

J. G. Wigley.   H. C. Barry.

W. Nicholson.   G. J. Selby.

Members of the Court of Common Council for the Ward of Cripplegate Within.

A. Hanley frank Ward Clerk

Cripplegate Complimentary letter to Harry Twyford, Sherrif of London, 1934 (Photographer Nick Locket).

Packing department 1960s.

Right: This cutting from last Octobers 'Drapers' confirms Slenderella's position in the market. (Reproduced by kind permission 'Drapers').

TOP 5
Best-selling nightwear brands of the week

1	
2	**Slenderella**
3	**Marjolaine**
4	**Pill**
5	**Hanro**
	Triumph

Drapers spoke to 50 independents about their women's lingeri

10 Drapers October 1 2010

Slenderella factory, Queen Street, Belper.

GS with Miss England.

Gary's Final Thoughts

I have alluded to the wonderful stories and achievements of so many Brettles staff I have known. So, around the time of the Brettles 200-year celebration, I decided that this splendid history should be recorded. The highs and lows of a progressive company are apparent through the chapters.

The story nearly ended in 1997, when after the Chilprufe takeover it was considered that the Brettles brand would cease to actively trade. I recall that, after taking my redundancy from Chilprufe and launching the Slenderella brand, a personal ambition was to bring the Brettles name back to Belper and re-establish it as a private company. This was achieved in 2003 after the Leicester business entered administration. We immediately developed a high-quality pure cotton underwear collection, quickly followed by a seamfree thermal range. Both of these groups of products enjoy a wide UK and export distribution. Add to this dressing gowns, pure cotton nightwear with lingerie, and the historic brand grows into the twenty-first century.

Interestingly, apart from consumer and historic interest, we have had offers to purchase the brand, one a substantial bid from a mail order catalogue. Naturally the 'not for sale' sign was shown. After all, many of us consider the custodianship of the brand to be priceless. The garments are also sold more extensively via the internet.

My recorded memories in this and the previous chapter are but a few recollections of one individual, which would not have happened without that first step through the Brettles revolving door. Thousands of people have enjoyed their time at the company over the years. To many it was much more than a way to pay the mortgage; in fact a lot of employees met their future spouses while working there. This book has given but a brief overview of a historic company and of its 'phoenix' that trades successfully today. As 'Custodians of the Brand' I know that all of my staff will work hard to ensure a healthy future. My thanks to them for their dedicated support.

Acknowledgement

Many thanks to Rod Hawgood, without whose diligent research, this book would not have been written. Also many thanks to Nick Lockett for his photographic professionalism.

Obituary

Sadly, just before the book was published we lost two former senior members of staff. Ernie Lovell, who made so many positive contributions to the sales side of the company. Also, former Managing Director, Tony Gray who was delighted to add his wide knowledge of the textile trade to the contents.

Both I'm sure would, have enjoyed reading the history of "Brettles in Belper".

11. CONFERENCE PHOTOGRAPHS

Glyn Bailey and Sandy Taylor(facing away from camera) Ian Lindsay was a key salesman for Slenderella in the 1970s,and also a major player in the Brettles sales force.

Roger Knowles organised the company cars, and operated the internal computer systems.

Sales office manageress Mary Bailey, warehouse Director Graham Newton. Credit control manager Peter Knight ensured the company maintained excellent cash flow.

Mike Base, Bob Ash(partly obscured) and Glyn Bailey.

Key accounts executive, Don Mcleish.

Tony Gray and the great organiser Elaine Lovell.

Jimmy Lewis added his wit and sophistication to several sales conferences.

Charles Powell, was greatly respected in the hosiery industry, and played a major role in the success of the factory.

Personel manager George Morley. Experienced sales force members Stewart Perrin and Fred Blakey.

Michelle Hobson and her team of professional models add glamour to one of the Belfry sales conferences.

Miss United Kingdom Michelle Hobson.

Above: Popular Irishmen in the sales force, Randal Ferguson and Laurie Reid discuss the 1986 knitwear collection with retail expert Bob Hoadley.

Stan Ferguson, the agent for Eire.

Above: East Anglian area manager Terry Purkiss was often asked to mentor the young trainee sales people.

Conferences were very important, twice yearly, in the company calendar, usually attended by over sixty of the company sales team and management. These black and white photographs are "stills" taken from VHS videos filmed in the 1980's. The quality is therefore somewhat lacking in definition but an important part of the story never the less.

Thoughtful questions from Mike Meredith and Graham Edwards.

Left: Ken Royle and Ken Mortimer considering the latest lingerie styles.

Right: Sales rep George Tunnicliffe was always guaranteed a captive audience when giving a presentation.

Twice salesman of the year Gordan Bayley.

The ever popular Glyn Bailey.

Sarah Emery worked tirelessly to implement new computer systems and expand the company's marketing profile.

REFERENCES

Chapter 1

1 Figures from pages 15–18, 1845 Report and 'Some Particulars of the Past' from *A History of the Machine-Wrought Hosiery and Lace Manufactures* by William Felkin, London: Longmans, Green, and Co., 1867.

2 Pages 164–165, *The Civil, Political and Mechanical History of the Framework Knitters in Europe and America* by Gravenor Henson, Nottingham: printed by Richard Sutton, 1831.

3 Page 299, 'A New Historical and Descriptive View of Derbyshire' by D.P. Davies (Belper 1811).

4 Ch 3–4, *The Strutts and the Arkwrights 1758–1830* by R.S. Fitton & A.P. Wadsworth, Manchester: Manchester University Press, 1958.

5 'William Strutt's Fire-proof and Iron-framed Buildings 1792–1812' by H.R. Johnson & A.W. Kempton.

6 Page11, *A History of George Brettle & Co. Ltd 1801–1964* by Negley Harte, published by the author, 1973.

7 'Ince's Pedigrees' f.212 and Strutt MSS, Derby Public Library.

8 Page 67, Fitton & Wadsworth, op. cit.

9 'Chevening: One of Derbyshire's Lost Arts' by Marjorie Blount, in *Derbyshire Life* Volume 17, January – March 1948.

10 Duffield Parish Church Marriage Register, 16th April 1759 ; Ince's Pedigrees ff.212 &223.

11 Page 13, Negley Harte op. cit.

12 Manchester Central Library: Strutt MSS, Belper Ledger 1792–1803, f.194.

13 Strutt MSS, Belper Ledger 1792–1803, f 194.

14 Confirmed by Kent's Directory for 1803 and for 1804.

15 Pages 15–16, Negley Harte, op. cit.

16 Brief Account of Ward Brettle & Ward by William Ward and John Finney, 1823.

17 Ibid.

18 Ibid.

Chapter 2

1 Brief Account of Ward Brettle & Ward by William Ward and John Finney, 1823.

2 Ibid.

3 Page 20, *A History of George Brettle & Co. Ltd. 1801–1964* by Negley Harte, published by the author, 1973.

4 Pages 263 & 275, 1845 Report to Parliamentary Commission, Appendix 2.

5 *Derby Evening Telegraph* article on 'George Brettle & Co. Ltd.' on 5th March 1954.

6 Ibid.

7 Page 47, *Yarns*, Volume 1, No.2, April 1929.

8 Page 25, Negley Harte, op. cit.

9 Page 32, ibid.

10 Brief Account of Ward Brettle & Ward by William Ward and John Finney, 1823.

11 Page 20, Negley Harte, op. cit.

12 Page 100 & 242, *History, Gazetteer & Directory of the County of Derby* by Stephen Glover, 1829.

13 From *Buildings of England: London* by Nikolaus Pevsner, Harmondsworth: Penguin, 1952.

14 Page 283, *Gentleman's Magazine* NS, clll, ii (1833), and *Derby Mercury* 11th September 1833.

15 Page 53, Negley Harte, op. cit.

16 Page 20, ibid.

17 Pages 76–77, ibid.

18 Probate 11/1856. & Page 58, Negley Harte, op. cit.

19 Page 62, Negley Harte, op. cit.

Chapter 3

1 Page 62, *A History of George Brettle & Co. Ltd. 1801–1964* by Negley Harte, published by the author, 1973.

2 *History, Gazetteer & Directory of the County of Derby* by Stephen Glover, Derby, 1829, quoted in 'Framework Knitting & Hosiery', web article by Mary Smedley.

3 Page 275, 1845 Report to Parliamentary Commission, Appendix 2.

4 Page 85, ibid.

5 Page 226, ibid.

6 Page 88, ibid, John Rogers quote

7 Page 238, 1841 Report from Select Committee on the Exportation of Machinery, Appendix 3

8 Page 85 of 1845 Report and page 382 of 1854–55 Report.

9 Page 275, 1845 Report.

10 Page 236, ibid.

11 Page 82, ibid.

12 Page 305, 'English Reports', Chancery XXVI.

13 Page 342, VCH. Surrey 3, 1911.

14 Article in *Derby Mercury*, 29th May 1867.

15 Page 276, 1845 Report, Appendix 2.

16 Page 279, ibid.

17 Page 70, Negley Harte, op. cit.

18 Ibid & ref 15.

19 Page 277, 1855 Report.

20 Page 263, 1845 Report.

21 Page 269, ibid.

22 Page 76, Negley Harte, op. cit.

23 Page 247, 1855 Report, Appendix 2.

24 Page 725, *Gardners History, Gazetteer of the County of Oxford* (Peterborough, 1852) and page 140, *Kelly's Directory of Oxfordshire* (London, 1899).

25 Page 78, Negley Harte, op. cit.

26 Page 248, 1845 Report.

27 Page 262, ibid.

28 Pages 21–24, *A.J. Mundella, 1825–1897: the Liberal background to the Labour movement* by W.H.G. Armytage, London: Benn, 1951.

29 Page 291, *History and Gazatteer of Derbyshire* by Samuel Bagshaw, Sheffield, 1846.

30 Page 562, 1845 Report, evidence of Thomas Whittaker McCallum.

31 Page 138, *Yarns* Volume 2, 1930.

32 Page 83, Negley Harte, op. cit.

33 *Derby Evening Telegraph* article, 5th March 1954.

34 Patent 918, 1870.

35 Page 85, Negley Harte, op. cit.

36 Page 60, *Derbyshire* by Nikolas Pevsner, Harmondsworth: Penguin, 1953.

37 Page 75, *I. & R. Morley: A Record of a Hundred Years* by Frederick M. Thomas, London: Chiswick Press, 1900.

Chapter 4

1 Will of George Henry Brettle, Principal Probate Registry, Somerset House.

2 *Kelly's Handbook to the Titled, Landed and Official Classes* for 1888 and for 1901.

3 Page 2124, *Kelly's Directory of Kent, Surrey and Sussex, London 1887*.

4 Page 88, *A History of George Brettle & Co. Ltd. 1801–1964* by Negley Harte, published by the author, 1973.

5 Pages 147–151, *The British Hosiery & Knitwear Industry: its History and Organisation* by F.A. Wells, Newton Abbot: David & Charles, 1972.

6 Page 89, Negley Harte, op.cit.

7 Will of Helen Twyford, Principal Probate Registry, Somerset House.

8 Page 140, *Dod's Parliamentary Companion for 1880*, 2nd edition, London, 1880.

9 1882 Partnership Agreement, quoted on page 93, Negley Harte, op. cit.

10 Page 13, *Yarns* Volume 3, No. 1, 1931.

11 Page 23, *Yarns* Volume 1, No. 1, 1929.

12 Page 99, Negley Harte, op. cit.

13 Letter written by 'Thomas Paul', reproduced June 1914.

14 Page 62 *Yarns* Volume 1, No.2 (1929) and *Derby Evening Telegraph*, 5th March 1954.

15 *Derby Mercury*, 11th April 1913.

Chapter 5

1 Will of H.R. Twyford, proved 13th May 1913, Public Probate Records, Somerset House.

2 Page106, *A History of George Brettle & Co. Ltd. 1801–1964* by Negley Harte, published by the author, 1973.

3 *Derbyshire Advertiser*, 16th January 1959.

4 Page 134, Negley Harte, op. cit.

5 'Framework Knitting and Hosiery', web article by historian Mary Smedley.

6 Page 170, *The British Hosiery & Knitwear Industry: its History and Organisation* by F.A. Wells, Newton Abbot: David & Charles, 1972; and Import Duties Act Inquiry data in 'The Hosiery Industry' in *Studies in Industrial Organization*, ed. H.A. Silverman, London: Methuen, 1946 (reprinted London: Routledge, 2003).

7 Pages 119–20, Negley Harte, op. cit.

8 Pages 7–9, *Yarns*,Volume 1, No.1, 1929.

9 *Financial Times*, 18th April 1930.

10 *Yarns*, Volume 4, No. 2, 1932: Chairman's letter following Editorial.

11 George Brettle & Co. Profit & Loss Accounts 1928–1940, Derbyshire Records Office.

12 Mary Smedley, op. cit.

13 *The Banker*, May 1929.

14 *Drapers Record*, 3rd May 1930.

15 *The Times*, 27th August 1936.

16 Page 134, Negley Harte, op. cit.

17 'Contact' newsletters, nos. 1 & 2.

Chapter 6

1 Pages 75–86, 'Board of Trade Working Party Reports: Hosiery', 1940.

2 Page 147, *A History of George Brettle & Co. Ltd. 1801–1964* by Negley Harte, published by the author, 1973.

3 'Personality Parade – George Brettle & Co. Ltd., Belper', *Womens Wear News* 1951.

4 Brettles Employees Handbook.

5 Memoirs of Mr Syd Clarke, Accountant.

6 *Derbyshire Advertiser*, 16th January 1959.

7 Pages 148–50, Negley Harte, op.cit and company accounts.

8 'Flimsy Girl', poem by Sally Goldsmith in 'Threads' collection.

9 Pages 148–150, Negley Harte, op. cit. and company accounts.

Chapter 7

1 'George Brettle of Belper', article in *Hosiery Times*, March 1967.

2 Visit to Arabian Gulf and Saudi Arabia, Report 17th November 1975. T. Hollingworth, L. Collins & W. Thorpe

3 Visit to Arabian Gulf and Saudi Arabia, Report 24th March 1976. T. Hollingworth, L.H. Collins & W.O. Thorpe.

4 Visit to Saudi Arabia, Yemen and Libya, Report October 1976. N.A. Henderson & W.O. Thorpe.

5 Minutes of Export Meeting at Courtaulds Distributors, Birmingham, 19th May 1980.

6 Page 37, '*Body Style*, Issue no. 6, November 1987.

7 *Belper News*, 'Brettles Supplement', 1986.

Chapter 8

1 Page 99, *A History of George Brettle & Co. Ltd. 1801–1964* by Negley Harte, published by the author, 1973.

2 Page 20, *Yarns*, Volume 1, No. 1, 1929.

3 Pages 34 & 44, *Yarns*, Volume 1, No. 2, April 1929.

4 Page 33, *Yarns*, Volume 2, No. 1, January 1930.

5 Page 46, *Yarns*, Volume 3, No. 2, June 1931.

6 Page 48, *Yarns*, Volume 4, No. 2, December 1932.

7 Annual General Meeting minutes, 1938.

8 Page 141, *Yarns*, Volume 2, No. 4, October 1930.

9 Page 102, *Yarns*, Volume 3, No. 3, October 1931.

10 Page 48, *Yarns*, Volume 4, No. 2, December 1932.

11 Annual General Meeting minutes, 1937.

12 Annual General Meeting minutes, 1938.

13 Ibid.

14 Ibid.

15 Oberon Annual Accounts, 1941.

16 'Contact' newsletter, No. 2, December 1944.

17 Annual General Meeting minutes, 1944.

18 *Derbyshire Advertiser*, 16th January 1959.

19 Constitution and Rules of Oberon Sports and Social Club, 1964 edition.

20 Annual General Meeting minutes, 1969.

Chapter 10

1 Andrew Miller, *The Earl of Petticoat Lane: From an East End Chronicle to a West End Life*, London: Heinemann, 2006.

APPENDIX 1

Partners and Directors

1762–1800 Ward & Son
John Ward sr. 1762–1800
John Ward jr. 1790–1800

1801–1803 Ward Sharp & Co.
John Ward jr. 1801–1803
James Carter Sharp 1801–1803

1803–1834 Ward Brettle & Ward
John Ward 1803–1823
William Ward 1803–1833
George Brettle 1803–1834

1834–1930 Ward Sturt & Sharp
John Ward jr. 1834–?
Benjamin Ward 1834–?
James Carter Sharp 1834–?
? Sturt 1834–? (a rival concern)

1834–1914 George Brettle & Co.
George Brettle 1834–1835
Benjamin Hardwick 1835–1843 (trustee)
Alfred Brettle 1843–1856
Edward Brettle 1843–1867
George Henry Brettle 1843–1872
Thomas Wilson Elstob 1844–1866
William Smithyman Bean 1867–1876
Parmenas Martin Burgess 1867–1879
George Dickson 1867–1882
Frederick William Sharp 1867–1876
Mrs Helen Brettle-Twyford 1872–1882
Isaac Hanson 1880–1901
John Scott 1880–1903
Henry Robert Twyford 1882–1913
John Henry Mallard 1883–1904

1914–1963 George Brettle & Co. Ltd
Lionel Thomas Campbell Twyford 1914–1920 (Chairman)
Harry Edward Augustus Twyford 1914–1964 (MD 1914–1960, Chairman 1920–1963)
Alfred Murrell Gibson 1915–1941 ; part-time 1941–1949
Frank John Rayson 1920–1933 (Company Secretary 1914–1933)

Harry Richard Twyford 1925–1954 (Joint MD 1945–54, Deputy Chairman 1951–54)
Alfred Page 1937–1941
Ernest Edward Hall 1941–1946
Henry Osmont Randall 1938–1959 (Secretary 1934–1959)
Wallace Hoole Inch 1946–1959
Ernest Henry Meredith 1950–1954
Walter Bennett 1950–1966
 Frederick Mills Welsford 1955–1964
Cecil George Gosling 1958–1971
Robert Bagshaw Wynne 1955–1964 (Dep Chair 1955–1963, MD 1960–1964, Chair 1963–1964)
P.A. Nash (Company Secretary) 1959–1963
William Bernard Ross Collins 1961–1964

Appointments after 1963

T.P. Jennison, Chairman 1964–1966
G.H. Tarrant 1964–?
Charles W. Powell, MD 1964–1969
J.L. Bush, Merchandise Director 1965–1969
Ivor Boyes, Merchandise Director 1965–1972
Jack Price, Financial Director 1965–1986
Charles Doerr 1965–?
Oswald Herbert, Production Director 1966–?
C. Gosling, Managing Director 1969–1972

Appointments after 1970

Ivor Boyes, Managing Director 1972–1975
Tony Gray, Merchandise Director 1972–1975 & 1981–1993
Tony Gray, Managing Director 1975–1981
Graham Newton, Merchandise Director 1975–1981
Gwyn Stevenson, Managing Director 1981–1996
John Simpson, Sales Director 1981–1989
Mike Moulds, Financial Director 1986–1996
Gary Spendlove, Sales Director 1993–1997
Bob Ash, Merchandise Director 1993–1997

APPENDIX 2

Assets and Profits

Ward Brettle & Ward

Year (y/e Dec)	Owed to Jn Ward	Net Assets £	Net Profit £	Rate %
1822	---------	93,634	(14,572)	(15.6)
1823	31,134	69,197	7,068	10.2
1824	25,978	84,352	15,154	17.9
1825	25,996	92,860	8,507	9.2
1826	25,669	104,836	11,974	11.4
1827	26,000	126,876	21,939	17.3
1829	26,000	161,044	17,083	10.6
1830	26,000	191,232	30,187	15.7
1831	26,000	215,947	24,713	11.4
1832	0	233,831	17,883	7.6

George Brettle & Co.

Year (y/e Dec)	Debts Due by company	Net Assets £	Sales £	Net Profit £	Rate %
1915	140,973	167,448	654,289	34,446	20.5
1916	58,528	201,746	610,577	34,298	17.0
1917	60,166	213,186	626,215	54,180	25.4
1918	68,598	267,390	898,108	95,966	35.8
1919	73,449	329,098	1,253,551	149,672	45.4
1920	197,619	351,111	1,563,093	141,119	40.1
1921	253,642	232,504	1,797,361	(103,836)	(44.6)
1922	163,248	232,505	1,108,094	(15,472)	(6.6)
1923	74,591	258,569	1,158,744	48,844	18.6
1924	71,739	274,541	1,096,191	29,408	10.7
1925	87,491	300,131	1,143,002	48,315	16.1
1926	97,552	309,965	1,233,929	41,267	13.3
1927	90,723	323,417	1,187,332	41,426	12.8
1928	99,276	347,770	1,204,775	53,699	15.4
1929	121,536	377,873	1,415,085	53,158	14.0
1930	117,257	395,441	1,484,340	49,278	12.4
1931	99,981	387,552	1,132,052	36,728	9.4
1932	80,421	382,604	1,172,199	28,381	7.4
1933	71,066	372,079	1,048,542	22,362	6.0
1934	76,341	372,681	1,066,497	22,990	6.1
1935	65,792	366,734	1,068,724	20,303	5-5
1936	70,078	363,795	1,043,703	18,289	5.0
1937	75,598	365,048	1,050,965	20,846	5.7
1938	67,721	364,964	1,053,790	22,189	6.0
1939	69,496	368,353	1,038,790	22,854	6.2
1940	79,904	385,080	1,220,697	36,981	9.6

APPENDIX 3

Sales by Department, George Brettle & Co.

In the early years, a high fraction of sales were wholesale, not actually produced by Brettles.

Year (y/e Dec)	Belper Cotton £	Other Cotton £	Belper Pants £	Other Pants £	Belper Produce £	Other Sales £	Total Sales £
1908	2,939	10,457	9,983	54,172	12,922	253,246	266,168
1909	3,529	10,701	9,934	55,314	13,463	270,035	283,498
1910	4,708	11,059	10,075	55,846	14,783	285,684	300,467
1911	7,270	10,203	8,237	26,263	15,507	306,222	321,729
1912	6,613	10,910	6,971	55,491	13,584	322,467	336,051

After 1912 it is not possible to distinguish between produce and non–produce, but closest comparative figures are given, plus a couple of new lines manufactured at Belper.

Year (y/e Dec)	All Cotton £	Under-Wear £	Ribbed U'wear £	Half Hose £	Total Sales £
1914	19,332	69,214	0	0	376,990
1915	21,320	162,169	0	0	654,289
1916	22,101	201,001	0	0	610,577
1917	30,161	135,237	25,979	0	626,215
1918	45,831	190,542	42,119	0	898,108
1919	55,218	241,948	59,032	0	1,253,551
1920	59,410	239,901	69,893	87,599	1,563,093
1921	76,541	249,638	81,906	130,878	1,797,361
1922	39,935	177,706	41,657	74,987	1,108,094
1923	43,790	210,413	50,416	83,013	1,158,744
1924	50,957	190,353	48,846	104,585	1,096,191
1925	59,942	188,429	47,700	124,478	1,143,002
1926	83,414	185,198	43,771	131,897	1,233,929
1927	99,285	171,216	36,300	124,427	1,187,332
1928	118,379	184,834	35,820	110,602	1,204,775
1929	139,094	189,491	43,530	113,874	1,415,085
1930	156,655	187,868	48,449	107,058	1,484,340
1931	131,767	185,313	39,140	86,944	1,132,052
1932	122,742	187,807	35,141	63,316	1,172,199
1933	108,818	155,497	30,914	54,519	1,048,542
1934	109,196	150,637	40,886	56,892	1,066,497
1935	102,627	147,374	43,186	57,917	1,068,724
1936	104,788	142,129	36,986	57,973	1,043,703
1937	112,625	140,149	39,071	59,625	1,050,965
1938	113,355	139,716	39,985	61,572	1,053,790
1939	119,318	144,199	36,641	61,663	1,038,790
1940	127,379	208,109-	44,545	63,355	1,220,697

APPENDIX 4

Key Indicators for George Brettle & Co. Ltd

Year (y/e Dec)	Net Assets £	Production £	Sales £	Net Profit £	Rate %
1941	396,551	?	1,201,162	30,473	7.6
1942	408,711	?	753,164	31,162	7.6
1943	410,266	254,286	620,293	30,058	7.3
1944	411,020	231,110	646,738	29,793	7.2
1945	411,514	235,570	674,123	29,535	7.1
1946	411,451	227,464	649,657	28,977	7.0
1947	430,609	270,528	780,362	31,214	7.2
1948	438,807	315,673	932,475	42,308	9.6
1949	493,434	428,674	1,283,502	54,409	11.0
1950	554,467	514,241	1,530,000	59,245	10.6
1951	620,848	630,016	1,883,739	88,099	14.1
1952	652,061	758,893	2,104,757	78,440	12.0
1953	620,631	547,517	1,637,859	48,794	7.8
1954	740,490	727,343	2,054,206	109,673	14.8
1955	800,733	820,785	2,198,604	126,298	15.7
1956	839,104	770,575	2,117,619	113,223	13.4
1957	823,241	701,346	2,024,358	70,066	8.5
1958	824,781	764,937	1,948,774	60,877	7.3
1959	807,373	594,475	1,850,402	40,817	5.0
1960	800,949	?	1,826,597	53,329	6.6
1961	824,653	?	1,959,513	75,985	9.2
1962	846,695	?	1,992,007	61,823	7.3
1963	832,451	?	2,053,225	52,981	6.3
1964	787,271	?	?	14,305	1.8

INDEX

Published in the UK by:
Slenderella Limited
Queen Street
Belper DE56 1NR

Tel: 01773 822340
E-mail: info@slenderella.co.uk

1st edition

ISBN: 978 184306 533 3 Paperback

ISBN: 978 184306 534 0 Hardback

ISBN 978-1-331-66549-6
PIBN 10042879

This book is a reproduction of an important historical work. Forgotten Books uses
state-of-the-art technology to digitally reconstruct the work, preserving the original format
whilst repairing imperfections present in the aged copy. In rare cases, an imperfection in
the original, such as a blemish or missing page, may be replicated in our edition. We do,
however, repair the vast majority of imperfections successfully; any imperfections that
remain are intentionally left to preserve the state of such historical works.

1 MONTH OF
FREE
READING

at

www.ForgottenBooks.com

By purchasing this book you are eligible for one month membership to ForgottenBooks.com, giving you unlimited access to our entire collection of over 700,000 titles via our web site and mobile apps.

To claim your free month visit:

www.forgottenbooks.com/free42879

English
Français
Deutsche
Italiano
Español
Português

www.forgottenbooks.com

Mythology Photography **Fiction**
Fishing Christianity **Art** Cooking
Essays Buddhism Freemasonry
Medicine **Biology** Music **Ancient**
Egypt Evolution Carpentry Physics
Dance Geology **Mathematics** Fitness
Shakespeare **Folklore** Yoga Marketing
Confidence Immortality Biographies
Poetry **Psychology** Witchcraft
Electronics Chemistry History **Law**
Accounting **Philosophy** Anthropology
Alchemy Drama Quantum Mechanics
Atheism Sexual Health **Ancient History**
Entrepreneurship Languages Sport
Paleontology Needlework Islam
Metaphysics Investment Archaeology
Parenting Statistics Criminology
Motivational

ELLEN TERRY'S COTTAGE, KENT, ENGLAND

THE HONEST HOUSE

PRESENTING EXAMPLES OF THE USUAL PROBLEMS
WHICH FACE THE HOME-BUILDER TOGETHER WITH
AN EXPOSITION OF THE SIMPLE ARCHITECTURAL
PRINCIPLES WHICH UNDERLIE THEM: ARRANGED ES-
PECIALLY IN REFERENCE TO SMALL HOUSE DESIGN

BY

RUBY ROSS GOODNOW

IN COLLABORATION WITH

RAYNE ADAMS

INTRODUCTION BY FREDERICK L. ACKERMAN, A. I. A.

PUBLISHED BY THE CENTURY CO.
NEW YORK - - - - - - - - - MCMXIV

ACKNOWLEDGMENT

To our friends, who have given us so freely of their encouragement and enthusiasm in the making of this book, we wish to give our thanks.

We are especially indebted to Frederick L. Ackerman, Richard Derby, Thomas Robinson, Robert R. McGoodwin, and William Roger Greeley for their co-operation in the planning of the book; to Alice Boughton, Edmund B. Gilchrist, Lillian Baynes Griffin, and Frank Cousins for photographs; and to Frances Delehanty, Howard Greenley, John D. Moore, Franklin P. Hammond, Henry B. Guillan, Bernhardt E. Muller, Jules Gingras, Henry Henderson and Gerald Wright for many drawings and chapter headings.

RUBY ROSS GOODNOW
RAYNE ADAMS.

TABLE OF CONTENTS

TABLE OF CONTENTS

INTRODUCTION

There are few things which concern us more intimately than the houses in which we live; fewer still are the things in which we take a greater interest than the homes which we individually own. The actual size of the house does not so much matter, and we may even venture the statement that the degree of interest which an owner takes in his home is in something like an inverse ratio to its size.

It is difficult indeed for us to create a house which is expressive of the owner, and at the same time consistent in all of its parts, true to a chosen style or character, and containing throughout the elements of good design, for the simple reason that we are still young as a people, our social traditions are not so well established as to indicate clearly what is to be our future, and in consequence, what will be the character of the homes which will result.

In our larger houses we are very likely to draw our inspiration from widely separate and distant fields, and we bring into them the accumulated art of the centuries past, and of the whole world. So it is no wonder that in these hustling times, when our days are filled with a multitude of interests, that we sometimes feel that we are strangers in our own homes. Then too, a spirit of pride and emulation is often wrought into the building of our larger houses, and often this motive, working unconsciously in the minds of both the owner and the architect, acts as a Chinese Wall, separating us from our ideals and the things which we actually accomplish.

It is likewise true that similar motives influence those of us who build small houses, but fortunately it is not true to the same extent. We lack the wealth of resource from which to draw; we do not possess the pecuniary means. The materials from which our houses are to be executed must be found close at hand, and they must be inexpensive. These influences, together with a multitude of others of a similar nature, tend toward the development of the smaller house along more intimate and more interesting lines. They tend toward the creation of a type, something more accurately expressive of our life and time, something more indigenous to our society.

In our American homes, particularly the smaller ones, we find that which we have characterized as a typical architectural expression of our day and people. In these homes we find an extremely wide range of expression. They are infinite in variety, as regards form or mass, style or character, and in the materials used. Among them we find a few really interesting and fine examples, but in the main, the small houses of our suburban and rural communities, scattered the length and the breadth of our country, are ugly; many of them are inexpressively ugly, and yet notwithstanding this fact, we do not hesitate to recognize them as our own, and strange as it may seem, we take a justifiable pride in them.

How can we explain this seeming paradox—that we have a vast number of ugly houses of which we are proud, which we take so seriously, and that we consider them one of the few characteristics and architectural expressions of our people? It is pertinent to ask: What is the underlying reason for our so generally accepting or assuming such an attitude?

There is no more accurate chronicle of a people than the buildings which they erect. Seen in perspective, they help to explain the nature of a people's religion and philosophy, and their social, moral, and political ideals as well. We can deduce from them their intimate thoughts and desires.

We have been a busy people,—conquering all sorts of physical conditions, endeavoring to solve an endless number of political, social, and moral problems,—and we have not given serious thought to the building of our houses. In the architecture of our day we have only sketched in, as it were, the many ideas which form the basis of our lives. As yet the forms are crude; we have not arrived at that point in the development of an architectural style or expression where it is possible for us to say clearly that this is true and that is false. In other words, we cannot distinguish the masks from the faces.

Let us, however, return to the reasons for our assumed pride in our houses. We can surely say that it is not their general appearance, taken as a whole, which justifies that pride. The last generation or so has certainly not built fine houses, when we compare them with earlier American examples. The fine work

of the colonial builders has been replaced by a crude effort of the recent contractor. The fine old farm houses of two generations ago have been replaced
by the motley colored forms of to-day. We have not much improved their plan
arrangement nor have we made them better adapted to their use. With the exception of a recent tendency towards simplification, our small houses for a long time
have been growing more complex; simple roof lines have been replaced by
forms resembling the clocks of the Black Forest. Little attention has been
paid to the general mass of the buildings, and we have substituted, in our en-
deavor to improve upon the old forms, an endless number of superficial and
unnecessary elements, in the main of exceedingly bad taste, such as is illus-
trated in the product of the jig saw and the turning lathes.

The reason for our satisfaction must be sought below the surface, for it is
surely not in the external appearance that we find sufficient evidence or a sufficiently good reason. There is something expressed in the *plans* of the houses
themselves, in the very arrangement of the plots of land upon which they
stand, which differentiates them from similar houses of Europe. They do not
express landlordism, but rather a group of democratic ideals. This is particularly and most clearly expressed in the plan, where is indicated, not as some
would have it, the aping of a more pretentious scale of life, but rather a direct
and vigorous expression of the effort to lead a life that is sociable, though
laborious.

It is this which we have expressed in our small houses. This is why, with all
their ugliness, they are characteristic of America. Is this not enough for a
new people to have accomplished? Is this not a sufficiently firm foundation
upon which to build?

Quite naturally we consider small houses as being in the nature of an individual or a personal expression only, something growing out of the mind of the
owner, the builder or the architect. A study of the history of the house from the
earliest times forces home to one the fact that it is a product or expression of
great social and economic forces.

It is not alone the taste of the owner or the architect which establishes the
general character of the house. It is rather that the general character of the
house is established by these forces, and those who actually build it in materials but modify the details already established by tradition. From the tree
house of the Tropic, the cave house of the North, and the later primitive house,
consisting of but a single room, down to the modern house of our own day, we
see these forces working; we see them changing,—the changes bringing greater
comfort to the individual. Precedent has been the determining factor in build-

ing, and as we look back, we wonder that a people could have tolerated in times past the stupid housing conditions under which they lived.

When we compare these old crude expressions with the homes of the present day, it is evident that we have gone a long way, and yet, who can state that a few centuries hence we shall not have evolved a type which will make our present achievement look as crude then as the log house of but a few generations past looks to us to-day?

Yet one may ask what has all this to do with this particular problem, and how can this help us in the building of better houses? Let us see!

It was but a few generations ago that local tradition alone influenced materially the design and the arrangement of the houses. There was not possible at that time the universal interchange of ideas which we possess to-day. There was not present the demand for community life such as we find characteristic of our civilization; the great industrial centers did not exist, and there were not present such conditions as we find in our great suburban communities,—in other words, the housing problem did not exist.

Many are the individuals and societies spending in total large sums of money upon stimulating the erection of better houses and providing for the working man houses of simple design, economical in construction, safe and sanitary, and many municipalities and states throughout the world—more particularly in Europe—are giving to-day very serious study and consideration to this subject. The task is difficult. There is a multitude of complex conditions entering into the problem. In bringing about better housing conditions and better houses from the æsthetic standpoint, the garden cities of Europe have been an important factor. These do not represent a complete solution of the problem, but they point in the right direction. Through these experiments we have been able to gain a great deal of knowledge.

The early efforts in garden city development were, in the main, along philanthropic or semi-philanthropic lines. In the more recent developments, however, there are a number of examples where the funds have been provided by the people themselves. It is in these latter developments that we find an architecture more accurately expressive of the conditions and more consistent in character, and we already see in these developments the possibilities of a better architecture.

The many efforts made toward better housing are aimed primarily toward providing better living conditions. This, in a word, means that houses must be built cheaply but at the same time of durable materials. They must be sanitary and wholesome, and what is of vital importance, they must be so designed as to meet the actual needs and requirements and to satisfy the reasonable demands resulting from a better education and an independence of spirit.

In these community developments, beyond providing for these things, a serious effort has been made along the æsthetic side. We realize that it is possible to do much toward raising the standard. The influence of good work surely tells, and it has a marked influence upon adjacent and even distant communities where the erection of small homes goes on through the effort of individuals only.

This effort, however, does not solve the problem. The problem of obtaining worthy designs of small houses is an exceedingly difficult one and at present, there seem to be few avenues open to the owner desiring to build a small home other than to secure the services of the speculative builder or contractor, or as he is sometimes termed, "architect," or to buy a book depicting one hundred hideous houses for one dollar.

The architect of ability,—and it takes an architect of such qualification to design a small home,—has not been able to do a great deal toward bettering the design of the vast number of our small houses which make the majority of American homes. His office, by necessity, is situated in one of the larger cities; his problems, in the main, are the larger problems of city and country, and about the only opportunity ever presented to him comes when he is called upon to lay out and design something in the nature of a garden city or a community development. The economic side of the problem has forced him away from being a material factor in its solution.

He sees these little ugly houses along our roads; he wishes that they might be otherwise, and yet it seems almost impossible to suggest a method of making them better.

A number of efforts have been made by the various chapters of the American Institute of Architects toward this end. There are at present a number of schemes under consideration looking toward providing something in the nature of scale drawings which could be purchased by an owner for a very nominal sum, these to be modified under the supervision of a competent architect, so as to adapt them to the varying conditions of site.

While all of these efforts are in a very preliminary state of development, yet they indicate the possibility of a solution. The Department of Agriculture at Washington has already started a department, the object of which is to study carefully the farm house problem to this same end, and already the work is well under way. There is no logical reason why the Federal Government, if properly supported in this excellent work, should not be a strong factor in bringing

INTRODUCTION

about a higher standard in the erection of buildings upon the farm, not only from the economic and social side, but from the æsthetic side as well. Many newspapers and periodicals have instituted competitions; many have been conducted under most excellent conditions. Much material of value has been published. The good, however, is so insignificant in its total amount as compared with the bad that as yet the influence is hardly felt.

This book is not an attempt to consider the housing question in general, nor to supply the prospective owner with designs or plans for small houses, but it is rather an attempt to present to the prospective owner of a home a few simple suggestions as to the best methods of attacking his problem and also a few hints concerning the great underlying principles of good design. It purposes to state these principles in such a way that they may be easily understood and acted upon.

All our experience in life shows that it is easier to criticize a bad thing than to construct a good one. Houses are no exception to the rule. We can easily see the errors in the work of others; we criticize with a spirit of bravado, but when we start something of our own, how grateful we are if some guiding genius tells us what to avoid! We all feel that we do not need to ask that we be not led into temptation so much as we need to be told how to avoid failure.

Nearly all books which deal with domestic architecture are put together with the idea of showing examples of good houses and plans which have merit, and from which the student or the reader may draw inspiration. This is only half of the story. It is not enough to point out what is good in art or architecture, we should point out what is bad also, and show by specific illustrations how the errors may be avoided. One of the purposes of this book is to present good and bad examples of domestic architecture, and to point out specifically many of the common faults in planning and in detail to which the inexperienced home-builder is liable, and which remain to commemorate his ignorance and bad taste.

FREDERICK L. ACKERMAN,
Member of the American Institute of Architects.

THE HONEST HOUSE

A queer fancy seems to be current that a fire exists to warm people. It exists to warm people, to light their darkness, to raise their spirits, to toast their muffins, to air their rooms, to cook their chestnuts, to tell stories to their children, to make checkered shadows on their walls, to boil their hurried kettles, and to be the red heart of a man's house and hearth, for which, as the great heathens said, a man should die.

G. K. Chesterton, in "What's Wrong with the World."

THE HONEST HOUSE

CHAPTER I

THE QUEST OF THE IDEAL HOUSE

YOU are going to build a little house, your first and only house, your home. For years you have dreamed and saved and scrimped with the rosy vision of your Ideal House luring you on. At last you have accumulated the hoard of dollars you fixed for your goal. Now you are ready to buy a bit of earth for your house, ready to approach the practical problem of the building of it. How are you to accomplish it? You cannot go ahead blindly.

You look about you at the hundreds of small houses built by people who have entertained ideals, just as you have, and you realize that a large proportion of these houses are poor in design, inconvenient in plan, and uneconomical in construction. What is wrong about it all, anyway? If a man has worked hard for honest dollars to build a house, why is it so difficult for him to accomplish an honest house? You wish to use your best knowledge and judgment to insure the expending of your hard earned money

to the best possible advantage. Presumably your neighbors had the same ambition. Why, then, are there so few small houses that are honest in construction, logical in plan, and attractive to the eye? Are there any means which may be taken to prevent deplorable results?

It is fair to assume that you do not rely on your own technical skill, in either design or construction. You know that you yourself are an expert in your own line of work; that your value to the community depends directly on your ability to serve them in this expert capacity. You are likely to apply this reasoning in the case of your own home. You probably believe that those people who are designing and building houses right along are the very people who can furnish you the expert service you need. So far, so good. It becomes, then, not a matter of whether you shall have help or not, but of what kind of help you shall have.

There is your neighbor who has recently built a house. You might learn from him

3

the methods he has pursued, and pursue the same yourself. But are you able to detect the faults in his advice? Sometimes owners are not wholly conscious of the defects in their houses. Sometimes they are conscious of these defects when it is too late to rectify them. Granting that your neighbor will give you the benefit of his experience, mistakes and all, does his house fill your particular requirements?

Suppose you wish to exercise your judgment, independently of your neighbors. You will find various kinds of assistance at hand. The most important of them are the magazines, the carpenters, and the architects. The magazines have done much to create a general interest in bettering small house architecture.

Much of your inspiration has come from the magazine articles on house building, probably. I know a man who confesses that for years he bought every number of a well known journal for women because he loved houses so, and this magazine often presented pictures of charming houses at ridiculously low prices. The trouble was that the houses could n't be built at the prices named; he discovered this when he actually tried to build one of them. Still, he argues, the magazine did much to stimulate his interest in house building, and so he does not altogether condemn its impractical advice.

Most of the architects I know are not so amiable about the case of the women's magazines. Their quarrel is with the misinformation supplied by glib writers who quote prices that may be reliable in an individual instance, but nine times out of ten the client who relies upon them finds that his is not the instance. He is unable to use judgment in comparing the quotations to his own locality, and without judgment tables of costs should be left entirely alone.

Some of the magazines are even running departments for the purpose of giving the readers expert professional advice. They print plans and elevations of different types of houses and of different costs. Frequently these plans are dimensioned, and could be executed effectively. The trouble is that each owner wishes to vary the plan in some way that shall more exactly fill his requirements, and in making the alterations he is very likely to lose whatever merit existed in the original design. If by any chance one of these houses should be built exactly as shown, it is very likely that it would be inappropriate to the locality.

A few of the magazines that have a desire to give actual help to the man who would build his own house employ consulting architects. When these men can give time and thought to the problems of individual home builders, the magazines will be doing a great work indeed. But such a service, if successful, would mean that thousands of problems would be presented to the staff architect, and he could n't consider them all. We are not living in the millennium, and magazine owners are not likely to employ more architects than editors, and it would undoubtedly come to this! So—make the best of the advice offered you, and then turn to the other possible sources of help.

Undoubtedly you have a neighbor who is a carpenter, or who knows a carpenter. We all have neighbors who are carpenters. Some of us, however, know things about carpenters which you, as a home builder, may not know. The architect knows that the average carpenter is not a designer; he cannot plan. That is, he cannot plan as conveniently as

4

THE QUEST OF THE IDEAL HOUSE

What could be more attractive than this charming old house, in Westchester County, New York, with its plain shingled walls? The shingles are laid in wide courses, about nine inches to the weather. Their irregularity gives an added interest to the house. Note also the unbroken roof surfaces, and the total absence of meaningless ornament.

should be for the amount you are going to expend on your house. He cannot make his hard and fast ideas conform to the peculiar requirements of every individual client. He lacks the flexibility to change his ideas, because he lacks the knowledge and the training which give flexibility. It must be remembered that I am speaking of carpenters who are architects, not of carpenters who pursue their own callings. There is no more honorable profession but it should not be confused with architecture.

The carpenter must always copy. Sometimes it is good work and sometimes it is bad work which he chooses to copy, or to adapt. In either case, it is a matter of chance, for the simple reason that he lacks the esthetic and the practical judgment to know good from bad design. Yet despite the fact that

he takes all his ideas from other people, he cannot be brought to admit that the other people, meaning the architects, are of any use to him or to the home maker. He seems to feel bound to defend his ignorance by repudiating the source of what knowledge he has. He usually has a lot of arguments up his sleeve against the architect. Here are some of them:—

(1) The architect is an additional expense. That is, the fee paid to the architect is simply so much money thrown into the ditch.

(2) The architect is a very arbitrary fellow, and will not allow the owner to have anything he wants if he can possibly prevent it. (This is of course a throw at the highbrow architect who no doubt exists, but who is far from typical of the profession.)

(3) The architect will take a month or

more to draw the plans, and this means a month or more wasted.

There are other stock objections which he advances also, which it is not necessary to enumerate. All of them, including the ones mentioned, can be answered adequately with facts greatly to the confusion of the carpenter. We shall make no attempt, however, to answer them here for our purpose is to help to bring about, not a dispute, but a thorough-going co-operative working policy in which owner, carpenter (and by carpenter we mean all the building trades), and architect find their proper places and rewards. If each can be brought to realize his dependence on the others, you will be in a fair way toward getting an ideal home for your investment.

It matters not whether you are going to build a four-room cottage or a forty-room house. The principles are the same. You might be able to learn these principles from reading and observation. You might find an intelligent carpenter who could copy a good house for you. And also you might go to a so-called architect and get a disappointing house. The chances are against you, unless you solve certain problems as an architect would solve them. The main questions you must answer to your own satisfaction are:

"What is a house, anyway? And what is the advantage to me of consulting an architect? How am I to know a trained architect when I find him?"

The architect's answer is lucid enough·

A house is primarily a building to live in. The idea in planning a house is to make it comfortable.

"Comfortable" means that the arrangement of rooms should be convenient, that the heating system should be so that the house can be made warm when one wishes, that the plumbing system should never fail to give hot water, that the windows should not leak, and that the cellar should be dry.

These things when well done give bodily comfort.

There is, however, another comfort, which has been called a "comfort of the eye."

Though your plumbing system is perfect, and your cellar dry, and your house warm, we still ask: "Is it attractive? Does it please the eye?"

The houses in which we live must not only answer the conditions of efficiency, but of good taste also.

CHAPTER II

THE VALUE OF THE ARCHITECT

YOU have only so many dollars for your house and as you count the precious hoard you wonder if you can afford an architect. What makes an architect desirable, anyway, when you have plans of houses of all styles and all periods to draw upon? When you have denied yourselves so much for this ideal house, dreamed and studied so for it, you feel you cannot afford to lose the best part of it—your comfort and satisfaction. And so you make a program of your requirements and begin to question if, after all your years of planning, you are n't just as capable to build your own house as an architect. You know what you want. Why pay another to tell you? Why should n't every man be his own architect? Just what is an architect anyway?

The science of building is the practical side of house construction. The art of designing is the other. That is why the architect, trained to consider both aspects, is more successful than the practical builder untrained in the history of art and design, or the artist untrained in the use of building materials.

Now, just as there are houses and houses, so there are architects and architects. To become a good artist it will readily be granted one must study long and assiduously; to become a good practical builder one must study and work with all the different building materials, must learn to put them together, must ascertain what their many qualities are. This also is a long study.

It is not difficult to see that an architect, who must cover both these fields, is not made overnight. The study of the practical side of building is admittedly long. What shall we say of the study of design, which is simply the development of good taste? The development may continue during a lifetime; there is no end to the study of good taste.

"But," some one argues, "suppose we are willing to give up our questionable plans and copy a good old house? Suppose we like a square brick house in Salem, or a stately white house in Richmond, or a clapboard cottage in our home town well enough to copy it? Suppose we have found just our ideal rambling house in England, or France, or Italy.

THE HONEST HOUSE

The Villa Gamberaia is one of the glories of Italy.

You admit that we build our houses on the traditions of these countries. Why shouldn't we reproduce these houses faithfully? Why consult an architect?"

Unless you can select every door, every window-casing, every molding; unless you can assemble exactly the materials that went into these old houses, how can you reproduce them? How can you build a closet or a bathroom in a symmetrical Georgian house? How can you get real timber-work in your Norman cottage without paying well for it? How can you get your windows scattered properly over the surface of your Italian villa and at the same time meet all the hard conditions of practical comfort demanded by a modern home-builder? How can you get the soft curve of an English roof-line without thatch?

The idea that a simple Colonial house can be copied by a carpenter is dangerous; the simplicity of those old houses was enforced.

"But this is dreadful!" some one argues. "You are condemning us to dreary boxes, safe houses of no character. What chance is there for charm and originality in a small house?"

There is all the chance in the world; as many chances as there are houses to be built. The most interesting house in America is the small country cottage, and it is also the representative house.

It is not generally understood that it is much more difficult to design a small house than a large one. A five-room cottage may be just as distinguished as a great house, but it takes a trained architect to make it so, and the trained architect usually has his hands full of bigger things. It isn't that he scorns the small house—he loves it. When he turns his hands to it, he does something supremely complete and charming. But he, like all the rest of us, is concerned with making a financial success, and he doesn't often find a client who wants a small house for a reasonable amount of money. The average client wants a large house for a very small and insufficient amount. And so there are very few *new* small houses that have both convenience and charm. There are thousands of lovable old ones— clapboard and shingle cottages, and field stone ones, and old brick ones. But the new ones are apt to be hideous things, mushrooms

8

that grow overnight from queer floor plans; lumpy bungalows; pretentious cottages of stucco or wood masquerading as manor houses. The smaller they are, the more attention they require, and the less they receive. Poor little houses!

All small houses should be good, because people love them so. We do not always resent the great ostentatious pile of masonry that the newly rich man builds for himself, because the chances are he has much space and many trees around it. But we do feel sad over the poor little houses that might so easily be beautiful.

The very small house shown on page 11 was designed by Mr. Charles Platt, who is known everywhere as a designer of great country houses. This little house has as much charm as his larger houses.

The Vanderbilt gate lodge at Great Neck, Long Island, is a triumphant expression of the trained architect. The inspiration is Norman. The timber-work is actual, not sham. The tiles came from an old middle-western church. The gargoyles are a fine example of the proper use of ornament. The roof line and the chimney treatment are so delightful that we feast our eyes on their fine

John Russell Pope, Architect.

Designed in the Norman style of half timber architecture, the Vanderbilt lodge, at Deepdale, Long Island, is interesting especially because of the thoroughness with which the design was carried out. The half timber is *real* half timber, the tiles are real old tiles, and the whole house has an aspect of age. There are few more perfect examples of small house design.

lines, but—when we come down to essentials —this is simply a five-room cottage, planned for a family of two people.

These two cottages are the finest possible illustrations of the trained architect's fitness for his profession, a fitness that comes from the pride of workmanship and the joy of work.

If, then, you are going to employ an architect (and it is the only sensible thing to do) you should submit all your ideas to his knowledge and training, just as you would rest your case with your lawyer, or trust your child to your doctor. You should go about the business of house-building with an open mind. You must look upon your house as a lifetime business. If you don't live in it always, some one will follow you. You must build for those people who will follow you, as well as for the immediate content and comfort of yourself. You should be free to tell your architect all the things you have thought out about your house, but then you should let the problem rest with him.

The architect's profession is based on an exact science. He must know the history of house-building. For instance, he must know the significance of the four styles from which we commonly draw our inspiration for our homes of moderate size and cost—the Colonial or Georgian, the Norman, the English and the Italian. Each style has its special value for adaptation and use. All are subject to the same general principles of good design. What these principles are, what things should be done, what rules observed that your house may be attractive, it is the business of the architect to know, and it is yours also from the minute you begin to plan your house. Good house-design is not obtained by him who has a practical mind only; it is essential that he also have an eye trained for beauty in things.

If you haven't taken the trouble to train your eye, if you don't know why one house is good and another bad, play safe. Stick to simple things. Be modest. See to it that your architect knows your desire for simplicity. This may seem drab counsel, if you are full of original and untried ideas, but until you have learned the rudiments of any art, go warily! Don't try to put on "lugs," and don't let your architect put them on. He won't, anyway, if he knows his business.

But, how are you to know? There's the rub! It is unfortunate that we accept the architect so casually here in America. In European countries it is usual to require an architect to hold a diploma, or what corresponds to a license, before he is fully entitled to practise his profession. Over there a man may build his own house from his own

First floor plan.

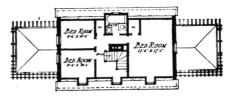

Second floor plan.

House on estate of Robert H. Schutz, Hartford, Connecticut.

THE VALUE OF THE ARCHITECT

Charles A. Platt, Architect.

This example of house design shows how great are the possibilities for an attractive small house. Note the beautifully proportioned dormer windows and the fine character of the details of this house, which is located on the estate of Mr. Robert H. Schutz, at Hartford, Connecticut.

plans, but if he employs an architect it is with the understanding that the term "architect" implies a special, serious training. We Americans demand this proof of the fitness of our lawyers, our doctors, and our dentists, but we have no hold on the men who call themselves our architects. We have not yet awakened to the consequent stupidities and atrocities that surround us and make us ridiculous to the people of older countries.

Down in Florida recently, in a municipal council, it was proposed that all buildings over a certain cost should be designed by an architect or an engineer, as the case required. This plan was defeated on the ground that any one of ordinary common sense could draw plans for a building! Is it a wonder we go

slowly in establishing an American architecture?

Any man who can drive a nail may call himself an architect, and perpetrate one dreadful house after another. The country is full of these untrained men whose taste is open to criticism on the ground of immaturity, to use no harder expression. Therefore, you who are about to build should investigate the standing of your architect, and go to him not simply because he calls himself so. For the time being you are entering a business partnership with him, and you should investigate what he has to offer as carefully as you investigate the title of the land on which your house is to be built.

It is unfortunately true that certain idiosyncrasies attach to some of the architects on the outskirts of the profession. It is equally unfortunate that these architects are the ones with whom the small home builder, directing his own course of procedure, is likely to come into contact.

In architecture, as in the other professions, individuals are marked off into classes by different attitudes of mind. The attitude of the specialist, the commercial attitude, the professional attitude and the attitude of the professional man who even in this practice is not a professional man merely, are the four usually encountered.

The specialist is the man who is doing a definite line of work for a particular class of people. The mill architect is a typical instance. He does such things as factories, warehouses, and large commercial buildings of a similar class. His knowledge is the knowledge of the engineer, rather than of the architect. It is unlikely that the mill architect will be either interested or successful in the designing of small houses.

The commercial attitude is simply that of the man who does something for some one, and gets paid for it. It is a typical tradesman's attitude. This sort of an architect feels that he has something to sell, and he means to get as much as he legitimately can for it. He performs his service in the briefest possible time, taking all the short cuts at his disposal, and paying out as little money in salaries as is consistent with the satisfaction, or what he calls the satisfaction, of his client. When a sincere, and not a cut rate, worker, he may be relied upon to do a workmanlike piece of ordinary work. Unfortunately, he is lacking in the finer perceptions of esthetic values. He cannot study a problem with sufficient reference to the location and

the client's peculiar needs. His work is likely to be all of a piece, and one house is distinguishable from another only by the difference in size and the kinds of materials used. He performs a legitimate service, but a service of a kind not calculated to raise the average quality of small house architecture.

The professional (perhaps it should be called ultra-professional) attitude is that in which the architect tries to force upon the client designs and ideas in which he, as a professional man, has the greatest confidence. He is preëminently a stylist. His work is the result of the particular faith that is in him. He is likely to be found among the highest class (socially speaking) of the men in practice. When he is a man of prominence and strong individuality he can undoubtedly force his ideas through.

The result, however, is likely to be unsatisfactory in the end, from the view of the client. Once in the house, the client finds numerous places that are not to his liking. Several of the rooms are to him unlivable, and after a while he comes to realize that he is occupying not his own house, but the house of his architect.

While the attitude of mind of this kind of practitioner is undoubtedly one to command respect, it commands the respect due to an artist who happens to be an architect, rather than to a home maker.

The attitude of mind of the architects who are not professional men merely, seems certainly to be the right one, from the point of view of the man who would build a home. It is also the dominant idea among those men who are doing the domestic work.

These men, so far as life is concerned, are, like the client himself, still in the making. They are near enough to the struggle for ex-

THE VALUE OF THE ARCHITECT

Derby & Robinson, Architects.

This house at Winchester, Massachusetts, is full of the placid charm of early New England Colonial architecture. Note the rather unusual but happy type of dormer.

istence to realize that happiness is the main point, after all, and that happiness is not confined to the kind of house in which a man lives. They believe, however, that happiness is materially qualified by the home. Just what these respects are vary in different cases.

The kind of comfort which comes from convenience is first of all, perhaps, with the average man. He has accustomed himself to a certain standard of living, and the conveniences which he demands are limited by this standard. An architect must find out what this standard is, and work with it in mind. He must not spend the limited means of the client on superfluities, even if they are practical superfluities.

On the esthetic side also there are standards. The true architect of homes is not disheartened by the apparent lack of taste in a client. He knows that in certain matters a client's ignorance is less than his own. He remembers always when he is commissioned to do a house for a client that it is the client's house he is doing. He is engaged upon it for a month or a year, but the client must live in it all his life. He does not spend time trying to force upon the client a hundred and one trivialities of design, his own singularities, perhaps.

He uses his best knowledge in the interpretation of a client's fundamental needs. He does not observe all of the whimsical wishes the clients advance, for these are often no more than the cut of a coat for a particular season. He goes below the expressed ideas, and finds out which of them have solid foundation. Taking these and a knowledge of the man (and by this should be understood the man's whole family), he retires to his office and applies his hardest thinking and his best skill to the designing of a home which the client can occupy in that comfort of body and mind which shall leave him free to the pursuit of his own proper life work.

In a word, he gives his client something to *grow to*, and not something to *live up to*. This (granting technical skill always), and a proper solution of all the practical requirements, is in our opinion the whole art of architecture as applied to home making.

It is certainly not to your discredit if you do not know all of architecture. You can't be held responsible because you have not educated yourself in all the arts. You have enough to do to educate yourself in that particular profession which gives you bread and butter. But you can acquire a certain knowledge of the simpler principles of architecture which will help you build your house wisely and well.

CHAPTER III

AMERICAN HOUSES AND THEIR EUROPEAN PROTOTYPES

WE have no architecture of our own in America; we are just emerging into the light. We are a population intensely satisfied with certain things. We are well schooled—that is to say we know our arithmetic, and we know how to buy and sell. We know that a house must have a bathroom and must be well heated. But few people have been taught that sheer utility is not the end of things. Few of us are taught to look for beauty, that the ultimate value of a civilization lies largely in what it contributes to beauty.

We hear a great deal about the improvement of the mind, and yet thousands of well educated people live in houses which are too atrocious for words. Some of them are not hypocritical in this matter; they don't know that their houses are atrocious. We condemn a man who wears showy clothes, but many of us don't care enough to notice whether the house he lives in is showy and vulgar, nor what there is about it that makes it so. Some day we shall appreciate beauty more. In the meantime we are all in a melt-ing pot. When we have melted a little more, and our economic system has become more stable, we shall have time to think whether the houses we live in are cheap or gaudy or pretentious.

The situation to-day is a normal one, when you consider the history of culture of the fine arts in this country. It is interesting to trace this history—that is, it should be interesting. If you would know the tendencies of our architectural design to-day, you should know something of the history that is responsible for these tendencies.

This country was settled principally by the English, the French, the Dutch, and the Spanish. All of these various contributory elements to the early population of the country brought with them their ideas and customs in the matter of house building, just as they brought their ideas of clothes and cooking.

The early ascendancy of the English influence in the colonies crowded out the expression of other nationalities in literature and art. Of course we still have some colo-

THE HONEST HOUSE

A little house at Garden City, Long Island, that has survived many generations of fashions in house-building. It will always be good,—because it always was. The long hand-split shingles are characteristic of early Long Island work.

nial work other than that of the English colonists, such as the Dutch colonial houses about New York, and the Spanish mission architecture of the Southwest and West. But by the time of the formation of the United States, the domestic architecture throughout the thirteen states was fairly Georgian in its character. We call it Colonial or Georgian, but really it is Georgian with a difference, the difference coming from the variation caused by the use of local materials, and by local climatic conditions.

The original colonial houses,—those built, let us say, in the seventeenth century for the most part—had hardly any characteristic style. They were built for shelter, for protection against the savages and the weather. Not only this, but their simple expression was due in part to the fact that building materials

were difficult to obtain. Timber there was in plenty, but saw-mills were few, and without saw-mills the mechanical labor of obtaining lumber from the trees was enormous.

Building stone was plentiful enough, but in many parts of the country, as in New England, the common stone, granite, was restricted in its usefulness, owing to the difficulty of working it. One may note that whereas New England is literally criss-crossed with stone walls, yet stone houses of the colonial period are scarce. In other districts, notably in Pennsylvania, stone was more generally used. It was of limestone formation and more easily worked.

From these indications you may easily see how the architecture of a country depends for its expression upon the character of the building materials which are most readily found and most easily worked.

In the days of early settlement the newly arrived settler copied his neighbor's cabin. Most of these early houses were of logs. The newcomer learned from the pioneer how to notch and caulk his logs, and how to cover his roof. In New England the log house was commonly built around a huge central chimney, since the climate was rigorous and the first thing to be looked out for was the provision of heat. In the South the warmer climate made the heating of a house less important than air and space, and so even in these early days there were differences in the fundamental requirements. As every one knows, the Southern house differs essentially from the Northern house and the Cape Cod cottage differs from the log cabin. Yet all of these types may claim to be native to a particular locality, and native as well to the country as a whole.

As the community grew in size, the individual fell more and more into the way of specialization. At this point he called in the carpenters and masons to do his house, and they copied for him the model which he chose. It varied only slightly from other neighboring examples which he might almost equally well have selected. The particular difference from others in the model of his choice was merely his slight expression of individuality as exercised in his own home. As a result of this, the houses of the older communities bear very striking resemblances to each other.

With the multiplication of communities and of their respective styles, expert service in designing or building came to have a broader foundation. It became necessary for the expert to be able to tell his client what was being done in other parts of the country.

Sometimes the client chose an example of work that originated in some other part of the country than his own. From this resulted a more or less general commingling of the styles.

It was seldom that the fundamental type for a particular place was altered, and it was still more seldom that the requirements of the individual were neglected. In fact, fundamental types and requirements of individuals became more and more pronounced as communities grew, and as various details of design and construction were adopted for general use. The most successful service was that which preserved the old styles and satisfied the individual requirements, and this

Old New England.

17

is the most successful service to-day also.

Undoubtedly this early architecture followed the national characteristics of the various groups of colonists. But in all cases, since they were built in a country still savage and economically poor, early colonial houses were characterized by an extreme simplicity. When a man feared to receive an arrow in his back while he was shingling his cabin, he did n't waste time on the study of proportion, or the refinements of design. The conditions necessary for the growth of the arts were lacking.

There were many elements of national feeling and aptitude among the original population of the colonies, but the leisure to develop this aptitude was lacking. By the time the country had been sufficiently organized on its economic side for leisure, the English colonists held an overwhelming predominance in the political state.

The English régime tended to absorb various political and social groups, and to extend its political influence over them. It also imposed' its conception of architecture upon the country.

At the beginning of the eighteenth century George I of England ascended the throne, and then began the so-called Georgian period of architecture. Naturally the contact of this country with England was as constant as the imperfections of ocean traveling would permit, and the colonies drew from England many artisans, workers in wood and metal.

As wealth increased in the colonies, architecture became more costly, more complicated, and more decorative in its expression. The models upon which this Colonial work were based were, generally speaking, the actual buildings in England with which the artisans were familiar.

This does not mean that you will find in America exact replicas of English buildings; it is rather that you will find the spirit of the work identical. The old Salem house shown on page 19 closely follows a common type of English cottage. Its gables and roofs are very true to the traditions. But it is interpreted in shingle and clapboard, whereas its English prototype was more likely of slate, stucco, or half-timber.

This tradition was continued throughout the colonial days, and there is no perceptible change from the Georgian type of architecture until long after the Revolution had established the independence of this country. Independent politically, the new country still continued to draw largely on England for its literature and art as well as for its trade.

It was not until after the War of 1812, after a new generation of native Americans had grown to maturity under an independent government, that the break with English tradition appears. The country had come doubtless to a full realization of its political independence, and to see the economic independence which could be based on the enormous national resources. We see here the beginning of our artistic independence, but this artistic independence began with faltering steps. For more than a century its logical and normal development was arrested and deflected by social and economic conditions peculiar to its history. It had started on the road to independence, but it was, in the course of the next century, to be nearly smothered by the very democracy which had brought it about.

At the time of the break with England, which became definite after 1812, we entered into the first period of our modern development. The revolution wrought by steam

This old gabled house of Salem, Massachusetts, shows beautifully the English architecture of the seventeenth century, transplanted in America. Its gables, its projecting second story and its huge chimney, can still be seen in the old English villages, only the materials, owing to local conditions, are somewhat different.

locomotion changed the country from a relatively compact group of states with largely homogeneous population, into a great territory, thinly populated, filled with incredible opportunities for wealth. The huge, unpeopled West was waiting to be exploited. In all directions expansion began. The farming lands of the Middle West and, subsequently, the discovery of gold in California drew the emigrant always westward. Immigration, which had been fairly noteworthy up to then, became unprecedented. The enormous country lying to the west of the Alleghenies began to be populated.

The colonies which later formed the original states had been under English domination up to the time of the second war with England. The school system, the social and political regulations were fairly well determined, and the standard of literacy and in-

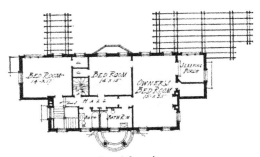

Second floor plan.

telligence was fairly high. Now with the expansion of the country there came an invasion of immigrants from other countries, from Germany, from Scandinavia, and later from Italy. This new population had for the most part come from countries where political rights, schooling and personal fortune had amounted to little. On entering America they became citizens. The vitality of the country was undoubtedly increased, but culture went into a decline, a decline of which the outer expression is shown in the depths of the artistic horrors of 1875.

In taking account of this eclipse of the arts, it is essential to remember two important facts connected with it. The first is the extension of the use of machinery in replacing hand labor. The second is the spread of the labor unions, to which we may accord a large share of responsibility for the decline of the skilled artisan. That these two developments have been a necessary part of our economic development will not be denied. That they have made for the destruction of interest in the arts, and especially architecture, is just as strongly affirmed.

One seeks for an explanation of the uniform attractiveness of Colonial work; the ab-

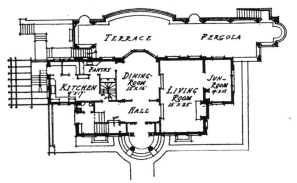

First floor plan.
House of William J. Henry, Scarsdale, New York.

AMERICAN HOUSES AND THEIR EUROPEAN PROTOTYPES

Franklin P. Hammond, Architect.

The William J. Henry house at Scarsdale, New York, is a fine modern expression of late Colonial work at its best. It is built of tapestry brick, red in color, with good variations. Note especially the proportions of the curved porch and the graceful dormer windows.

sence of vulgarity; the exquisite sense of proportion—qualities so often lacking in modern work. Often one hears the question: Who were the real designers of the Colonial architecture? Perhaps the best answer to be given is to be found in "Colonial Architecture for Those About to Build" by Herbert C. Wise and H. Ferdinand Beidleman.

"Who were the real designers of the Colonial monuments? It is difficult to conceive of a doctor drawing the design for Christ Church, or a lawyer and Speaker of the Assembly that of the State House. A knowledge of architecture being then considered part of every gentleman's culture, however, it is easy to picture these leading men of the community in the rôle of connoisseurs, having drawings made under their guidance by others; and after so doing, producing or submitting the design at the official meetings where a course of procedure was to be determined. The names of those other persons who actually handled the T-square and triangle are lost in obscurity.

"We believe them to be the more intelligent carpenters of the time, some of the men who banded themselves together, as we have seen, 'to obtain instruction in the science of architecture.' It was such a motive that

21

made the Colonial carpenter a thinking be-ing, that added some ability at drawing to his skill to construct. His dividers labor-iously transcribed the proportions of Vi-truvius, Serlio and Scamozzi from the al-bums of classic forms. A few old English works on architecture were also his compan-ions. One of the most valued of these was Batty Langley's 'Builder's Director or Bench-Mate,' which the title-page announced as a 'pocket treasury of the Greek, Roman, and Gothic Orders of Architecture made easy to the meanest capacity by near 500 examples, improved from the best Authors ancient and modern.' There were also the four books of Palladio, esteemed by Englishmen and por-trayed by Isaac Ware and others. We can imagine the Colonial carpenter conceiving a proposed building with Sir William Cham-bers' time-honored work open before him, referring also to the designs of Sir Christo-pher Wren, James Gibbs, Vanbrugh, and Sir Robert Taylor. We can picture him zealously striving to do what the Brothers Adam were simultaneously essaying in Eng-land: 'To catch the beautiful spirit of an-tiquity and infuse it with novelty and va-riety.' This meant translating into wood many of the forms originally conceived for stone. In the process it was but natural,— it was necessary indeed,—to attenuate the antique proportions. By such an avenue there arrived the invention and freedom of Colonial architecture, that true novelty that sacrificed neither beauty nor dignity. The public did not demand originality. What

was proper was acceptable. Of all mechan-ics occupied with building, the greatest gen-eral knowledge of all crafts, in addition to special knowledge of his own, resided with the carpenter. Add a practical knowledge of working in the three dimensions to famil-iarity with the graphic forms in books, and the possessor was quite in the position to be-come the architect of an earlier day."

In a brief summary, the history of culture in this country is largely this:—weak in the beginning, it developed early a quasi-English character. Its dependence on Eng-land was overthrown, along with political dependence, and it was finally overwhelmed by the expansion of the country, and the in-flux of people of alien thought and speech who came to this country in the search of wealth and freedom. The introduction of machinery and the subsequent disappearance of skilled hand labor completed the unfor-tunate situation.

To-day we have at our hands scores of ma-terials to use in building, we have hundreds of appliances to make our living conditions better. Our contact is no longer with one country. England is no longer the fountain head. We draw from all the world. Our architecture is English and French and Span-ish and Italian. It will never be American until the home builder accords to the archi-tect a position of responsibility at least as great as that which he gives to his tailor, and until he insists that the architect shall have been trained before he practises his profes-sion.

CHAPTER IV

THE PRACTICAL PROBLEM OF HOUSE BUILDING

THE people who inherit ready made houses and acres never taste the finest joys of home-making. The dreams that come when you have finally decided to go ahead and buy a little land and build a house upon it are the most enchanting dreams you will ever enjoy. Anything is possible, in this golden period. You can decide to buy a hillside site with a view, and build your house to fit the site. Ten minutes later a valley site with a brook seems more desirable. You remember an old house in your scrap book that puts an end to both hillside and valley, and so the dreams and plans change again and merge and change again, and there are so many possible selections— sites, and styles, and materials, and color. How are you ever to find the home that will be peculiarly your own?

It seemed so easy, before you had money enough to go ahead. You had a site securely fixed in your imagination,—its picturesqueness was fixed. Its boundaries were vague, unreal, elastic enough to accommodate any of the houses you dreamed. There was the placid old Virginia house that had all the

lure of family and ancestry. There was a little Japanese cottage built among the beach grasses of Long Island. There was a timber and plaster house you saw once in Kent, a thatched roofed Tudor cottage covered with ivy and roses that seemed the absolute fulfilment of your ideal. There was a wondrous rambling Spanish house near the City of Mexico with a looped roof line that held you enthralled. There was a gray shingle farmhouse in the Connecticut hills with a stone wall and an apple orchard. There was a little mushroom of a house on a Massachusetts hillside, and a little octagonal California house built on the sea—there were dozens of delectable houses. It seemed so easy to choose one and make it your own. All that worried you was the wherewithal to realize the chosen house.

The trouble is, when you see a house that pleases you, you see it as a part of its entourage. You see the hedges and the shrubs and the flowers that have taken so long to grow. When you go about building your own house you will have to separate all the things that another man has done for his house from the

THE HONEST HOUSE

"Westover" on the James River, in Virginia, is a placid old house that has all the lure of family and romance. It is really Georgian in character, though we commonly call it Colonial. Note its extreme simplicity. Its air of elegance comes from its exquisite proportions.

house itself. . You will have to buy an undeveloped site, and see the litter of building for long months before you can see any chance of beauty. And this is a bitter pill to swallow. The chances are that all the houses that pleased you had been growing for years, that the land was bought when land was available at low prices and building materials cost little. When you are forced to compromise on your site, forced to give up the brook and the vista for a small rectagonal lot with a few trees on it, you feel that there is no light ahead. You have to give up your daily dream of picturesqueness and put in your waking hours considering the practical problems of accessibility, and drainage, and expense, and neighbors, and water supply. These things must be settled before you can buy your site and go ahead with your plans.

The consideration of neighbors is important, but may be made too much so. You will be a neighbor yourself, remember, and you can't demand any more of your neighbors than you give them. They got there first. If you would know who is a good neighbor, look to the parable—it was a Samaritan in that case. Your neighbors may be closer than you like, but there are other elements beside the neighbor necessary to a good neighborhood. The school, the playground, the railroad station, the prevailing breezes, and the various kinds of public service—water, gas, electricity, telephone, and sewer—are of great importance.

It is far wiser to buy enough land for comfort, and to wait a year to build your house, than to economize on your site and regret later that it cannot be expanded. If the site is to be in a section largely built upon, or divided into lots for building purposes, it is better to buy two lots and afford only a tent, than to buy one, build a house, and always look, feel, and be cramped. A house can be enlarged. A lot cannot. If you expect to

24

have an automobile later, when you prosper, plan it in the beginning. Leave room for it on the site, and be sure of an adequate approach, lest later you find it an impossibility.

Some people I know, who were tired of living in a New York apartment, bought a large lot on the top of a wooded hill on Staten Island. They were not ready to build their house, but they built a garage big enough to house them comfortably. Some day there will be a house on the crest of the hill, and later there will be an automobile. In the meantime they live in perfect comfort in the garage, and plant flowers and vines and fruit trees for the years to come. A little vineyard is already growing on the sunny side of the hill. This is an infinitely better plan than buying a small lot and building a small house would have been.

If you are to build in the real country the consideration of view is important, but if your lot is to be one of hundreds in a suburb or a small town there are more important considerations. Many people go into a new house and say, "But there is no view!" In a little while, when they have lived in the house a few weeks, the view is forgotten. A pleasant and interesting foreground is of much greater moment twelve months in the year than the sight of a distant landscape.

As far as topography is concerned, a level lot is always capable of excellent treatment. A lot sloping down from the street gives the advantage of large cellar windows at the back, and a door instead of a bulkhead. A small lot sloping down toward the street is usually disadvantageous. Such a lot can be made very attractive to the eye, however, by a good architect.

From a standpoint of picturesqueness, the more irregular the lot, the better. Any interesting features—rocks, trees, a precipitate slope—can be turned to advantage by the architect. But building a house to fit an irregular site is obviously more expensive than building a house on a flat site. The questions of retaining walls and excavations must be considered.

The position of the house in relation to the points of the compass must also be reckoned with. Very often it occurs that the view you want to get is to the north, and that is unfortunate, because your living rooms have to be to the north, which means they are harder to heat in winter. If possible you should ar-

A rambling English house that owes much of its picturesqueness to its thatched roof, its large wall spaces, and its surrounding hedge and shrubbery.

THE HONEST HOUSE

Robert R. McGoodwin, Architect.
A pleasant foreground is of much greater moment than a distant landscape. The difficulties of the irregular site of Mr. McGoodwin's house at St. Martins, Philadelphia, have been overcome attractively by the use of stone walls.

range your house so that you can get the living-rooms on the southern exposure, and where this cannot be done some kind of sun parlor or porch should be arranged on the side of the house that will be most accessible.

A south exposure gets little or no sun on the longest summer days. A north exposure gets the early and late sun, the east and west the forenoon and afternoon sun, but the south receives none, as the sun passes through a point near the zenith rising north of east and setting north of west. The south for the living-room, therefore, gives warmth in winter and comfort in summer. The ideal orientation for the dining-room is southeast.

When you have finally chosen the site of your house, real work begins. The selection of the site was not such a difficult problem after all. It resolved itself into a matter of getting as much land as possible within reasonable distance of your business. But the house! Now come the real indecisions, the tempting comparisons, the agonizing necessity of selecting one thing from a number of others. You know by now that you can never realize the full measure of your ideal house: you have already compromised in buying the site. Now

26

moments of despair will distress you, but you are still in the golden period. You are still the potential builder of a house that will be a real home for your family, and that is a very fine accomplishment, no matter how much you may have to compromise.

What kind of house are you to build? You may have a large family or a small one. You may need a house with four rooms, or twelve. You may need a nursery, a library, a workroom, an office, a billiard-room or other special rooms, or combinations of some of these rooms to meet the requirements of the likings and needs of your family. Some of the members of your family may have very decided likes and dislikes which may modify your problem greatly. The size of the house, the style of architecture, whether it is to be a two story house, a bungalow, a house with sleeping porches, a house without porches— all these are special conditions to be dealt with.

There is a common fallacy that if a man

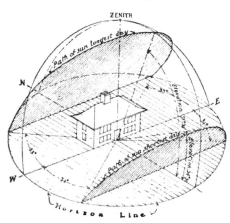

This diagram shows a house facing south, and its relation to the sun's course.

has a section of land on which to build a house, and money enough to build it, he has only to go to an architect and turn it over to him, and to-morrow a plan will be perfected. "Plan a good house for me," the patron says. "I can spend ten thousand dollars." And if the architect seems a little dismayed, the client thinks he does n't know his business.

The only way to go about the serious business of planning a house is to present to the architect a list of your requirements. You may formulate your own plan, or he will do it for you, given plenty of time and intelligent co-operation. Whether you are going to build a new house or alter an old one, first of all you must consider carefully your family needs.

Out of all these many possibilities, there is one certainty which appears. *Before you can begin building, you must know what you want*—that is, what your practical means dictate as the necessary practical conditions that your house shall fulfil. In other words, you must establish a *program*. The more clearly you can decide upon what you absolutely do need the simpler the solution of your problem will become.

Suppose you have decided upon the number of rooms and the general requirements of your house. Let us suppose that your family consists of five people, and that you wish to keep one servant. You feel you need for your house these simple requirements:

On the first floor a living-room, dining-room and kitchen, with pantry and service dependencies. On the second floor, three bedrooms, a nursery and two baths. And, either in a wing, or in a third story, a servant's room and attic. This is a brief statement of the common requirements of home builders.

So far, so good. But how large are these rooms to be? Obviously, this depends on two things. Their size is limited by the size of the house, and this in turn is limited by what you can afford to spend. Here we come to one of the crucial problems which confronts you: how much can you afford to spend for your house?

Let us see if we cannot arrive at an answer indirectly. Consider the houses in your neighborhood. Select one which pleases you most in general mass and size, materials and finish. Find out what this house cost to build.

Let us suppose it cost $5,000.00. Figure roughly the cubic contents of this house. This can be done very easily. Let us suppose that the house in question contains 25,000 cubic feet. Then, obviously, the cost per cubic foot is 20 cents. Now, if you have $4,000.00 to spend, you can have a house the cubic contents of which is about 20,000 cubic feet. In other words, the dimensions of your house might be approximately 25 feet wide by 40 feet long by 20 feet high, or it might be 50 feet long by 20 feet wide by 20 feet high, or whatever dimensions would give approximately 20,000 cubic feet.

The picture on page 29 will help explain how to find the cubic contents of a house. This house consists of two parts:—the main portion, and the porch attached to it. We assume that the cellar goes under the whole house, excepting the porch. The contents of the house under the main roof from the cornice line to the ridge, as the section shows, is equal to the width of the house times its length, times one-half the altitude of the roof, this being the volume of a prism. It is equal to $21' \ 6'' \times 24' \ 0'' \times 5' \ 6'' = 2{,}838$ cubic feet. The contents of the re-maining portion of the main block of the house is equal to its height times its length, times its width. It is equal to $17' \ 0'' \times 24' \ 0'' \times 21' \ 6'' = 8{,}772$ cubic feet. Adding these we get a total of 11,610 cubic feet. Calculating the contents of the porch similarly we get about 1,050 cubic feet. Now, since the porch is not finished like the interior of the house, and since it has no cellar underneath it, we may count its contents as only a third of what it actually is. This rule follows practical usage and will be found to be fairly correct. Counting the contents of the porch as 350 cubic feet, and adding it to the previous figure, we have for the total contents of the house, 11,960 cubic feet. If the house is to cost 20 cents per cubic foot, which is the price your neighbor paid for his house, then the approximate cost of the little house at the top of page 29 would be $2,392.00. There! It isn't so very difficult to find what a house should cost, is it?

You can repeat this calculation in reference to other houses in your neighborhood which differ in materials and finish from the house you have just considered, and in this way you can arrive with fair accuracy at the size of the house and general type of material and finish which the money you have to spend will enable you to get. You might calculate the price per square foot, but this method is far less accurate.

This gives you a better idea of building costs in your own neighborhood than any table of costs, but you cannot go ahead on this rough basis of estimate. You must also decide on the materials you wish to employ, and the way in which you wish your house to be finished. The cost of the house will be proportioned to its size, its materials, the

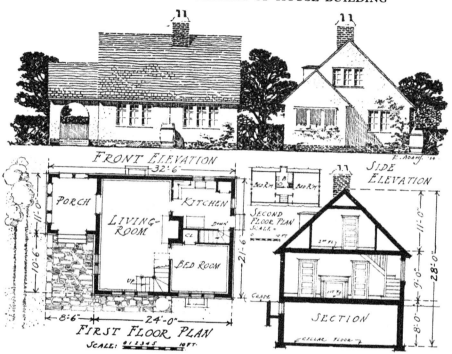

"How much will a house like this cost?" See page 28.

cost of labor and its excellence of detail.

A brick house costs more than a wooden one, because bricks are more expensive than wood. A house faced with tapestry brick costs still more, because tapestry brick is more expensive than the ordinary kind. Two stucco houses built from the same plan may be extraordinarily unlike, because one has been done by an unintelligent builder and has the general effect of thin gray cardboard, and the other has been finished by an artist, with a plaster of a pleasantly rough texture. If you wish the best results, be prepared to pay for them.

Similarly, the success of a house may depend as much on the seemingly unimportant details of hardware as upon the use of the materials selected. I have known many delightful small houses that owed much of their charm to the excellence of their shutters, their ironwork, hinges, and so forth. You can spend a fortune on such fascinating details and preserve the modesty of a small house— if you have the fortune. So decide just how important these things are, before you decide on the materials of which you will build your house.

A great deal is said about the usual increase

over the estimated cost. Why should the architect be blamed for this? You should boast of it, for it is simply an index to the growth of your conception of what a house should be, during the progress of construction. No one with an alert mind can fail to become immensely educated during this experience, and the results of this education are bound to show in the increased cost.

The only way you can avoid making changes in your original plans is to run away from your house while it is building. Go abroad, and no extras will be incurred

When you have worked over your practical living requirements; when you know approximately how large your house is to be, your program is still incomplete. You do not yet know what shape the house will have, whether it is to be long, or short, or L shaped, or a high house, or a low one. This will be decided largely by the site you have chosen. The relation of house and site is usually not enough appreciated. You may have gone on the assumption that you can design your house and fit it to any site you please.

The earlier American houses that we all admire so much were practically free from the considerations that you have to face. You have to work ten times as hard to get a simple effect, because your problem is so much bound by limitations. You don't own all out-doors; you are fortunate if you have bought an ordinary building lot, that pathetic modern *pied-a-terre* that takes the place of your grandfather's great estate.

If your land is flat and your property is indefinitely extended you can put your house anywhere, and you do not have to worry about special conditions, such as expensive foundations which result from the differences of grades, and all that sort of thing. But few of us are so fortunate as to have extended lands on which to build.

As to the kind of house you will build on your chosen site, you will have to decide first between a high house and a low house. A high house is usually less expensive than a low one, but it is almost never so satisfactory. If you have to build in a depression, a hollow, it is permissible to put up a higher house than otherwise, but in general a high house is unattractive. It is interesting to note that the English and the French, geographically so close to each other, have totally different con-

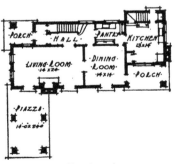
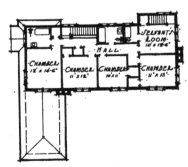

First floor plan.   Second floor plan.
House for Mr. Eugene J. Lang, Scarsdale, New York.

THE PRACTICAL PROBLEM OF HOUSE BUILDING

Eugene J. Lang, Architect.

In Mr. Lang's house at Scarsdale, New York, broad clapboards are employed. The placing of the windows under the long roof, and the general horizontal expression of all the details, gives the house a low-lying quality.

ceptions of domestic architecture. Modern English houses are usually low-lying and pleasing, rising out of the ground as if they grew, while the houses of France are often high and stilted in appearance.

When you have located the position of your house approximately on your lot so that it fulfils to the best advantage all the practical considerations above named, you have fulfilled the important steps preliminary to the program necessary in building your house.

You have considered the living requirements, the cost, and the size of the house you wish to build.

In all these matters it is well to take the advice of a competent architect, but if his services are too difficult to obtain, in following this program you will have gone through the very steps that the architect himself would go through if he were handling the work. By well considering your problem at the start you will avoid painful errors later on.

John Russell Pope, Architect.

The Vanderbilt Gate Lodge, Deepdale, Long Island.

CHAPTER V

THE VEXATIOUS MATTERS OF PROPORTION AND BALANCE

WHAT do we mean when we say that a thing is out of proportion? No expression is more familiar. Yet, if any of us were pinned down to define *why* it is out of proportion, we would find, on reflection, that it is so because it does not conform to some standard. We judge everything by a standard. When we complain that our daily bread is n't like that made by our maternal ancestor, we are referring to a standard. If we see a man whose legs and arms are very long, we say he is badly proportioned. Yes, but we do not criticize the length of arms and legs in a gorilla. Length belongs there. We have different standards of proportion for men and gorillas.

You could go further; even in the different types of mankind, we make classifications. We do not judge the beauty of the Chinese woman by the Caucasian standard. So in the infinite variety of the forms and colors and materials with which the arts deal, we make the same distinctions; we classify things and we judge them according to a standard. This standard, in every case, is what we call our sense of proportion.

In architecture we have been taught that the classic orders have certain proportions. The height of the column, for example, is given in terms of its diameter, and variations from the accepted rule usually are condemned on the ground that their proportions are not good. The Corinthian column, such as that shown in the Salem house on page 34, is ten diameters high. It has the classic proportions. No one will deny that a column so proportioned is attractive.

Contrast this column with that shown on page 35. Examine the two. The propor-

First and second floor plans of the Vanderbilt Lodge.

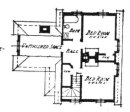

Photograph by Frank Cousins.
This detail of a charming old Salem portico is full of the grace of the best Colonial work. It adheres closely to the classic tradition.

tions of the latter column are such that the trained architect would say unhesitatingly that it is ugly.

Is the mere fact of the variation from the Colonial model enough to condemn this particular column? Certainly not. The picture of the Henry house on page 21 shows columns which vary from the first example quite as much as this column does, and yet

the Henry house columns are well proportioned. Like those of the Salem house, they are beautiful, and yet the proportions are different. What does this mean? Is n't there any such thing as proportion? If the correct proportion of so common a thing as a column is in doubt, can we have any canon of proportion for any of the forms of architectural design and composition? Is there then no standard to which we may conform?

The answer is that proportion is and always must be *an individual matter*, varying continually with the development of the mind of the individual. Like good taste, it is a chimera. At the merest attempt to define it as a permanent standard, it eludes us.

While, however, our conception of proportion and taste is individual, we ourselves are subject to the influence of heredity and environment. We see with the eye of those who have gone before us. We are bound to the past in the matter of our esthetic perceptions, as in all others. We live in communities, and our individual minds reflect the thought of the collective body. If you were born in Turkey, you would be likely to profess the Mohammedan religion; if in Persia, sun worship. If you lived in Russia, the steep roofed and domed architecture would seem to you the natural expression in that art. We all grow up to the general standards of our local surroundings.

We find that the architecture of one community differs from that of the next, just as we find different ideas of government. But these ideas resemble the molten metal in the melting pot: they are in continual flux. Nothing is fixed. The ideas of certain individuals rise to the surface, and a new style is formed. In proportion to the force of the new individuality and of the social conditions at the time, the new style, the new conception, makes a strong impression. And what was popular yesterday becomes unpopular to-day.

What is our guidance in all this confusion? For those of us who believe in the possibility of progress, the single answer is: *study.* If we are to improve on the past, if our art is to have a better and more just relation to our every day life, we must know what mistakes have been made in the past. In this way, we shall learn what is essential, what is superfluous, and what is necessary to our architecture.

The more we study a subject, the more sensitive we become to certain distinctions. The farmer recognizes by sight the different qualities of soil. The coin collector can tell the period of a coin by its general appearance. The physician detects symptoms which are invisible to the layman. The architect sees distinctions of beauty in the varying proportions of design. All this is a matter of training. And when a body of men devote their time to the study of any subject, they come to an agreement on certain fundamental principles. These men all go through certain stages of vacillation and inexperience, but the majority finally arrive at certain definite conclusions. These conclusions are at best only working hypotheses; they are subject to change and modification at any time. But on them we base our system of education,

of government, and of all our industrial and social life. And by such a concurrence of opinion, certain principles are recognized in art and architecture.

If we realize that in order to have good architecture we must study for it—that is a great gain, but what do we mean by "study"? How does one go to work to study? Is it simply a matter of buying a certain number of dry and tedious books which deal academically with the history of architecture? Is it a matter of memorizing the dates and styles of various buildings?

It is not. One of the greatest stumbling blocks in the matter of popular understanding of architecture is the academic history of the subject. For the most part these histories are written without color or style. They are erudite and stilted. They approach the subject with the intellect alone. They point out facts to be memorized. Not one, to my recollection, states the fact that the appreciation of the art of architecture is a matter of training the *eye.* To study architecture is primarily a matter of training the eye. "Does this please the eye?" is the ultimate question which architecture asks.

The more you use your eyes, the more you classify your impressions, the more you become accustomed to fine distinctions and to essentials, the more you are able to answer the questions intelligently. Who would consider for a moment the contention that music should be appreciated by reading about it? The way to appreciate a sonata is to hear it. The way to appreciate architecture is *to see it.*

You can develop your appreciation of architecture wherever you are by simply stopping to consider what looks well, and what does not, and why.

35

THE HONEST HOUSE

William G. Rantoul, Architect.

This house, built for Mrs. Emmerton at Salem, Massachusetts, has much of the character of its old neighbors. It is beautifully studied throughout. Note especially the proportions of the classic doorway.

What do we aim to reach in our study? The criterion of good architecture is its *fitness*. It is all summed up in the word "character." In designing anything, we must try to express its character. You know houses which look like prisons to you. The houses are built as residences, but they look like jails. Imagine the lives people would live in such gloomy places! And yet, the same houses by the changing of a few proportions might become attractive dwellings, with the character of homes.

If you wish to have an understanding of architecture you must study to find what best expresses the character of the building. In doing this you will come to realize that with certain types of architectural design you cannot avoid following certain general proportions. If you wish to reproduce the character of a Greek temple, your columns must have the proportion of Greek columns, and you must know what these proportions are. And so with all styles of architecture.

If you wish to get the effect of a certain style you must understand what proportions the various elements bore to one another. We thus reach an understanding that there is a reason for designing certain things in certain ways; that in so designing them we are attempting to express the character of the building of which they are a part.

Let us make a brief summary of what has

THE VEXATIOUS MATTERS OF PROPORTION AND BALANCE

gone before in this chapter: We have seen that the sense of proportion—like the sense of good taste,—is an individual matter, but that it is influenced by the community in which the individual lives; that the standards of good proportion, as of good taste, are similarly variable; that our guidance in this confusion is *study;* that in this way we arrive at working principles on which we base our system of education and training in architecture; that the way to study architecture is through training the eye to note distinctions of form and color; that the aim of this study is to enable us to grasp the character of a building, to realize what is essential and what is not.

While we have seen that proportion is infinite in its range of variation, we may ask if there is no principle more "fixed" than this shifting one. Yes, there is the sense of balance.

Whereas the sense of proportion, like the sense of good taste, depends directly on our local influences, on the character of the community in which we live, on the ideas current about us, on our particular training in art, on

our having studied in Rome, or in Paris, or in London, or in some other locality which is circumscribed with limitations, there is a deeper sense essential to good design, which has its foundations much more permanently established. This is the sense of balance. What do we mean by it?

Everything in nature tends to grow about a center. A tree tends to grow straight about a vertical axis. A tree that has been bent by the wind gives the impression of instability. We know that it is held in its position from falling over by the straining roots, but it looks ill-balanced to the eye. And yet the tree tends constantly to right itself and grow straight again. It is a law of nature that any object tries to come to a condition of rest, of equilibrium.

The most simple illustration of balance is that of the grouping of windows in the wall of the house. But do not confuse "symmetry" with "balance."

In this country the symmetrical arrangement is often seen in Colonial architecture, which follows classic tradition in the disposition of its detail, its windows and columns. The unsymmetrical arrangement is found at its best in the English cottage type which, not employing classic motifs, is naturally more free in expression. The symmetrical arrangement gives an impression of formality, dignity, and reserve; the unsymmetrical, something more intimate in character.

The house that a child draws is generally symmetrical in the disposition of its windows. Unless you know pretty well the meaning of balance, when you come to arrange your windows in unsymmetrical fashion you are likely to produce a house with very restless character. The moment you cut loose from the safe mooring of symmetry you are nowhere!

Compare the house on this page with that on page 36. The general scheme of windows is similar, yet the sense of restfulness shown in Mr. Rantoul's house is totally wanting in this example. The central motif and the over-large dormers are especially vulgar.

37

Just because you have chosen an accidental arrangement, you must not think that your windows can be scattered over your walls like pepper out of a shaker. Such an accidental placing of windows usually results in

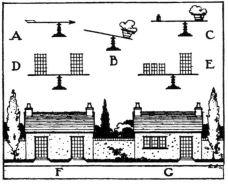

a frightful exterior that is as spotty as a calico horse.

An accidental or unsymmetrical façade must be balanced just as surely as a symmetrical one.

Look at the pictures shown on this page. Fig. A shows an arrow with a stone head and a feathered tail. We all know that this arrow balances when held as shown, for the weight of the part of the right equals that on the left. Let us go a little further. Figures B and C show a flower pot on a board held similarly. In Fig. B the flower pot is too heavy and tilts the board; in Fig. C we have put a small weight on the left hand side which restores the balance. In Fig. E instead of a flower pot we have put window sashes on the board, a big one on the right and three small ones on the left, and the balance is maintained. In Fig. D we have put equal sized windows on each side, and again the balance is preserved.

These mechanical illustrations may be applied to the window treatment of the wall of a house. Fig. F shows such a house with the window composition shown in Fig. D, and Fig. G shows a house which has the composition shown in Fig. E. In both cases we say that the composition is *balanced*, but in Fig. F it is *symmetrical* and in Fig. G the composition is *unsymmetrical*.

Note, then, that in these house designs *the windows balance about a vertical axis.*

Let us go a step further. Let us take for our subject not only the composition of the windows, but the whole house. In Fig. H is shown a house similar in design to the Vanderbilt Lodge. It is, as one can readily see, an unsymmetrical composition. It consists of two distinct elements. To indicate them clearly they are shown separated in Fig. I. The vertical element is marked X and the horizontal Y. In a well designed composition they should balance. If we diminish

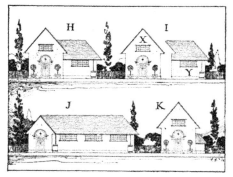

the gable too much relatively to the wing, as is shown in Fig. J, the balance is destroyed; similarly if we diminish the wing it tends to become a mere accident, as is shown in Fig. K.

And so we arrive at another architectural

38

THE VEXATIOUS MATTERS OF PROPORTION AND BALANCE

Joy Wheeler Dow, Architect.
A very daring example of unsymmetrical treatment is Mr. Dow's house at Summit, New Jersey. It is eminently successful. The detail of this house is worthy of careful study.

axiom: *An unsymmetrical composition implies a contrast, but the contrasting elements must make on the eye impressions of approximately equal importance, or the balance will be lost.*

If you wish to have an unsymmetrical design for your house, or an unsymmetrical arrangement for your windows, train your eye by looking at different schemes and ways of arranging windows and wall surfaces, and you will arrive at a conception of what is meant by balance.

If, after all, some profane critic remarks "that all this sort of theory ends nowhere," it is only necessary to remind him that he must have a theory of his own in order to condemn another. It all comes back to the fact that in judging architecture, we have to have a standard—and this standard is our sense of proportion.

THE HONEST HOUSE

Mellor & Meigs, Architects.

This house, built near Philadelphia, is an excellent example of the picturesque English type. Unsymmetrical in its design, its elements are well balanced and the impression given is a restful one. The high chimney in the corner is extremely effective.

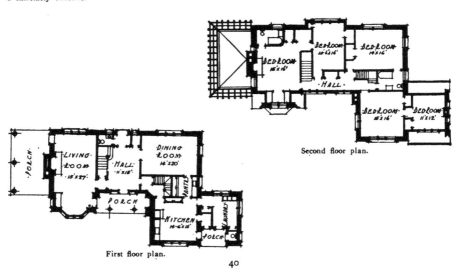

Second floor plan.

First floor plan.

CHAPTER VI

THE USEFUL AND THE BEAUTIFUL

UNFORTUNATELY, when we have considered the matter of proportion and balance, we have not done with all the vexatious problems of architecture. There remains the question of the relation of usefulness to beauty.

A flower pot will serve as an example. It fulfils the obvious purpose of holding earth so that a plant can grow in it. It can also be transferred easily from place to place. From the botanist's point of view it makes very little difference what the shape of the flower pot is, provided the drainage and practical considerations are good.

Suppose we paint two or three colored bands on a very plain flower pot. Obviously we have not changed the practical conditions for the plant's growth, but we have changed the appearance of the pot. To what end? In the·hope, not of making the pot more useful, but of making it more at-

tractive. Our artistic judgment may be good or bad, but the desire to make the pot more attractive is the motive of the decoration.

The settler in the clearing builds a rough log cabin. The boards he uses are rough hewn, the windows are only holes in the thick walls. As time passes and the dangers of attack and the difficulties of living become lessened, and his contact with civilization better, he builds another house. This time he is able to get more finished material and he builds, let us say, a shingled house, which has, instead of the rough plain door, a more elaborate doorway with a simple cornice over it. He pays more attention to the finish of the cornice and the other parts of his house. He has added these refinements simply to make his house look more attractive, not to make it more useful.

It is important to remember, however, that

41

THE HONEST HOUSE

An old log cabin in the Tennessee Mountains.

just because this builder has substituted for his rough log cabin a house in which the design has been more considered, it is not necessarily more attractive. It may be far less so. The old log cabin on this page has an attractiveness which may be lost in a later elaboration. The builder may have had no taste at all, and the new house may be very ugly compared to the old one.

It is evident that a useful thing may have the qualities of attractiveness, or of unattractiveness. Take as an illustration the plan of a small building shown at the top of page 43. It is exceedingly simple. It is built over a spring and serves to shelter it. So far as the plan goes it is perfectly arranged. But how does the building itself look? On this plan it is possible to get a great variety of elevations. Either of the houses shown beside the plan satisfies the condition of protecting the spring from the weather, and giving adequate access to it for the visitor. And yet, these two houses are ugly. The first is barren, and the second is fantastic. Compare them with the design of the spring house shown below. Notice how modest,

how simple, how well proportioned it is. And yet so far as the consideration of *utility* is concerned, it is no better than the others.

What is true of this spring house is true in a larger sense of all dwelling houses and of all architecture. For the most part, when the untrained layman begins to think of his own house which he is going to build, he begins with the plan, and considers the number of rooms that he needs. That is right enough so far as it goes. Only he must remember that he can get the same conditions of arrangement and the same number of rooms equally well in a house that is ugly, or one that is attractive. The plan, certainly, is important, but the impression we carry away with us of a house usually comes from what the eye sees,—the shape, the materials, the color, and the location of the house.

You see, then, your house has two definite aspects to the architect. It is both a "visible" and "invisible" house, which means simply the difference between the arrangement of your house on plan, and your house as the eye sees it.

Look again at the sketch at the top of page 43. In the center is shown the plan of a small building. What does this plan tell us? It tells us that there is to be a single room in the house, that it is entered by a door and lighted by two windows. And that is all. It doesn't tell us what the house will look like. It doesn't tell us how high up the windows are, nor how high the house is, not what its roof is like. The plan arrangement is the *invisible* house. In this book we are particularly interested in the *visible* house. The trouble with most houses is not so much that they are badly planned as that they are unpleasant to look at. For

any floor arrangement there are many interpretations of façade possible, good and bad, and we shall arrive at the good solutions only as we understand the dangers and pitfalls of design. What are these dangers?

For centuries, writers on architecture and the fine arts have been disputing the theories of design. Different schools of design have been established and widely different theories taught. In this country the student of architecture is trained to a conception of beauty under theories which are different from those by which the young French or English student is trained, just as again the French training is different from the English, and so on. And in addition to this confusion of training there is the point of view of the individual student with theories all his own.

However, just as we differ in our ideas of good taste, of what is attractive and what is not, just so we differ at *all* points. We have different ideas of government, of philosophy and of ethics. How do we go to work to clarify our ideas in these fields? We study history. We approach the problem by the historical method, and we find that after long lapses of time certain institutions have a social value; they continue to be useful to the succeeding generations of men.

For instance, we are all pretty much agreed that theft is undesirable. We accept certain things as established. They form a working basis for our practical life and we make such progress as we can.

Let us go a step further. We have seen that a house may be useful and ugly, or useful and attractive. The ideal is always to combine these latter qualities. Whatever our individual taste may be, we must come to the point of establishing certain fixed aspects of house design. To think clearly and comprehensively on the subject we must reduce it to its simplest terms.

To study the problem of house design, we must agree first on the elements which enter into it. Look at the two very different

43

THE HONEST HOUSE

In "Witchwood" Mr. Dow has caught the character of Colonial architecture. The entrance door is like the famous Witch Door at Salem. The porch is an interesting variation in porch design. The foreground is unfortunately rather bare.

houses shown on pages 44 and 45. What have these houses in common?

To begin with, they all have *wall surfaces* which are penetrated by window openings. These walls and windows are of different heights and shapes, and the arrangement is different in each case. Each house has its "fenestrated" walls.

Besides this each house has a *roof*. The roofs may be different in shape and construction, but each house has its roof.

As we look closer, we make out a certain number of smaller parts. The houses have doorways, chimneys, porches, shutters, etc., —these are the *details* and incidental parts of the design.

Then we see that these houses are built of different *materials*—wood, brick, stone, and stucco are used in them.

Each house has its own *color*. Unfortu-nately in a black and white reproduction this cannot be suggested easily. This color may be the natural color of the material, or of an applied nature, but whatever it is, each house has its color.

Finally, there is the setting of the houses, their relation to the background and fore-ground, to the planting of their gardens—in a word, the *entourage*.

What is true of these houses is true of all houses. There are certain elements which occur in every house, and they are few in number. They may vary indefinitely, but they can be classified and through these classifications we may learn to avoid certain mistakes in designing our houses.

Understand clearly that this is no "sys-tem" of design. There is no royal road to learning to design well. It is a matter of hard and continual work. Every architect

THE USEFUL AND THE BEAUTIFUL

It would be difficult to find a small house which gives greater satisfaction than the gardener's cottage at "Krisheim," Dr. Woodward's estate near Philadelphia. Its simple stucco walls and its happy setting give it great charm. The roof surfaces are unbroken by dormers, and yet the house is adequately lighted.

who has studied seriously makes some kind of classification of principles, and bases his work upon this conception of the relation of the different elements of his art. In assuming the above classification, it must be said at once and most emphatically that this classification is only analytical. It is artificial, but it is artificial only in the same way that any method of instruction is bound to be artificial.

In studying geography, we separate the mountains from the plains, the plains from

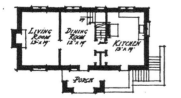
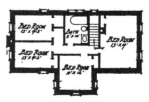

First and second floor plans of the gardener's cottage at "Krisheim."

45

the valleys, the valleys from the rivers and the rivers from the sea. And yet in nature, all these form a part of a united whole. They are all interdependent, and are in reality indissolubly linked together. We make an abstraction of the word "river" and we take it out of its setting, but in reality the river exists only in connection with its banks, the valley in which it lies, the plains and the mountains which form the valley, and so on.

So in architecture the correct conception of design is that of an organic whole. The plan, the section, the elevations of the house should all be thought of together. Perhaps it is impossible to do this absolutely, but we should come as near to it as we can. However, as in geography, it is impossible to think of all the elements at once. We make a kind of classification of the elements that we are to deal with. In house design, we have these invariable elements, capable of unlimited variations in their expressions: the walls and windows, the roof and the details, the materials, the color, and the entourage. We shall take them up one by one, and try to find out what are some of the common mistakes of interpretation.

John Russell Pope, Architect.
A detail of the Vanderbilt Lodge at "Deepdale" showing the carved gargoyles.

46

CHAPTER VII

THE ENTOURAGE OF THE COUNTRY HOUSE

IT is no longer necessary to preach the joys of country life to the right-minded American. He dreams of his some-day home to such good purpose that eventually he realizes it. But the consideration of the entourage of his country house is new to him. It savors of that expensive new-comer, the landscape gardener. He fears that some elaborate foreign fol-de-rol will be brought into his decent American domain, and he will have none of it. Besides, he argues, his house is a good one. His lawn mower clicks from morning until night. He has proper walks with orderly flower beds bordering them. What more could a man want?

Your foreigner dreams always of his house and garden as a well considered whole. No matter how small his little place may be, he finds some way of enclosing it, of making all of it a part of his family life. He works from the outmost boundaries in, with his house always as his point of departure and point of arrival. The disposition of the houses and gardens that surround his place,

his own hedges and walls and walks and gardens—everything that is a part of the landscape immediately surrounding his house becomes as important as the house itself. He knows that until his house fits comfortably into its site, until his trees and gardens and vistas hang together in a harmonious series of pictures, until his place offers his family a maximum of privacy and repose and beauty, he has not made the best of his entourage.

Our architects have done everything in their power to hasten the appreciation of the entourage. They are hampered, however, by the average man's determination to spend so much on his house, and to let his "grounds" take care of themselves. It has n't been long since the popular measure of a country house was its expensiveness, and the number of acres around it. If beauty was considered at all it was the supposed beauty of closely clipped lawns spotted with geometric flower beds. Garden architecture was limited to a deplorable mixture of summer houses and bridges of unfriendly styles. Garden ornament meant a few terrible statues of cast iron or granite, and the last word in magnificence was an elaborate fountain.

With the growth of country life a new feeling has come about, and where a dozen years ago there were only a few houses and gardens that "belonged," to-day there are hundreds of entrancing domains that disprove all the old arguments that you can't make a perfect garden in America. The three influences that have brought about the new consideration of entourage are the architect, who wishes to see his house placed to the best possible advantage; the American's habit of travel, of adapting the best things his foreign neighbor has to offer to his own uses; and a really genuine pleasure in living out doors, which must inevitably bring about a desire for the same repose and privacy in his garden that he demands to-day of his house

For these hundreds of houses that have well planned entourages, however, there are tens of thousands that have no relation whatever to their surroundings. Nothing is more extraordinary than the indifference of the home builder of the average suburban town to the planting about his home. For every cottage that is set attractively in its surrounding garden, there are hundreds that stand solitary, without so much as a sunflower or a blueberry bush by way of foliage. The idea back of this bleakness seems to be that a house is a man's business, and a flower garden is merely a woman's frill, to be added if she feels equal to the work of it.

Of course, a house situated in the forest far from any neighboring house can be treated more freely than a suburban house located in close proximity to other houses. This is also true of an isolated man. When he is alone, he can do as he likes. But few of us build in the forest; most of us have to build near our neighbors, and it is necessary to consider the problems of our entourage all the more carefully. We must make our house harmonize with its surroundings, and we must better them, if possible, by taking advantage of all opportunities for co-operation with our neighbors. You should consider the entourage before you begin to build your house.

Perhaps the site is already wooded; in that case much of your work has been done for you. But more often the lot upon which the house is to be put is barren, or nearly so. The actual house itself, the house which is enclosed within the four walls, is only a part of your problem. If you wish to get the greatest attractiveness out of your house design, you must consider it in relation to the possible planting and the development of gardens, etc., which your lot will permit. You must consider the approaches, the placing of out buildings, the views from certain windows—everything. If you have a very small place, every inch of it should be made to count. Flowers should be kept close to the house, or lattices, or hedges, or walls, and a certain feeling of space preserved.

This badly proportioned and over-elaborate house is set squarely in a barren lot. Privacy is impossible.

48

THE ENTOURAGE OF THE COUNTRY HOUSE

Wilson Eyre, Architect.

"Fairacres" at Jenkintown, Pennsylvania, is an ample house that fits serenely into its setting. A mass of shrubs gives privacy to the living part of the house. It is possible even for small houses to get similar protection.

In considering the approach, you are met with the problem of placing the house on the lot, since the approach presumably leads from a public street to the house. There are two ways in which we can place the house that are typical of American and European custom. In America a small house is usually set far back from the public road, and the space between the road and the house is given over to a lawn or garden open to the passer-by. On a larger lot the house will be set half way with the same open lawn in front and a vegetable garden in the rear.

Surely we are all agreed that the charm of home life lies in its privacy. No one wants strangers looking into his house. Why should he deliberately bare his gardens, his lawns, to the public gaze? It is not a snobbish selfishness, this enclosing one's own. It is rather the common-sense practice of people who live simple, sane lives. We have too long lived in a careless neighborliness that passed for democracy. We have sacrificed our possible gardens, throwing them all together into an unbroken greensward, "for the benefit of the town." This is very commendable in a closely settled suburban town, but even then there is a possibility of developing the side and back yards into an enclosed garden. Hedges and lattices can be used with discretion. The humblest house, with a little careful planting, will take on dignity and charm.

In European towns it is common practice to plan the house so that it turns its back on the street and faces its own gardens. This arrangement gives all the advantages that any entourage can offer—privacy, and repose, and an attractive garden space.

If your plot of land is very small and you

THE HONEST HOUSE

John Russell Pope, Architect.

No detail of small house architecture is so neglected in this country as the garden wall. This house and garden is located on the Vanderbilt estate on Long Island.

wish your main rooms to face the street, you can arrange to have adequate planting between street and house, and in this way screen the family rooms. Rooms so placed will receive the maximum of noise and dust, however. Of course if your interest is such that you have to have a constant view of the happenings on the street, you are not interested in this argument for quiet and privacy.

A wall is the finest thing a man can bring to his entourage. It should be of the same material as the house—stone, or stucco, or brick—or, if the house is of wood, it may be of cobbles, or it may be a graceful lattice with a hedge planted against it. In old European gardens the wall is never forgotten. It is a part of the general plan, often continu-

ing the very house walls, always giving picturesqueness and privacy. Against it grape vines and small fruits are trained. It forms a shelter and a protection, it makes a home a man's own, and it is a convincing argument that it is built for permanency. It is looked upon as a heritage.

In building a wall, the question of expense must be considered. Many of us would prefer a high stone wall covered with a thick growth of green and blossom to a house, but we *have* to have the house, and we usually give up the wall. The hard working people who built miles and miles of stone walls all over the old farms of the colonies built with their hands, and our hands are too untrained, too occupied with other things. But cement—that magic means of accomplishing a desired effect at small cost—has made walls possible for many of us.

Walls with green things growing over them and slender gardens of old fashioned flowers creeping along them are much more interesting than fine gardens spread open, public park fashion. Who does n't thrill at the occasional patch of color seen through a thick hedge, at the adventurous roses that clamber over a high stone wall? There is always an element of mystery, of remoteness, hanging about a wall of any sort. The beauty of it is that such a wall gives the family within a chance to live their own lives,

and it also gives the passer-by a chance to dream.

Hedges are a godsend to those of us who cannot afford walls. We have only recently realized that we can have a respectable hedge of privet in two or three years, at very small expense. The clippings of our hedges have been transplanted as hedges for our neighbors, and so the custom grows.

Gateways give the necessary glimpses of the pleasure that lies within our walls. Who that has had the thrill of peeping through the great iron gates into one of the old gardens of Charleston, or Augusta, or New Orleans, will ever see a garden so fair? I remember

Photograph by Lillian Baynes Griffin.
Here house, garden and water come together on the shore of Long Island Sound in a delightful and informal intimacy.

realizing my favorite fairy story, when I was a very small person, in an old Augusta garden. The high iron fence was completely covered with vines and roses, but there was an open place just big enough for a small head to be poked through, and beyond lived The Sleeping Beauty. I saw her fountain, and a red and yellow parrot that perched on its rim, and a very elaborate peacock somehow much more royal than those on my grandmother's plantation, and a black-green magnolia tree heavy with white blossoms. Back of the fountain a long whitewashed stone house rambled along, and hundreds of make-believe people lived there. I never saw the Beauty, or the Prince, though I surprised the parrot and the peacock often, but I was always sure they were just beyond the vista afforded me. When travelers talk of walled English gardens, and sculptured Italian gardens, and adorable French ones, I remember my perfect glimpse. To this day I am thrilled with expectancy at the sight of an enclosed garden. It always has a beckoning quality that allures.

The entourage is elastic in its possibilities—for every house there may be a garden that will "belong." On Cape Cod there is an old gray shingle house that I know, just one story high, with a grape vine growing all over the roof, with little square panes of glass, and a dark green door and a soft little yard of uncut grass, and gray palings with honeysuckle spread over them. There is a rustic arbor (it would be a pergola now) of weathered gray railings running all around it with a narrow brick terrace beneath, and literally hundreds of grape vines covering house and arbors and the palings of the old fence. The grape vines actually creep along the roof tree and festoon the chimneys. It

is the most adorable little house you can imagine, but it would be as humble as a gray alley kitten without the soft uncut grass and the grape vines.

On the North Shore of Massachusetts there is a great house that belongs in its entourage just as surely. A little park of pine trees screens the place from the public road. Once past the pine trees you enter an enchanted domain of intimate gardens, with mysterious paths that lead you to the tennis court, or a pergola, or a rose garden, or a geometric color-mass of vegetables, lying like a brilliant colored flag in a sunny sunken space. All the paths lead to the house, as paths should. You go through the long hall and come out upon another garden, a brick terrace with grape vines covering the beams above it, and formal box trees in great Italian jars along its rim. This terrace drops to a walled garden filled with rose and blue flowers, and this in turn drops to the sea. You sit upon the high terrace and look out over the rose and blue blossoms to the sea. Even the vistas are your own. Were you under yonder distant little white sail, you'd be sure that this enchanting garden and the house above it had sprung from the blue water, so perfectly does it all hang together.

It takes an architect to plan a proper house, but any one who is willing to think a little and work hard may develop a very beautiful and satisfying entourage for his house. It is a consoling thought that although the detail of your house may be unattractive, its arbors and gateways badly designed, you can plant trees and shrubs and vines that will cover the ugliness, and your house will become a transformed thing that belongs to its garden.

Many houses that seem dignified and fine to us are in reality commonplace and depend

THE ENTOURAGE OF THE COUNTRY HOUSE

entirely on the surrounding foliage for their beauty. I remember one old place that always seemed remote and beautiful because I could see only a bit of the dingy yellow house through a thick tangle of evergreen trees—magnolias, and cedars, and low shrubs that had been transplanted from the woods. Queer old people lived there, and so there was no excuse for a small person to explore its mysteries. It gave me a shock of disappointment years after to realize that the house was worse than commonplace in itself,—it was a dreadful mustard colored pile of clapboards, with gingerbread trimming around its porches. But that mattered little, for the rose vines and ivy completely covered the ugliness of the jig-saw work, and the trees crept close to the house and protected it from the passers-by. It was not a house, but a "place," with an important and comforting entourage that saved its secret from discovery.

We can perhaps never have the fine luxuriance of growth around our houses that the English gardens have, but we can have something very pleasant, if we will work for it. Rose vines and hedges and grass and old fashioned flowers grow quickly for us, and lattices and pergolas add to the charm of our little houses. We can manage everything quickly except trees, and we can have pretty good trees if we study the soil and plant the trees that are quickest in growth. We can plant those for our own pleasure, and a few slow growing ones—oaks, elms and such—for the pleasure of our grandchildren. There is no excuse for barrenness.

We can't have the delightful brick walks of English gardens, with grass growing between the bricks, because the bricks will freeze in winter and bulge up. But we can

Mellor & Meigs, Architects.
The rose-grown lattice adds greatly to the attractiveness of Mr. Meigs' little cottage.

have flat stones of irregular shape laid in the grass Japanese fashion, and they will keep their places. We can have walks of bricks laid in cement or in sand, instead of ugly ribbons of gray cement, or we can have soft earth paths with a little gravel in them instead of terrible white-washed walks. We can have borders of little flowers and ferns instead of tiresome arrangements of zig-zag bricks or shells or bottles or white-washed stones.

No place is too small for some sort of flower garden, an arbor or a lattice, a pool, a stretch of greensward, a little space for vegetables. We may realize the wall fountain, or the pergola, or the sun dial, or the little pool we have always planned, but we must never crowd things. Repose is the beginning and end of a garden.

Formal gardens are rarely entrancing. They are admirable and orderly, and they afford us plenty of flowers for the house, but they seldom give us sheer ecstasy, as a proper garden should. The real pleasure of planting flowers lies in placing them where they will follow something. A rose covered arbor is much more charming than an orderly "bed" of roses. Long shallow masses of flowers following the rim of a terrace, or a wall, or the rim of a pool are always successful. A large entourage may include a dozen gardens—formal ones, wild ones, vegetable ones, but on a small place it is best to plant flowers where they will supplement the trees and shrubs, and tell in striking spots of color.

We can all have flower gardens, and we can all avoid flower "beds." It is all very well to fill your garden chock full of flowers, so that there is no room for grass or walks or anything else. A mass of flowers is always lovely, just as a field of weeds is lovely. But if you have a well planned garden your flowers should be *against* or *around* things, in

A rustic arbor that leads to an old-fashioned flower garden.

long shallow borders against a hedge, or a terrace alongside a brick wall, or around a tree. The only other way of handling masses of flowers is to make a formal garden of them with walks and a sun dial, or a tree, or a bird bath in the center. Nothing is more unfortunate than a great stretch of green lawn dotted with isolated crescents and stars and circles of flowers.

The house must always be the heart of the entourage, and the paths should all lead to it, but they need not go directly. Winding paths may go pretty much as they please, if they are accompanied by shrubs and flowers to invite strolling, but straight walls should always lead to something. It may be an arbor, or a pool, or a sun-dial, or a bench against a lattice wall, but it must lead to something. There should be a vista of something pleasant at the end of all the walks that lead directly from the house. This is often achieved by placing the main walks in line with the windows of the living-room, or dining-room, so that the eye can follow the walk to the picture that lies at its end.

Probably no one ever planned his ideal entourage without including a little brook, or a glimpse of the sea in his plan. We yearn so for the sight of water, and if we can afford it we sometimes compromise by bringing an elaborate fountain into the garden to take the place of the little brook. But fountains are dangerous things. They are usually vulgar in their noisy display and their mechanical elaboration. A pool with a simple rim of stone or cement or marble set deep into the grass will give greater joy. A round pool eight feet in diameter, or a rectangular pool five feet by eight, is quite large enough to serve as a mirror for the trees and flowers about it. It may have a tiny spray of water

THE ENTOURAGE OF THE COUNTRY HOUSE

Designed by H. T. Lindeberg.   Albro & Lindeberg, Architects.
Here is a formal garden which is also entrancing. The walls, the pool and the prim box trees are all formal in their disposition, but a long garden of everyday flowers relieves the formality by its gaiety.

from some little figure in the center, a fruit tree twisting over it, a bench beside it, and a school of gold fish within it. It will afford us never failing color and motion, and it will cost little more than a pair of the awful cast-iron vases your grandfather bought for his garden.

Garden furniture is tempting, and here too we must go warily. Cement has made possible to all of us reproductions of fine old Roman and Greek benches and fountains and jars. It is hard to resist them, but an over-crowded garden is as sad as an overcrowded house. Too much garden furniture destroys repose. Indeed, the small place with one garden bench, and a sun dial, and a pair of Italian oil jars placed where the creamy whiteness will tell against dark green foliage is in much better taste than the elaborate entourage that includes all the marble temples

and fountains and benches and bridges that the landscape architect can devise. Modesty is an essential to repose.

The house is the final, as it is also the first, consideration of the entourage. It must fit comfortably into its site. The brutal line of the foundations must be softened with a mass of shrubs. Ivy will creep over its wall, and pull it more securely into place. If the house is low upon the ground, and we can enter it without climbing, we are fortunate indeed. If the house is much higher than the main garden, terraces will do much to bring it into the general harmony.

When the house has finally grown into its surroundings, and ivy has softened the newness of its lines into mellowness, when trees and shrubs have been planted where dark shadows are needed, and flowers massed where they will be most effective, then will come to pass an intimacy of house and garden that will make the perfect entourage.

Do not be discouraged by the thought that it takes time for bushes and trees to grow. Of course it takes time, but once the tree is planted, it needs little care. Who that has n't planted trees can know the excitement of watching the first apple ripen into maturity? Who that has n't planted a rosebush can know the thrill of the first rose?

Charles Barton Keen, Architect.
Entrance gateway at Strafford, Pennsylvania. Note the generous proportion of the arch and simplicity of the design.

CHAPTER VIII

CONCERNING COLOR

HAVE you ever gone along one of the streets of a suburban town and noticed how each house is painted without any regard to the colors of the neighboring houses? First we have a red house, then a white, then a chocolate, and then a gray one. If these colors were light, soft tones, such as one sees in the multi-colored towns in some of the tropical countries, it would not only be pardonable, but very desirable. But nothing could be further from picturesqueness than the aspect they present. The colors are hard, decided, cheap and unsympathetic.

Don't be afraid to have the color of your house bear some reasonable relation to the color of your neighbor's house.

Don't think you get an artistic distinction by making your house picturesque or noticeable by violence or eccentricity.

The thing that strikes the European most forcibly on coming over here is the lack of harmony between houses put up in the same neighborhood. A man builds his house in his own way, and next to him will be a neighbor who has a different type of house,

and who has developed his garden in his own way.

The reason that European cities, especially those on the Continent, are so skilfully developed is that certain despotic rulers have said, "We are going to put a boulevard from here to there without asking anybody's advice or consent about it." Whereas, in America, the only way this could be done would be by unanimous public opinion, and on esthetic matters public opinion is very difficult to awaken.

Nevertheless the intelligent house builder must realize the advantages of making his neighbor's property benefit his own, and to do this means study and consideration and co-operation.

Much of the attraction that the old European towns has for us exists largely because of the character of the houses, homogeneous in both design and color. The harmony of design comes from the custom of observing the traditions in building. Harmony of color comes largely from the use of local building materials.

Each building material has a color of its

own. Nature endows it with that color. The common building stones such as limestone, sandstone, granite and marble all have their characteristic colors. Bricks, though artificial in that they are made by man, preserve the natural color of the sand and clay that goes with them. Wood, the commonest building material of all, has its pleasant range of neutral colors, but unfortunately we associate wood always with paint, and so the value of its natural color is rarely seen.

It is extremely difficult to consider color in its relation to architecture, for color lies so much in the eye of the beholder. And it is difficult to convey an idea concerning the use of color through the medium of a black and white page. To many people "color" suggests instantly paint, something applied to the surface of the house. To others, "color" is an elastic term including a hundred things —the effect of the house and its entourage, the color Nature has given and man has applied.

If you seek to analyze the spell that your favorite house always casts upon you, you will find that much of its fascination lies in the harmony of color of the house and its details, its surroundings. You have probably treasured such a house in your imagination, a house that seemed exactly right to you. It may have been a pink stucco house in the Azores, or a salmon-colored villa in Sicily, or a dove-colored English cottage with velvety thatched roof. It may have been nearer home, an old whitewashed, broad-shingled farmhouse in a pink and white apple orchard, or a cottage of clapboards silvered by the weather, with masses of hollyhocks crowding against it. Wherever you saw it, it entered into your soul and became a vision to be cherished; and you planned a some-day house very much like it. The point is, you considered the green of the trees and vines and grass, the hues of the flowers, the very clouds and sky, along with the house. It was the harmony of color that got into your memory and stayed there. Else why do we not go into ecstasies over the houses we see in winter? We don't. Ideal houses are visualized in full color.

You may succeed in avoiding all the common pitfalls of design so far as your architectural detail is concerned and then wreck your house by the use of bad color. You can avoid this only by studying assiduously the possibilities of your house and its relation to the neighboring houses. If your place is large enough, of course the neighboring houses need not enter into your consideration at all. Then you can work out a harmony of house and garden that will declare your good sense and your understanding of the community in which you live.

One of the finest examples of a color plan in our architecture is the country place of Mr. Albert Herter at East Hampton, Long Island. Here is a large, rambling house, built so close to the sea that the blue-green of the water and the clear blue of the sky are deliberately considered as a part of the color plan. Mr. Herter's idea was to get, if possible, the effect of a house in Sicily, and so he built the house of pinkish yellow stucco and gave it a copper roof. The sea winds have softened the texture and deepened the color of the walls to salmon, and the copper roof has been transformed into ever-changing blue greens that repeat the colors of the sea. In front of the house there are terraces massed with flowers of orange and yellow and red, and back of the house there is a Persian garden built around blue and green Persian tiles,

CONCERNING COLOR

Photograph by Lillian Baynes Griffin. Slee & Bryson, Architects.
This stucco house at Tokoneke, Connecticut, shows vivid contrasts of color which are fascinating. A mass of black-green ivy climbs over the creamy stucco. Note the ruggedness of the plain walls and the sense of graceful intimacy which is given by the Italian bas-relief on the ivied wall.

and great blue Italian jars. Here flowers of blue and rose, and the amethyst tones in between, are allowed. Black green trees and shrubs are used everywhere, with the general effect of one of Maxfield Parrish's vivid Oriental gardens.

It is a far cry from this intoxicating harmony of color to a shabby genteel villa of an Italian peasant on the Long Island railway, but somehow the peasant's house seems almost as wonderful to me, it is so frankly a courageous attempt at realizing an ideal

house. I pass the house every day, and in the few seconds it is within my sight I find new pleasures, a new amusement.

The house is a large, squarish box, spang against the railway tracks, but it has been treated as seriously as if it were an imposing villa with spreading acres. A high wall covered with stucco has been built to enclose the yard, which the ambitious owner is struggling to make into a real garden despite the cinders and smoke and heat. In the meantime, huge colored vases at least a story high have been painted on the walls of the house, vases with spiral-like leaves and flowers in gay colors. On the large gate posts are clumsy urns, with feeble flowers growing in them. The gate itself is a strange affair of odds and ends of iron patched together, but what matter? On the arbor real grape vines grow, and the vegetable garden gives real color.

A huddle of little out-houses, "dependencies," runs along one wall, and I am sure they are somehow a part of the dream. The dream, by the way is clear to me: here is a prosperous Italian who has always had a vision. Prosperity gave him courage to accomplish the villa that must be as much like an old-country estate as possible. In the frankest, simplest fashion he has set to work to embellish his house and his wall in the gay color that expresses his happiness. All around him are hideous little mustard colored shoe-box cottages of clapboards, with not a twig or a tree for solace, but they do not discourage him. Somehow he has accomplished a splash of real interest and good color in a dingy railway yard, and I rejoice with him and wish we had more like him.

The charm of the cities of Spain and Italy and of warm countries generally, lies in the ever present evidence of warm colors. The tones of the walls are light,—light grays, pale yellows, pale pinks and greens, and the appeal to the sense of beauty which they make is irresistible.

In the temperate climate in which most of us live, we run to two extremes. In New England, where granite is plentiful, one sees frequently the house of a bluish steel-colored cut stone, than which there is nothing more gloomy in the whole world. Then on the other hand, there is the New England farmhouse, painted white with dark green blinds, but of a whiteness which only the light of heaven can equal. It is a cold white, with a bluish cast, and against the dark greens of surrounding trees it shocks one with its intensity and austerity.

Let your grays and your whites be warm, and your effects will be happy. The white needs only to have a blush of yellow in it to take away the frozen aspect, but that slight blush is what makes the difference between amiability and harshness. Avoid bluish tones always, for they give an impression of bleakness. This is a matter perhaps of psychology, but certainly it is none the less true that we always associate our ideas of winter and of the cold landscape with bluish colors. And so with the somber tones in our stone and brick and stucco walls.

But, after all, the natural colors as they occur in the different building materials, such as stone and brick, are all relatively subdued. Probably you think of an exception to this, and remind me of the bright colors of certain marbles. We do not, however, use these marbles in every day houses, and our common building materials are not endowed with brilliant colors. Even if they are sometimes strong and displeasing, time and weather gradually soften their bad qualities. The real color problem of the usual small house is the painter and his paint.

In the field of artificial color, the possibilities for ugliness are unlimited. The colors which the house painter can wallow in range from the deepest piratical black to the most screaming vermilion, and whereas nature endows each building with one color, the painter can make your house look like a kaleidoscope in a few days' time.

The ordinary house painter, armed with

three pots of different colored paints, varies only slightly from a maniac in his conception of decoration.

We have all seen rows of small wooden cottages, badly built and badly designed, that became relatively attractive by being painted in one uniform color. The same cottages painted in bright reds, greens, purples and browns look more frightful than words can tell.

Good advice to follow is this: if you have a shingled house, it is well to let the shingles take a natural weatherstained color. If it is necessary to give them protection stain them with some silver gray stain which approximates the weathered effect. Or you can paint the shingles. Generally speaking white is best for the shingled walls, and with this you can have your outside shutters, your flower boxes, and your lattice work painted warm tones of brown or gray or green. It is best to paint the whole house uniformly, save for these details.

For the ordinary simple house of clapboards, no color combination has been found more satisfactory than white walls with

Charles Barton Keen, Architect.
The restful impression given by these houses at Strafford, near Philadelphia, is due to their harmony of color and form.

61

THE HONEST HOUSE

shutters of some greenish color. If you feel yourself at all uncertain on the matter of color, paint your house white. Avoid heavy colors like chocolate, slate gray, and red for the colors of your walls. Don't be afraid to have your house conform to the houses of your neighbors. Don't think that you get artistic distinction by making your own house an eyesore. If your ornament is unstudied and bad, to silhouette it by using two contrasting colors, is simply to make your house a thousand times more hideous than it need be. In the days when cheap wooden ornament of the jig-saw, gingerbread type was prevalent it was customary to emphasize this ornament by the use of paints of different color.

Even if your trim is good, it is best not to emphasize it. In no other way can you make your house look cheap so quickly as to afflict it with stripes and rectangles of painted trim. The roof has one color, the walls another, and the shutters and doors have still another. That is enough. Nothing is more unpleasant than a house with the first-story walls painted one color, the second story another, the triangular space of the gable ends another. Such houses have been called the "shirt-waist-and-skirt-houses," and the term fits. They are usually further embellished by painting the piazza lattice and railing still another color, and of course the roof has something awful to declare before the color-plan is finished. Often you will see such a house sitting impudently between two self respecting colonial houses, affording a contrast which only a blind person could look upon without shuddering. I shall never forget passing such a house in a sweet old village on Cape Cod, where its very existence was a libel. A little South-

ern girl was with me, and though none of us said a word, she looked at the house, sniffed, and said, "It looks like a nigger preacher's house!"

It is a great misfortune, this lack of consideration of our neighbors. For too long we have ignored them. Each man has built as he pleased. Beside a house of the English style he has erected one of the formal classic colonial type, and his neighbor has built a house of the Spanish mission type, and so on, thus producing a disharmonious jumble of color and design.

Happily, this reckless disregard of neighborhood is passing. We are beginning to co-operate, to pull our little towns into pleasant completeness. There are several garden cities already begun, planned on the English and continental schemes, and at least one town is far enough along to be an object lesson to thousands of people. This is Forest Hills Gardens, Long Island, a much misunderstood community that owes its being to the Sage Foundation.

The popular conception of this place is that it is a model village for working men. It would be much more interesting if it were, but unfortunately land in the immediate

Too many colors are used. The columns are badly spaced and like the stone wall, they are out of keeping with the rest of the house.

62

CONCERNING COLOR

Photograph by Lillian Baynes Griffin.   Wilson Eyre, Architect.

The first floor of Mr. Goodnow's house at Forest Hills Gardens is very near the ground. This gives an impression of intimacy and informality on entering. The house looks as though it grew out of its surroundings. Note the admirable texture of the stucco. The woodwork of the porch is stained a deep brown, the tiles are red and the stucco is a light gray, tinged with the slightest suggestion of green.

vicinity of New York is too expensive to permit the charming cottage colonies so successfully fostered in England. Forest Hills Gardens is within nine miles, and fifteen minutes, of the heart of New York, and this means that a man must pay as much for the little bit of ground on which he would build, as a good house would cost in a more remote community. But there are enough people who appreciate the excellence of a little town that is planned for the future to make the enterprise successful. You may object to being restricted yourself, but it is heavenly to know that your neighbors are restricted as to color, and design, and the many things that are so unpleasant at close range. You are willing to pay more for a small house that fits into its landscape, its neighborhood, than you would pay for a very much larger house in a town where every house is a law unto itself.

Much of the charm of Forest Hills

Gardens comes from the color of the materials used. Some of the color is undoubtedly unfortunate, but as all the houses must be fireproof this makes for excellent color. Fireproof houses are most commonly expressed in brick or stucco, which almost always have good color and pleasing texture. If your stucco goes wrong, you can tint it. If your bricks are ugly in tone, you can whitewash them. Good color is always easy to obtain in such materials.

It is almost impossible to build wooden houses close together and get a harmonious effect. Indeed, we recall very few successful streets of wooden houses, except the quaint old village streets that are lined with rows of gray and white and faded green houses, pulled together comfortably by old trees and placid gardens. But when you begin assembling houses that are vertical rather than horizontal in expression, you have a difficult problem. The architects who have planned Forest Hills Gardens had this problem to solve. They do not permit three or four houses to be built on a line, for instance.

The two end ones may be set near the street, and the two inner ones set far back toward the edge of the lots, and so a pleasing irregularity is gained. Houses of timber and plaster, houses of a composition cement of dull browns and reds, houses of brick and field stone and stucco are all there, but the architects have decreed that all the roofs shall be of red tile, and so the community is united. As one of the architects says, the little houses are all satisfyingly different, but their roofs are all singing the same tune.

As with the house design, so with the garden. Each garden is considered as a part of a perfected plan, and the planting around the house assumes its proper importance as a part of the picture. The result is a delightful mass of color that will grow finer always. As ivy covers the houses and the gay little gardens grow up around them we shall have a fine exposition of what may come to pass when every man considers his neighbor.

In the meantime, most people are forced to live in neighborhoods that have grown

Compare this restless row of badly designed houses with the street of modest white houses on page 61. Compare them also with the group of houses on page 65.

CONCERNING COLOR

Wilson Eyre, Architect.

These houses, built at Forest Hills Gardens, are grouped so that all share in the enjoyment of the enclosed garden. A detail of the house at the right is shown on page 63. The middle house is a twin house.

without plan, and must make the most of situations that are most discouraging. You may have bought a lot with a magenta house of many turrets on one side of it, and on the other a sprawling house of mustard yellow stucco, and terrible tiles of a red that swears at the magenta. What sort of house can you build that will soften the vulgar conflict of your neighbors' houses? How can you separate your own house from its ill-bred fellows?

Of course the only real separation possible is planting—trees and shrubs and hedges. But after you have done all you can with the frame of the picture that is your house, you must study color as related to the neighboring houses before you can go ahead.

As to the matter of choosing your colors, it is possible here to give only the slightest hints, because each house presents its own special difficulties. Nevertheless whether your house is of stone or brick or shingle or stucco, there are certain combinations which it is well to avoid. These combinations are those made by the association of uncomplementary colors.

You know what is meant when we say that crimson and scarlet clash, that they do not look well together. Under ordinary conditions this is true of scarlet and crimson, because they are not complementary colors.

What are the complementary colors then, and how shall we know them? This could be answered simply by giving a reference to any text book on physics, but text books of that kind are always forbidding. Briefly, the theory of color is this: white light, or sunlight, is made up of seven or, we may say, six colors. These are called the colors of the spectrum. You see these colors in the rainbow, or through a prism of glass.

There are three primary colors, red, blue, and yellow; the secondary colors, orange,

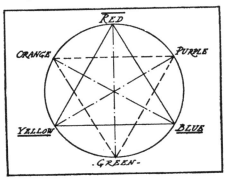

violet and green, may be derived by the combination of the primary colors. Thus if we have some blue paint and some yellow, we can mix them and the resulting color will be green. In the figure on this page, yellow, blue, and red, each at an apex of the triangle, represent the primary colors; green, orange, purple, which form another triangle, are the secondary colors. Thus, if you will notice, green lies half way between blue and yellow, orange half way between red and yellow, and violet half way between blue and red. Now those colors are complementary which lie diametrically opposite each other. Thus orange is complementary to blue, purple to yellow and red to green. These colors can be used successfully together, that is, side by side. The nearer two

colors approach, such as green and orange, or yellow and orange, the more difficult they are to use together.

Many difficulties will probably present themselves to your mind! First for instance, that there are a dozen different reds, and a dozen different blues, and so forth. Which of these are you to take as the standard for comparison? The answer to this is found in the spectrum. The yellow which forms the standard is that yellow which has no green and no orange. And so for the other colors.

Another difficulty is, how do we account for such colors as gray and brown? These are composite colors, and if you will look closely at a gray you will see that it is a blue-gray, or a yellow-gray, or a red-gray, and so with the browns. Thus these so-called neutral colors may be considered as having the color of that primary color which is most prominent in them, and associated accordingly.

This explanation is of course very incomplete; the science of the combination of colors is involved and difficult. But if we can be content with simple color combinations, we have nothing to fear and much to gain. It takes an artist to plan a house of many colors, but any of us can accomplish a house of some soft tone, with individual detail of colored lattices, or shutters, or what-not, to satisfy the personal equation. With a background of neutral tone, we can experiment with occasional splashes of brilliant color in our gardens, and here, after all, is where vivid color really belongs.

CHAPTER IX

THE MATERIALS

IT is all very well to tell a man that a masonry house is cheaper in the long run than a wooden one. But the run is so long! The immediate necessity is so imperative! It is hard to convince a man who has only so much money to spend, and who wants a lot for his money, that he should wait until he can build a fireproof house.

He knows that masonry construction is more durable and from certain points of view more sanitary. Brick, terra cotta, field stone, or concrete will make a house that will last beyond his time with little necessity for further outlay. But he sees all about him the wooden cottages of people who lived a hundred years ago. These cottages have lasted. They are attractive. The price of building such a house is not prohibitive. These are the arguments with which he consoles himself.

Still, the cost of a house should be figured as an investment of capital. The cost of painting clapboards or siding, and of re-shingling, is large. Six hundred dollars extra to build of brick means thirty dollars

a year interest. To keep a wood house painted means as much as this, and there will be repairs in addition, to say nothing of depreciation in value.

When the insurance companies reach a stage of intelligence (and they are leading the people in this), it will be considered good business not only to build the walls of masonry, but to build the house fireproof throughout. We burn up some three million dollars' worth of property per annum, and insurance does n't pay for a cent of the loss—it only makes us pay for our own carelessness and the carelessness of others.

We are agreed that on all practical points of view, save that of initial cost, masonry construction has the advantage over wood frame construction. But from the point of view of appearance, the matter is not so easily settled. The old clapboard Colonial house with its white painted walls and its green shutters remains one of the most charming expressions of small house archi tecture.

A house builder under primitive condi tions built his house of local materials, and

67

a great many historical styles were developed in the materials or capabilities which were found in the locality. The difficulty of transportation forced builders to use their ingenuity in solving their problems. We do not have to do this to-day. As an instance, the early builders of Colonial houses in this country had to import some of their building material from England. The facilities for transportation were, however, very feeble, consequently Colonial builders had to turn to local materials to satisfy their needs. The cheapest and easiest material to get was wood, which was plentiful and of very good quality, whereas in the European countries it was both scarce and expensive. Wooden houses therefore sprang up all over the Colonies as a result of the economic situation.

To-day the facilities of transportation are so great and the number of building materials so multiplied that there is a temptation to build largely from a surplus of material. The supply of wood is of course diminishing, and is forcing the builders to use some form of masonry construction.

This is, in some ways, a very good thing,— it has a tendency to produce a more solid architecture!

In coming to the matter of materials in which we can express ourselves, there is a variety to choose from. Suppose you build a frame house; you can express its exterior in stucco, clapboard, shingle, or half timber. If you build a masonry house its exterior can be expressed in stucco, brick, or stone. Each of these materials has its own character, its own limitations, and its own application. The eye judges the house by its appearance, rather than its *construction*.

The use of shingles for exterior covering is, one might almost say, indigenous with America. If shingles were ever used in England and the European countries generally, they had long given away to the use of slate and other materials by the time of the colonization of this country. The forests of our new world offered such an abundant supply of wood that the wooden frame house with its shingle or clapboarded exterior was a natural and easy development. Until something like fifty years ago,

When this attractive old house at Hartsdale, New York, was built, there was a plentiful supply of shingles of good quality. They were more durable than the shingles you can buy nowadays.

THE MATERIALS

This house for the Misses McVean at Great Neck, Long Island, is unusual in its design and charming in its simplicity.   Eugene J. Lang, Architect.

wood was still plentiful, and no one thought of the danger of its becoming scarce.

As late as 1870 hardly any one thought of planting new trees to replace those which were being so ruthlessly cut down. In the European countries the forestry regulations have been in force for hundreds of years, and wood has been greatly prized for so long that it has become an established custom to plant a tree when another is cut down.

So far from being appreciated was this attitude in this country that when, about 1870, a New Englander, inspired by the system of forestry practised in France, bought a number of deserted farms in New Hampshire, and planted hundreds of thousands of pine trees, he was called a visionary! Had there been a few such visionaries about a hundred years ago we would have had a system of forestry insuring the country with a rotation in the production of lumber. We should be sure of getting wood of good quality, cut from large trees instead of having to use wood cut from small trees still filled with sap and therefore being impermanent for building purposes. Only recently have measures been taken by the government for the increase of our forests, and for reforestation.

What is the bearing of this on shingles? Just this: that whereas shingles were once a fairly durable house covering, they come to

Photograph by Coutant.   Parker Morse Hooper, Architect.

Few houses in America have so much quality as has this house designed for Dr. Abbott at Cornwall, New York. The balcony is a somewhat daring feature but it is beautifully studied. The first and second floor plans are shown below.

be less and less so, because it becomes harder and harder to get them of good quality, and of sufficient length.

The older houses were shingled with hand-split shingles about eighteen inches long. These can still be obtained, though they are expensive. They make a much more interesting house covering than the shorter machine cut shingles, which in virtue of their reduced length, cannot be laid so as to expose more than five inches to the weather. On page 5 is shown an excellent example of a Colonial house with hand-split shingles

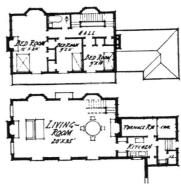

laid about nine inches to the weather. The effect is charming. Wide courses of shingles are generally more attractive than the common narrow courses, in which the shingles are laid only six inches to the weather.

One of the commonest misuses of shingles from the point of view of good design is seen in the attempt to reproduce with them elaborate architectural forms. Houses of this type belong to the post-Richardsonian school of domestic architecture, common to the eighties, but happily belonging to our past. I am quite sure there will never be another epidemic of such houses, but unfortunately many of them are still with us. They are seemingly built for inflammable purposes, but fire has passed them by, and they linger to torment us.

Another misuse of shingles is the would-be decorative scheme, where scalloped shingles are used along with ginger-bread and jig-saw work. Nothing could be more ugly or more trivial. Another misuse is seen in the combination of shingles with other materials for wall covering, a familiar sight in closely settled suburbs, where the lower part of every house is clapboarded and the upper part shingled. This treatment, by the way, invariably invites a shocking application of paint.

As for clapboards, the type of wide clapboard used in the old Long Island farmhouses gives an excellent effect, far better than the type of narrow clapboard used commonly in New England. An excellent example of the proper use of the wide weather clapboard or siding is shown in Dr. Abbott's house at Cornwall. The wide courses give interest and vigor to the façade.

In the real old English houses of the half

timber type, the timbers expressed the actual frame construction of the house. These houses were constructed of heavy joists, and the spaces between them were filled in with brick and sometimes covered with stucco. In our modern methods we have n't the honesty (or perhaps we should say the money!) to use real timber in our half-timbered work. We frame our wooden houses which are going to be half-timber on the exterior, just as we frame them when they are to be covered with a shingle or stucco, and then we apply our false half-timber to our frame. This false half-timber work consists often of only $\frac{7}{8}''$ boards, and under the action of the weather they tend to twist and warp and go to pieces generally, all of which is too painfully evident if one looks somewhat critically at most of these houses.

This practice of false half-timber work is not altogether reprehensible, but when we have a modern house of real timber work built as is the Vanderbilt Lodge, there is a certain satisfaction in viewing it, a satisfac-

In this old English house, the timber work expresses the actual frame construction of the house.

tion which comes from seeing a thing well done.

There are ever so many schemes possible in the handling of half-timber decoration. We say decoration rather than construction, because the real construction of our houses is concealed. In the old Norman work the pattern of the half timber was the natural expression of the construction. Notice that a horizontal piece is laid under the sill of the window and over its head; similarly the slanting pieces were put there to brace the frame, and so on. Therefore, as a general rule it is well to design a half timber house as though the half timber had a real meaning structurally. This tends to make the design look serious and reasonable.

In the English and Norman work, the timbers were spaced rather close together. This was done because it gave strength and solidity to the building. In some of the modern American work designed by untrained builders who knew nothing of the antecedents of half timber work, the design is frequently skimpy, the spaces between the false timbers too great, and the false timbers have no apparent structural relation to the window openings, or to each other. Such

houses usually look as if they had been striped with brown pasteboard, or smooth satin ribbons.

The use of stucco is very old, and it is used very generally throughout Europe, largely because it is made of lime, and lime is abundant everywhere. Moreover, the use of stucco on masonry walls has a distinct advantage inasmuch as stucco can always be re-applied, and an old house made new. In this country, where we have excessive heat and excessive cold, stucco has to meet difficult conditions of expansion and contraction, and it is consequently still somewhat imperfect. Still, if the stucco cracks here and there, it can be patched, and that patch instead of being ugly is often a picturesque addition. Certainly much of the charm of the old European stucco houses lies in their battered condition, their delightfully varying color.

There is a sad superstition in America that a house should look as though it were taken out of a band-box. The moment it becomes shabby enough to be interesting, it is painted and varnished until it shines. Of course we must keep our houses tidy—but not too tidy. If they are of wood, we have to repaint them

 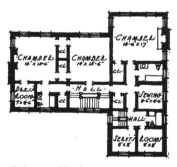

First and second floor plans of Mr. Raymond's house at Manchester.

James Purden, Architect.
Note the complete lack of useless decoration in this interesting house of Mr. Robert L. Raymond at Manchester, Massachusetts.

lest they fall to pieces under the attacks of the weather, but when they are of brick, or stone, or stucco, there is no excuse for our frenzied housecleaning. People actually tear down the shrubbery and friendly vines that were struggling to make their houses beautiful in order to apply a new and unnecessary coat of paint!

I know two stucco houses of approximately the same cost and plan, in the same town, and there is all the difference in the world to any one possessed of the seeing eye. One house was planned for years by its owner, and finally the plans were turned over to a sympathetic architect. The house

is placed as close as possible to the street, to gain privacy for the garden in the rear. The long line of the house is parallel with the street, which gives it added interest, and this line is emphasized by a wall which begins under the front windows and runs along past the end of the house, enclosing the laundry yard. The house sits low on the ground, and although it is not yet two years old, it has all the subtle charm of an old English cottage. The texture of the plaster is very rough, slapped on by a skilled hand, and just enough black was put into the creamy mixture to take away the "new" appearance. The unobtrusive outer trim is painted a neutral blue-gray. The red tiled roof has the character of an old one, for the tiles have not that unvarying redness that is so deplorable. Brownish ones, and purplish ones, and black ones have been spotted among the dark red to give a shadowy variation of color.

The other house was equally well planned, but it has been set at right angles to the street, so that you get an impression of the bolt upright end of a narrow house. It sits up from the ground with a deliberate frame-

The doorway of "The Cloisters," an old house at Ephrata, Pennsylvania. The stucco is of good color and a most interesting texture.

work beneath the first floor that says obviously, "This is the basement." But my main quarrel is with the horrid smoothness of the stucco, the neat yellow expanse that looks more like the eggshell plastering of an interior than an outside wall built for weather. The trim on this house is very heavy, very much emphasized, and it is obviously false. It is stained an even, chocolate brown. It is supposed to suggest a bit of half timber, but it really suggests brown satin ribbon, neat and thin and temporary. The roof of this house is blatantly red, every tile a perfect mate to its neighbor. Certainly it is a "new" looking house, and should be quite right for the people who wish to live in band-box-new houses, but even to the unpractised eye it is disappointing.

From the point of view of good design, the main difficulty with stucco is its color, and the next is found in its limitations when used otherwise than in flat surfaces. In other words, stucco is not adapted for the small house unless the details be extremely simple. Nothing is more disagreeable than a dark bluish, or dark brownish colored stucco. This danger can be obviated usually by the use of white sand and white cement, for it is essential that the tone be light. Light grays, with a suggestion of yellow or green, are warm and cheerful, and show off stucco at its best. The quaint pink stucco houses of Southern France, of Italy, of the Azores, and of so many fair countries are not for us, for their color is tempered by climatic conditions, but we may at least aim for a pleasant deepening of some cream or gray tone.

It is well to keep the surfaces of stucco walls plain, because it is difficult to express

Edward B. Gilchrist, Architect.

This house is located at St. Martins, Philadelphia. Note the large areas of blank wall, the interesting texture of the stucco, the fine grouping of windows, the generous proportions and mysterious charm of the arched doorway.

detail in stucco without getting into trouble. It is worth noticing that in the attractive stucco houses of English architecture the walls are kept severely simple and the detail, in order to give contrast to the stucco, is found in the dark stained wooden cornices, window frames, and bay windows. Mr. Dow's house shown on page 39 is a beautiful illustration of this use of detail.

Brick is one of the most attractive of building materials, provided two things are observed: the brick must be of good color and it must have good texture. The brick used in the early houses of this country were imported from England, and were no doubt imperfect from the point of view of technical composition, but they had and still have more attractiveness than the majority of our modern bricks, judged at least by our modern standards. Their very imperfection of manufacture gives them a texture and a variety of color which is extremely interesting. This is also true of the first bricks that were made in this country, which were crude in color and texture, and therefore wonderful in composition in mass.

About 1870 the so-called "water pressed," or smooth faced brick came into use. It was smooth, unvarying in color, and usually of a dead salmon-colored red. During the time that this brick was in fashion, brick houses were unattractive, so far as their design depended on the material. Only recently has it become recognized that the variation of color and texture in a brick wall is one of its charms, and we have to-day a variety of bricks which are beautiful in their color and rough texture. The best of these are the so-called tapestry brick.

The chief mistake in the use of brick is in its misuse in connection with stone. Frequently brick is used for the general wall surfaces of the house, and the window sills, heads, trim, and so forth, are made of terra cotta, marble, or lime stone. Mr. Greeley's house at Lexington, Mass., is an example of an excellent brick house which is quiet and

reposeful. It has an almost complete absence of stone ornamentation. Compare it with the agitated little house shown on this page in which the repose is all lost in the confusion created by the stone decoration.

A house should be one thing or the other; it should be brick *or* stone. One of these materials should predominate if it is to be restful. Nothing is more vulgar than the emphasis of decorative forms which are totally unrelated.

The color of bricks is most important, and the old fashioned red bricks are the most satisfactory in the long run. They have a rough uneven surface which will permit the weather to work its changes agreeably. The worst colors are the deep blues and browns, purples and magentas, because they are cold and unsympathetic in effect. In combining brick with other materials the color should be carefully considered. Do not put crimson-red brick with orange colored sand-stone, or salmon colored stone. Go back always to the old Colonial work, and notice how simple and how sure is their sense of color in brick work.

Stone, in spite of its abundance, was not so extensively used in Colonial architecture

An overworked little house.

76

THE MATERIALS

William Roger Greeley, Architect.
Mr. Greeley's house at Lexington, Massachusetts, is quiet and restful in design. Note that the entrance vestibule is at the ground level. Note also the enclosing wall for the service yard

as might be imagined. It was used most in those districts where limestone, which is easily worked, was readily accessible. There remain, however, many excellent stone houses, notably those in the vicinity of Philadelphia. An example of such stonework is shown on page 79. The walls are eighteen inches thick, and because of this, the windows may have very deep reveals. This depth of reveal may be taken advantage of either for the exterior or the interior; in either case, it gives added interest.

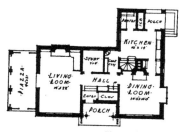 

First and second floor plans of Mr. Greeley's house.

THE HONEST HOUSE

Savery, Sheetz & Savery, Architects.
Mermaid Lane Cottage at St. Martins, Philadelphia, is a fine example of the house built of local stone.

For the small house, cut stone is usually too expensive to be considered, though one finds occasionally a combination of cut stone and rubble stone. It is in the simple rubble wall that the small house architecture of this country has found its completest expression.

There are mistakes to be avoided in the use of stone, as in all other materials. The difficulties commonly met with in this material are first, the manner in which the stone is laid and second, the color of the stone. Contrast the beautiful wall shown on page 82 with that shown at the bottom of this page. In what does the difference consist? The stones in the wall shown in the first figure are laid horizontally, and rest evenly on their beds while in the other case the stones form a crazy pattern which is restless and futile.

If the color of the stone which is accessible to you is not warm and cheerful, it is better to build your house of some other material. Warm gray limestones tinged with yellow, green and pink are attractive, and grow better with age. Field stone which has long

submitted to the influence of sun and storm, often acquires an attractive character. Marble of the whiter kinds in order to be attractive must have also warm pink, yellow or greenish tones in it to be agreeable in color. It should never be bluish in tone. The stones with the deeper colors, such as red and brown sandstone and the dark gray and dark blue limestone, are best avoided. Nothing is more lugubrious than brown sandstone, which, in addition to being ugly, is very friable.

We have confined ourselves to the consideration of shingles, clapboards, stucco, stone and brick, in this discussion. There are, in addition to these, two other building materials used for the exterior of houses

This shows how *not* to build a stone wall.

78

which are fairly common, concrete and glazed terra cotta. There are still other materials, such as the decorative tiles used in Mexico, the tile being applied directly against the masonry wall. But this material has been little used in this country, and, while its possibilities are many, it falls without the scope of this book to give it more than passing notice.

Of concrete there is this much to be said: Constructively, it is an excellent material, and its color (usually a dull blue, brown or gray), makes little difference provided that it is covered with a warm colored tint. As for the concrete block, however, it may safely be said that it would be difficult to find anything much more ugly. If the concrete block house, which looks like a German toy block house, were covered with stucco of a uniform tint, it would be passable. Glazed terra cotta is used generally for the purpose of imitating stone, and serving in its place, and as such it does very well. Its use in domestic architecture, especially of the smaller type, has been restricted, and so it is only necessary to say that what has been said about stone applies to the use of glazed terra cotta.

Finally we come to a most important matter, the juxtaposition of materials. Materials in themselves are far less frequently abused by the untrained builder than when they are put in intimate association in the same building. That is where most of the mischief enters. If you will look at the good examples shown in this book you will find that most of them are built of one uniform material. It is saddening to note the tendency of the amateur home builder to mix unrelated things. The untrained builder seeks for interest in complexity. He multiplies his forms, his colors, and his ma-

Mellor & Meigs, Architects.
Note the stonework in this cottage near Philadelphia. The white paneled woodwork set in the reveal of the doorway is beautifully studied.

terials. His house is composed of all the motifs he can think of. He uses three or four different materials and, finally, he paints his house two or three different colors. All simplicity is lost.

The effort of the trained architect is to get back to a simple expression of his idea; to find the interest of his design in the refinement of its proportion, and the skilful use of detail developed at the salient places.

In combining materials, then, it is necessary to remember that from its very constitution masonry does not knit with wood. One kind of masonry is fastened to another with cement, whereas wood is fastened to another piece of wood with nails.

To show what is meant by saying that two materials do not knit, let us take a practical example. Consider the house shown on this page. In this house, which is a clapboarded house painted white, the red brick chimney seems to cut right through the side of the house and gives one the impression that with a slight push from the other side it would fall away. Compare this with the house shown on page 81. Here the chimney holds the same relation to the house design, but it is of the same material and color as the house and consequently it gives the impression of belonging to it.

In the first case, the brick of the chimney and the wood of the house do not knit. Nothing holds them together. From this we can make a generalization.

With materials differing so completely in character as wood and masonry, we get a feeling of stability when the joint between them is a horizontal one, and not a vertical one. When wood rests on brick, as for example the wooden second story wall rests on the stone first story wall in the house on page 82, we feel that gravity acts to hold them together, and that the weight of the wood holds it in its place.

Of course this is only a matter of theory, because in practice we know that a chimney is stable, whether it is red or white in color, and we know that in house construction the second story wall is n't built with reference to its weight. Nevertheless this theory has its practical side, which is simply this: the impression which the eye gains in looking at such a building as that shown on page 82 is that the chimney does not knit with the house. The eye also decides that it is reasonable for different materials to lie horizontally upon each other, and the eye is the final judge of architecture.

The relation of wood to stone is an important one. When it is necessary to cope a stone pier, such as a piazza porch, with wood, the stone work should not be rough and angular. The strictures which have been expressed on the matter of joining wood and masonry apply in a much more limited sense to the joining of one form of masonry

This charming little cottage is reminiscent of the old villages of New England.

THE MATERIALS

DeArmond, Ashmead & Bickley, Architects.

Note the distinctive simplicity in this house for Miss Mary C. Gibson at Wynnewood, Pennsylvania.

wall with another, simply because they have much in common in their character.

So far we have considered only the materials used for walls. There remains the important question of the roof and its covering. Of all the roof coverings the most common is shingle, and undoubtedly this is one of the most satisfactory so far as looks are concerned. The gray, weather-beaten shingle roofs of some of the old colonial houses, colored by mosses and lichens, have an attraction which is very appealing, but the fact that they are not fireproof causes them to be regarded with suspicion by many house builders. Then, too, they must be renewed once in so many years, which is expensive to the modern economist. So we turn generally to one of two types of roof covering, slate or tile.

Slate is permanent and fireproof, but it is usually cold and unsympathetic, in color. The best roof covering is unquestionably flat

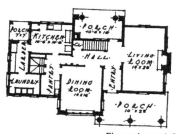
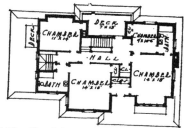

First and second floor plans of Miss Gibson's house.

shingle tile. In the old European tile works, as in the old European brick work, the manufacture was imperfect. The tile was of a rough texture, unglazed and soft baked. The consequence was that while they satisfied the conditions of permanence and fireproofing, they also permitted age and weather to beautify them. The roofs resulting were symphonies of color. Their tones varied from light orange to warm browns, and through these colors, the greens and grays of the mosses and the lichens played.

In this country until recently tiles, like brick, have been too hard, too smooth, too colorless to be interesting. Recently, however, shingle tile has been made with a rough texture and good color. Little can be said

in approval of the so-called mission style of round tile, such as is seen everywhere on ponderous near-Spanish houses. This tile is always ugly and awkward, and its constant convolutions are very tiresome.

Of the other types of roof covering, such as asbestos shingle and various patent roof coverings, it is only possible to say that they are practicable. Certainly they are nearly always ugly. Nothing is more sad than an asbestos shingle roof with its dull, monotonous red or sickly green, and its thin unbroken evenness. It has a surface that one could almost skate on. Some day this surface and texture may be improved, and we may have an asbestos shingle of good color, and thickness enough to be interesting.

Charles Barton Keen, Architect.

Note the excellent stone work in this Germantown house at Garden City, New York.

CHAPTER X

WALLS AND THEIR OPENINGS

AFTER all, what is the wall of a house? First of all it is a protection against the weather; secondly, it is a construction to insure privacy.

The early builder, long before he came to cope successfully with the problem of roofing his house, realized that his walls insured him against the attacks of the enemy, gave him shelter from the weather and afforded privacy for his family. Then he added a roof to further protect himself, a roof consisting, probably, of skins of animals. In the walls of his rough dwelling he made a few openings —rough windows and doorways to give him light and air. And so came to pass an elementary home.

This primitive home is a type of dwelling which exercises a fascination upon most of us even to-day. Don't you remember as a child, in reading stories such as "The Swiss Family Robinson," a certain thrill of satisfaction when the adventurous castaways succeeded in establishing a rough shelter for themselves? Have you not experienced

while camping in the woods the excitement of improvising such a shelter? It exercises your ingenuity to obtain and fashion the material for the rude walls and roof. Far away from villages and shops you must make the best of such material as you can find. Finally, however, the shelter is finished; your few belongings, your stores, and clothes are moved into it; night falls; a huge fire is started and you contemplate the surrounding blackness with security and content. To a certain extent you are living as the primitive home-builder lived. After all, what you have done is simply to construct some walls with an opening or two in them and a roof overhead. And this was primarily just what the first house-builder constructed.

In this rude beginning we have the earliest form of domestic architecture, and in its essentials the most pretentious dwelling of to-day varies from it only in the interpretation of these elements. In the diminutive building shown on page 84 we see a wall with a

rough opening in it, and in the background—a palace. It is obvious that in the most elaborate architecture the façade is, in the last analysis, only a wall punctured by openings. If these openings are arranged so as to produce a balanced effect, the façade has attained a large measure of the essence of good design. There are, of course, many other considerations which enter into its design, but the placing of the windows in the walls so as to produce a happy effect, is one of the very first problems.

To show how the character of a building varies, not only with the arrangement of the windows but with their size, examine the houses shown on page 85. In enlarging the window openings relatively to the wall spaces between them, we lighten the appearance of the building. We let in more air and light.

It is easy to see that one of the essential considerations in designing your house is to get the window openings just right in size, not too large and not too small. If you make them too small, your house will suggest a prison; if too large, it will look like a greenhouse.

Somehow we associate our ideas of home with a certain snugness, a certain security. It is this quality which makes the difference in character between a public building and a home. Seated around the great fire, with the doors securely locked and the strong walls of our house about us, we get a feeling of what the French call the foyer,—of what the English call home. This feeling vanishes for most of us, if we try to imagine such a scene in a house which is all windows.

In a word, it is all summed up by saying, as is pointed out in Chapter V, that in architecture the important thing is to express the *character* of a building. On looking at a building we should be able to say by its appearance to what purposes it is put. We ought to be able to tell a greenhouse from a jail and a jail from a dwelling house. Nothing tends to express the character of the building so much as the treatment of the walls in relation to the openings in them.

In a greenhouse the openings are large; in a jail, small. It is not a question of the *kind* of window you use; it is simply a question of fixing the amount of window space relatively to the wall space and thus to find a treatment which will express the particular character of a building.

It is interesting to look a little further into the conditions which determine the difference in the treatment of walls and windows in different countries.

The walls of a house protect the inmates against heat and cold. In addition to the heat and cold which come from the outside atmosphere, the house also receives its light from out of doors. There is protection against cold by the use of artificial heating in the house, but there is no such protection against excessive heat.

In hot countries where the light is intense, and the heat excessive, the window openings are very small. In extreme northern countries, and in countries where glass is expensive, and fuel scarce, the windows are small again. In temperate countries the windows are made as large as possible, to let in much light and air. Thus you see that the matter of the size of the windows in a house has a direct relation to the climatic conditions.

Of course these climatic conditions tend less and less to influence our house design, because with modern appliances, we are able to combat more or less successfully the conditions of heat and cold. The point to be made is this: you cannot expect to retain the character of certain types of architecture if you go to work and change the very things which gave them their character.

It is important that you should not confuse the wall itself with the decoration of the wall. The essential thing to remember in designing a house is that you have a simple wall in which you are going to make simple openings. The use of pilasters, of band courses, of window frames, etc., are all of secondary importance. They belong to the decoration of the wall surface, and are not essential. It is important to recognize the beauty of the wall in itself. How often we have admired the crumbling wall of a deserted house over which the vines and lichens have grown. Time and exposure have given to the old stone color and texture, a richness which comes only with age.

So much for the theoretical aspects of the wall and window treatment of the house. A very practical matter is the placing of the windows.

Generally the people who are planning their first house begin with a consideration of the plan arrangement. I have seen dozens of people in the first flush of their pride as landowners, and invariably they seize pencil and paper and begin making squares that are

supposed to indicate rooms, and choppy little lines to indicate windows and doorways. Later they perfect these amusing plans and work out room sizes laboriously, with the aid of a simple scale of measurement. But of the exterior they think not at all. Where will these windows and doors find themselves? That is a mystery they expect the architect to solve, and woe be unto him if in solving it, he sacrifices their room arrangement! I do not decry the making of plans —it is one of the finest pleasures a man can have,—but I do wish his imagination would soar upward to his second story, to his roof. A crude elevation would be quite as much fun

to work out as a crude plan, and would give him so much more respect for his architect.

In my magazine experience, I have had hundreds of plans sent in to me with requests for criticism. These plans usually are incomplete and hasty, and of course any intelligent criticism is impossible, because nothing has been submitted to show what the house is to look like.

How is it possible, looking at such a plan, to tell whether the windows are going to work out right, whether the roof is possible,—in a word, whether there is any design to the house at all?

The correct way to work at such a problem

Photograph by Frank Cousins.
The old Henry House at Germantown, Pennsylvania. Note the beautifully proportioned windows.

is this: suppose you want a house which has a living room, a dining room and a kitchen on the first floor and two or three bedrooms on the second floor. Usually you will have been inspired by some house which you have seen, and liked. Perhaps it did n't altogether suit you, but it gave you a point of departure. Suppose that you want an arrangement in which the living room and dining room are adjacent. As soon as you have drawn that much, you realize that you need windows in these rooms. Where are they to go? Well, the average person just indicates them any-where, without reference to anything. That is wrong. The thing to do is this: when your little sketch is drawn, make a rough study of the elevations as is shown at the bottom of this page. This will tell you where your windows ought to go to look well. Then check on your plan so that they agree in po-sition with the windows on the little sketch elevation.

This does not mean that the position of the windows is fixed. You have only made one little study, and before arriving at the design you should make a great many such studies, always checking the plan and the elevations. Not only is this true in the con-ditions of the windows, but it applies to the roof and to all the elements that go into your house design. It is the only way to work intelligently. If you work simply by con-sidering the plan arrangement, you will in-variably get some terribly complicated and impossible plan for which no ingenuity could possibly devise a respectable elevation.

So far in this chapter the window open-ings have been considered in relation to the wall in which they form the openings. I have tried to point out that the essential character of the home lies in its security and shelter, that in order to express this charac-ter the openings of the walls must be neither too large or small, and finally I have tried to show how in designing a new house you must constantly consider how the windows which you so easily locate on plan are going to look in elevation. So far nothing has been said about the types and kinds of win-dows and doors which we can use.

I wonder if ever a woman planned her ideal house without a vision of wide-flung casement windows, ivy framed, with broad inside sills holding orderly pots of red gera-niums, and a bird cage somewhere in the background? Of course there are no win-dow shades and no wire screens in sight. Flies and mosquitoes do not frequent ideal houses.

Men plan differently. They always think of the sensible side of things—of adequate light and air and all that. They bring us to earth with practical considerations and ar-guments for and against casements, or double

PLAN OF 1ST FL.   END ELEVATION   SIDE ELEVATION.

Edmund B. Gilchrist, Architect.

The planting about this house is so successfully done that, although the house is still very young, it has the appearance and charm which age and time give. Note the plain wall surfaces which contrast happily with the planting.

hung windows, as the case may be. I know one man, however, who always specifies casements when he possibly can (of course he is an architect), because he says the text of his career is the image called to his mind by the poets' songs of the magic casement. He sees a small window in a high tower flung wide open, with a fairy princess hanging out. A more definite examination gives him an impression of a charming arrangement of small panes of glass. No one, however realistic, could conceive the possibility of poetic imagery lying in a double hung sash consisting of two huge sheets of plate glass!

Architects should be also artists, and artists have such visions. If your architect insists on huge sheets of glass, instead of begging you to consider small panes, there is something wrong with him. I *know*.

In the chapter on wall openings we considered windows as mere penetrations, but they must also be considered as decorative, or marring, details. From a historical point of view the window in the primitive house was an opening to admit light and air. At first a simple hole in the wall, it finally came to be glazed, and then the refinements of window design began.

The early English and French cottages from which we draw so much of the inspiration for our American homes were built in a period when glass was expensive. Life was lived out of doors, and when night fell the family went to bed, since artificial light was scarce and expensive. Partly to protect themselves from the rain and snow, men made the windows of their houses small and few. Look at the typical old cottages shown on pages 5 and 25. Notice how small the windows are as related to the wall surfaces, and how charming the cottages are, because of the mystery, the intimacy of those quiet walls.

When glass became less expensive and it became possible to have large windows, a new condition was brought about which still obtains. The modern architect must keep the picturesqueness, the sense of hominess, the sense of privacy which these old cottages gave, but the house must have more windows. People demand windows everywhere! Each room must have two and often three, and the houses of to-day are designed so as to answer these conditions. Then the layman wonders why our small domestic architecture is not picturesque, like the old English and French cottage architecture.

The small country houses of England have small windows and large wall spaces. This is also true of Spanish houses, but the Spaniard has the excuse that the sun is so bright and the day so hot that thick walls and small windows give relief. It is curious that the Englishmen should have built in the same way, for the climate is exactly the opposite of that of Spain. Perhaps the price of glass, or the old window and door tax, caused this.

Drawn by B. E. Muller

In northern Italy you go through a great many small towns where the windows are boarded up, and the Italians have even gone so far as to give the effect of windows by painting them on the outside walls. You may remember having seen in Italy the painted figure of a man leaning against a painted doorway.

At the beginning of American housebuilding our windows were good,—they had to be good because no one had attempted to apply the principles of vulgarity and ostentation to them. (Principles is too good a word,—what is its antonym?) Then, about 1880 some malignant fiend decided that windows had been decorative long enough, and introduced into American domestic architecture that hideous atrocity which we know as the plate glass window, the window which makes every house in which it is used pretentious, dismal and uninteresting. For a shop window the big pane of glass has its utility. It is a public window. It invites us to examine it. We all look into it to see what is exposed. But is not this the very opposite of what we should demand of the windows in our home? The modest retiring aspect of privacy should be the quality which distinguishes a "home," and this is destroyed when the house has windows of huge sheets of glass.

In America we have not had the difficulty of the window tax, and with the introduction of electric light—a desire came over the country to have the maximum of light by day as well as by night, and so plate glass windows were introduced because they gave a great deal of light. The fact that they absolutely destroyed the beauty of the houses where they are used, meant nothing to their perpetrators. An epidemic of plate glass made most of our houses as badly open to the gaze of passers-by as if they were shops.

I remember as a child, with the smugness of childhood, classifying the social desirability of people on the basis of whether or not the windows of their houses were of plate glass. I disdained the small panes, I thought them old fashioned and that only poor people had them in their houses.

Many old cottages which the American traveler admires so much when passing through English villages are very lovely—from the outside. The traveler rarely sees them from within, and he does not realize that their defect lies in the lack of light and air the interior enjoys. He sees a low, rambling cottage with an overhanging roof of moldly tiles, and a few small casement windows, and much ivy, and he decides his architect must give him an English-style house of exactly this sort. He is sadly disappointed when his architect tells him that the interior of the cottage is as black as your hat, and that these visible charms can't be introduced into our American houses without sacrificing sunshine and air and comfort.

But if English houses are defective through a lack of light, many American houses err in the other direction. You must understand that this is not a criticism against well-lighted rooms, but against the disposition of too much window space in one place. Often in American houses the privacy that should belong to the home is destroyed by badly placed windows on or near the street, which enables the outsider to look into the house.

If we could only make up our mind to the radical idea of broad wall spaces and few windows, we could get along with small window openings. The Boardman Robinson house on page 164 is a fine exposition of this. Here is a long rambling house with large wall spaces broken by small casement windows. It is most adequately lighted and ventilated, and yet it has the picturesque and

Photograph by Frank Cousins.
   This detail of the door and windows of the old Robert Morris House at Philadelphia may well serve as an inspiring model. The small window panes are charmingly proportioned.

intimate character of an old-world house. It has great charm, absolute convenience, and all the comforts.

The window divided into small panes possesses much more decorative interest than the single pane sash. Look at the houses shown on page 109. The first is without interest; the second has windows that look like windows, and not like great black holes, or characterless shop windows.

The defense of the large pane of glass is commonly based on two considerations:— the small pane window is more difficult to clean, and the muntins between the small panes obstruct the view. If one were to be logical he must also do away with the open fire-place because it is responsible for a certain amount of dust in the house, whereas steam or hot water heating is more scientific. And if the muntins obstruct the view, so also do curtains obstruct it. To be logical these should be done away with also. But we are not quite so foolish as that. We keep the open fire-place, because in spite of its inefficiency as a house heater, we like to see the open fire. We decide that its cheerfulness makes up for its dust. And so with our curtains. They do obstruct the view, but the window looks bare without them, and we can see enough.

With these strictures we pass from the subject of plate glass windows. The offense does n't lie in the fact that the windows are of *plate* glass, but in the hideousness of an unbroken expanse of glass. Very large studio windows are often filled with large sheets of glass, but they are small in comparison with the wall opening, and they are, after all, divided by muntins.

Windows made up of large single panes of glass are uglier than windows subdivided into small panes, but unless the small panes are well managed they can be pretty bad, too. In ordinary house design a window with wooden muntins has panes eight by ten inches. As a rule a rectangular pane is more attractive than a square one, a vertical rectangle better than a horizontal one. The simple rectangle of ordinary cottage windows is much more satisfactory than the diamond shape, or any of the fantastic sub-divisions, be the muntins of wood or of lead.

The leaded diamond panes in the old English Tudor houses are very delicate and graceful, but these windows were large, and vertical in expression. Diamond panes that are squarish and separated by thick wooden muntins are very unpleasant.

Do not have windows of one sort in one part of the house, and windows of an unrelated family in another. It is possible to use double-hung sash windows and small casement windows in the same house with excellent effect, *if* the general character of the windows is the same.

If your house is two stories and a half high, your windows would ordinarily be larger— that is, taller—on the first floor than on the second. Consequently the panes of the sec- ond floor window may be less in height than those in the first, but the width of the panes should be kept and the windows will belong to the same family.

There are three kinds of windows in common use: the double hung, which is the familiar window, the two halves of which slide up and down; the casement which opens into the house; and the casement which opens out.

Of these three types the advantages and disadvantages are pretty much as follows:

The double hung window is more practical in a very small house where outside shutters and inside screens are required, since its operation does not interfere with either the swinging of the shutter or the screen. Its disadvantages lie in the fact that one can utilize only half the opening. Its advantage lies in that it may be opened solely at the top or bottom. From the point of view of good looks it is invariably the least attractive of the three types.

The casement opening in is generally less weather proof than the double hung window, or the casement opening out. It also consumes part of the room space which would otherwise be useable, since it has to swing into the room. Its advantages lie in the fact that it can be used easily and it gives you the full value of the window opening.

The casement opening out is weather proof and looks well open or shut. Its disadvantages lie in the fact that it is less easily managed from inside of the house than is either the casement opening from the inside or the double hung window. It is difficult to arrange outside shutters in connection with it, and in summer the problem of screens becomes an abomination. There are now, however, contrivances that make it possible to

Designed by H. T. Lindeberg.

Albro & Lindeberg, Architects.

This house presents interesting and excellent detail throughout. It will repay the most careful study.

open the windows by using a small lever that runs through the lower part of the screen.

Doubtless as we become more appreciative of the beauty of the casement "flung wide," our American ingenuity will devise still better mechanical means for manipulating the shutters and screens. Casements must ordinarily be smaller than double-hung windows, because they are supported by their hinges. It will take a group of casements to admit the same light as two or three ordinary windows, but the ordinary windows give too much light usually—else why do people curtain them so resolutely?

Study the old cottage architecture of Eng-

land and France and notice how simple the forms of the windows are. In the Colonial work, it is true, you find examples of semicircular and elliptical arched windows, and occasionally in gambrel roof houses you find quarter circle windows. But the great majority of windows are plain, straightaway, rectangular openings, with little effort to elaborate. It is always well to avoid triangular, hexagonal and oval windows. Especially unpleasant in modern work is the recurrent oval window with its elongated key stones, invariably made of wood. Many otherwise good houses are spoiled by this silly little oval window that is inserted in the wall without thyme or reason. It may light a closet or a dark corner of a stairway, but surely the architect could devise some better opening. Too often the oval window has not even this excuse: it is merely a strange expression of a misguided ambition to decorate; to beautify. Almost always it goes with another dreadful sin against good taste—colored glass.

There is a general superstition that the stair hall window should be filled with colored glass, and this idea has ruined many stair halls that would otherwise be good looking. We all remember the houses that have come to us from the dreadful period of the seventies and eighties, when blue and green and orange and purple glass was used with terrible effect. If you feel you must have stained glass in your house, study the subject thoroughly, and then use it sparingly. Of course if you are a connoisseur in glass, that is different. You will understand what stained glass *is*. Otherwise, let your glass be of good quality, transparent. Cheap stained glass is a sure way to vulgarize the appearance of any house. It is a two edged sword: it betrays you to the world outside, and it is always with you inside your house. Shun it.

There are accidental effects that are worth recording, while we are discussing colored glass. Any one who has visited Boston remembers those quaint old houses on Beacon Hill with their windows filled with panes of violet glass. This is one of the delightful things that came by accident, for the violet tones came from some chemical action in the glass. There are dozens of other reasons for it, one hears a new one on every side! One theory is that these Simon-pure Bostonians conceived the idea of living in a violet light for ethical reasons. Another theory is based on the hygienic value of violet rays. But the

truth probably is that the glass started out innocently as plain glass, and Nature, the baffling chemist, did the rest. It is safe to say, however, that a man who deliberately planned to fill his sashes with panes of violet glass would make an awful mess of it.

The bay window and the dormer window are special types which merit special attention. Both these occur in a great variety of forms, and both are hideously designed in the ordinary house built by a contractor. The common mistake is to make the bay window too heavy. A bay window should always show some kind of support under it. If the walls of the bay window cannot run to the ground, as shown on page 155, then it should be supported by brackets, or a series of moldings.

As for dormer windows, the great error lies in making them too monstrous. Nothing takes away from the serenity of a house so much as great dormer windows, too big to be dormers, and too small to be gables.

The dormers not only are frequently too large but they are nearly always badly designed. Compare the dormer of the house shown on page 36 with that shown on page 37. Note in the latter house how heavy are the pediments crowning the dormers, and

What a roof ought *not* to look like.

94

note further how much narrower in the dormers shown on Mr. Rantoul's house is the space on either side of the window sash. These dormers are beautifully proportioned. In the ordinary dormer a common fault is seen in the too great projection of the roof of the dormer. Look at the example shown on page 118. What could be more hideous than the great flaring overhang of the dormer roof? Compare these with the modest dormers of the house shown on page 119. Still another distressing use of dormers lies in overdoing the number of them. The dormer windows in the house shown on page 94 destroy absolutely all sense of restfulness and give the house a very unhappy and agitated appearance.

A word of caution should be given: it is well to finish the side walls of the dormer window in the same material as the roof. Thus, if your roof is shingle, let the shingles be carried around on the side walls of the dormer. This makes them more inconspicuous and knits them to the roof.

The grouping of windows is done most successfully in the English country house work, and well repays study. One thing that has to be remembered, however, is that a group of windows makes the application of outside shutters impossible, unless the windows are spaced so far apart that they lose the feeling of being grouped,—and shutters are very attractive additions to the house.

In placing the windows in relation to the floor and ceiling, remember that the upper part of the window lights the room, and that the nearer it is to the ceiling the lighter the room will be. As a general rule the head of the window should come to within about eight inches of the ceiling, and the sill within two feet four inches of the floor. This ap-

plies, of course, to the usual windows. Special windows may be high from the floor.

Shutters have much to do with the attractive appearance of the house. The most charming ones are the old, faded blue-green ones. The old painters did not achieve this delightful color deliberately, they used a green paint in which the yellow was weaker than the blue. The yellow faded out, gradually, leaving much of the more lasting blue, and so those delicious blue-green tones came to pass. Recently paint manufacturers have had the good sense to copy this accidental color with excellent results. Gray, white, French green, and sometimes even blue shutters are used with interesting color effect nowadays.

In most of the newer country houses the downstairs windows are grouped to give greater light, and no shutters are used, but the upstairs windows are placed at well studied intervals, with wide-spread shutters that help balance the grouped windows below. One seldom sees solid shutters on the ground floor, nowadays, but occasionally in clapboard houses one sees batten or solid shutters on the first story, and slat shutters on the second story.

It is much better to stick to shutters of one type for the whole house. Undoubtedly the heavy, solid old shutters, with their graceful panelings, were most attractive to the eye. But for real use they are a nuisance! The happy compromise is the shutter that has a panel at the top in which a little tree, or a crescent, or a bird, or what-not has been cut, and the lower two-thirds slatted. These shutters admit sufficient light and air, and are very attractive folded back against the house walls. They give the house an old fashioned home-like character.

THE HONEST HOUSE

"An old fashioned character." Does it seem reactionary, this praise of the old fashioned? The significance of "home" depends upon its long tradition; on the idea of a place of well established security and peace. It takes time for such a tradition to grow. If you are to build a new house let it be so designed that you will catch in anticipation something of what time will bring. You can achieve a suggestion of this character if you consider carefully the design of your windows.

An old farmhouse in Normandy.

CHAPTER XI

THE CONSIDERATION OF THE ROOF

THE average untrained home builder is inconsiderate of his walls and windows, but he is positively indifferent to the designing of the roof of his house. It seems to be a failing of untrained architects, and all carpenters, as well as of the home builder. One of the most famous professors at the École de Beaux Arts in Paris had the habit of saying, when he was called upon to criticize a student's plan, "How are you going to roof it?" He realized that the student had n't thought of how he was going to roof it, and that in all probability it was impossible to roof the proposed building reasonably.

It is very easy to draw a pleasing floor plan, given plenty of pencils and paper, but when you try to visualize a house built upward from these floor plans you find yourself hopelessly involved. You can't decide how the rooms on the second floor will find themselves, and the roof disappears into the clouds. You can't even imagine it, except as a poetic, friendly covering that will somehow fit itself comfortably over your house.

The trouble is, it won't. The trained architect has a hard enough time with it, and the untrained builder finds opportunity for a thousand mistakes in solving the problem.

How, then, are you to design your roof? The architect sighs in despair as he tries to answer you. If you asked: How do you go to work to design your windows or your façade, or your chimneys, or what not, his sigh would be as heartfelt. How can you separate the designing of one part of a house from that of the others? You can't! He can't! You have to grope and grope until you find your vague dream-house gaining form. Then the form grows more definite and becomes style, and when you have your general style decided, the details of roof and windows and chimneys suggest themselves, little by little.

One thing you are sure of: you must have a roof, and it must be a good one. Who of us has n't said: "As long as we have a roof over our heads—" The very spirit of hospitality hangs upon the proper consideration of the rooftree. Your roof and your hearth

97

must be unfailing in giving you shelter and warmth, if you would make the most of your house.

The two types of roof in general use are the flat roof and the roof composed of slanting surfaces. It is with the varieties of the latter that we who build small houses are particularly concerned. We seldom use flat roofs, for ours is a country of rain and snow. We associate round roofs with Eastern temples and Eskimo huts. But everywhere we see three types of sloping roof: the gambrel, the gable, and the hip. Almost all our houses are roofed with these types, or combinations of them. Illustrations of each type are shown on pages 16, 19 and 31 respectively.

It seems easy, given only three types of roofs, to select one and play safe, but just as there are only a few kinds of windows and a thousand vicious ways of misplacing them, so there are so many mistaken ways of handling your roof that you have good reason to beware the seeming simplicity of "putting in your thumb and picking out a plum"—be it gable, gambrel or hip. You can design any one of them so that it looks like a pasteboard crown or a heavy load of tile or shingles.

Go out into your neighborhood and see if you can't tell a good roof from a bad one. Study first the little good and bad sketches on this page, and then exercise your powers of criticism. It is good for you and it won't hurt your neighbors.

The three houses on this page all have gambrel roofs. Mr. Jones's roof is bad because its lines are flattened out and weak. Mr. Brown's roof is a hundred times worse, because it is spread over a three-story house, and the eaves of a gambrel roof are best never more than one story from the ground. Mr. Green's delightful little house, on the contrary, has a pleasantly proportioned roof of logical lines.

The slope of your roof depends on the style of your house, the arrangement of your plan, the climate, and many other such conditions.

The gable roof lends itself to the necessities of houses built in climates where snow is plentiful. It is the roof most used, and it is the easiest of the three types to construct. It has its difficulties, however. You have to be careful that it does not project too far over the face of the gable wall. The roof that extends too far looks like cardboard. If it hugs the wall and is finished with a

At the left is Mr. Jones's House; at the center Mr. Brown's; at the right Mr. Green's. The roof lines of the latter are designed by the method shown on page 102.

Joy Wheeler Dow, Architect.

Mr. Dow's house at Summit, New Jersey, is full of unusual detail. Note the leaded glass windows, the plain, steep roof, the strong contrast between the stained woodwork and the stucco walls.

simple molding, the effect is usually happy. Compare the projections of the roofs of the houses shown on this page. One looks like a slipshod arrangement of pasteboard. The other roof fits its house perfectly, and the narrow molding is as clean-cut as if it had been modeled by a practised sculptor.

I don't think, however, that any photograph or drawing could give adequately the bad impression which a great flaring roof gives in reality. There is something so heavy and brutal and common about such a roof, that one must get the impression of the actual house as it exists in three dimensions to appreciate the gravity of this fault.

As for the pitch of the roof, it is better to make the slope somewhat over forty-five

degrees with the horizon, than to have it just at forty-five. For houses in the English style generally a steep-pitched roof such as is shown in Mr. Dow's house above is most in character. From a practical point of view it is rarely safe to risk a roof with a

99

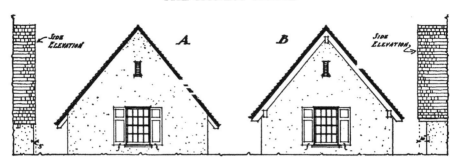

pitch less than twenty-five degrees, if it is to withstand rain and snow.

There are four common ways in which the gable roof is terminated at the gable wall. These are shown on this page. The first termination of the gable is common in English cottages, and is usually used on a house with stucco walls. The second is frequently used with half timber construction, and the third with stone or brick walls. The gable termination shown at the right at the bottom of the page is a special problem, and will be considered in Chapter XIII.

It seems dry, does n't it, to spend much time on small matters like moldings? Actually, although it may be difficult to believe, it is the lack of understanding of such details that is responsible for so much bad architecture. Let us, as patiently as we can, consider each of these gable terminations in order. So far as (A) is concerned, the most reprehensible error to which it is liable has already been noted in the preceding page. It consists in giving the roof too great a projection over the roof of the wall. As the drawing shows, the projection under ordinary circumstances should not be more than three inches.

The type of gable finish (B) is called the barge board termination. The barge board is the large flat board which runs parallel to the roof, and projects from the wall. It is supported by brackets. In much of the English and French construction the barge board is highly ornamented, but this decoration is not essential. If this type of termi-

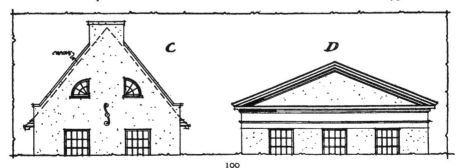

nation is to be used, it is important to remember three things:—do not let your barge board project too far from the face of the gable; do not make it too large, and do not fail to support it by brackets.

There is little that needs be said here concerning the third type of termination (C). It is one of the most attractive of all gable terminations, and is used extensively in brick colonial architecture, and in English stone construction. The roof is contained between the two gable ends, and shows only at the eaves. In using this gable termination the

The barge board in this house is brutally large. Compare it with the barge board shown on page 45.

lines of the coping should always be simple. Compare the simple and effective coping of the houses on pages 21 and 88 with the horrid accentuated coping of the house on page 76.

Finally we come to the last type (D). It is the classic pediment, and is common in the larger Colonial work. In this case the projection from the face of the gable is the same as the projection at the eaves. For the ordinary gable roof the projection of the roof at the eaves must be greater than at the face of the gable—and amounts usually to about twenty inches. But the rules for the classic pediment and cornice are much more rigid.

You remember, I am sure, some old Colonial or Georgian courthouse with its imposing front of huge, white-painted columns. The columns, without doubt, remain clearly in your mind. As a child, I remember wondering how anything in the world could be so big as the columns of just such an old courthouse. I don't think I ever tried to look to see what was above the columns. Of course, I knew the building had a roof,—but how that roof ended above the columns I never stopped to notice. And my attitude was n't so different from that of grown-ups. At any rate, it is safe to say that over the columns was a cornice and pediment,—in fact, the pediment looked something like (D) on page 100. Of course, the courthouse with the columns required a complete cornice and pediment to conform to the classic models from which it is copied. In the case of small houses, such as that shown on page 86, where no columns are used, it is customary to modify the cornice and to omit the architrave and sometimes the frieze, and when the corner of the house is reached, only the upper moldings are continued up the edge of the gable. Notwithstanding this modification, the moldings should have the character of the classic moldings. To know how to use these moldings, you must understand something of the classic tradition. What that tradition is we shall take up when we come to the chapter on columns.

We now come to the gambrel roof. In general, what has been said regarding the gable roof applies to this also. It is best to have only a slight projection at the gambrel end of the building and a much larger overhang at the eaves. In the best Colonial work this rule always obtains.

A very special difficulty, however, confronts the designer of the gambrel roof. On page 98 I pointed out some of the characteristic errors to which the gambrel roof is liable. It is evident that the chief trouble lies in the determination of the slope of the roof surfaces. They must not be too steep or too flat.

We very often see unpleasant gambrel roofs, such as that at the top of this page. How shall we go about to make a better one? There is a general rule which will be found to give good results for average domestic work.

In the figure at the bottom of this page let AB represent half the width of the house. Let us suppose the width to be 25 feet, which is that of many small houses. Let B be the edge of the outer molding of the cornice which projects 20 inches from the wall face.

With the point A as a center, strike the arc of a circle as shown in the little diagram. Draw the top line of the roof tangent to the circle at an angle of thirty degrees with the horizontal line. Then join the tip of the eaves with this point of tangency as shown. To make the roof graceful it is well to have the lower line slightly curved at the eaves.

An example of a badly designed gambrel roof. Note the awkward projection of the roof beyond the face of the walls.

Now you have to test this roof in relation with the floor lines, especially the second floor line, to determine if the necessary dormer windows will take their right places. By a series of simple experiments you will arrive at a good roof slope.

In the house shown at the top of this page the roof lines are stiff and harsh. The pleasant sweep of the roof at the eaves, so familiar in the old houses, is absent. The old Dutch Colonial roof is worthy of great commendation, but it is easy to lose all the charm of this roof by bad lines.

The third type is the hip roof. It is called "hip" because of the rafters which run up diagonally from each corner to meet the ridge, and into which the other rafters are framed. With this roof there is only one mistake to watch for—the overhang of the eaves. If the overhang is too great, the roof will look like grandfather's hat on a small boy. It is usually a good plan to bring the eaves down as near as possible to the heads of the windows. This gives an impression of lowness, and low houses usually have much greater charm than high ones.

So far in this chapter the difficulties which are peculiar to the design of the gable, the

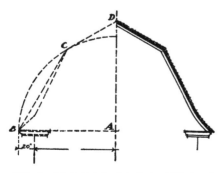

This shows a method for designing a gambrel roof.

gambrel and the hip roof have been considered.

These three types of roof are distinct, and in building any house it is well to avoid combining more than two of them. It is usually best to use one type. Let your roofs, as much as possible, belong to the same family. Thus, if your main house is roofed with a gable and you have a projecting wing, do not use a gambrel roof on it. Do not make a salad of your house top. As a rule the roofs which go together are the gable and hip roof, and the gambrel and hip roof. Do not mix the gable and gambrel. It has been done, but it is rarely satisfactory.

It is almost impossible to get much length for roof line in a small house, but wherever it is possible it is to be strongly recommended. A little cottage one room deep and one story high that is placed parallel with the village street is more pleasing than a very much finer house that shows you only its narrow end. Often one gets a finer effect of length of line in a small cabin that sits low on the ground than in a house that has

Here the roof fits the house, and the relation of the eaves of the roof to the second story windows is good.

worked hard for beauty. Look at the long restful lines of the house shown on page 65 and compare it with the agitated roof lines of the houses shown on page 64. Nothing could be more restless or unprepossessing than these, and yet they are no worse than other houses one sees every day.

When your house is small, try all the harder to get your roof simple. Sometimes this is achieved by the combining of two small houses into one, so as to get an expression of length, as is shown on pages 132 and 133. Let your roof be as undisturbed as possible.

Look again at "Fairacres," on page 49. The roof has one long, unbroken ridge. "But," you say, "this is a huge house; how are you going to get a long ridge-line with a small house, the plan of which is square?" Well, if your plan is square, do not roof it with a hip roof; if possible, use a gable. Better advice is this;—Try to design your house so it will not be perfectly square in plan. A pyramidical roof on a small house is always unpleasant;—such a house is that shown on the bottom of page 118. One way out of the difficulty is the twin house scheme

This house, with the exception of its roof, is like that shown at the top of the page. Note the too great overhang of the roof.

THE HONEST HOUSE

already spoken of in the preceding paragraph. After all, for all you can tell by looking at it, "Fairacres" might be such a twin or triplicate house.

Avoid dormers which are so big that they destroy the design of the roof like that shown

Another illustration of bad roof lines. If the dormer has to be so big, why try to have a gambrel roof?

on this page, where in order to gain room for the second floor the dormer is made so large that only two thin ribbons of the gambrel roof are left. In a case like this, it would have been better to give up the gambrel roof, and make a simple, two story and a half house. A recent atrocity is the double dormer,—one dormer on top of the other. If it were carried a little bit further with still another dormer on top of the second one, the roof would look like a wedding cake, or a Chinese pagoda.

So much for the design of your roof. The consideration of the material is also important. What is the roof to be made of —shingles, or tiles, or slate, or thatch? And what is its color to be?

Lately there has been an effort to shingle roofs in curving lines, imitating thatch. Thatch is a charming miracle of nature and of architecture that should n't be imitated, as a matter of fact. But occasionally a mas-

terly architect comes along and accomplishes a wonderful effect. Mr. Harrie T. Lindeberg has accomplished some really satisfactory roofs with thatch-like curves. One of these is shown on page 105. Usually, the thatch imitations are very distressing, and at best the woven shingle roof invites criticism on the ground that it is an imitation.

The everyday roof is made of shingles, left to weather a soft gray. Certainly for average wooden houses this is the most successful treatment, and the least expensive. The only sensible variation of color is to stain the shingles wood-brown, or soft green. Brown shingles seem to belong to certain bungalows, and green shingles are very pleasant on the little white cottages that sweeten the country landscape. But the eccentric roof is always to be avoided: red shingles are somehow always terrible, whereas red tiles are almost always pleasant.

The temptation of gay-colored roofs is hard to resist. I have seen one blue roof that gave me great pleasure, and the blue-green copper roof of Mr. Herter's house at East Hampton, Long Island, is a rare sight, but the best roof for all neighborhoods is the uneven red one of flat tiles. When we planned a little house for Forest Hills Gardens, I had so long dreamed of a white and green house, with green tiles on the roof, and a whitewashed chimney with green stripes around its top, and green lattices, that it was difficult to yield to restrictions. But to all my arguments that it would be cool, and fresh, and just as fireproof as if it were red all over—the architects said me nay. All the houses must have red roofs, to pull the place together. I recognize their wisdom when I go through other towns, with

THE CONSIDERATION OF THE ROOF

Designed by H. T. Lindeberg.

Albro   Lindeberg, Architects.

Nothing could be more charming than this glimpse through the shrubbery showing the excellently designed lattice. Note the way in which the shingles are woven.

vari-colored roofs spread out like a crazy quilt.

Our roofs belong to our communities as well as to ourselves, and it is only fair to make the best of them.

Yes, we have "to make the best" of our roof. Do you know that every roof represents a conflict? We try to cover our house simply, we know that a simple roof costs less and looks better than a complicated one, but we also wish to utilize the space under the roof. We begrudge the space lost by the slanting surfaces. If you cannot afford to use the space under your roof for an attic, try to choose a type of plan and roof which will permit you to utilize the space without spoiling the exterior appearance of your roof. I remember a house in which the roof was so arranged that the attic was n't quite high enough to stand up in without bumping one's head. Yet it was so *nearly* practicable that for twenty years, the occupants bumped their heads in the attempt to utilize it. Finally they burst through the roof with huge dormers,—with the result that the appearance of the exterior of the house suffered appallingly. There is no rea-son why your roof should not be a practical as well as a beautiful one, if you take time to think it out. But don't be *too* practical.

Wilson Eyre, Architect.

Nearly all modern half-timber houses are built with a machine-like finish in the half-timber work. Note in this drawing of the house at Jenkintown, Pennsylvania, the irregular, hand-hewn character of the timber. The charm of half-timber work lies largely in this rough suggestion of strength.

CHAPTER XII

DETAILS OF SMALL HOUSE DESIGN

TO refresh your memory turn back to page 44. You will see that we planned to discuss the elements which enter invariably into the design of a house. Whatever kind of house you have it must have some kind of setting or entourage; it must be one color or another; it must be built of some material and it must have walls with openings in them and a roof overhead. These are the important elements which we have dealt with. In addition to these there are certain other things to consider. For example, your house usually has chimneys which are visible; it usually has leaders for the rain water; it sometimes has balconies; it always has at least one exterior door. Moreover, columns may be used in its design, and it very likely has a porch.

After all, it is the consideration of the various details which makes or mars your house. We have seen in the preceding chapters on the walls and windows and the roof that bad design consists largely in the way in which the window and the roof were treated in detail. A badly designed dormer window, a hideous porch, an ugly chimney, will go far to destroy any merit your house may otherwise have. It is these smaller things which are sometimes the most vicious.

I remember an old stable I used to pass on my way to school. It was an unpretentious affair; rather low lying and hidden by trees; but I never paid any particular attention to the modesty of its retreat. Over the large door was carved a sunburst. Do you know what a sunburst is? It is a piece of ornament representing the rays of the sun and usually semi-circular in shape. This one in particular had a yellow center, from which orange rays flashed out over a blue background. It sounds frightful, doesn't it? Yet I used to look at it with equanimity. In passing the stable I always looked at the sunburst and wondered in a dull way how such things were born. I know now. And I know this one small detail in the design of that old stable completely counteracted the charm which the building otherwise had.

One doesn't need to take so violent an example as a sunburst, however, to make the point clear that it is the character of the detail of your house which largely makes or breaks it. Look at the old house shown on

THE HONEST HOUSE

The sunlit porch of this old house at Mt. Vernon, New York, is very inviting.

this page. It was built almost one hundred and fifty years ago. It began simply. Probably at first it had neither porch nor dormers. The general proportions of the house were excellent. The window openings in the front wall were well disposed, and the roof was terminated at its gable end with the modest molding so commonly used in the early Colonial work. Then the house began to submit to a number of "improvements." A porch was added. The posts of this porch are very simple; their designer, moreover, had sentiment enough to make the cornice over the post small and in keeping with the unpretentious gable termination. So far so good. The appearance of the house was doubtless benefited by the addition of the porch. Then the dormers were

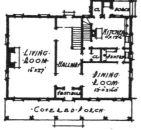

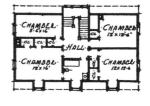

The first and second floor plans of the Mt. Vernon house. Note that the second floor plan is modified and that three dormers are shown instead of four.

added—and half of the charm of the old house was destroyed. Why? Because there ought to be no dormers? Certainly not. But because the dormers are too big, because there are too many of them and because they are awkward in design. Compare for instance their large pediments and heavy moldings with the charming and delicate cornice over the posts. This is what I mean by saying that it is detail that counts.

I am going to press this matter further. The old Mount Vernon house started out well and was damaged subsequently. Suppose, on the other hand, we start out badly. Suppose we have a house like that shown at the bottom of this page. The drawing was made from a photograph of an actual house. What is wrong with it? Compare it with the house at the top of the page. The shape of the two houses is the same, they have the same number of windows, the roofs are alike, and yet the upper house is attractive, and the lower one disagreeable. What is the reason? Look a little closer and you will no-

What the house below might have looked like if its designer had known more about architecture.

tice that instead of a heavy round tile roof with fantastic brackets at the eaves, the upper house shows a simple flat tile, or shingle roof with simple moldings at the eaves. Instead of the eaves being high above the heads of the second floor windows, they are brought close to them. Instead of the huge awkward dormer windows in the roof, smaller ones have been substituted. Instead of uninteresting single panes of glass, the window sash is divided into small panes. Instead of a pretentious and more or less useless porch, a simple hood has been placed over the entrance door. Instead of the house being raised high out of the ground, a terrace has been used to bring the house close to the ground, giving the pleasing impression of the house growing out of the ground, and therefore belonging to the landscape and not looking like a hat-box placed on the floor.

So you see there is much in the way we design these various details.

Before taking up the matter of doors, columns and porches, which are, after the various elements already considered in the previous chapters, the most important mat-

Modern American Domestic architecture,—alas!

ters in house design, I am going to touch on two or three others of lesser importance. First of these is the chimney.

In the older cottages of England the chimney was usually made much of. Often it took huge and uncouth shapes, but usually this resulted from the fact that many and large fireplaces had to be accommodated. However that may be, when the colonists settled this country they brought with them the tradition of the huge chimney. It was customary in the old New England houses to place the chimney in the middle of the house, —and then build a house around it. In this way the occupants of the house were able to utilize the chimney for as many as four fireplaces, and thus keep the house warm. It is not until comparatively late that the chimney became a decorative feature. When the Colonial brick house developed, the chimneys were often arranged at the end of the house, in the manner shown on the Henry house on page 21. This treatment is typical of old Southern houses, where the wide hall usurped the center of the house, and at least two large chimneys and often several smaller ones were necessary to heat the large, high ceiled rooms.

As has been pointed out, when wood and brick join each other horizontally, the wood upon the brick, gravity acts to hold them together and if they don't "cohere" in any other way at least the weight of the wood holds it in place. Therefore in a wooden house it is well not to expose your chimney on the outside. Often space on the inside is at a premium, and this pushes the chimney out. When it is thus pushed out it can at least be painted the color of the house, or treated in some way to make it inconspicuous. Of course in a brick or stone house the danger

rarely arises, since the chimney is usually of the same material as the house proper, and consequently belongs to it.

So far as the design of the chimney is concerned, whether it is to be a chimney which shows its full length or one which starts from the roof, it should not be too high. Perhaps the only criticism one can make of the excellent house shown on page 70 is the too great height of the chimneys. The tops of the chimneys should not come much above the main ridge line. It is best, if possible, to have your chimney intersect the roof at the ridge or near it, or to have it located on the face of the house wall, either at the gable as on page 21 or at the side wall as on page 40. It appears in this way to be tied to the walls of the house. When, however, it emerges from the roof as shown in the house on page 48, the result is usually less happy. As to the elaboration of the design, of course a chimney like that on the Vanderbilt Lodge shown on page 9 is very beautiful, but such chimneys are difficult to do well.

Balconies are unfortunately little used in this country, chiefly for the reason, I suppose, that their place is taken by porches. And yet nothing is more charming than a well designed balcony such as is shown on page 70. And a balcony such as that on Mr. Dow's house on page 39 will appeal readily to the imagination. In France and Italy where it is common to use small iron balconies the charm of the house is greatly added to by their use. Moreover, a balcony such as that shown on the Villa Gambreria on page 8, though it is nothing more than a railing between the jambs of the windows, has a considerable practical value. Inside this room, one can open the windows and feel that he isn't altogether "cooped up." If the balcony is large enough to walk upon this impression is largely increased. Small iron balconies like this are beautifully adaptable to houses built in the Italian style. But in the best examples the iron work is severely simple; just plain square rod about half an inch thick, set about three inches apart. Such balconies should be adequately supported, but the brackets, if brackets are used, should not be gross and heavy. Frequently one sees in American stucco houses the floor of the balcony made of a huge slab of concrete supported by blocks of concrete each large enough to support the world. The essential qualities to search for and to express in designing a balcony are delicacy and grace.

The leaders of your house should receive ample consideration. We have the habit in this country of conducting our roof rain water to cisterns. In England they let the leader run into a rain-water barrel,—which is an infinite improvement, because a rain-water barrel properly treated is a very interesting object. We used to use rain-water barrels, too, but they have somehow fallen into disuse; and even at their best they were rarely developed as the English have developed them. The sketch on page 29 shows such a rain barrel. It adds a spot of interest to the design, and is a far more effective thing than a simple leader which disappears in the ground. Of course we can't use rain-water barrels for every leader, but it is well to remember that the barrel is a charming motif to make use of. The best leaders are those made of copper. If it is possible to do so, it is very desirable to use leader boxes. They, too, give interesting spots of color. A very interesting example is that shown on the Vanderbilt Lodge on page 46.

Now we have done with chimneys and balconies and leaders. We come to the important matter—the door—of your house. I have reserved it for the last because it relates in its design to columns and to porches, two subjects taken up in the two following chapters.

The most formal of all doorways is the classic type. The opening is usually half as wide as it is high, and is surrounded by an architrave door jamb, usually molded. This is surmounted by a frieze and cornice and sometimes by a pediment, as is shown on this page and on page 36.

Inasmuch as these doors are derived from the monumental doors of the classic tradi-

An old classic doorway at Annapolis, Maryland. Note its simple dignity.

111

THE HONEST HOUSE

This old doorway which belongs to a house in Pittsfield, Massachusetts, is a fine example of the modest Colonial doorway. The eight panel door and the side lights are characteristic.

tion it is absolutely essential that the man who attempts to design such a door should have an understanding of that tradition.

The Salem type of doorway which we have shown on page 113 has a somewhat freer expression. Here it is possible to get an expression of width without having to increase greatly the height, because we are using a triplicate motif instead of a single motif. It is best, however, that the side lights be narrow, and that the door itself maintain the general proportion of its width being one half its height. One of the common mistakes made in this kind of doorway lies in the inaccuracy of the ellipse. The ellipse should

be a true one, or as closely approximate to it as possible.

The exterior door should be painted to match the walls or the shutters, or should be stained and waxed to a quiet, flat tone. Avoid doors of golden oak or mahogany, and shun big panes of plate glass. A door should not be so spick and span as to suggest the interior of the house, and varnish and plate glass are sure to give this suggestion.

If you are absolutely sure of yourself (and this surety comes from a keen appreciation of the daring things done by artists and architects who *know*) you can take liberties with your doorway. On a certain grimy, dusty

DETAILS OF SMALL HOUSE DESIGN

Photograph by
Frank Cousins.

The Andrew Safford house at Salem, Massachusetts, can boast one of the most perfect doorways of the later Colonial period. In these Salem houses the walls and windows are kept severely plain and the doorway is treated elaborately.

street in London there lives an artist who chose to make his house peculiarly his own. He had his doorway lacquered Chinese red, and gave it a huge knocker. Certainly the neighborhood should bless him. But a New York man who made over an old stable tried very much the same thing with sad results. He paneled his great door, and painted it a gay, deliberate green. Before the next night it was covered with chalk and pencil drawings by the unappreciative youngsters of the neighborhood.

Can't you remember your friends' houses by the impression you received of the doorways? We recall so many delightful doorways: pleasant, homely ones of ordinary green boards with old hinges and latch strings; serene and gracious white painted ones, with shining brass knockers; quaint Dutch doors, cut in half, the lower half being closed to keep dogs out and children in, the upper half opening upon a pleasant interior; dark doors studded with nails, suggesting a great hall and complete privacy within. All these are good doorways: they beckon you to come and try them. But the dreadful doorways, always hung on the inside with much lace and colored silk, or filled with near-stained glass! We prefer to forget them. You know them all, anyway.

It is easy to have a good door in your house by emulating the simple and effective doors of the old houses we have mentioned.

Designed by H. T. Lindeberg.   Albro   Lindeberg, Architects.
    The difficulty in designing a hooded doorway lies in the danger of making the moldings too heavy, and the hood too big. This detail from the house for Mr. R. S. Carter, Hewlett, Long Island, is a well studied example.

CHAPTER XIII

THE COLUMN AND ITS CORNICE

WE employ columns so extensively in American architecture that it never enters the head of the ordinary man that there may be essential differences of proportion and design. "A column is a column—just as a house is a house!" That is his point of view. It is because of the commonness of this point of view that there is so much bad architecture.

Indeed, in some parts of the country a man who has lived his working years in a plain box-like house, usually builds a new large house with a lot of columns, when Fortune favors him. The towering columns serve as evidence of his prosperity. He has huge porticos with tiers of columns built all around his house, all kinds and shapes of columns.

Let us leave him with his gigantic house and its multitude of columns, and turn our attention to the reasons which justify the use of columns. Let us try to understand their real meaning. The column is almost always used in the design of porches and as it is almost invariably associated with some kind of cornice, it will be profitable to consider them together.

The element which gives greatest difficulty to the untrained designer in the detail of a house is the column and its cornice. The column is used everywhere—for porches, entrances, porticos, and pergolas, and for this reason it deserves the most serious consideration. Often an ugly house can be made attractive simply by correcting the hideous detail of its columns and cornices.

A column is a very beautiful thing, used rightly. But do you know a good column when you see one?

Perhaps your own house has "classic" columns surmounted by some kind of cornice. Do you know that such columns, from an architectural point of view, are simply posts designed to hold something up, but that they must have certain definite dimensions of height to diameter, and equally definite relations with the cornice above and with the adjacent columns? Perhaps you have never thought about it.

It is well at this point to remark that for small domestic architecture the use of classic columns is not absolutely necessary. Our early Colonial architecture and the simple English cottage which charms us all rarely employed columns. It was only with the introduction of the more monumental type of Georgian architecture, such as was built in the later Colonial days, that the column was used extensively. Its use even then was confined principally to the Southern colonial work of the large and formal type. For the small domestic architecture of to-day the only place where the column is indispensable is in the porch and the pergola.

In any case if you decide to use columns, be sure you employ them rightly. If your house is not of the pretentious sort, the simple square post treated as one sees it in an unassuming farmhouse will give you the most satisfactory and pleasing results for your porches.

To use the column rightly you must understand something about it. Let us look for a moment into its history.

Every one is familiar with pictures of the Parthenon. It is not necessary to reproduce it here. From the days of our history and geography lessons it has been so familiar that we have ignored its relation to our affairs. If we thought of it at all, it was as we thought of a picture of the Sphinx—as something with which we had no concern!

Forget that you have seen the picture of the Parthenon before, and consider it with a

new interest. After all, it is only a composition of columns, but they are so beautifully proportioned that they make a deep and lasting impression on the student of architecture.

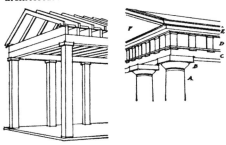

The building at the left looks like the framework for a garage or a boat house, and yet it is not different from the primitive type of wooden building from which, somewhere in the Orient, at some time in Mesopotamian history, the Parthenon and all the classic orders sprang. Beside it is shown a sketch of the Parthenon columns. The wood posts correspond to the stone columns. On the wood posts rest strong beams which support cross beams, the ends of which are visible. These in turn carry the roof rafters.

This wooden structure represents primitive construction. Gradually the unpermanent wood was replaced by durable stone, and although the two building materials are very different yet it is easy to trace in the stone temples of antiquity survivals of the earlier wood construction and wood detail from which they came.

At first the column was only a post, made doubtless of a tree, or a bundle of reeds, just as the cornice was originally nothing but the rough projecting edges of the roof covering. From these simple beginnings arose what we now call the Doric, the Ionic and the Corinthian orders, which are distinguished from one another most readily by their characteristic capitals.

Under the Greeks and Romans these orders were developed and perfected. When, after the long night of the Dark Ages, the Italian Renaissance came, certain architects, inspired by the renewed interest in the civilization of Greece and Rome, undertook to classify and measure the various proportions and parts of the ancient temples, in their design. Among these architects was Vignola. He established a system by which the dimensions of the whole order, that is, the height of the cornice, the projection of the cornice, the size of the capital and base, and so forth,—are given in terms of the size of the diameter of the column near its base.

In Chapter V we considered the matter of proportion, and we touched on the classic orders as examples of "fixed" proportions in architecture, and of a canon of proportions which has been accepted by the great majority of trained architects in all countries. To-day in the schools in this country the student of architecture is first set to work to master thoroughly the elements and proportions of the orders, and the system of Vignola is commonly employed. The student is taught to combine columns with other motives, such as arches, doorways, and the like, and this method has been adopted because after several thousand years of study and criticism, the most highly trained architects are agreed that these orders express a perfection in their proportions which can be bettered only by genius. Geniuses are rare!

If we put ourselves in the position of the student, we shall understand some of the

things there are to learn concerning the orders.

The next thing to notice is that a column is not simply a straight shaft, cylindrical in form, nor is it like a tree which diminishes in diameter as it goes up. The column has a slight curve. This curve is called the entasis of the column. If this curvature becomes great enough to be noticeable, it is unpleasant; it is simply to give the column more grace and strength. Many stock columns carry the entasis to excess, as is shown on this page. It finds its extreme in the cigar

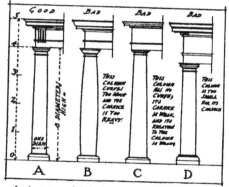

At the extreme left is shown the Doric column according to the proportions established by Vignola. The proportions of the Ionic and Corinthian columns have similar systems of proportion.

shaped column, which is most unpleasant. In the real Roman orders the curvature is hardly perceptible.

On the other hand, pilasters are given no entasis; they are usually made the width of the column at its necking. A fine example of the Doric pilaster is shown on page 91.

A common misuse of columns lies in their application to porches of the type shown on page 118, where the column rests on a railing and is only about five feet high, and usually

If you use the classic pediment, let it have the right slope. If you use columns let their proportions be right.

thick out of all proportion. No misuse of the column is more common or more hideous. If you are to use columns, respect their dignity and let them come to the floor. Use the column without a pedestal, and it will gain dignity and grace. It is almost a safe rule to say that no column should be less than eight feet high, if it is to be used in exterior work, and provided it makes a pretense of keeping the proportion of the classic orders.

Do not make the mistake of having a column in the center of the portico. This has an unpleasant effect. A column should never come in the center of the front of a house. One should feel the center of the colonnade open and inviting. It may come in the center of the side colonnade, however, —as witness the Parthenon.

For the relation of the arches of the columns, for the spacing of columns, and for the full development of the orders it is necessary to refer you to treatises which deal with these problems. It is an extended study which unfortunately lies without the province of this book. We are simply trying to give an indication of some of the common mistakes which are made by the untrained

builder who does not realize the fixed proportions of the orders. A trained architect can advise you wisely about your columns.

In Chapter XI, in considering the termination of different kinds of roofs, the gable roof in which the classic cornice is employed was mentioned. In using this cornice the great danger lies in getting the cornice too big for the house. The sketch at the top of this page shows two houses which are identical save for the design of the pediment. On the right the slope of the pediment is like that of

Another example of every-day American architecture. It has so many faults that it is hard to find anything good at all about it. Note particularly the stunted columns and the ungainly stone arches.

118

THE COLUMN AND ITS CORNICE

Designed by H. T. Lindeberg.
Note the refinement of the detail in this house at Hewlett, Long Island.
Albro & Lindeberg, Architects.

the classic examples. On the left the pediment is much too steep. We frequently see this error in American work. It is an error which arises partly from our ignorance of what the classic proportions are, and partly from the fact that we have changed the slope to meet the hard conditions of our climate. The Greeks and Romans had no snow to contend with, and their roofs were not subjected to the tests of harsh weather. But in changing the slope of the pediment to the requirements of climatic conditions we have completely spoiled it. So, if you are going to use the classic pediment, give it its right slope, and find some way of making the roof tight. Otherwise don't use it; use some type of architecture which adapts itself more easily to the conditions.

In dealing with columns we have touched on the most difficult subject which this book has to present. The architecture of simple walls and the architecture of columns present very different degrees of complication, To use a comparison: it is not hard for any of us to understand the simple melodies of Schubert; it is very difficult to understand the intricate architectonic structure of the Bach fugues. We can all hope to understand something of the little steep-roofed English cottage, with its simple and free lines. Those of us not architects rarely have the time or patience to understand the immense difficulty of using columns rightly. Therefore it is well in small house design to use the column as sparingly as possible unless you are willing to take the time to unravel its mysteries. Unfortunately this is not widely appreciated and everywhere about us we see architecture of which the house given on the bottom of page 118 is a sad example.

THE HONEST HOUSE

Where columns are used in connection with the cornice, it is easier to determine the size of the cornice, because we know that it should have a certain relation to the column. Where, however, the columns are omitted, how are we to determine how big the cornice should be? Perhaps one of the best ways would be to study the façade as if it were to have columns, and then remove the columns.

It is very difficult to give definite information concerning the proportion of columns. It depends largely on the type of building which you are designing. The best thing to do is to go to the examples which are shown in the books written on the subject of domestic architecture by competent architects, and study the cornices used on these buildings.

Ford, Butler & Oliver, Architects.
This house for Mr. Mestre at Sheffield Island, Connecticut, is interesting because of its long ridge line and its simple roof.

CHAPTER XIV

THE PLEASURE OF PORCHES

THIS business of living out-doors has brought about a change in our ideas of house building. We have actually found it desirable to drop Show and embrace Comfort. From boxlike houses with no porches at all, or porches so narrow as to be useless, we have jumped to an embarrassment of porches.

We were once content with a long front porch where we sat in six green rocking-chairs with six turkey-red tidies at our backs, and gossiped as the neighbors passed. And we sat in our best clothes, and busied ourselves with company sewing—lace or embroidery or such. We did n't take the darning basket to the front porch. We did n't even go there in the morning. The porch was reserved for afternoons and good clothes. We sometimes had a back porch, but that was n't intended to be enjoyed; it was a place for churns and milk-cans and fuel and so forth. The cook did n't think of sitting there.

In short, most porches were then ugly and meaningless excrescences, built for show. The only good ones, from an architectural standpoint, were the neat little stoops of New England cottages, with their two stiff settles and their formal air, and the great verandas of the classic Southern houses. Southern porches have always been pretty good, because they have always been used; and now people everywhere are insisting on living a part of every day outdoors, and porches everywhere are becoming noteworthy. When we plan a new house, we feel that we must have an entrance porch, very small and very formal; we must have a great living porch opening from the living room, a porch that may be screened with glass in winter or wire net in summer; we must have an ample porch for the servants, and we must have one, or two, or three sleeping porches up-stairs! We demand so many porches that the poor architect tears his hair, for the solution of the problem of porches is probably the greatest trial the American architect has.

The architects of England and France solve the problem easily: they simply have no porches. They sometimes have what the average American home builder would regard as an apology for a porch, an entrance hood which is very small and narrow.

In the early American work also, the porch was largely absent. In the most pretentious Georgian houses of the Southern states there were façades consisting of colonnades, and the effect of these porches was usually imposing, but the floor space afforded was usually small and narrow as compared with the modern porch and piazza. The wide spreading piazza is something distinctively American, distinctively modern. That it is a wonderfully comfortable institution, no one will deny. That it is a difficult matter to design is admitted by those who have tried to do it. The architect declares that our determination to have many porches will be disastrous. What will become of the style of the house? he pleads.

I don't know what will become of the style of the house, but I do believe that if we really enjoy living and eating and sleeping outdoors, our domestic architecture will have a chance at a style of its own at last. Simple, honest living conditions have always produced simple, honest architectural styles. Something very desirable will come from our recognizing the need . of bringing outdoors into our houses. Witness the delightful style of the Mexican and Spanish houses, with their open courts and patios, which came from this same problem of bringing outdoors in. We may make many mistakes in arriving at this new style, but if we have the courage of our common sense and employ trained architects, we shall finally add something to the sum of traditional architecture and decoration. We will find in ourselves that rarest quality—originality.

It requires great ingenuity and restraint to add porches to a well designed house. Look at the photographs shown in this book. The houses that please you most have no porches at all, or very small stoops. There are notable exceptions, such as Mr. Lang's house at Scarsdale and the cottage on the Tracy Dow estate. There are many enclosed porches, "sun rooms," but the old porches tacked upon a house without rhyme or reason are conspicuous by their absence. Two or three of the Colonial cottages have porches, it is true, but on the newer houses they are missing.

The two usual types of porches are the screened room incorporated as an integral part of the house and the porch that is built against the finished house. Of course the porch that forms a part of the house itself is much easier to treat successfully. It takes away a minimum of light from the living room, it can be glazed in winter and screened in summer, and it is ample enough in size to make it comfortable.

Another porch that seems to be a part of the house proper is that which is obtained

This represents the idea of a seaside cottage as the architect of 1880 conceived it. Note the ugly posts and the fantastic railing.

THE PLEASURE OF PORCHES

Photograph by Coutant.   Designed by H. T. Lindeberg.   Albro & Lindeberg, Architects.
Do not let the beauty of the setting of this small house on the estate of Mr. Tracy Dow at Rhinebeck, New York, blind you to the excellence of the house itself. The house is so designed as to take full advantage of the slope of the land. The roadway passes on the upper side of the house.

by letting the roof project over the porch, as is shown in the cottage on page 108. This is one of the earliest types of porches, and still one of the most attractive. There is also the modern example of which Mr. Dow's cottage is an excellent illustration.

A type of porch which has come lately into favor is that shown on pages 31 and 127. Here the porch is made into a separate construction, almost like a little house in itself, and it is an excellent solution of a difficult problem.

The different types of porch have certain things in common and it is in the interpretation of these things that most mistakes are made. They all have some kind of roof support, usually consisting of a series of posts or columns. If columns are used it is necessary to see that they follow the rules for the use of columns, which were touched on in the foregoing chapter. If the supports are wooden posts, a wide variation of interpretation is possible. Usually, however, for small domestic work, a simple post five inches square spaced about six feet from the next post is an excellent solution. It is simple, unpretentious and adequate.

THE HONEST HOUSE

It is possible to use stone, stucco, and brick piers, but stone piers used in connection with a frame house of which the exterior is clapboarded or shingle, are usually disagreeable because they suggest unnecessary brutality in the use of materials. The main trouble with masonry piers is their size, and unless they are of the same material as the house they will look awkward and bulky.

Often it is possible to use an arcade treatment. In the old Italian work most porticos are so designed, and nothing is more attractive. They have this fault: the arch cuts off a certain amount of light from the rooms behind the arcade, but the rooms can be lighted sufficiently by proper treatment.

If possible let your porch floor be of brick or tile, rather than wood. Cement may be marked off in squares and a tiled effect is secured at small expense.

All porches have some kind of cornice. We have touched on the subject of cornices, and what applies to the house cornice applies here also, except that the porch detail should be finer in scale than that of the house cornice which is much higher up and naturally more important.

If you use lattice, use a simple design such as is shown in Mr. Embury's house, or Mr. Lang's house. Do not go into florid and meaningless forms.

So much for the ordinary porch. Now for the sleeping porch, which like the *porte cochere*, is one of the nightmares of the architect. Why? Because in a small house the sleeping porch means that we are going to get

Howard Greenley, Architect.
The small arcaded porch of the gardener's cottage on Mr. C. A. Coffin's estate at Locust Valley, Long Island, is full of charm. The roof which is cut off on the gable end might better have terminated in the usual way.

Aymar Embury, Architect.

The use of the gable on Mr. Embury's cottage is questionable, but the house as a whole is agreeable.

a great, black, gaping hole in our wall, or in our roof. Nevertheless, it is possible to treat a sleeping porch attractively. The best ar-

First floor plan of Mr. Embury's cottage.

rangement, perhaps, is the treatment of it as a loggia, as is shown on page 126.

If there are enough trees about the house it is much easier to manage a sleeping porch, for if it can not be seen from the street or the garden proper it is not a source of worry to the architect. I once visited a house in New Jersey which had an upstairs porch that is most successful. It is broad and long, and is roofed at each end. The center of it is open to the stars, like a court. The great trees swish over it, and of course if it rains the sleeper can retreat to the sheltered ends. This porch is an exception, however, and was made possible by the fact that the house is built against a steep hillside, and by the great trees that screen it.

The large veranda which is to be used as an outdoor living room should be at the side or back of the house, if possible. In front

Eugene J. Lang, Architect.
One of the best ways to treat the difficult problem of the sleeping porch is that shown in this house at Scarsdale, New York. The use of the Palladian motive is a happy one.

we do not need more than a little square porch with two trim settles for a bit of talk with the parting guest. The real business of living outdoors is reserved for a more private place. Haven't you had the doubtful pleasure of calling on your friends only to find the whole family lounging in the hammocks on the front porch, scattering hurriedly, when you come up the front walk? This is not the most hospitable reception in the world, but what else can you do when there is only one veranda, and that a very public place?

The porch must not only be inviting, it must give you the comfort it promises. It must be as cool, as clean, and as gay as you can make it. A screen of some kind is imperative, whether it be a lattice covered with vines, awnings, or hanging screens of bamboo, or slat-like strips of wood. Screens

not only offer shadow: they temper the heat of the sun.

Standing screens of latticework are very successful if they are planned well and securely placed, so that they will not be pulled awry by the growth of the vines upon them, or by the strength of the wind. Where roses are to be planted around a porch, these lattice screens are the best solution of the problem. Last summer I saw a veranda one end of which was screened with a white painted lattice filled with small glass panes. This house was on the sea, and the wind was so strong at this particular exposure that the glass screen was necessary as a real shield. You can sit on this veranda and have the pleasure of looking out at the sea through the glass, and at the same time you are protected from the southwest wind. This is an attractive but rather expensive screen.

You can do what you like with color

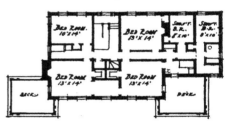

First and second floor plan of Mr. Barrett's house at Concord.

THE PLEASURE OF PORCHES

An attractive solution of the porch is to treat it as shown above in this house for Mr. Barrett at Concord, Massachusetts.

Derby & Robinson, Architects.

schemes inside your house, but when you are planning the color scheme of your porch you must consider the colors Nature has given you to build on. The best of all colors for porch furniture, awnings, and so forth are white, gray, brown, light green, and very dark green. The light green should be the color of green apples, or green peas or lettuce —if you are uncertain of the tone I mean. The dark green should be the soft velvety tone of the evergreen tree—the boxwood, olive, gardenia, japonica, laurel, or any such green. Yellow is a good porch color, properly used. Red is extremely popular, and extremely dangerous.

For some strange reason, four porches out of five seem to have turkey-red cotton cushions on the chairs, and red-and-white-striped awnings, the only excuse being that turkey-red is advertised as a "fast" color, and it is believed, by people who do not think for themselves, to be "cheerful." Why should we bring this warmest of all colors into the place that is supposed to be coolest and most restful? These are the people who plead for the combination of red and green, arguing that "this is a nice contrast."

Certainly if we could manage our reds and greens as Nature manages them, we might be pardoned the use of this combination. But we can't do it, so we had better leave it to Nature. She will do it for us in a flower-box of red genaniums and white daisies. We will get all the red we need in such flowers, and in the plain earthenware pots, and perhaps in the dark red-brown tiles of our floor. We must remember always that green is the dominant outdoor color. Nature provides pleasant greens, and we must not destroy her fine harmony by introducing vivid fabrics colored with cheap dyes. Our awnings should be green and white, or gray and white—some cool color; our cushions and rugs and things of green, or brown, or gray—the natural tones of wood, or stone, or foliage.

A masonry house will probably have its porches floored with tile, bricks or cement, but most of the wooden houses will have porches made up of ordinary boards. When you are painting such a floor, tones of gray are good, and certain shades of green are also pleasant. If any rugs are used they should be rugs that will not be injured by rain or dirt.

The furniture-makers are giving us really charming furniture for out-of-doors, and it is hard to decide just what we will have on our ideal porch. I think there should be a Gloucester hammock of green and white drilling, fitted with green cushions and mattress; a wing-chair of willow with a big pocket for magazines; a large Canton hourglass chair with a tabouret of the same type beside it; a chair built on the lines of the familiar steamer-chair in willow or rattan; a long bench painted dark green (this bench may be eight or ten feet long, and it will serve as a table as well as a seat when there is company); a chest or settle with box seat for tennis-rackets and such; one or more tables of green painted wood or willow; several large jars of green things, and a bird-cage.

Surely, if there is ever an excuse for having a bird in a cage, I think one might be excused for having one of those enchanting thrush cages of orange-colored reeds on one's living porch. You need n't have a thrush in it; have any bird you please. The cage itself is such a charming thing that any bird would be happy in it.

A wooden settle with a box beneath the seat to hold outdoor things, or a long chest of painted wood, will be found most useful on any living porch. Such a settle or chest offers a great chance to young people who have been studying the applied arts, for here is a fine opportunity to decorate a simple straightaway object with some bold scheme of design and color.

Don't allow your porch to become untidy. Have as much freedom and gaiety and informality as you please, but none of the shabby disorder that is so distressing. The cushions, for instance, should be covered with water-proof cloth if possible, and then with whatever you choose—denim, linen or chintz; but the outer covers should be made to button on so they may be washed. Cushions that have faded or "run" in unsightly streaks are unpleasant. Gaudy, sagging hammocks of many colors and untidy fringe are also unpleasant, but the modern Gloucester hammock is a comfortable resting-place by day and a bed by night. It is the ideal porch hammock, because the lines are logical, and you are screened while you are resting.

CHAPTER XV

THE PLAN ARRANGEMENT

WHEN you start out to design your house the probabilities are that you do not worry about its looks so much as about the arrangement of its rooms. You want your house to have an attractive exterior, but that is the architect's business, and you are sure that you can do as you please with the plan arrangement. So you get out a calling card and draw your floor plan on it, as casually as you'd make a memorandum, and all the king's horses and all the king's men can't alter some whimsy that you give that first rough plan. The poor architect is expected to possess a legerdemain that will enable him to develop any sort of house from your proposed floor plan.

An architect told me recently that in one of his recent houses he gave three French windows to the living-room, two on the south side and one on the east. There was no view on the north side, and no windows were needed there. Besides, the architect considered that the wall space was necessary for furniture, and that the exterior appearance of the house required a blank wall to make the design effective.

"But we are building the house for comfort, not for looks, and we want a cross draft in this room. After all, it is only your opinion that the windows will spoil the looks of the house!" said the client. So the windows were put in and the appearance of the house was spoiled. The house has been occupied several months now, and the north windows have never been opened. The occupants forgot all about the cross draft the moment they had bullied the architect into spoiling his façade.

It is difficult to realize that whatever you arrange for in plan is going to affect the appearance of the exterior. If you reflect, you will realize that there is no valid reason why your plan and your exterior appearance should not both be good. But to get them, you must not be bigoted; you must not make unreasonable demands of the architect. You must expect to make concessions.

In any problem dealing with any subject, it is possible to impose conditions which make a good solution impossible. So when you are thinking of your room arrangement, you must also be thinking of what this particular room arrangement is going to force you to accept for the exterior of your house.

You must think of your house as having three dimensions, length, breadth, and height.

We are accustomed to think of our houses in two dimensions only, mainly because our architects offer us only floor plans and elevations, blue prints that we are supposed to visualize into an attractive mass. Only the trained eye can imagine a roof line, for instance, from a cold and regular blue print. If we only had some one to make little clay models of our proposed houses how delightful it would be!

Last winter, a young English architect came over with the extremely sensible idea of making models of houses in clay. He was an artist as well as an architect, and his charming little models of Devonshire cottages and spreading Tudor manor houses were most convincing. His theory is that client and architect should work together while the model is being made. If his client insists on a certain group of windows, he can show the effect of those windows in the clay model, and the client is convinced.

Surely nothing can be more interesting than to watch the dream of your little house gain form, to see the roof lines find themselves, to find this chimney absolutely beautiful and that window a surprising defect. It savors of magic to see the architect thumb your roof into more poetic lines, and soften the window frames until they look like weather beaten stones. If you plan to build a wing, some day, he models the wing now and fits it to the house, and you know exactly what your house will look like when all your plans are realized. These little models are irresistible. You cannot but agree with their maker that eventually every one who

plans a good house will have a model made before he makes fatal mistakes. Hasten the day!

Your architect would like to show you a model, you may be sure. But his office is not organized to produce models, and so he must do the best he can with the meager information you give him. Given the survey of your site, he would much prefer a long letter setting forth ideas to a crude plan of *your* proposed plan. You can propose a hundred plans later, but unless you have a clear idea of the arrangement of your rooms you'd better let him do his own groping at first. Send him all the information you can —the amount you can spend, the number of rooms you must have, and get just as much of your personality over to him as you can.

A woman went to an architect I know and said that she wanted a house with a staircase of the curved balustrade sort. That was all she could offer to help him. The architect was set adrift on an ocean of possibilities, and made dozens of sketches of different house designs only to find that none of them were satisfactory. He had been given no real guide post or indication, because his client was either unable to define her wants to him, or too lazy to find out what they were for herself.

Another client gives him a problem pretty much as follows:

"We must have a huge living-room, no matter what happens to the rest of the house. We will do without a real hall—a tiny little box of a place will serve—and we will do without a proper dining-room, and have a breakfast room instead. The breakfast room will be sun parlor and conservatory as well, with flowers and vines and a tiled floor. It must be very gay and sunny, with *comfortable* chairs and a gate-leg table and a built-in dresser for our blue china and pewter, and magic sliding partitions that will make it a part of the living-room. We will have most of our meals alone, and sometimes one guest, or two—but only a dozen times a year will there be as many as six people or more—then we can "repair" to the living-room and eat on the great black oak table.

"We will do away with the conventional kitchen. Please plan us a compact laboratory of a place, with a big laundry in the basement that will serve also for overflow kitchen things. We will never require more than one servant, so the kitchen may be *very* small. People who build kitchen closets and pantries are such idiots—having wide shelves eighteen inches apart, when many narrow shelves close together and a few deeper ones at the bottom would hold all the utensils and provisions for a hotel. Please plan a long cupboard in the laundry, with an ironing board that will swing down, and many six-inch shelves below it that will hold irons and wax and holders and such. And the long outside panel will be painted with —with—I don't just know what, yet. Something gay, with yellow and orange in it. And there will be many shelves in the laundry, where I can display my cherished tins and jars and things full of provisions and jellies and jams. There will be one vermilion chair for the washlady, and quite a lot of color, for it must never become a dreary place.

"And there must be casement windows everywhere, and thin glass curtains, and thick inside curtains of shimmering stuffs that will be drawn at night, and no window shades. And many closets—a cedar lined one for linen, and so many in the kitchen. The kitchen must be fairly walled with closets and drawers."

Essentially a woman's letter, but the architect gets a feeling of her real needs, her personality, the quality of her family's life, and he has inspiration to go ahead. The flowers and vines and pewter and ironing wax and jellies are not in his specifications, but they linger in his imagination and become a part of the invisible house that gives him inspiration.

You probably have just such personal ideas. Note just what you wish to spend, and just what these personal idiosyncrasies are, and then go ahead. Before you reach the end you will probably have reasoned yourself out of believing that certain of these idiosyncrasies were very important, after all!

Of course we not only have our idiosyncrasies, but we usually have a lot of them. Unfortunately, when we come to build we have to forego a good many of them,—simply because the house isn't big enough to hold them all.

There are two kinds of houses, big and little. This may seem a most arbitrary classification. So it is! Nevertheless, it holds true as a basis for discussion. Obviously, when you have money enough to build a fifty room house, the possibilities of arrangement in plan and in elevation are far greater in their variety than when you have money enough to build only a six room house. If we except cabins and camping cottages, it is rare that we build a house with less than five or six rooms. The house with from five to ten rooms is the home of the average home builder. It costs from $3,000 to $15,000, and we call it a "small house."

It is noticeable that a great many small houses are square, or approximately square, in plan. A common type is planned with a central entrance hall, and the second floor hallway is thus reduced to a minimum. With a rectangular house, longer in one dimension than in the other, the second floor hallway must usually be longer. But what is saved in space in the square plan is usually lost in appearance. The square plan house is less flexible and less suitable to a variety of room arrangements. Moreover, the longer house will as a rule give a better looking house for the reason that one gets the impression of a dominant sense of direction. Of course this does not mean that a square house is always bad. The house shown on page 29 is excellent, but of course in this particular case the impression of length is gained by the addition of the porch.

A group of small single houses placed at regular intervals along the street has something discouragingly monotonous about it. In many suburban communities where land is expensive, the houses have about twenty feet or so between them. These houses, often built on speculation, are usually of about the same size, and the impression they give altogether is of an overcrowded community.

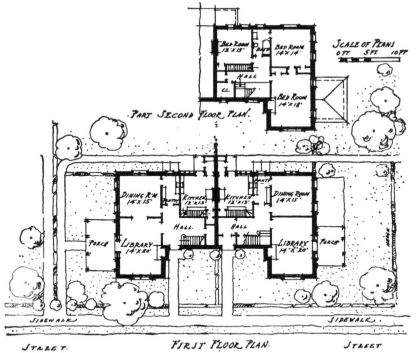

Floor plans of the twin house shown on page 133.

This house, located at St. Martins, Philadelphia, is a fine solution of the twin house problem. The plans are shown on page 132.   Edmund B. Gilchrist, Architect.

The space between the houses is too small to count as a real breathing space, and the houses are too far apart to look like a continuous building. Many architects are turning to the type of dwelling called the twin house as a solution of this problem, two houses being gathered into one building complete in itself. Such a plan is shown on page 132. Sometimes as many as five houses are planned in this way.

Under this system, it is easy to see that the space which would exist between separate houses goes to augment the space between the twin building and its next neighbor, and in this way we get a piece of land and an air space which is big enough not to look cramped. That is the first benefit gained from this type of house. The next is hardly less important. By joining two small houses into one, we are able to get a greater variety of expression for the elevations of the house, a long roof line. This is tremendously important. The charm of the low lying English cottages often consists in the long unbroken roof line.

A house may have either an "open" or "shut" plan. The Colonial house with its central entrance, its staircase in full view as one enters, and the living-rooms all opening from the hall and all visible to the visitor, is an example of an open plan. In a house planned like this, there is little or no sense of privacy.

The "shut" plan is one such as is shown on this page. When the visitor enters, he sees little except the room in which he finds himself. He does not penetrate at once into the privacy of the house. He is received, so to speak, in a waiting room.

These two types correspond to the types of humanity which we meet every day. Some people like the sense of privacy, and others don't care. As for me, I am sure I should always declare for the shut plan when

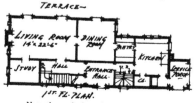

Note the seclusion of the living quarters.

133

it is possible to get it. This type of plan has an importance in its relation to the surroundings of the house, as has been touched on in the chapter on the entourage. It enables the house to turn its back to the street, and to reserve its better rooms for its garden.

In most English country houses of any pretense, a forecourt is always arranged for the reception of visitors and strangers. The house and its garden are screened by trees and bushes from this entrance court, so that the sense of privacy is not destroyed. If you are a guest or a privileged person, you are taken out into the garden.

Most American houses are so planned that the only privacy is on the second floor, and when an unwelcome visitor comes, every one is forced to flee to the security of his bedroom to escape detection.

With these general observations over, I am going to note some of the essential things which should be striven for with a view of convenience in your room arrangement. In order to have your house beautiful as well as convenient, you must resign yourself to make concessions on both sides, and it is necessary to look at what constitutes the essential practical conveniences. You should not be forced to sacrifice the appearance of your house to obtain these.

Economy of space is most important, since it has a direct relation to the cost of the house. Often houses are built with rooms that are never used. I know of a house in New York which has a small reception room to the left of the hall as you enter. The only person who has ever been known to go into it is the maid who dusts it. Everybody else rushes into the living-room which opens directly upon the hall. We all know the country house parlor which is entered even less frequently; which through the livelong year preserves its chilly respectability and is disturbed only at rare intervals on the occa-

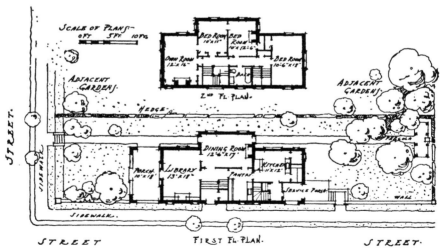

These plans, of which the elevations are shown on page 135, will repay careful study.

THE PLAN ARRANGEMENT

·STREET ELEVATION·

Edmund B. Gilchrist, Architect.

This house is so planned that it "turns its back to the street," thus giving its fine rooms the advantage of facing the garden. The garden elevation is shown below.

sion of a funeral or a wedding. That parlor is waste space.

Build your house to live in. Count on using *all* of it.

You can waste space by the bad planning which results in long second story hallways, in kitchens which are too big, and which require many steps to cross, in badly shaped rooms into which it is impossible to arrange ordinary furniture conveniently. All these mistakes of plan cost money, and they can all be avoided.

Nothing is more uncomfortable than a long narrow room. In a bedroom of this shape, one has always the feeling of sleeping in a hallway. In general, in a small house of from six to eight rooms, the living-room should not be less than 14 feet wide and at least 22 feet long; preferably more. The dining-room, unless it is to be used only as a breakfast room, should not be less than 11x12 feet if it is to be used by more than four people.

The kitchen is variable; it should be planned in reference to the size and needs of the house and particularly in relation to the question of servants. If the house is to require one servant, the kitchen can be made

·GARDEN ELEVATION·
135

as small as 9x10 feet, if it has adequate closets and ice space in addition.

For the bedroom, the closets are best arranged between rooms, so that the rooms shall be of good shape, always rectangular if possible, and without any closets or strange angular forms projecting themselves into the rooms.

A clear height of 8 feet 6 inches is usually adequate for small house rooms.

If you contemplate the employment of one or two maidservants, the house plan should be considered as having two distinct divisions:—the living and service quarters. In the latter are grouped the kitchen with its dependencies, such as the pantry, laundry, service porch, and servants' bedrooms. If the house is of two or more stories, the service quarters should, if possible, have an independent staircase.

Of an eminently practical nature are the matters of heating and plumbing. The installation of these two systems adds greatly to the cost of the house, and should be reckoned with from the beginning.

An attempt should be made to keep the plumbing fixtures in close proximity. You can easily see that if your house is planned so that your kitchen is on one side of the house, the laundry on another, and the bathroom on a third, your water supply pipes have to run a considerable distance to connect to various fixtures. If they are near together you save the expense of this piping.

This applies also to the heating system. If your heater is placed in a central position under the house, you will get better use out of it and you will not have to pay for long runs to connect distant parts of the house. This, of course, is Utopian. It is not always possible so to arrange your plumbing and heating, but it is worth the effort.

It is well to note here that when you begin to plan your house, you must keep in mind the uses to which your house is to be put. If it is to be a farm house, it must be planned as a farm house. If it is a suburban house, it must be so planned.

By this I mean, that if it is to be a farm house, it is well, for example, to have the side entrance into a vestibule lavatory, so that heavy boots and coats may be removed there. Also, if you have a growing family, you must plan your house so that it may be expanded; so that it can be added to without spoiling its beauty or its convenience. For this reason, it is well to keep your house as simple as you can in plan. A complicated house plan is always difficult to modify.

The front hall must be reduced to a minimum in a small house, so as to serve only for stair and coat room accommodations. The

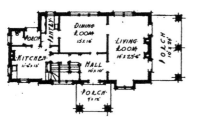 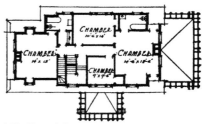

First and second floor plan of Mr. Dayton's house.

An excellent modern example of the Dutch gambrel roofed house is Mr. Dayton's house at Wynnewood, Pennsylvania.

De Armond, Ashmead & Bickley, Architects.

hall may even be omitted, and the front door opened into the living-room with the coat closet and the stairs on one side of the room. To insure protection against the weather on entering the house, the entrance can be under a covered porch. The living-room should face the south. It should be light, but you must beware of too many windows and doors.

A complete lay-out showing every piece of furniture accurately drawn to scale in its proper place should be made previous to building. Wall space is essential for the placing of furniture.

Light and room are necessities. A fireplace can hardly be called a luxury. It means many things to the room. It affords good ventilation; it is the best ornament a room can have, it is a place for a clock and candlesticks; it gives out warmth and good cheer; it gives a raison d'être for the hearth rug, the symbol of a home, it provides a place to hang the stockings on Christmas Eve, and finally it generously offers a place into which to throw all kinds of waste papers.

The dining-room should have an easterly exposure, as the only family meal at which it is possible in winter to have the sun is breakfast and this is also the time in the day in winter, spring and fall, when the warmth of sunlight is most welcome. In the dining-room it is a fine luxury to have a bay window if you can. The room should open from the hall or living-room, and should be directly accessible to the kitchen. It may be made a thoroughfare from the kitchen to the front door, although this is not an ideal arrangement. A fireplace here is of much less importance than it is in the living-room.

The kitchen should be a laboratory pure and simple, if the mistress is to use it alone. If it is to be used by a domestic it may be a combined laboratory and living-room. Direct access from the kitchen should be had to the cellar without the necessity of going out of doors. It is a bad thing to put the cellar stairs so that one has to reach them by going into the pantry. The plan at the top of this page shows the design of a kitchen arrangement which may serve as a basis for the discussion of what a kitchen ought to be.

It is a model which in actual experience would be modified in a hundred ways to suit the conditions of the particular problem. It shows:—

(a) Ice-box with door to permit filling from the outside. Mechanical refrigerators are better than the ordinary ice-box, but they are not yet made and sold at reasonable prices for small houses.

(b) Fireless cooker. This should be combined with the range, if the latter is a gas range.

(c) Range. It is preferable to use a gas or electric range, insulated for fireless cooking. An oil range is an alternative.

(d) Sink. A pantry sink set into the mixing shelf is a convenience.

(e) Cabinet. Whether "built in," or merely set against the wall, such a cabinet, supplemented by a cupboard under bread shelf, and pot-hooks and shelves over range and sink, provides place for utensils and supplies.

(f) Slide. A slide from the dining-room opening upon bread shelf for the passage of dishes is very convenient. This slide is shown dotted on the plan at the end of the shelf near the dining-room door.

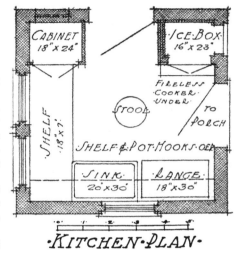

·KITCHEN·PLAN·

(g) Stool. From this stool everything in the laboratory can be reached.

The larger and more usual type of kitchen is commonly used also as a sitting-room for the "domestic." It should be laid out in principle like the laboratory kitchen. A good solution of the larger kitchen is to use the laboratory kitchen with an alcove or additional room to be used for a service dining- and sitting-room.

The cellar should extend under the whole house if possible, and should be adequately lighted. An exterior entrance to the cellar should be arranged. If the land slopes, the cellar can be lighted by windows on the side of the house which is the highest out of the ground. If the land is flat, it is far better to use areas, so that adequate light will be obtained without the necessity of raising the first floor level high above the ground. Many houses are so designed and the result is that the houses have a very stilted appearance. Page 118 shows such an example.

The piazza or covered porch, in regions where the southwest is the prevailing summer wind, should be on the northwest, or on the east of the house. It lends itself to a greater variety of uses if it is broad and short,—that is, if it has the shape and size of a room,—than if it is long and narrow. It is also much more easily decorated and much more distinctly a part of a private house. If it is built so that it can be screened in, it will afford still greater variety of use.

The bedrooms of the house should be like hospital wards, if one can use the word hospital without running the danger of suggesting unpleasant things. They should be clean, gay, simple and airy. In any bedroom much depends upon the closet. Size alone is only a part of the need. Closets should be designed with special fitness for the clothes to be accommodated with drawers, poles and presses. Wherever possible, outside ventilation for the closets should be secured but this does not mean that small, eccentric windows are permissible.

The sleeping balcony or sleeping porch is a valuable adjunct, but I believe it is no improvement on a good bedroom, if it is built with a solid rail and sash to fill the openings. These effectually hinder the free movement of air, which is the only virtue of out-of-door sleeping. An open balustrade, with screens of light canvas or duck above it permits of free passage of air and allows the sun and air to keep the floor and all its corners sweet

and dry at all times. The duck screen can be swung from the ceiling during a shower, and let down during a snow storm.

The bathroom nowadays takes care of itself. It is as much standardized as a telephone, with its white porcelain and white enamel. If possible, the tub should sit squarely on the floor, so that there will be no difficult cleaning. There should be a large mirror and a large medicine cabinet, not one of those silly shallow boxes that refuse to hold a fat bottle. There should be an ample supply of towel rods, and if a towel closet can be managed it will be a great convenience.

Discuss and amplify all these things with your architect, and you will probably get a very good house. The temptation to quote an architect who is still a friend of all his clients' is great. The architect is Mr. Harrie T. Lindeberg, and he disproves the adage that you can't build a proper house without making an enemy of your client. His theory of successful house planning is this:

"If you wish a successful house, give your architect a free hand, not into your pocketbook, but into your confidence and faith, believing he will work many times the harder, knowing that you trust his judgment and stand behind his decisions; and when all is said and done, and your house is built, and you are proud of being its owner, give now and then a little credit where it is due, and don't be guilty of that bromidic speech, 'We designed the house ourselves; the architect just drew it out for us!' "

THE HONEST HOUSE

Photograph by Coutant.   Parker Morse Hooper, Architect.
Dr. Abbott's house at Cornwall, New York, is an example of small house architecture at its best.

CHAPTER XVI

GOOD TASTE AND COMMON SENSE

BEFORE you begin considering the interior of your home, you must consider your own point of view. You must take stock of yourself, and discover just what you have to put into your house that will make it a home. *Things* won't do it.

A home is not so much a place as it is a state of mind. Lots of people who own houses haven't really homes, and, by the same token, lots of us who have a tiny apartment or even a mere hall bedroom have homes in the real sense of the word. We will take the homes and home feeling for granted. I assume that what we all want is to make our homes a little finer and cleaner and more beautiful.

By finer I mean more genuine.

By cleaner I mean freer from shams and imitations.

By beautiful—well, that is a word that holds its own meaning for each of us. There isn't any better word, if you apply it honestly.

Women who have a healthy interest in their surroundings, who realize that no real growth is possible in an unfriendly, jarring atmosphere, who see the intimate relation of environment and family life—these are the women who have fundamentally good taste. They need only an honest self-analysis to become real home-makers.

The woman who asks for help and admits that she doesn't know everything, can develop her sense of appreciation so that her life will be full of a genuine joy that she has never before realized. And this applies also to men. Men are interested in developing the interiors just as women are interested in the building of their homes. Somehow the greater interest in the practical problem belongs to the man, however, and the job of making the house decorative and comfortable is the woman's. And so one falls naturally into discussing certain subjects with men, and others with women. But every subject discussed in this book should be of equal interest to both.

Cheap and changing fashions have done much to deter American women from real appreciation of the principles of home making. Prosperity has come so easily, and there is such a fatal facility of imitating good things, that we have ever changing epidemics of fashions in house furnishing that are disastrous to the development of taste.

There are always new developments and improvements in certain house furnishings, as in everything else, but there is no such thing as the "latest wrinkle" in good taste. If your grandmother left you a kitchen chair that was made a hundred years ago from a good model, it is better than the "latest" chair of gilt legs and tawdry satin, or any chair constructed from a worthless model to meet the needs of women of no taste. But if she left you a chair that was ugly when it was new, age has n't made it beautiful.

It is the women who try to follow the fashions in house furnishings who have the dreadful, dishonest houses that flourish all over America. It is these women who have furniture of every style, of every wood, of every period, jumbled together in rooms equally bad.

The intelligent woman when she buys a chair demands that it shall be comfortable to sit upon, beautiful to look at, and simple and sturdy of construction. Even given these things, it must be suitable to her needs or it is not the chair for her. It must be in harmony with her other furnishings and in scale with her husband's means.

There are French chairs of damask and carved wood that are comfortable, beautiful and of exquisite workmanship, but they are not suitable to the needs of the woman who lives in a small house. Suitability is the first and most important law of good taste. If a thing is suitable it must necessarily be comfortable and beautiful and of sound construction.

Oh, the dishonest and pretentious spirit in which so many women furnish their homes!

And the pity of it is that they are proud of their shams, their imitations, their petty hypocrisies. They glory in being a little more magnificently gilded than their neighbors. The only excuse for them is that they are bewildered by a sea of things of no value. "Bewildered" is a nicer word than "stupid."

How many houses we all know that have not violent paintings and grotesque crayon "portraits" on the walls? Is your house innocent of them? None of these things are beautiful. You know that. Every one knows it. They are on our walls because they imitate the real things, because they are "done by hand!"

There are thousands of beautiful prints and engravings to be had for less money, and yet we are contented with imitations. A print is not an imitation. It is a mechanical copy, and it does n't pretend to be anything else. But a print gives us the picture the master painted, and a cheap imitation gives us merely an absurdity that is neither copy nor cartoon, that has neither beauty nor value.

We live in an age of just-as-good-as things. We hear daily of the high cost of living, of the shallowness of religion, of superficial education, of untrained daughters, of dissipated sons, of tired husbands, restless wives. Much of this discontent, I firmly believe, comes from the prosaic matter of badly chosen chairs and tables and wallpapers. A red wall-paper with fiendish scrolls gives a man mental indigestion just as surely as fried foods give him the other kind.

I believe that the houses of women who are "pizen neat," who have uncomfortable chairs placed just so, who have no logical center for the family gathering, no reading light, no books and magazines, no real touch of home—these houses will result in disap-

GOOD TASTE AND COMMON SENSE

Edmund B. Gilchrist, Architect.

Could anything be more suggestive of cool tranquillity than this charming picture of the library in Mr. W. W. Gilchrist's house at St. Martins, Philadelphia? The fireplace with its front of artificial stone, framed by an adequate molding, does not need the customary mantel-shelf. Note the entire absence of unnecessary ornament.

pointing children. Who could blame the youngsters for preferring other people's houses?

Did you ever know a real, shabby home room, with plenty of books and couches and big chairs and flowers in the window, swarming with happy children? Did n't you get a thrill of the real spirit of home from it? If you have a real home room, the children of your neighbors will get happiness from it, as surely as your own.

If we could all follow William Morris's advice, and have nothing in our houses that we did not know to be useful, and believe to be beautiful, how clean and genuine our children would be!

Lose your temper in a stately, well-ordered room, and you will be shamed by the very dignity of your surroundings. Go into a sunshiny family room when you are despondent, and your mood will change; it can not resist sunshine and good cheer.

You have n't time for petty jealousies if you are surrounded by simple furnishings and quiet colors and well-used books and excellent pictures. The friendly spirit of the room gives you new poise, and petty things are forgotten.

And—you could n't think great thoughts in a dirty, cluttery room, for if the great thoughts were there, you would be busy making decent surroundings for yourself.

It is true that in the last generation we have gone far on the road to good taste, but think how far we had retrograded! Think how beautiful were the simple houses of our great-grandparents,—beautiful because of their enforced simplicity, perhaps, but beautiful just the same. They had the things they required, and nothing more.

Thirty years ago women were so far from this simplicity that they hung gilded shovels and clothes-pins in their parlors. The sitting-room, the living-room, and the drawing-room were too "old-fashioned" for this gilded period. "Parlor" was the word.

The accomplished ladies of the period filled their parlors with "tidies." They tied ribbons on chair backs, around vases, and I have heard of a lady who tied ribbon around the newel-post of her staircase! They painted snow scenes on the tin tops of lard-cans, and sunflowers on empty wine-jugs, and cattails inside honest mixing bowls. It is hard to conceive of the colossal stupidity which made this epidemic possible, and yet we have modern epidemics of china-painting and burnt wood and crude stenciling that are almost as bad. I suppose we always shall have them until we open our eyes and use them.

The best way to open our eyes to the essential differences of good and bad taste is to hold hard to our sense of humor, and to let sentiment go. The excuse of sentiment covers much that is banal and meaningless.

More than any other one thing, it retards the growth of good taste.

Last winter a number of us who were interested in the advancement of the decorative arts arranged an exhibition of bad taste. We were inspired by coming upon a large statue of the Venus of Milo with a clock in her stomach. The Venus reminded us of all the atrocities in bad taste we had observed, and we decided an arrangement of very bad objects would be much more impressive than all the good things that ever were.

We did not purpose to laugh at our grandmothers, or ourselves: we planned to present a retrospective view of the art of home decoration from which instruction and amusement might be gained by the sensible visitor. We showed the things that had gone before rather than the things of to-day because we wished to amuse our friends. There is nothing amusing in our modern cut glass, our gaudy lamps, our disgusting ornamentation of things that were bad to begin with, but there is always amusement in bad things that happened a long while ago. A lamp made to-day of stag antlers, a quart of glass beads, and a few yards of puffings of silk saddens us. A lamp made many years ago of a milk jar covered with putty and encrusted with a hundred odds and ends —nails, ear rings, sea shells, buttons—affords us unholy mirth. So we showed the things of many years ago, depending on the imaginations of our visitors to point the parallel.

The exhibition was approved by over a thousand visitors. Its lessons went home. But there were disgruntled dozens who called the wrath of their pet newspapers down upon us because we "violated sacred sentiment." They were entirely unable to

GOOD TASTE AND COMMON SENSE

Harrie T. Lindeberg, Architect.

This bedroom in the Boardman Robinson house at Forest Hills, Long Island, owes much of its charm to the substantial old furniture. A gay, English chintz covers the four-post bed. The French windows lead to the sleeping porch.

distinguish between filial sentiment and esthetic appreciation, and they found themselves in the ridiculous position of defending bad taste.

Good taste comes slowly, but it is the final standard by which our homes must be judged.

When you study other people's houses and analyze your own, consider always your own needs.

Ask yourself: "What sort of home is suitable to me, to my husband, to my children? What furnishings do I actually require in my house—not my neighbor's house, but my own house? What things have I

that will grow more beautiful the longer I live with them? What things have I that are worth leaving to my children?"

And, having worthy things, what sort of house have you to place them in? Are its walls pleasant in color? Are they real backgrounds for the life that must be lived in· your rooms?

Are your floors made to walk on, or are they piled with rugs upon rugs?

Are your windows fulfilling their object of giving light and air, or are they draped and redraped with dusty curtains of no utilitarian or artistic value?

145

Is your woodwork grained to imitate some wood, or is it real wood, waxed to a soft glow? And if it is n't real, why have n't you given it a coat of honest white paint?

Are your fireplaces real, or shams?

Is your piano a piano, or is it a catch-all for fringed velvet and motley bric-a-brac?

Happy the woman who has a few good things to build upon, for a good thing is always good—you may be sure of that. It may not be always suitable. For instance, a spinning-wheel that was both beautiful and useful a hundred years ago is not at home in a city apartment nowadays, but it is the usefulness that has passed. The beauty lives always.

The training of the eye is a long process, but most amusing! Its lessons are never tedious, though they are sometimes very shocking, but you live through it all and watch your appreciation grow as though it were a wonderful plant. You cannot see actual growth, but you discover by looking back from day to day and from year to year that there has been growth. You find yourself in a room that yesterday seemed unobjectionable, and to-day you resent its ugliness. You look at a vase that you once thought beautiful, and realize that it is impossible. When you know that the room is ugly and the vase is impossible ask yourself why it once appealed to you, why it now offends you, and if you can answer you have traveled far toward good taste.

An old hooded doorway at Germantown, Pennsylvania. Note the delicacy of the moldings.

CHAPTER XVII

THE SHELL OF THE HOUSE

THE average woman's idea of beautifying her home is to buy new things for it. She covets a rug like Mrs. Brown's, a cut-glass punch-bowl like Mrs. Jones' and brand-new furniture like Mrs. Robinson's. She thinks if she could only add new household gods her home would be a very fine place. She does not concern herself with the possible beauty of the house itself. It does not occur to her to work at fundamentals first, to begin at the shell of her house and work inward.

By the shell of the house I mean the walls, floors, ceilings, woodwork, doors, windows, mantels, cupboards, and in fact all the architectural details that make or mar the interior of a house. The placing of a picture-rail is of more importance than any amount of new furniture, and a too elaborate mantel is worse than any detached possession.

There is one period in house-building when your house is potentially as beautiful as you care to make it: when the shell of it is ready for the workmen who will smooth its rough edges and make a home of

it. I love to visit a house in the rough, to wade through sand-piles and climb over heaps of timber, to explore and speculate on this promising home in the making. There is a great fascination in the rough frame of so much possible beauty and happiness. We are free to wander through it, to anticipate closets here and bookshelves there, to hang its skeleton walls with the pictures that mean beauty to us, to fill its fireplaces with log fires, to cover its floors with magic rugs, to people it with congenial friends—in short, to make believe a home for ourselves.

How many houses I have enjoyed in the rough, only to shudder over them when they were finished and filled with unworthy things! I have a strong sympathy for the architect who plans beautiful interiors for people of no appreciation. It must be hard to plan an honest house for linen-and-gingham people and then have them try to live silk-and-plush lives.

Many of you have houses already, probably, and do not wish to make structural changes. You may not be able to have new

Samuel Howe, Architect.

During the past decade the bungalows have become popular with home-builders. Most of them, however, have little value from an architectural point of view; they are too frequently overornamented and awkward in design. This bungalow of Mr. Howe's has the merit of unpretentiousness. Its plan, somewhat modified, is given at the bottom of this page.

doors and windows and mantels, but you can improve those you have. You can determine the finish of your walls and ceilings. You can make your floors good or bad. You can at least empty your rooms, one at a time, of furniture, and go to the root of your troubles. When you have made the best of the shell of the room you'll be so pleased with the restfulness of space that you will be tucking your excess furniture away in the attic, instead of coveting new things.

Of course, if you are planning to build a

THE SHELL OF THE HOUSE

new house, anything is possible for you. It does n't matter how little you have to spend: "Good taste builds a house for peasants to live in." It is n't the lack of money that makes so many houses commonplace, it is the lack of forethought. Few of us will build more than one house in a lifetime, therefore we should build it wisely. I approve of building your house with words and pencil and paper. It does n't matter if you are n't going to build for five years, or ten, you can read books on architecture and decoration, you can fill note-books with observations of the mistakes and successes of your friends, you can make scrap-books of house plans and photographs and such, and when your house is at last realized it will be well worth while.

As with the exterior, so the interior of your house will be a success or not depending largely on whether the detail, architectural and other, is good. The three rooms which ordinarily have the most detail in them are the hall, the living room, and the dining room. In these rooms it is not uncommon to have fireplaces, wainscoting, cornices, beamed ceilings, and built-in furniture in addition to the door and window trim which is common throughout the house. Now all these elements are architectural, and they need as much consideration as the details on the outside of your house.

A room consists broadly of three elements, the floor, walls, and the ceiling. Of these the walls of course present the greatest opportunity for bad design and bad treatment. In the treatment of the room, to give an impression of lightness, keep the tone of your floor darker than your wall, and your walls darker than the ceiling. The theory of this treatment of the interior finds its parallel in an out-of-doors landscape. If you look first at the ground and then raise your eyes slowly, you will see that the ground and the immediate foreground with its bushes and grass has a stronger value than the distant fields and hills, and the value of these fields and hills is stronger than the value of the sky at the horizon, and the value of the sky at the horizon is stronger that that of the sky higher up. This is why the arrangement of an oak floor covered with dark blue or green oriental rugs, with the walls papered or tinted in some tone of light gray or light yellow and the ceiling

Drawn by Charles S. Chapman

There is fine dignity in the uncluttered spaces of this room in the Casa Blanca, San Angel, Mexico.

THE HONEST HOUSE

Photograph by Lillian Baynes Griffin.
This house, on the north shore of Long Island Sound, fits well into its surroundings.

treated with the plain white or the faintest tinge of color, gives an impression of gayness and space.

If you wish to have an interior which is gloomy, keep the ceiling darker than the walls, and the walls darker than the floor.

Not so long ago people generally refused to admit the presence of floors in their houses. They concealed them with carefully fitted velvet carpets, thick of pile and gaudy of coloring. They pretended to like walking on beds of cabbage roses and bows of ribbons. They even added insult to injury by piling rugs upon carpets, and insulted the hearth by flinging a rug representing a life-size collie dog, done in red and green and brown, before it. They did n't question the wisdom of having dogs and sheep and flowers beneath their feet—but accepted them as being finer than plain boards, because their neighbors accepted them.

Then came the wave of interest in sanitation, in hygiene, and the dreadful carpets gave way to expensive parquetry floors. The floors probably had intricate patterns of different colored blocks of wood. I have seen may parquetry floors that were quite as bad as flowered carpets. The parquetry man has a devilish ingenuity, as any one who will take the trouble to enter his shop can see. He can execute squirrels cracking nuts, palm-leaf fans, American flags, lilies-of-the-valley, and lions in the jungle, all in many colored woods. But do you want picture-puzzle floors? I don't think so. Good honest boards, well polished, with just enough rugs to give warmth and softness, are good enough for any house.

I am not condemning parquetry floors. Those made of blocks of wood of uniform size and of not too abrupt a gradation in color are very good. The floor to be avoided is the conspicuous floor, the floor that ceases to be a background and jumps up to meet you when you enter the room. A floor of bricks or tiles is beautiful, because we ex-

150

pect bricks and tiles to come in small squares and oblongs. But we expect lumber in long pieces, and a floor composed of boards that have been carefully cut apart and then put together again reminds us of the mere man who pondered over the eyelet embroidery that occupied his wife: What could be the wisdom of punching holes in cloth just to sew them up again?

If you have an old house with floors made of wide boards, paint them. Hardwood floors are preferable to painted floors, but painted boards are infinitely better than carpets. One of the best houses I know is a New England farmhouse now used as a summer home by people who appreciate its good points. It was necessary to lay new floors in the bedrooms, but the downstairs rooms were floored with eighteen-inch boards, entirely too fine to be discarded. The old house is square, four rooms to a floor, each room wainscoted with plain white boards on three walls and paneled to the ceiling on the fireplace wall. The woodwork is all white, the walls painted a soft robin's-egg blue, and the wide boards of the floor are painted a bright leaf-green. This treatment, with simple New England furniture, rag rugs, Swiss curtains, open fireplaces with well used brasses, and huge jugs of wild flowers, is somehow exactly right. You feel that the green boards are responsible for the rightness of it.

It might be safely said that all New England ceilings are too low, and all Southern ceilings too high. The cause is obvious: the New England house was built to conserve warmth in winter, and the Southern house was built for summer comfort. Architectural effects were n't often considered in either; perhaps that is why they are so good, despite their ceilings. Carpenters were content to be carpenters in those days, and they built for utility and comfort. They had n't begun to pretend to be architects.

The matter of the height of your ceiling depends to a certain extent on the amount of window space you have. It was the fashion formerly to make the story heights considerable. In the period of 1880 a room height of eleven feet was not unusual, whereas now in modest country work a room height from eight to nine feet, except for a very large room, say over sixteen feet by twenty-five feet, is generally recognized as adequate. One great advantage of the lower room is that it is much easier to decorate. If you use a beamed ceiling, count your ceiling height from the bottom of the apparent beams, and do not make your beams project much from the ceiling. Beams four inches deep and five inches wide spaced about two feet on center is an average good arrangement for a span of fifteen feet.

The treatment of a low-ceiled room is simple: the wall color should meet the ceiling, with a narrow molding as dividing line.

There are many ways of lowering a too-high ceiling. The simplest method is to drop the picture-rail four or five feet, and treat the wall-space above the rail as a part of the ceiling. Then you will not be conscious of where frieze-space stops and ceiling begins. The eye will travel no higher than the picture rail.

The other method is to have a simple wainscoting three or four feet deep, painted or stained to match the rest of the woodwork, and a smaller space between picture-rail and ceiling. Wainscotings are very good in any high-ceilinged rooms that have cream or white woodwork, but a wainscoting of dark

Drawn by Charles S. Chapman

Here brown woodwork is used with brown beamed ceiling and cream washed walls. Note the generous width of the settles, the "built-in" cupboard, and the English treatment of the fireplace.

wood is too formal a finish for any room, except halls and libraries, or living-rooms with dark tinted walls.

The treatment of your ceiling should be determined by the finish of your walls and woodwork. Plain whitewashed ceilings are always safe, but a cream wash is better than dead white, just as cream paint is better for woodwork than white. Pure white is the most difficult of colors for the amateur decorator. It should be used sparingly.

If you are fortunate enough to have a beamed ceiling, the beams should be scraped to the grain and waxed. I have seen brown oak beams in a room finished in white wood-work, and the effect was excellent, but usually it is better to have beams and woodwork of the same wood and finish. If you have brown oak woodwork and beams, the plastered space above the picture-rail and the spaces between the beams may be cream or yellow or gray or tan. If your beamed room has mahogany doors and furniture and white woodwork, paint beams and ceiling white.

The next stumbling block is the window and door trim. Here is where the carpenter designed house again betrays itself; because in it the trim is almost sure to be too heavy and the moldings too coarse. There is no need of using a "stock" molding, which is

152

almost invariably ugly. One of the cheapest and best looking window and door trims is shown below (A). It is not only inexpensive, but is easy to put in position. The double hung window as it is generally built requires a width of trim of at least five inches to cover the plaster. It can be designed so that it will be narrower, and as a rule the narrower it is made, the better it looks.

If your trim is of this type, the flat part of the trim may be kept narrow by using a back-molding as shown (BB), and thus gain the necessary width.

There is a saying that " interior detail cannot be made too small in scale" and while it is an exaggeration, there is much truth in it. Keep your trim as small as you can, and keep it simple, if you wish to get an attractive and restrained effect.

If the trim is painted white it can afford to be molded, and the moldings can be finer in scale, than if it is stained. With stained woodwork the shadows of the molding do not stand out clearly, whereas with white painted woodwork the trim may be so flat that it may seem bald and uninteresting.

If you wish to stain your trim, go warily. Dark woodwork is an absolutely compelling precedent: you have to follow its demands. Chestnut, or oak, or redwood, or whatever wood you please may be used with excellent results if you plan every stick of your furniture to harmonize with it. Otherwise, there is great danger of clashing effects.

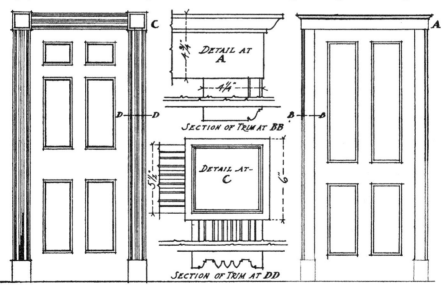

Both these types of door trim avoid the necessity of mitered corners. The examle at the left is taken from an old house on Long Island. Its charm rests on the excellence of its molded section. It is better, however, in small houses to employ as narrow a trim as possible; 5½" is a maximum width; 4" to 4½" is far better. For general purposes for doors and windows the trim shown at the right is excellent; easy to construct and effective in its simplicity. Note the paneling of the doors.

If you have been tempted by some arch fiend of a "painter and decorator" (generally a near-American who does n't speak English and who believes that a cut-out border of pink roses or purple grapes is the last word in wall decoration) to stain all your woodwork to imitate mahogany, for instance, I pity you. You have set the mark of indifference upon yourself. A birch chair may be stained to imitate mahogany, and it may remain unobtrusive. But the moment mahogany woodwork asserts itself we "look it in the grain." It must be real. There is the chance of changing the chair, you see. The woodwork is a fundamental, and should be what it seems.

This does not mean that your woodwork will lose in character if you paint it. Paint is paint—if it is applied properly. It may be streaked and wiggled to imitate graining and knot holes, and it becomes a nameless thing that has no excuse for being. We are accustomed to think of painted woodwork as being white, cream, or French gray, but given proper consideration there are many other colors that may be applied to the trim of a room. Yellow, putty-color, a dull green-blue, a gray green or a yellow green, —all these colors may be applied to woodwork if the color of the room is worked out skilfully.

I know a kitchen in an old Long Island farmhouse that has dark blue woodwork and pale gray plaster walls. The dark blue doors are relieved by gray trees painted upon them. The room is very successful. There is a room in another house where the walls and woodwork are painted bright yellow, and the curtains are of a blue that has a tinge of green in it. Another has the woodwork painted cream, with an orange line outlining door panels and moldings. A little cottage has all its walls washed with dull green and all its woodwork painted a very much darker shade of the same color. All these rooms were planned by people who understand color, and therefore were able to do as they pleased.

This freedom that comes with sound taste applies also to staining woodwork: gray, green, and even violet may be rubbed lightly into raw wood by a man who knows what he is doing. If you are n't sure of yourself, stick to neutral colored paints and stains. Avoid imitation mahogany *always*, but use brown or gray stains on almost any wood you please. If you have real oak or chestnut trim, by all means give it the effect of oak or chestnut, if you don't care for painted trim.

Granted that you are willing to choose all your furniture and rugs and wall-papers to go with oak or chestnut woodwork, avoid varnishes if you would keep your self-respect. Almost any wood may be stained lightly and waxed, and it will be good in effect, but there never was a wood that would stand a thick coat of varnish. Polish it as much as you please, stain it judiciously to heighten the shadows of the grain, but don't varnish it.

There is a deplorable fashion in the South and West that has sprung from the vogue of yellow-pine woodwork. This is to make the floors, ceilings, wainscoting and woodwork of a room of yellow-pine boards, oiled or varnished to a slippery degree, and to plaster the walls a ghastly white. The floors will take on a good color with age and use, but the shiny ceiling, eternally threatening, is unpardonable. Yellow pine may be made very beautiful by rubbing in a tan or gray or brown stain, but in the natural finish

An excellent adaptation of the English type of small houses. The plans, shown below, are carefully thought out.

Howard Greenley, Architect.

it has the color of a bar of laundry soap. No matter how good your furniture may be, yellow pine kills it.

The only thing to do with such a room is to paint every bit of the wood, except the floor, white or cream. If the varnish were not so thick you might stain the woodwork and paint the ceiling white or cream, but whatever you do, paint the ceiling! It will' no longer hang like a pall over your room. And do something to those ghastly white walls! If you don't like wall-papers or colored walls, if you are waiting for your house to settle, paint the walls a soft cream or tan or gray. White walls are as mistaken as oiled pine ceilings: all physicians and ocu-

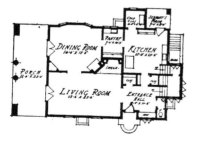

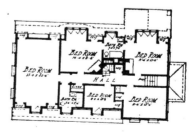

lists deplore the distressing effects of the white glare on the nerves. There is no reason in the world why white should be considered cleaner for walls than cream or tan or yellow.

There is another mistaken ceiling treatment that has been brought about by catalogues of wall-papers probably, and this is to paper ceilings with moiré papers, or papers sparkling with stars. Moiré suggests a watered surface, and why should we wish our ceilings to remind us of the rippling of waves? As for the stars—go outside for them. Forego the indulgence of a papered ceiling, and buy a better paper for your walls.

These are the general first considerations of the shell of the house—floors, ceilings, and woodwork. The treatment of walls will be discussed in another chapter.

There is another subject which really should be considered while the house is in the shell, and that is the matter of built-in furniture. It does n't matter whether your house is still in embryo; whether you are making over an old house planned and built by some one else, you can make it very much more your own by building certain things. You may have lived in your house for years, and still find there are advantages in built-in furniture that you cannot afford to disregard.

To be good at all, it must be very, *very* good. Otherwise, it is n't furniture. Granting that it is well designed, well constructed, and a logical part of the room, its case may be summed up pretty much as follows:

It is more interesting than "detached" furniture because it has a flavor of the designer's personality, a suggestion of judicious planning.

It is more dignified, because it has been planned for permanency.

It is more decorative, because it has been considered as a part of a whole, and therefore has an architectural relation to the room.

It is more reposeful, because it keeps its place as a part of the wall.

It is more durable, because it cannot be mauled about by the careless.

It is more economical because it may be constructed at a nominal cost of labor and material, and, once finished, it invites no further outlay.

Built-in furniture is very good in a small room, because it takes and keeps its place as a part of the wall, and increases the floor space. It is advantageous in a room of great size, because it then becomes of architectural importance, and may be of great decorative value in mass and color if its conception is in scale with the architect's conception of the room as a whole.

Built-in furniture, on the other hand, is for the permanent home, not for the transitory one. If you are n't satisfied with the house you live in, you 'd better buy things you can move.

It must be *well* built, because you cannot change it as you would an unsatisfactory chair or table.

It must be logically placed, because there is no latitude of change in a room that has been so furnished, and what normal woman does n't love to move furniture about? So it will be best to build in only the things that belong inevitably where you place them.

It has a dignity which must be respected; it will not stand being "prettified." Give it no laces and ribbons, or you 'll destroy its reason for being. Its restraint and formality must be preserved. The ideal built-in

Drawn by C. S. Chapman

This fireplace is in a remodeled barn near Brookhaven, Long Island. The treatment of the useful little cupboards is ingenious and decorative.

furniture represents great simplicity and perfect craftsmanship.

For so many years we women were slaves to bulky things! We did n't think for ourselves. Our classic houses had too much of geometrical exactness to permit closets, or window-seats, or open book-shelves, and we meekly endured the colossal furniture that was thrust upon us. Some of us still endure —more 's the pity! There are still incredible houses where ponderous wardrobes serve instead of closets, and heavy bookcases tower to the ceiling, with dim glass doors effectually concealing the books.

Have n't you seen those beautiful old secretaries with diamond-paned doors, and on the broad projecting shelf the collection of family bric-a-brac which had to be removed piece by piece before you could open the door and get a book? Such bookcases were not very encouraging to the children's love of reading. Surely there could be nothing more sensible than open bookshelves, with the friendly books spread out invitingly and the mosaic of their bindings adding to the decoration of the room. And yet I know many people who protest at open book-shelves.

The smaller our house, the more necessary it becomes to consider its possibilities. We must not forget that the fireplace with its surmounting mantel, the windows with their broad sills, the closets and cupboards, are all architectural furniture, and must be studied in relation to the detached objects to be brought into the room, as well as in relation to the window-seats, the settles, the open book-shelves, that will become a part of the room. A closet with well placed shelves and glass doors becomes as definite and useful a part of the furnishings of the dining-room as the chairs and table. The chimney-piece invites book-shelves in the recess flanking it, and the book-shelves invite settles, and so an ordinary corner becomes a place for foregathering The turn of the stair invites another settle, with a woodbox beneath its seat. A group of windows invites a long window-seat, with a latticed paneling that conceals the necessary, but hideous, radiators. The kitchen, of course, is practically made up of built-in furniture. It needs no argument.

Every angle of the house should be given the furniture it invites, and convention should be subordinated to ingenuity. When the house is finished it will be pleasantly furnished: only tables and chairs will be immediately necessary. You can wait comfortably for the things you really want. There will be no temptation to rush in and buy recklessly, and in the fullness of time you will be able to furnish your home with "finds" that will become real household gods.

Kilham and Hopkins, Architects.
Here advantage has been taken of the steep slope of the hillside in order to give an interesting and unusual appearance to the house.

CHAPTER XVIII

A PLEA FOR THE HEARTH

BEFORE we go further into the treatment of walls and windows, of woodwork and built-in furniture, I want to talk about the most important feature of the shell of the house: The Hearth.

I like to think that all houses, no matter how dreary they may be at times, become homes once a year, at Christmas. If happiness does n't fill your house at Christmas there is something radically wrong with the house or the people in it. I wonder if the fault is with the house? I wonder if it is built around a hearth?

There was a time when the hearth was to the house what the heart is to the body; when the hanging of the crane was the symbol of the birth of a home; when fire-glow was the evening light; when the spinning wheel whirred here, and the meals were prepared here, and the hooded cradle was snug in the shadows of the settle; when family traditions and folk songs and fairy tales and prayers were handed down from one generation to another; when the problems of the family and the nation were discussed here; when the passing traveler was welcomed for the sake of hospitality, and for the sake of news of the world outside. The hearth was the foundation. The home was an elastic place built around it.

The hearth stood for something more than mere physical comfort then. It stood preeminently for family loyalty, and we must be skilful indeed to give our children this saving quality in the mechanical shoe boxes that jerry-builders thrust upon us and call "homes."

Certainly none of us wishes to revive the primitive customs of our ancestors. We are vastly better off materially; we understand hygiene and sanitation and many things our forebears had no time to contemplate. We read by well-shaded lights and save our eyes. We buy our cloth ready spun and woven, and have no regret for spinning-wheel days. We are done with the drudgery of the crane and its ungainly pots, and we no longer require the services of the warming pan—we treasure it for decorative purposes! Our houses are as warm as toast, Aladdin-warm,

THE HONEST HOUSE

Edmund B. Gilchrist, Architect.

This shows the advantages of a well-arranged foreground. The house is Mr. W. W. Gilchrist's at St. Martins, Philadelphia.

and we have no material need of the old-time hearth.

But—there is another side to the picture. Are the fairy stories in gaily covered bindings as wonderful as were those we heard from our mother's lips when we were children? Do the illustrations compare with the marvelous pictures we saw in the flames? Can the modern wedding trip be as soul-satisfying as was the ceremony of the hanging of the crane? Are the newspapers more interesting than were the travelers from the outside world? Are grandfather's Memoirs, bound in tooled leather, worth as much to our children as the family traditions those other grandfathers passed on to the crackle of the logs and the flare of the flames? Have we any such logical home center, where we may meet and talk, or listen, with the feeling of home and family strong within us?

Think it over: when you were a child, did n't most of the things that really mattered have the hearth as background? I am sorry for our modern children, with their orderly lives and their rigid routine and nothing to touch the spark to their imaginations. Poor dears! What chance have they in our smug, shiny little houses that are so empty of tradition? Material things have improved amazingly, but if we have lost a jot of the strong feeling for family that should be ours, all our gain is as nothing, for the happiness of the whole world depends upon the conservation of family life.

Two of my friends, young married people, recently built a house in a suburb of New

York. They had lived for years in apartments, and were quite happy until the children came, and then, Mary said, she had to have a real home with a Hearth. She couldn't tell her children fairy stories beside a steam radiator, and, more important still, she wanted them to say their little prayers at her knee before an open fire.

So the house was built and became a home, because thoughtful people made it. The home room was planned to last forever and ever, the walls paneled with brown oak, with many built-in bookcases as a logical part of the paneling. Many windows flooded the room with sunshine, and the furniture was comfortable and simple. The whole room led up to a great chimney-piece, with an open fireplace of red brick. At right angles to the chimney-piece was a huge settle, roomy enough for comfort. The climax was the portrait enclosed in the paneling above the mantel-shelf, a charming old gentleman with white hair and ruddy cheeks and smiling lips.

Mary confessed to me that she bought him! She said she didn't feel that a home was a real home without a grandfather or a

This mantel is in the dining-room of Mr. W. W. Gilchrist's house at St. Martins, Philadelphia. Note the air of simplicity given by the unframed painting.
Edmund B. Gilchrist, Architect.

great-aunt or some nice old person who could teach the children the things that only old people can teach. She was the young daughter of a younger daughter, and so the family portraits had gone to others, and when she needed an ancestor she calmly went forth and bought him. She calls him the General, and Sir, and all sorts of lovable names, and the children call him Uncle Jim. They are in the secret and quite approve of him, and he—well, Mary declares that he positively twinkles with joy at his adopted family.

"He stands for dignity, and Sunday-quiet, and time-to-live," says Mary; "and just let me tell you that we mothers of this mechanical age have to give our children a feeling for these things. My home is a home, thanks to our love for it, and the Hearth, and Uncle Jim. We have open fires on cool evenings the year 'round, and on winter Sundays, and on all our birthdays and high days. I have n't a piano yet, because I can't afford that and logs too, but at this stage of the game open fires mean more to children than music. We have story-tellings and songs and beautiful times before the fire. The children hear all the legends and stories we heard when we were children, and they can hang up their own stockings before a real chimney at Christmas, which is every child's divine right.

"I could sing for joy at the development of their imaginations, for they tell me amazing stories of things they see in the flames. Can you imagine a child telling his mother a story out of his own insides, as Billy says, before a radiator? I can't! I tell you there is nothing that can take the place of the Hearth."

Now Mary is what I call a real home-maker. She feels the Spirit back of the Thing.

I suppose that to the mothers who have real homes this chapter seems unnecessarily strong. But I have seen so many false mantels, and filled-in fireplaces and hearthless houses lately that I am alarmed at the trend of it all. I appreciate the high cost of living and the formidable cost of coal and wood, but we can always find a way to enjoy the things we very much desire. The very poor have no hearths, perhaps, but they can make the kitchen stove a substitute, and find in it something our expensive "false mantels" can not give; something to gather around. No one ever had a desire to pull his chair up to a false mantel or a radiator.

A living-room without a fireplace is unsatisfying, but it is infinitely better than a room that is dominated by a false mantel, of the kind so often seen in apartment-houses, and indeed in thousands of private houses. A false mantel is a dreadful imitation of an honored tradition. It is a mere excrescence, with no grate behind the elaborate "bronze" fire-front, no flue, no excuse for being. The jerry-builder knows that traditions die hard, and this is his way of giving you a hearth.

You can forgive people who tolerate one of these mantels in an apartment, because you know that often the landlord admires the thing and refuses to allow its removal. But how can any man tolerate such a sham in his own house? Somehow, one feels that a man will be honest in his own house, even if he does blink at shams in other people's houses.

Contrast these sham mantels with the big homelike chimney-pieces on pages 152 and 157. Does n't the one with the settle sug-

In this remodeled Colonial house the huge fireplace has been preserved intact.   Note the flagstone floor.

gest a good book and a basket of apples and a long winter evening? Does n't the other one—the more informal brick one, with its useful little cupboards—suggest real warmth and hospitality?

Granted that fuel is a luxury; could n't you provide an open fire for your family on gala occasions? How did we ever dare eliminate the hearth from our homes, I wonder? I dare say the day will come when some one will invent a system of illumination that will make sunshine unfashionable, and a system of ventilation that will result in windowless houses, to those who lose all the spirit of home-making.

And yet I think there will always be homes where the hearth will be the honored center of things. Even in New York, where the cost of living is felt most keenly, and home-making is most difficult, I know many people who put up with the inconveniences of old-fashioned apartments that they may have fires in open grates. Old Father Knickerbocker provides wood for his children at a small consideration—in his municipal woodyards. Surely, then there is no part of the country where fuel is an impossible luxury.

The French have a thrifty custom that is very pleasant for people who have a little fireplace and no fuel for it. They save all the waste paper and dried leaves and flowers, and every evening make it into a "fagot." The fagot is made by emptying the contents of the waste-baskets upon several thicknesses of newspaper, rolling up the paper until it becomes a "log," and twisting the ends tightly. Then the fagot is wrapped with a cord, placed in the fireplace, and a light is touched to each end. In a moment there is a wonderful fire.

Try it, and you will soon become a connoisseur in fagots, and discover that orange-peel makes a wondrous blue flame, and that laurel leaves crackle delightfully and that for special occasions a few chunks of old rotting wood will give a flare worthy of a Fourth-o'-July fireworks-maker.

What can we bring into our homes that will give the beauty and cheer of an open fire? Music and books and good appetite and sunshine and sound sleep and clear water —all these are essential luxuries in our homes, but the supreme luxury is the open fire on the hearth.

So I plead for one real fireplace, as big or little as you please, and an occasional fire in it. It will be worth any sacrifice you may have to make for it. Have all the radiators you need, but have also this one hearth, where you can gather your children around you and teach them the things the hearth has stood for for hundreds of years: a place where Christmas is Christmas, where stockings can hang, and where, in the long years to follow, the children may come in their day-dreams, and bless the memory of the place you made home.

Harrie T. Lindeberg, Architect.

The Boardman Robinson house at Forest Hills, Long Island, is unusually successful in its suggestion of old world picturesqueness. Note the unbroken roof surfaces, the plain walls and the ample chimneys.

CHAPTER XIX

DETAILS OF INTERIOR DESIGN

JUST as windows, doorways, porches and chimneys determine the appearance of the exterior, so do the chimneypieces and their mantels, the staircases, doors, and the lesser details such as hardware and lighting fixtures add to or detract from the attractiveness of the interior of your house.

We have considered some of the architectural details of the interior, such as the built-in conveniences that are a part of the shell of the house, but there are so many things still to be said that it seems hopeless to do more than count them off on our fingers, and leave their real consideration to you.

The design of the staircase is almost always a stumbling block. If the staircase is in evidence at all, it is the most important thing in sight. If you don't wish it to dominate your hall, or living-room, you can keep it out of sight by having it go straight up between two walls. Indeed, in a small house where there is to be only one stairway, this is the ideal arrangement. It makes for privacy, obviates draughts, and simplifies to a certain extent the heating of the halls into which it opens. Given plenty of light and headroom, an enclosed staircase is most desirable.

Of course, there will always be houses in which the treatment of the staircase will follow the traditions: Colonial houses with their wide, long halls, would seem queer without their long stairways of white spindles and mahogany handrails. Certain houses of the English type will always invite open stairways with interesting screenwork of oak taking the place of spindles.

Study the staircases of the good houses about you. Study their columns and posts in the same spirit in which you examine out-of-door columns and railings. The same principles apply to both. It would be possible to go into great detail, but the main thing to remember is that the usual defects lie in over-ornamentation of the stairposts and balus-

165

trades. Observe the modest detail of the staircase on page 167. It is a lesson in sensible detail. The staircase in the Colonial hallway shown on page 185 is equally good, but of an entirely different type. Here there is a gracious quality in keeping with the broad spaces of the Colonial hall.

A staircase coming directly into the living-room is a mistake, unless the family is very small indeed. There should be at least a possibility for privacy, even if it be obtained by the use of a screen or a curtain cutting off a small stairhall. If there are several living-rooms, this is not so important, for a chance visitor may be left in some other room until the family room is ready for him.

All staircases, whether they be conspicuous or concealed, should have easy treads and should be reasonably broad. It is necessary not only to provide for people with eccentric headgear, but for the occasional moving of trunks and furniture, and so the headroom should be more than ample. Otherwise, you will pay for it with badly scarred walls.

Ordinarily, stairs stained in dark tones have oak treads and risers. Where white woodwork is used the handrail and treads are usually of oak or mahogany, and the spindles and risers of white.

Doors are of great importance, architecturally, and must be treated accordingly. In a small house it is usually best to have all the doors of uniform size, but wherever possible it is advisable to place closets where their doors will not invite chance callers. It is very embarrassing to open several closet doors when you are trying to find your way out of a room.

Doors for large spaces are often difficult to manage, and there is a never ending discussion as to the merits and demerits of fold-ing and sliding doors. French doors filled with small panes of glass are deservedly popular, because they protect us from draughts without cutting off light and the sense of space that comes from long vistas. Provision should always be made for curtaining glass doors, however, as there are times when privacy is welcome in any room.

There is an architectural axiom, "never make a doorway without a door," which is often violated, and occasionally with reason. Often a large opening between two small rooms is a great improvement. The opening ceases to be a doorway, however, when it is large enough to be of real service, so perhaps the axiom is not violated after all. Certainly the many "open doors" of certain houses, openings with only flimsy curtains to cut off noise and draughts, are a nuisance.

The consideration of the chimney-piece and its mantel might easily fill a book, so varied are the possibilities for good and evil effects. The decorative value of the chimney-piece is not sufficiently appreciated by most home makers. The chimney breast should be treated architecturally, as a part of the woodwork of the room, and as a fitting frame for the center of interest—the hearth.

There are more dreadful mantels to be seen to-day than ever before, cheap stock mantels, seemingly designed in a lunatic asylum, are turned out by the thousands. New suburban houses are flooded with the most atrocious, unstudied mantels imaginable. Again the word of caution is, play safe! Use only the simplest motifs. The familiar mantel found in so many Colonial houses is an excellent one. Such mantels are shown on pages 161 and 183. It is not true that a mantel is good just because it was

DETAILS OF INTERIOR DESIGN

Edmund B. Gilchrist, Architect.

No part of the interior is more difficult to design than the staircase. This example, taken from a house at York Harbor, Maine, is most commendable for its simple straightforward detail.

built in Colonial days, but it is safe to say that if its design is simple it will prove acceptable. The more complex it gets, the more it incorporates columns of unusual shape and strange supports, the more likely is it that you should leave it alone.

It is always safe to avoid ready-made mantels that have superstructures of mirrors and shelves, like the corner what-not. After all, the chimney-piece is the important thing, the mantel is a part of it. The chief duty of the mantel is to frame pleasantly the opening for the fire.

The chimney-piece that projects into the room should have a certain reserve, an appearance of strength and dignity, and this effect can be obtained by the simplest method, by building a rectangular opening for fire and paving it with plain bricks; by carrying the framework—be it wood, or plaster, or brick, or tile—around the opening and crowning it with a plain mantel-shelf if the lintel of the fireplace is set flush with the walls of the room. The hearth need not project into the room more than sixteen inches from the face of the fireplace.

The space between mantel-shelf and ceiling may be filled in with paneling if the design is carried to the cornice, or the space may be used decoratively for a mirror, a good picture, or a plaster cast. If the frame of the fire opening is flush with the wall, the space above the mantel-shelf may be treated as a part of the wall, and the decoration will suggest itself when you look through your belongings for just the right picture, or mirror, or whatever seems most suitable.

Until recently, it was impossible to get tiles for fireplaces. We were offered thousands of ridiculous little dabs of white cement with thin colored glazes that were sold as "tiles," but they are libels. These fancy little tiles are associated with cabinet mantels, and are an insult to an honest tile maker. There are three factories that I know of making beautiful tiles at reasonable prices, tiles that are good enough for any house. They copy the fine old Dutch and Spanish and English tiles, and of late they have begun copying Persian ones that are objects of art in themselves. If you can't afford such tiles as these, use bricks for your fireplace and hearth. Avoid fancy brick, and use good red ones, the cruder and rougher the better.

It is well to remember that the mantel is a structural part of the room, and should be made of the same wood used for the doors and window frames and so forth. It is not to be treated as a thing apart, as if it were a grand piano or an easy chair. A mantel of oak, introduced into a room of walnut woodwork, is in a distressing position. A mantel of mahogany in a brown-oak room is just as mistaken.

The old-fashioned marble mantel was not so bad as the modern cabinet mantel, because, despite its bleakness and its chilling effect, it was simply formed to fit around a real fire, and it had no hideous overmantel. And, furthermore, a marble mantel was to its owners a sort of object of art, a thing apart from the woodwork of the room. White painted woodwork, a white marble mantel, and a quaint gilt-framed mirror filling the wall-space above the shelf—this wasn't an undignified combination. The marble might be very bad from the standpoint of an architect or a sculptor, but it was at least dignified in effect.

There are princely American houses where old marble and stone mantels may be used, but these mantels are really works of art, and are treated as such. They are the product of master sculptors, and are perfectly at home in dark paneled rooms. Lately, makers of cement and terra-cotta have copied many of these old mantels, but no matter how good the copies may be, they are out of place in little houses. A huge drawing room or hall or library may welcome such a mantel, but in a small room it would be an absurdity.

The Colonial mantel, however, would fit almost any room where white or cream or gray woodwork is used, or it would be good in brown or gray stained wood. The first principle of this mantel is simplicity, and the square panel between cornice and mantel-shelf offers a tempting space for decoration. An old portrait flanked by mahogany candlesticks would be suitable for it, and one can imagine a quaint circular mirror or a good cast being equally good. Or, if you liked, you could leave the square panel to its own decorative devices. I recall one mantel of white painted wood with the space between mantel and ceiling filled with a white paneling. The center panel was framed in a slen-

DETAILS OF INTERIOR DESIGN

H. Van Buren Magonigle, Architect.
The Gardener's Lodge on the estate of Franklin Murphy, Wendham, New Jersey. The design of this house, which in general is excellent, would be improved, perhaps, by the omission of the horizontal band on the gable end.

der molding. Lighting fixtures of brass were placed at the extreme edge of the molding, and the only effort at decoration was a blue Chinese vase of field grasses on the mantel-shelf.

The bungalow is responsible for the chimney-pieces made of field stone, or rough brick, that are omnipresent nowadays. Such a chimney-piece is at home in a real bungalow or in a mountain camp, where rafters and beams are exposed, but can you imagine anything worse than a towering mass of stones in a room where polished furniture and silk curtains are used?

Recently I saw a fireplace that would hold a five-foot log, with the chimney-piece towering to the rooftree and disappearing through

the rafters, and on the slab of granite that formed the mantel-shelf was a row of cut-glass vases! I felt sorry for the poor, insulted old chimney-piece.

Finally, there is the question of hardware and lighting fixtures. Hardware is an almost hopeless subject. The best you can do is to select the very simplest door handles and hinges offered you. American makers have not yet gone in for careful design in hardware, more's the pity. The French and English hardware shown at the Metropolitan Museum should be an inspiration to our designers, but the designers await the public demand, and people who have opened their eyes to the badness of many details, such as lighting fixtures, are still content with spun-brass door-knobs and hinges and so forth. Buy the simplest thing offered you, and let it go at that.

Lighting fixtures are being improved rapidly. It is possible to buy reproductions of most of the good ones from France and England now, if you are very judicious in your selections and if your purse is long.

It is always the tendency to underrate the expenses of lighting fixtures, when the plans of the house are being made. One hundred dollars seems a liberal apportionment for a small house of, say, seven rooms. But there are unexpected difficulties. It seems very simple to go forth and buy lighting fixtures —until you see the innumerable varieties offered you. And the good ones are as rare as the proverbial needle in the haystack. You must determine whether ceiling or side lights are best, and whether direct or indirect lights will best fill your needs. Your architect will probably decide much of this for you before you go forth to buy, but the chief difficulties and advantages may be considered here.

There are two kinds of illumination commonly in use to-day. They are called direct and indirect lighting. By "direct" lighting I mean that the light shines directly in the room, so that you see it. For example, when you are out-of-doors with the sun shining overhead you are enjoying the best kind of "direct" lighting. When you are in the house, let us say in a room on the north side, where the sunlight does not reach, you are enjoying diffused lighting. The source of light is not visible, and we call this indirect, or semi-indirect, lighting.

Now in our houses we have to use feeble imitations of the sun. We use, most of us, electric light. Even the strongest lights we can use are feeble compared to the light of out-of-doors, and the rooms we live in are too small to admit much light. We have to face this difficulty, to look at the source of light, whether we want to or not. Out-of-doors, in the full sunlight, the sun is so far away and yet it is so brilliant that we don't have to look at it. In fact, we can't look at it for more than a moment, or we become blinded.

We are not blinded by the intense glare of the lights in our rooms, but we are greatly annoyed when the lights are so placed that they shine in our eyes. One of the first principles of good lighting is to use that method of lighting which will adequately illumine our rooms, and to select fixtures that will veil the source of the light as much as possible.

In recent years the system of lighting called "indirect" has come into common use. In its simplest terms it means only this: you place your lights (the incandescent bulbs) in a bowl and hang this bowl from the ceiling. The light is thrown up to the ceiling and reflected back again to the walls and floor of the room. If this bowl is opaque, this method is called "indirect." If translucent, so that the bowl itself is softly lit, it is called "semi-indirect." In this way the source of light, that is, the brilliant incandescent bulbs, is hidden.

For this system it is imperative that the ceiling be cream or white, so as to reflect the light to the greatest advantage. Moreover, the walls should be fairly light in tone. If your ceiling is dark in color, you will succeed in lighting only the ceiling, and nothing else.

The light obtained from indirect lighting is diffused, and is good only for general illumination. It should be supplemented by special wall or baseboard fixtures conven-

A light in the center of the room, at the level of the eye, blinds one to the size of the room.

to use a center light in a small room of this kind. This center light is almost sure to take a position about as high as a man's head, and consequently the light of the fixture itself is always in one's eye. This means that the size of the visible room appears diminished. Now you want to make the room look as large as possible, and with a light in the center this object is defeated, because you never can look past the light. If the light is very bright, you see the other side of the room very imperfectly.

On the other hand, if the room is lighted by side lights, or bracket lights, you see all parts of the room clearly, and the light is

Lights disposed along the walls give a restful effect.

iently located, so that when a brilliant concentrated light is necessary lamps may be used.

Having accepted as an axiom of good lighting that the source of light should be veiled as much as is consistent with obtaining good lighting, the next important thing is to place the lights to good advantage. In a large room with a high ceiling the problem is much less difficult than in a small room. By small I mean the ordinary dining-room or living-room such as is found in a small dwelling house, a room perhaps fifteen by twenty feet in area and nine feet high.

In general it is a most unfortunate thing

171

more agreeably diffused. It is advisable to have as many wall lights as possible, and to use center lights only in such places as the kitchen, where overhead light is really valuable.

In using wall-lights you can employ semi-indirect lighting, screening the incandescent light with a shade of some sort. The best shades are those made of silk. There are many fanciful types of shades made of different materials, such as metal, leather, glass, and parchment. Often they are decorated by hand-painted designs, but they are nearly always too dark or too gaudy, or too something. The most successful shades are of silk. When you cannot get silk, use paper; those made of the yellow silks and the yellow papers are most attractive. The glass shades made of gaudy stained glass are usually utterly offensive; the colors are garish and crude.

Choose your fixtures always for their simplicity. Choose your colors always for their delicacy and their harmony of combination. The reason that yellow is an advisable color is because it looks well under ordinary conditions of daylight as well as when the electric light is turned on.

Avoid very ornamental fixtures—at least till you have made a study of ornament. Unless you feel that your knowledge of the forms employed in design is considerable, play safe. Choose the simplest thing that you can find. In doing this you will never lay yourself open to the charge of vulgarity in your taste. Remember that in

these matters you have to rely on your own judgment.

Curiously enough, you will find the simplest fixtures are either very cheap or very expensive. All the ornate fixtures are priced at medium low or medium high figures. Have the courage of your taste and demand the least expensive modern fixtures, if you can't afford the reproduction of the severely fine old ones. Often a three dollar fixture that is commonplace in spun brass is excellent in a pewter or bronze finish, and the cost is no more.

No matter how good your lighting fixtures may be, you will need a certain number of special lights, lamps or tall candlesticks, for reading. If your supply of electricity is stable, it is sensible to have a few base plugs in each room in the house, so that a reading lamp may be attached at will. If your electric lights have a habit of failing you at inopportune times, oil lamps and real candles are necessary. The principles of decoration are the same: the shade should never be too heavy for the lamp; the lamp itself should never be over-ornamented; a candlestick should be graceful, with a shade that has some relation to it, and so on.

Beware of too great a flood of light. It is very trying to most people's eyes. Learn to enjoy shadows. Have your wall lights so screened that they will give you an even diffused light for ordinary occasions, and have special lights when intensity is desired. The comfort you will enjoy will repay you for your painstaking work.

CHAPTER XX

THE TRADITION OF WOOD PANELING

WE may borrow ideas from the European and the Oriental for the small elegancies of our houses, but for the substantial things we depend on the English tradition. We may feel ourselves quite superior to our English neighbors in many things, but we must admit that when it comes to building a home the Englishman builds best; because he places his family first, and determines to make a house that will be home to his family for generations. We build small houses, or buy them, and then when we can "afford" it we buy bigger ones, and on and on and on! Not all of us, but an appalling number of us look upon our homes as temporary stopping places en route to a vague affluence. We do most things very much better than we do our houses.

We think of the things that make old English castles and manor-houses distinguished for their beauty as being remote from our possibilities. The superb oak furniture, the historic paneling, mellow with age and hard usage, are not for the likes of us! And yet, the humblest Tudor farmhouses that are left have the same dignified paneling, the same well-built furniture, made by the hands of the ignorant themselves. We assert that we are the most "efficient," the most "successful" people in the world, and yet with all our efficiency we can not embellish the interior of our houses with our hands. We cannot build a joint stool, or plan a panel wall. In sharpening our wits we have forgotten how to use our hands. The unlettered peasant can produce furniture that will last for hundreds of years, but the carefully educated son of America is unable to put up a kitchen shelf for his mother.

Now this matter of paneling. It seems expensive and remote to most of you, and yet it is within the means of the average man who builds a house. Of course, the cost of paneling varies with the locality, but machine-made lumber has lessened the cost everywhere. There are few sections in America where there is not plenty of lumber available at reasonable prices. Except in the desert country of the Southwest, there are dozens of native woods to be had in all localities that are suitable for paneling. The country is full of little sawmills where you can have your lumber finished to order, and it would be the simplest thing in the world for a man to plan paneled walls for one of the important rooms of his house—the hall, stairway, living-room, dining-room—which could be executed by any carpenter. Once paneled, it will last forever. There will be no after cost.

The trouble with us is we have not learned to look about us, to utilize the materials nearest us. We have so many beautiful woods—ash, oak, elm, birch, maple, poplar, yellow and white pine, chestnut, cypress, cherry, walnut, the California redwood, and other local woods, all suitable for interior woodwork. The English ideal of paneling is oak, but certainly many other coarse-grained woods are very beautiful when properly stained and waxed. New woods have an unpleasant rawness, and with the exception of a few of the more expensive woods (notably walnut and cherry) they should be stained before being waxed. Even the woods of the most beautiful grain and color are improved by an application of a light stain, because a stain brings out the lights and shadows of the grain as nothing else can.

We have seen so many houses with woodwork of yellow pine covered with a thick coat of shellac and then a coat of varnish, applied directly to the raw wood. The result is a hideous, cheap, glaring and glassy wood. We have seen other houses which had trim paneling of the same wood with a little brown stain rubbed in, and then an application of black wax, and the effect was as good as an English oak paneling. Hardwood should always be waxed, never var-

nished. The glare of the varnish kills the soft mellow quality of the wood.

In old England, before paneling was used, walls were rough and primitive masses of stone and mortar, hung with arras and tapestries and leather to keep out the cold. The first paneling (and indeed much of modern English paneling) was hand-cut and carved, the result of great labor and thought and nicety of workmanship. The paneling of a family was handed down in the wills, along with the plate and the tapestries. If the family moved to another home, the paneling was moved too.

Paneling began as a wainscot at the bottom of the wall, with the heavy hangings above it, and as the beauty of cleanliness and comfort became appreciated the loose hangings were removed and used as isolated decorations, and the walls were lined with carved oblongs of wood to the line of the ceiling, or to the line of a frieze. It is said that Henry III was the first king to use paneling, and he embellished the wood with gay colors and gold. From this painted paneling to the simple rectagonals of oak of Elizabeth's time is a great jump, and many beautiful and elaborate patterns of the intervening periods are still in evidence.

The Elizabethan paneling might be called the standard English paneling, because it is to be found in thousands of English houses, old and new. The wall is made up of rather small rectagonal panels, framed with a flat and narrow molding. On page 176 I am giving a working drawing of this paneling, with approximate dimensions. Sometimes the oblong is larger, and sometimes smaller, but whether it be found in Powis Castle or an humble farmhouse the proportions of the panels are much the same.

THE TRADITION OF WOOD PANELING

Edmund B. Gilchrist, Architect.

An effective example of formal interior design. It shows the hallway leading to the dining-room in a house at St. Martins, Philadelphia.

I have seen this pattern used in ever so many small houses lately, and it is always good, whether it be stained brown or gray or painted cream or white. I have seen a room with the pattern on a foundation of pulp board, the oblongs framed with two and one-half-inch strips of wood, the whole painted white. This, of course, reduced the cost of paneling to a nominal figure, and the effect was very good. Some one may argue that such a use of pulp board is not honest. The chief use of paneling is to give the walls of a room dignity and beauty. I should not advocate the combination of pulp

board and wood when the wall was to be stained, but when it is to be painted cream or white or gray what difference does it make?

White painted paneling is a perfect background for furniture of woods of fine grain —walnut, mahogany, rosewood, and so forth. The first vogue of white paneling was in the time of Queen Anne, when much of the heavy oak furniture gave way to the elegant new woods, and it became necessary to find a new background. Obviously, oak paneling belonged to oak furniture, and so white paint was applied to paneling of cheaper woods, and was quite in keeping with the

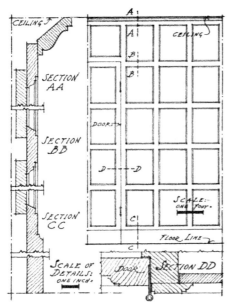

The important things to remember in designing a paneled wall are:—the shape of the panels and the widths of the stiles between. The panels should have a width about two-thirds their height, and the stiles should not be, in general, over three inches wide.

satiny furniture and the soft damasks. The crude tapestries and the sturdy oak furniture and the velvety brown of oak paneling is first in every Englishman's favor, however, and always will be.

The linen-fold pattern is as well known as the plain rectangular panel, but the old linen-fold work was always done by hand, when every man was his own carpenter, architect, and furniture maker, and now it is so expensive that it is seen only in the more costly houses. Certain English firms supply the linen-fold paneling carved by hand, but it costs about two dollars a square foot. The same firms supply a plain rectangular

paneling at about fifty cents a square foot. You may now appreciate our advantage over the Englishman, for we can panel our walls at a fraction of this amount. I have seen recently a Colonial hall, long and wide and high of ceiling, paneled in white rectagonals for twenty dollars! Old wood and home labor made this possible.

The linen fold is not available for many of us Americans, but it is full of suggestion to the man who likes to use his tools. I saw a beautiful oak chest made up of squares carved in the linen-fold manner, built by a young student of a technical school. An over-mantel made of small linen-fold panels is also very beautiful, and easy of accomplishment.

In a house recently built on Long Island there is an enormous living-room paneled in chestnut. Ordinarily chestnut is expensive, but in the localities where the chestnut trees are dying, the lumber can be bought for very little, and these people were wise enough to seize this opportunity. Chestnut has a wonderful rosy tone in its natural state, and a soft, gray stain has been rubbed into the paneling, showing rosy lights.

There is a house in Boston in which the huge living-hall is paneled with cypress, an upright paneling of broad boards running from the baseboard to the frieze line. Narrow boards of the same wood are applied where the broad boards meet, just as the narrow boards are applied to the rectangular paneling, except in the upright paneling they run straight from the baseboard to frieze line, where they are finished with a projecting molding of the same wood. This cypress paneling had a little brown stain rubbed in and was then waxed, and the effect is very soft and mellow.

THE TRADITION OF WOOD PANELING

An unusual farmhouse paneling composed of old pew doors came to my attention recently. Only a little while ago, it seems, the old village meeting-house was torn down, and of course the old lumber went for a song. The owner of this farmhouse, who had the seeing eye, bought all the pew doors and paneled his dining-room with them. The dining-room has quaint corner cupboards, also, and the effect of the diamond panes and the graceful white panels is very pleasant.

We are all familiar with the old New England farmhouses that had at least one wall, usually the chimney wall, made up of white painted wood paneling, and the other three walls plastered and papered. This treatment is always pleasing in an old house, but it would be mistaken in a new one, unless the new one happened to be a replica built to please some lover of quaint old cottages.

In Westport, Connecticut, there is a colony of artists who have bought old farmhouses and remodeled them, keeping the open fireplaces and big timbers and beams, but adding many modern conveniences—sleeping porches and hardwood floors, and adequate heating systems.

Most of the houses are a hundred years old, or thereabouts, and have heavily beamed ceilings, and that of course invited paneling. I wish you could see those paneled dining-rooms—all planned by the artists themselves, and executed by local workmen. The walls of one charming dining-room have a white painted paneling of an upright design, similar to the one shown on this page. This paneling is finished at the top with a molding broad enough to be used as a shelf, which is just the place for a collection of Colonial things—pewter and brass, and such—that are in keeping with the room.

Another house has a low-ceiled dining-room with most interesting woodwork. This house was built in 1730, and the new owner is very proud of his huge brown beams. The room is paneled with cypress of a brown tone. One whole wall is given up to two big china-closets, with a door between. An-

Drawn by C. S. Chapman

Here a simple rectangular paneling in brown oak is used effectively in connection with the English bay window.

other wall is broken by the chimney-piece, and a third by a glass door which leads to the sun-room.

The space between the top of the paneling and the ceiling of the fourth wall is filled with a row of little casement windows, about fourteen inches deep. In the center of the wall, just opposite the fireplace, the panels are recessed to make room for a long radiator, and in the space left between the top of the radiator and the top of the paneling, about thirty inches, are built two long shelves which may be used as warming-shelves, but usually hold pitchers and tea things.

A soft-toned curtain hangs just under the lower shelf, hiding the radiator, and the effect suggests recessed bookshelves. So much of the wall space of this room is filled with the cupboards, radiator space, windows, doors, and mantel, that very little paneling was required.

These old farmhouses often have paneled walls in the most unexpected places. Often three outside walls of a long room are plastered, and the fourth wall—that leading into another room or a hallway—is made up of oblongs of wood, usually painted white.

The stairs are finished with an upright paneling that creeps up, one board at a time, like the treads, and now and then you will find little cupboards and cabinets hidden in these stair-panels. The paneling beside the chimney-piece usually hid a cupboard, corresponding to the oven on the other side. That is one of the fascinating things about wood-paneling—it invites secret cupboards or patent ones, little cabinets for a few treasures or big cupboards for magazines and books and smoking things.

There are so many excellent stains and wood-dyes and wax-oils to be had now, you can experiment on a board of your chosen wood.

Oak furniture may be treated in a dozen different ways, from the soft grayish stain to the black-brown, but if your woodwork has a brown tone, light or dark, and a dull waxed finish, you need not worry about the harmony. The many shades of gray and brown are best, usually, but in a bungalow an upright paneling might be stained one of the many wood greens. If you are to use mahogany or such fine-grained furniture, your paneling may be stained a soft gray, or painted cream or white.

There is another method of paneling that is much used in modern American drawing-rooms, indeed wherever fine French furniture is to be used. This paneling comes to us from France, and Miss Elsie de Wolfe has been largely responsible for its vogue in America. The French method breaks the walls of a room into a series of large and graceful panels by the use of narrow moldings applied directly to the plaster. The plaster, it goes without saying, must be *good*. If it has n't been done by a man who knows his business, it will crack, and that spoils everything. The woodwork and the moldings of a room paneled in this manner are painted a faint shade lighter or darker than the walls. Cream, ivory white, putty-color, and French gray are the colors used, and the paint is invariably flat, affording a suave background to elegant furniture.

CHAPTER XXI

THE DECORATION OF WALLS

THE fundamental principle of mural decoration is: Walls are backgrounds. Keep that in mind and you cannot go far wrong. The surface of the wall is supposed to be flat, and this flatness must be preserved, but structurally a wall has thickness as well as length and breadth, and therefore this solidity must not be concealed by flimsy coverings. For instance, if you paper a wall from ceiling to floor with a flowered paper it would look as unstable as a muslin curtain, but if there is a baseboard at the bottom of the wall and a cornice or molding at the top, the strength of the wall is obvious, and you can use any paper or decoration you please.

The most distinguished wall treatments—the hangings of tapestries and other textiles, the tooled leathers, the beautiful painted panels of the mural artist—are not within the province of these articles. The average householder employs two methods of wall covering, wood paneling and plaster. We have discussed the possibilities of wood paneling in a former article. Plastered

walls may be divided into three groups: the walls which depend upon the natural color and uneven texture of the plaster for decoration, the walls that are painted or distempered, and the walls that are papered.

If you are building a new house, pay a little more for an expert plasterer and do without wall-papers. A good wall offers opportunity for real decoration, but an imperfect wall must always be covered with paper or textile in order to become a background.

Papered walls are very good indeed when the paper is carefully selected after due consideration of the uses of the room, the exposure of the windows, and so forth, but papered walls cannot be compared with painted walls for cleanliness and dignity if the plaster beneath the paint has been properly applied. We see so few good painted walls that it seems hardly worth considering them at all. Most people take it for granted that the plaster will crack and settle. They wait patiently until that ordeal is over and then paper the walls.

Plastered walls are very pleasant when

179

left in the natural color of the plaster. In every locality this color varies, according to the sand used. Sometimes the plaster is a pale biscuit color, sometimes a clear gray, but usually it is a soft tan. The colors may be varied indefinitely by the addition of a little pure color when the plaster is being mixed. The grain of the plaster is like the texture of a fabric, pleasing in its roughness.

Given a good plastered wall, you can do many things. You may paint it cream or gray or tan, using a flat paint always, or you may tint it with one of the many cold-water paints sold for the purpose. A painted or distempered wall may be broken into large panels by the use of a narrow molding, the molding being painted the same tone as the walls, or a lighter tone of the same color. Walls so painted should always be light in color.

Whitewashed walls are all very well for tropical countries, but they are the most difficult of all walls to make beautiful. An artist can plan a room with white walls and achieve something worth while, but an amateur cannot. In the first place, the glare of white walls is very bad on the eyes. Again, white is not a background color, it is too cold and downright; you cannot get away from it. Walls are primarily backgrounds, so there you are. White may be softened and mellowed by mixing a little yellow with it, and it becomes cream or ivory or buff, suave and aristocratic. But dead white walls are never pleasant. A white marble bust, or a white porcelain figurine outlined against a darker background is distinguished in effect, but the same object placed against a white wall would be pale and as uninteresting as skimmed milk. White is one of the precious colors, and should be used sparingly and skilfully, and not for large areas.

In some parts of the country, notably the extreme South, walls are always whitewashed. This treatment is either very good or very bad. If a room has white woodwork and a few pieces of handsome old furniture, white walls give it a severe formality that is commendable in a warm climate, where the inclination is to let things go.

White plastered walls with dark woodwork are distressingly glaring. Such a room requires masses of green things to make it homelike. I know one Georgia drawing-room that has white walls and ceiling and woodwork, and a floor of wide boards painted a dull green. A faded old rug of no particular color, a square piano, a davenport and several chairs of dark mahogany, and one old portrait above the mantel furnish the room. It is not necessary to comment on the quality of this room; few churches give you a feeling of greater quiet and reverence.

One can imagine whitewashed walls being very appropriate to the stucco houses of Mexico and southern California, where the glare of the sunshine is tempered by thick walls and embrasured doors, and windows and many hanging vines. There the interiors have the atmosphere of sun-rooms with tiled floors and light furniture and many growing plants. I am told that in those queer little islands, the Bermudas, every householder is required by law to whitewash his walls twice a year. The inhabitants are largely English people, and they know the decorative value of chintz, so they temper the glare of too-white walls by hanging lengths of gay fabrics against the whitewashed surfaces, as we would hang pictures.

I had the entire lower floor of my own

THE DECORATION OF WALLS

Wilson Eyre, Architect.
The pergola at "The Garth," Strafford, Pennsylvania. Note the effective contrast between the vines and the white columns.

house painted a flat, soft gray, walls and woodwork. I considered having a slightly darker tone for the woodwork, but decided that it would serve merely to emphasize the smallness of the rooms. One unbroken tone would make the hall, living-room and dining-room one large apartment in effect. Unwisely, I gave the painter a scrap of soft velvet carpeting of a delightful gray-tan, the color of a little woolly animal, and went away serenely expecting him to get just that color. He did n't. He got a deep middle tone of gray that is very lovely on sunny days, and when it snows in winter, but at night it darkens to a deep gray. I love the

quiet tone of it all, and I actually like the deep shadows at night.

With this deep gray as background, I have been able to use strong color in small things. I made a deep orange velvet cover for the living-room couch, and several large pillows are covered with this orange velvet and an orange and gray figured challie. There is a small table, painted black, at the head of this couch to hold a lamp and smoking things. The lighting fixtures are all of pewter, almost exactly the color of the walls. The reading lamp is made of a creamy-white jar, with a shade of orange colored silk. This color, which lies between red and orange, is

181

repeated in many small things—in the picture over the mantel (a color print of one of Jules Guerin's French chateaux), in many of the book bindings, in a little lacquer vase, and in flowers. Somehow there are always flowers to be had of orange and red and salmon color. Just now my vases are filled with fat rose hips and bitter sweet berries that will last all winter.

The dining-room, which is really a part of the living-room, has the same color plan. Oak furniture of a warm, waxed brown, linen colored curtains; a rug with much old red and dark blue in it; a gay Carl Larrson color print with splashes of his wonderful red; an orange lacquer tray and a big green jug of yellow flowers on the sideboard; and a blue and yellow Spanish bowl on a square of Chinese red brocade on the table. Everywhere spots of old blue, Italian yellow, orange, and deep Chinese red against the gray walls.

Upstairs, the gray walls and woodwork continue in the hall. There is a group of four windows on the stairs, bringing light and air to both floors, and in order to pull the two floors together and bring a little color into the gray hall I had long side curtains made of gray challie, with Japanese figures of flame red and very dark blue in it. These long curtains are beautiful by day and by night. The flame red is repeated in a number of pictures—black and white prints with mats of Chinese paper exactly this color, and narrow black frames. No other color is needed in the hall.

If the walls of your house are too badly scarred and cracked to be painted, there are hundreds of excellent papers to be found. For most rooms plain papers, or papers plain in effect, are best. For long hallways and occasional rooms there are fascinating figured papers, reproductions of the landscape papers of the early nineteenth century, of the grotesque Chinese papers, or the tapestry and foliage English papers designed by William Morris and Walter Crane, and hundreds of gay bedroom papers that are almost irresistible.

I admit the temptation of figured papers. When I go into a wall-paper shop I have the same greedy feeling I have in the early spring when hundreds of flowered muslins and sweet-smelling linens are spread out in the shops. I should like to buy dozens and dozens! But flowered wall-papers become very tiresome if you live with them long, and you would n't want to wear the sweetest rose-sprigged muslin that ever blossomed for years and years.

When you buy wall-papers, consider the rooms in which they are to be used. Consider also the rooms that connect one with another, for your open doors will bring about discord or harmony.

Figured wall-papers are not to be condemned wholesale; many of them are beautiful. The main thing to guard against in selecting your paper is too realistic design. The more fantastic and conventionalized the paper is, the better the result will be. A realistic wall-paper is dreadful for the simple reason that walls are supposed to be flat surfaces, and "natural" objects destroy this flatness. The trouble with most people who use figured wall-papers is that they are not content to let the design of the paper decorate the room, and they pile on pictures and mirrors until the general effect is that of a grotesque crazy-quilt.

One of the most beautiful halls I have ever seen had a paneled wainscoting about

THE DECORATION OF WALLS

Harrie T. Lindeberg, Architect.
The dining-room of the Boardman Robinson house at Forest Hills, Long Island, has walls of pongee color and woodwork of cream-white. Black chintz curtains patterned in birds and flowers are used in the casement windows.

four feet high, a whitewashed ceiling that dropped two feet to a picture-molding, and the space between filled with a Chinese paper made up of impossible trees and vines and flowers, with hundreds of gorgeous birds perched among them. This paper was copied from one of the rare old hand-painted papers of a century ago. The ground color was a deep yellow. Each length differed slightly in design, there were different birds swinging on different colored branches, but the flat arrangement of the background and the brilliant plumage of the birds and the queer greens of the branches gave the effect of an orderly, well-balanced design. Of course no pictures are used on a paper of this

kind, and the furniture used in the room with such a paper must be carefully chosen. This particular hall had furniture of black oak, and rugs of plain green velvet, just the tone of the branches. This is an example of a daring paper well used.

In my own little house I have used a paper very fantastic in design, but very subdued in color, with excellent effect. The room in question is an upstairs sitting-room, with four big windows that give us vistas east, west, and south. The design of the paper is made up of peacocks with sweeping tails, perched on flowery boughs. But it is the softest paper in tone, in color, in quality. It has no sheen. The colors are dull blues and greens and gray-mauves on a dark gray ground. The woodwork has been painted a light blue-green, just the color of the tail feathers of the peacocks. The ceiling was supposed to be of shimmering silver, but it does n't shimmer, and sooner or later I am going to go over it with a thin coat of gold. That will make it lovely. The furniture in the room includes a black oak desk, a black oak table for books and magazines, a pair of old Japanese chests of black and gray cedar, and a large day bed painted blue-green.

The color of this room is so joyous it does n't seem possible that it took so long to plan it. The curtains were easy—a lovely Japanese chintz of blue and green and silver, with the silver dominant. This stuff looks like a brocade, stiff with metal, but it costs only fifty cents a yard. The rug was a hideous thing of velvet—a gift—heavy of pile and shocking in design. I had it dyed black, jet black, and it is very fine indeed, not gloomy—it is soft and deep and warm looking, and throws all the other colors in the room into proper importance. I tried all sorts of colors on the day bed, and they were all too low in key. Finally I brought out a piece of deep sulphur yellow velvet, and it was just what the room needed. So I made a cover and pillows of it. There is also a pillow of the curtain stuff, and another of yellow with Chinese figures in it. Later, I brought in several things of vivid flame color and peacock blue—and a tall gray jar of real peacock feathers for my desk, and now the room is full of color but not in the least jarring.

There are hundreds of papers of good design and color in the market to-day, papers decorative enough to carry rooms far toward

beauty. The power of selection is all that is needed.

The hall is the most formal and least used part of the house, and therefore the very place for papers of bold design. The old landscape papers that were planned for the halls of Colonial houses are being revived, but they are suitable only to those long halls with doors opening just so, and stately staircases, and massive mahogany furniture. The hall shown in the illustration on page 185 is admirably planned. The white of the woodwork and the polished wood of the stair and the furniture is perfect with the dark landscape paper.

There are hundreds of foliage papers on the market. Some of them have designs in the tapestry colorings, and are very alluring. They may be used as friezes above the wainscoting or paneling of a hall or dining-room. Recently I saw a hall in a city house papered with a foliage paper made of many gray and white leaves, and the effect was very cool and prim. A similar paper of green leaves would be delightful in a country cottage hall, used in combination with white paint and green painted furniture.

Of course this does n't apply to halls that open directly into living-rooms with no doors between them. A bold paper should always be used in a room that has doors that open and shut.

Be careful of your bedrooms. Bedrooms invite gay papers copied from old English chintzes and French fabrics of the eighteenth century. You can do almost anything you like with your bedroom, but it must be planned just as carefully as the other rooms of the house. If you have a collection of small pictures and photographs you cannot put away, paper your walls with a plain

THE DECORATION OF WALLS

Drawn by C. S. Chapman

A Colonial hallway with its generous staircase, and large wall spaces decorated by an old-fashioned landscape wall-paper.

color, as gay as you please, and be happy. You will lose your good spirits and friends if you cover your walls with a paper of large design, and then cover the paper with photographs and bridge score-cards, and calendars and odds and ends.

In selecting my own wall-papers, I decided to give up pictures and odds and ends and to have just the paper I coveted for my own bedroom. All my bedrooms have cream-colored woodwork and cream ceilings, by the way, and so it was necessary to select papers with cream grounds. My bedroom paper is a reproduction of an old Japanese one with all sorts of legendary flowers and trees and temples and birds upon it. The prevailing colors were soft jade green and mulberry, on a cream ground. The dressing table, the chest of drawers, a high back chair, and the wooden bed were all painted exactly the green of the little islands in the paper.

There is to be a little green bedside table, and a bedspread of cream, and a large rug of cream and mulberry, when I find them. The little rug I have is a wee one, but it is exactly right in color. The dressing table has a glass top inset, and under it I have a length of green and blue and silver cloth. All the little bottles and things on the dressing table are of queer Chinese blues and greens. I picked them up in Chinatown. The curtains are of a sunproof material of silk and linen, of mulberry with little yellow threads in it.

Another one of my bedrooms is papered with a plain clover pink paper. The furniture is lacquered black, the woodwork cream, and the chintz an English one with birds of paradise and funny flowers in dark red, clover pink, dull green and yellow on a cream ground. Another little room has an old-fashioned paper sprinkled with little baskets of blue and rose posies. Here I used a black chest of drawers, and covered the bed with an old blue woven coverlet. You see, so much of my house is gray I feel I can afford gay papers in these rooms.

The shops have been very proud to offer figured wall-papers and chintzes to match, the last few years, though why any one should wish to have so much of the same design in a room, I cannot understand. The plain wall-paper always invites figured chintz hangings, and the figured paper invites plain colored hangings.

I once spent a night in a bedroom that was supposed to be a "sweet-pea room" by its misguided owner. The walls were covered with sweet peas, millions of them, so violently colored as to be a libel to the fragile butterfly flowers that inspired the paper. The curtains were of a sweet-pea chintz "to match." The furniture covering and the hangings were of the same chintz, and every innocent wooden space—drawer fronts and chair backs, and so forth—was painted with more sweet peas. I never wanted to see another sweet pea when I left that unhappy room!

Another custom the shops have thrust upon us is the scalloped border for bedroom papers. I am so tired of pink-rose wall-papers with carefully scissored and scalloped borders in bedrooms! The nicest thing about roses is that they are n't prim and careful, and they do not repeat themselves. I am sure we should all grow frightfully tired of them if we had every petal in replica.

But the color of the rose—that is different. That we may take for our own and enjoy. When I was a little girl we called soft pink "pink," and that dreadful candy-pink that is so vulgar we called "pank."

Rose color is as different from pink or pank as orange is from canary. I always think of them as pinks and panks now, the pleasant and unpleasant tones. Rose is a young girl's own color. Another good pink is the shade the Chinese use so much in their porcelains, and the English use so much in their chintzes—a deep pink with a hint of gray in it. This is really my clover pink.

Gray and tan are good wall colors, but they absorb the light most extravagantly. I like brown walls when they are of paneled wood, but usually brown is not a pleasant color in paper.

There is a dark tobacco-brown paper (Japanese of course) that is lovely in texture, soft and changing and shadowy, and not very expensive, but the ordinary brown papers are coarse, and dirty looking. A cool tan is much pleasanter.

Gray papers are charming in south rooms. I saw a wonderful room lately with walls covered with gray Japanese grass cloth, woodwork stained a silver gray, and ceiling covered with that silvered Japanese paper that is so indescribably lovely. There was much color in the room, in small things, but the effect of it was as refreshing and cooling as a group of silver birches in a deep wood. You could shut your eyes and feel the color.

Brown and buff and cream and tan have been the well-bred friends of homemakers for years, but gray has just recently come into its own. Gold papers are sometimes good, when they are made by Orientals, but domestic gold paper usually has a greenish tinge, and blackens unpleasantly with age. A room with one of these tarnished papers has the effect of plated table-ware when the silver has worn off—it tempers your pleasure.

The gold-leaf and silver-leaf papers of Japan are very beautiful, and are much used by artists for covering ceilings and screens and occasionally for walls, but gold-leaf papers must be used with discrimination, and the hangings used with them must be carefully chosen.

Gold papers are more often used successfully on ceilings than on walls. Many a gloomy hall would be vastly improved if its ceiling were washed in gold, or covered with gold paper. Gold invites Chinese red lacquer, and bronze green velvets, and dark waxed oak furniture. The silver paper that Japanese artists use so well is a perfect background for violet, and old blues, and pale yellows, and vivid light greens. Grass cloth is a sort of betwixt-and-between stuff that has the sheen of gold or silver and the texture of coarse linen. It costs more than wall paper, but it lasts well. Grass cloth has horizontal lines, and should not be used in low-ceiled rooms. In silver-gray, gold, cream, tan or buff it is an unobtrusive background for good furniture.

Drawn by C S. Chapman
These rooms have the serenity which comes from bare floors and plain walls. A glimpse of the Casa Blanca at St. Angel, Mexico.

Blue is the nicest color in the world, the heavenly color, but it is not for walls. It is too precious a color for large spaces. Think twice about blue. Blue hangings and porcelains, and gray or tan or cream or buff or sage green walls, and rugs with rose and more blue—you could make hundreds of color plans with blue as the dominant color, but it is n't necessary to spread it out on your walls. Blue and white figured papers are all

right, for then there is more white than blue, and a bedroom with such a paper and white woodwork and furniture and muslin curtains would be as sweet as a spring morning. Blue when used as a house color should always be a soft blue or a darker Chinese blue. Baby blue is a feeble color for decorative purposes.

Green and red have been so long and so badly misused that I 'd rather say, do not use them at all, than give any advice that will lead to the perpetration of further misdeeds.

Green we love because Nature loves it so, but we bring greens into our houses that Nature would not tolerate. The strong greens and the strong reds are best left outdoors. There Nature takes care of them, and masses other greens with them.

But for interiors we had best use the derivatives of these colors, and use the pure greens and reds only in embellishing soft-toned backgrounds. In a sunroom or a room with many windows you can use an amazing amount of green but it must be the right green.

The outdoor greens are only suitable for sunshiny rooms that are to be treated as outdoor rooms. For interiors blue-greens and bronze-greens and sage-greens and black-greens are best. They should be used as blue is used, with some softer color for background.

Yellow is the pleasantest of all wall colors. Books have been written in its praise, of its aristocratic influence in city drawing-rooms, of its sunshiny atmosphere, of its smiling suggestion of prosperity. You could not get very gloomy in a room with walls of warm yellow. But—there are yellows and yellows! I once knew a man who protested that blue was blue; you could n't get away from that!

Now every woman knows that blue is a most versatile color; it is a hundred things, pleasant and unpleasant, but you cannot mix blues recklessly and expect harmony.

Yellow also has to be handled with careful thought and consideration. If it has a creamy tone, it is suave and gracious, just the color for a painted wall that is to be broken into large paneled spaces by narrow molding.

If it has a rosy tone, it is delicious enough to eat, smiling and gay and full of the cheer of sunshine, and the proper color for the walls of the family living-room. If it is deeper, with a leaning toward orange, it will be superb in a darkened north room, with heavy brown furniture and much cream paint and muslin and an occasional splash of coral red, or flame red, as you prefer.

Green-yellow is ugly and depressing, like a sour smile. I have seen canary yellow used with mauve and gray in a French wall-paper, but I should not like to live with it. Sulphur yellow is also ugly in large masses. But both these yellows can be used successfully by any one who can handle color.

Orange, pure and simple, is a magnificent color, but it should be used sparingly. Too much of it is distressing. A cream bowl of orange flowers and green leaves against a creamy-yellow wall—that is one of the things that makes one appreciate the gift of eyes!

CHAPTER XXII

THE RIGHT USE OF CURTAINS

ONE of the New York papers recently contained a scathing editorial on the city women who make cave-dwellers of their families by having curtains, and then more curtains, and more curtains, so that whatever light and air may be outside, very little ever gets into the rooms of the city house.

The editorial was well deserved, for the present mode of curtaining New York windows seems to be to hang an expensive lace curtain flat against the glass, the full length of the window; inside that, there is usually a holland shade (as if the many curtains were not enough!); then another pair of lace curtains, looped back to give just a little triangular view of the glass curtain; then a pair of very heavy velvet or brocade curtains, lined and interlined, hanging straight or looped slightly and finished with a deep fitted top, similar to the hideous lambrequins of the Victorian era of decoration.

By the time all these draperies have been adjusted there is very little chance for light or air. The editor in question remarked that

while the people of the tenements are forced by law to have a certain amount of light and air, the cave-dwellers of the brownstone houses have no one to say them nay, and so bring up their pallid families in air-tight houses.

The city woman is not peculiar in her dread of light and air. Every little town has a goodly number of houses with windows always tightly shuttered. I have seen tidy cottages in New England with windows that have not been opened in years. There was a time when people had to pay taxes for the privilege of windows, so much for each window. One can imagine that those early windows were really appreciated, that they were allowed to give their full measure of light and air.

Perhaps some day, when health is just as much a matter of law as honesty, it will be a misdemeanor to be ill or cross, and a tax will be imposed on closed windows!

You can walk along the street and "size people up" by the way they treat their windows. When you see huge vases of artificial flowers between the lace curtains and glass, for outsiders to enjoy, you may be sure the people are "showing off." Closely drawn curtains and shades pulled down just-so suggest a too-neat housekeeper with a dread of light and air, or a room too fine to use.

Rooms should n't be too fine to use. Here is a house with lace curtains at the parlor windows, ragged net ones at others, and shabby dotted swiss ones at servants' rooms and basement—you know very well what to expect of the people behind the windows. Then you come to a plain little shoe-box of a house, such a humble little house no one would think of looking to it for a lesson in decoration, and you find real windows, shining and clean, with fresh white curtains hanging straight and full, and green painted window-boxes full of growing things fastened to the ledges outside. You know the dwellers in the little house are nice people, and that they appreciate the privilege of windows.

Windows are intended primarily as dispensers of light and air, but like all architectural details that are of practical value, they are also of the greatest decorative importance. Too many windows are as bad as too few. It is n't that we need so many more windows, but that we need a better grouping of those we have. That is one thing the modern architect does supremely well: he makes the most of windows inside the house and out. Instead of spotting the exterior of a house with many windows, badly proportioned and badly balanced, he groups the windows so that they decorate the exterior and make the interior a place of sweetness and light.

The single windows in Colonial houses are placed with geometrical precision, and are dignified in effect, but in so many nonde-script houses the windows are spotted singly over the surface with no apparent rime or reason, and are very ugly. Often these scattered single windows may be pulled into a group. For instance, if a room has one side wall broken by two windows, about four feet apart, the space between may be filled with a new window. The room will be much pleasanter, and the exterior will have a new interest, for the three windows will form a logical break in the wall. People are always "improving" their houses by adding bay windows, which usually look like expensive excrescences, when by expending about the same money and a little more thought they could make the whole house more interesting by pulling the scattered windows into well-balanced groups.

A group of windows often invites a broad window-seat. The window-seat may be constructed to cover a long, low radiator, with a lattice for the heat to filter through. Such a seat should have a long fitted pad, mattress fashion, of some fabric that will be in keeping with the other fabrics and colors of the room, and that will fade to an agreeable tone, for fade it will, you may be sure of that. However, grays and browns and tans fade to even pleasanter tones than they had when they came from the dye-pots.

In a small dining-room a group of windows will invite a square or an oblong dining-table, placed at right angles to the window-sill. I have often watched women scramble for the tables nearest the windows in tea-rooms and restaurants, and yet their own dining-tables are always placed exactly in the middle of the room, no matter how small or how gloomy it may be. It is not always practicable to place your dining-table under the windows, but when it is—do it! **You**

THE RIGHT USE OF CURTAINS

Mellor & Meigs, Architects.

This fascinating detail of the entrance to the office of the architects in Philadelphia is full of helpful suggestions for small house work. The casements are of metal.

can make the room even more delightful by building a long shelf under the three windows, and having a row of plants on the shelves. You will always have fresh green things, and you'll always feel that mealtime is a gala occasion.

The dining-room in my own little house is really a part of the living-room, and I did not want it conventional, with a table set squarely in the middle of the floor, so I

placed the dining-room table against the east wall, under a group of four windows. The table is a reproduction of an old English refectory table, seven feet by four. It was much too large to be placed in the middle of the floor, but is most successful under the windows. We pull the chairs up around it, and look out the windows. When the dog wood is in bloom, or when the first snow storm comes, we can offer our friends real

191

In this drawing note the method of screening the radiator which is under the seat. Note also the picturesqueness of the window arrangement with its small panes and simple hangings.

entertainment with their dinner. Then indeed do we appreciate the privilege of windows. There are so many trees outside that there is no glare in your eyes, facing the light, and our friends find it a very happy arrangement. You can see how it is placed in the photograph on page 199. On gala occasions we pull the table out into the middle of the floor and seat twelve people comfortably. But there are few such occasions.

If you have a bay window in your house, use it! Take down the heavy curtains and draperies, and remove the marble-topped table with its fine vase that has been viewed by passers-by for these many years, and make the little recess a useful place. A big armchair and a sewing-table, or a broad window-seat with narrow shelves for books at the ends, or a low table with a big chair on each side of it—any of these combinations will make the recess most inviting. If it has a sunny exposure, you can easily make a flower room of it. In this case, take down all the thin curtains and build many

shelves to hold plants. A lattice may be built around the windows, and ivy trained over it. This, of course, if there are other windows in the room. The flowers will darken the room slightly.

Don't permit curtains that will interfere with the pleasure of living. The best curtains in the world are made of sheer white swiss muslin. You can be sure they're always clean. You aren't worried about people looking in, and if you want to look out you can pull them aside.

The most beautiful windows are treated architecturally, and require only a heavy side curtain that may be drawn at night. Made up of well-balanced sashes subdivided into rectangular or diamond panes by leads or small moldings, such a window is a joy in itself. It doesn't need curtains. If you can afford the glass that is uneven in quality (amber is the nicest color of all) your window will be a jewel, as full of changing color as an opal. I love those stately old houses on Beacon Hill in Boston, with their panes

THE RIGHT USE OF CURTAINS

of violet and lavender glass. If one of these precious panes is broken the Bostonian's heart is broken also, and he seeks until he finds another piece of misty gray or lavender glass that will fit into his window.

If your house is built with thick walls ask your architect to see that you have broad interior window sills. Nothing adds more to the attractiveness of a room than a row of flower pots on a broad window sill. Somehow I can't imagine an English cottage casement window without a very crisp white muslin curtain and an orderly row of red geraniums on the sill. A bird sings merrily in a yellow reed cage, the flowers always bloom, the curtains never lose their crispness, in my imagination. This vision of mine has been fostered by the pictures of hundreds of artists, and grim reality does not change it. Therefore, this must be the ideal window treatment—all poets will agree with me!

We are so cursed with flies and mosquitoes in America that we can't consider our window curtains until we have arranged for wire screens. Window shades are almost as great a nuisance, but we can do without them by having two sets of curtains. Window shades temper the light, and are usually necessary to bedrooms, even if you manage to do without them in the living-room. If you must have them, be sure that they look well from the outside of the house. If they are tan or ecru or linen colored they will not be objectionable, but if they are white

Wilson Eyre, Architect.
The kitchen, when well considered, may be gay and cheerful,—as it is in this house at Forest Hills, Long Island.

or dark green they will be very glaring. Of course if your house is painted white, you can use white shades, but be careful not to get a sickly blue-white.

It is almost impossible to use a holland shade at a casement window. The wire screen is almost as difficult. If you have the screen placed outside the window, you can have a built-on window-box outside, but the casement will have to swing in. If you have the casement swing outward, the screen will have to be removed every time you wish to open or close the window.

Casement windows are best curtained with thin white net or muslin, shirred at the top and bottom on small brass rods so that the window may be opened without the vexation of flapping curtain. Casements made of leaded panes of colored glass do not require thin curtains. A heavy curtain that may be drawn across the window at night is all that is necessary.

A heavy curtain has great possibilities for beauty. When you choose the fabric, select some stuff that is good in design and texture, especially at night, for while almost any heavy curtain is attractive enough when pulled to one side in heavy folds by day, when it is drawn at night it should be even more so—it should be decorative. I like a curtain that shimmers at night, a soft fabric with silk threads, or one of those lovely Japanese cottons that are printed in metals and dull colors—bronze and silver, orange and brown, on a tan ground. Such fabrics cost no more than ordinary reps and velveteen.

The day of lace curtains has gone forever. This is one of the reforms of which we are *sure*. Despite the fact that millions of pairs of lace curtains are sold each year, no one that you know buys them. Really,

there might be an adage: By their lace curtains ye shall not know them!

I am so often asked "how long parlor curtains should be," or how new curtains are made, or whether curtains are draped. The treatment of window curtains is exceedingly simple because it is invariably based on common sense. The drapings and puffings of other days are unknown to the modern decorator. The main things to remember are:

Glass curtains are nicest when they are of white or cream net or muslin or scrim. Natural-colored linen scrim also is good. A two-inch hem on both sides and the bottom and a two-inch casing at the top are the usual finish. Sometimes they are finished with hemstitching, if you care to take the trouble.

These thin curtains are strung on a small brass rod and are hung as close to the glass as possible. The lower hem barely escapes the sill at the bottom. The curtains may hang in straight folds, or may be pushed to the sides by day. If they are made of net, it will not be necessary to push them aside, for net is thin enough to see through. Ruffled curtains, crossed and looped back, often appeal to us just because of their cleanly, fresh appearance, but plain ones are nicer. Ruffles belong on wearing apparel, not on house-furnishings. Occasionally one sees muslin curtains finished with an old-fashioned ball fringe. These curtains are usually held back by white cords during the day, but they should be released from the cords at night.

Windows that go all the way to the floor of course should have glass curtains that barely cover the glass and side curtains that just escape the floor. French windows are treated differently; here two small brass rods must be used on each panel, confining the top

THE RIGHT USE OF CURTAINS

and bottom hems of the thin curtains. Casement windows are often treated in the same way. Small casements may have short sash curtains, loose at the bottom. If the casements open out, the white curtains are often eliminated and inside curtains of silk or linen or cretonne are fixed to the inside window trim. These curtains are made with plaited valances.

When side curtains of chintz or such a fabric are used at the double-hung windows there may be a fitted valance, or a plaited ruffle at the top of the window. This valance should have its own rod, so that the chintz curtains beneath it may be drawn together at night. Many people string the valance and side curtains on the same pole, and while this is n't exactly as it should be, the framing of the gay chintz is very nice to look upon. If several rooms open together, and the wall treatments are the same, the side curtains should also be the same.

When glass doors lead to an outdoor dining-room, or a little conservatory, or an enclosed piazza, the effect is very pleasant indeed, because you can enjoy the sunshine and flowers and the feeling of outdoors while you toast your feet by a real fire within. Usually these glass doors are made French fashion, of two long narrow sashes, each two

Designed by H. T. Lindeberg.   Albro & Lindeberg, Architects.
The windows of this house are so designed that they are full of interest. Note the way the curtains are arranged for the French windows. The house as a whole is full of suggestions, and its well-studied detail may be easily applied to small house design. It is located at White Plains, New York.

panes wide, and many panes deep. The best method of curtaining the sash is to shir a soft white or cream stuff—muslin or net— on small brass rods, the top rod being placed at the second bar from the top, and the lower rod being placed at the very bottom of the glass panes. This leaves an open square of four panes at the top of the sash.

Plan your windows for sunshine and air, and then refuse to have a wall-paper or a rug that will not stand the test of the sunshine. This is a pretty good rule for the furnishings of your house. And if you are willing to spend your money for *quality*,— even if you have to deny yourself certain things you like,—your house will reflect the wisdom of your action.

studio near Hartford, Connecticut.

CHAPTER XXIII

BEFORE YOU BUY YOUR FURNITURE

HOW many women really decide what the furniture of their houses will be?

There is a nice theory that when a woman has a house to be furnished she has a neat little list of all the things she will require in that house, and all she needs is a few days' time and a certain amount of money and an obliging salesman, and her house will be furnished. There may be women who have actually bought the furniture originally planned for their houses, but I have n't known them.

Certainly most of the women I know have had this grave matter decided for them by some particularly good piece of furniture that has come to them, and this piece of furniture gradually influences the equipment of the rest of the house. It may be a grand-father's clock of mahogany, or an old rose-wood table, or a walnut sofa, or a quaint old oak chest, or even a Chinese vase or a French etching. But its influence is inevitable.

Houses cannot be furnished in a few weeks, or a few months, save by experienced decorators. If you plunge in desperately and do all your shopping in a few days, as so many bewildered young brides do, you will want to begin eliminating your mistakes before the year is out. Hasty shopping is always a series of compromises, no matter how carefully you have planned it before-hand.

Why are we so afraid of our houses seeming bare and empty? Why are n't we honest enough to buy things as we actually require them? Why do we apologize for the kitchen table in the dining-room, when the fine old chairs explain the situation? Any one with an ounce of imagination will know we are waiting until we can afford the proper table for those chairs, and why should we concern ourselves with people who have no imagination?

There are so many of us who really want simple things, and yet we compromise by buying things that do not measure up to our standards. Because the greatest number of women are content with things of hideous de-sign, wicked color and abominably cheap execution, the rest of us, who really want simple and durable things, sigh and compromise because, we argue, "Here is my house ready and waiting. It must have this and that at once, because other women's houses have this and that. I'd like to look further, but I am so tired, and, after all, this is the best thing I have seen!" Haven't you made this compromise, over and over? And haven't you finally thrown away half your hastily purchased furniture in sheer disgust? I have!

If you start out with the determination to have mahogany furniture only, or oak, or walnut, or whatever you may like, your house will be absolutely unobjectionable, but you won't have very much fun with it. If, however, you have a few pieces of furniture that you love too much to give up, and you have to search and search for every new thing you buy so that it will be friendly with the old things, your house will be a much pleasanter place to live in.

The furniture that most of us buy may be divided into four groups:

First, wooden furniture that is oiled or waxed so that the grain and color of the wood is its own decoration, such as oak, mahogany, walnut, and so forth.

Second, wooden furniture that is covered with paint and lacquer or gilt, such as the quaint Colonial furniture with flat ground colors and decorations of posies and garlands, and the lacquered Chinese furniture in which conventional decorations of gold are applied to a ground of green, red, or black lacquer, and the simple models painted or enameled in one tone.

Third, the furniture that is covered wholly or in part with tapestries, leathers, chintzes and the many less expensive fabrics.

Fourth, the light-weight furniture that is constructed of reeds, rattan, and so forth, that comes to us from China, the Philippines, the weavers of Europe and our own willow-craft workmen.

Of late another sort of furniture has been put on the market that will some day be useful to many of us. This is the cement or terra-cotta furniture made from old Italian models, and most suitable for gardens and hallways of stucco houses, but we need not concern ourselves with this furniture in this chapter.

You can associate furniture of each of the first four classes pleasantly in one room, if the design and color are in harmony. For instance, you can use a mahogany table and chintz-covered couch and willow chairs and a chest of drawers of painted wood in one room, or you can use oak furniture, tapestry-covered chairs, a black lacquer chest and Chinese reed chairs together. The Oriental lacquer furniture and the Occidental painted furniture are not friendly, just as oak and mahogany are usually unfriendly, but any one of the decorated woods may be combined with any one of the stained and waxed woods if the selection is made carefully.

If you had a piece of black-and-gold lacquer furniture, for instance, you would be careful to select a covering for your upholstered chairs that would be of plain color, or of a design in keeping with the design employed on the lacquer. It would be silly to associate chairs decorated with primrose garlands and lacquered furniture covered with fantastic temples, ships and Chinamen, in the same room. And yet either of these chairs, if used in connection with oak or mahogany furniture, would be very pleasant.

Wilson Eyre, Architect.

This view, taken in Mrs. Goodnow's house at Forest Hills, Long Island, shows a portion of the living and dining rooms. Note the use of hangings to give color to the walls.

Fortunately, we are no longer forced to buy sets of things. We buy a chair because it is comfortable and because it is beautiful, but we do not wish to repeat the chair. We would rather have a second chair of a different kind. The only room that really invites a "set" of chairs is the dining-room, and there is a great opportunity for gaiety and charm in this erstwhile formal room if you go about its furnishing in the right spirit.

Ever so many new houses are built without any real "dining-room." If the family is small and their life is simple, a huge living-room with a corner for dining is sensible. In my own house the dining- and living-rooms are practically one, so I avoided all the ugly "dining-roomy" things, and I keep the glass and china in the kitchen.

We have to be careful about mixing woods that depend on their grain and polish for their beauty, but there are so many lovely things in willow and rattan, in chintz and tapestry coverings, that we may associate with our fine polished woods and get remark-

199

able effects. There is something so very dreary about a proper room, with a set of furniture carefully matched, and sets of pictures and vases and books—not an accidental anywhere!

The secret of the association of furniture is: Harmony of color and line and design. Oak and mahogany are both beautiful woods in themselves, and if darkened by age and usage they may be used together, but if the oak is very brown and the mahogany very red, each cheapens the other. The oak seems coarse and colorless, and the mahogany seems impossibly red and shiny.

If your living-room is paneled or wainscoted in oak, and you have a particularly good Stuart chair with turned legs and cane inset to build on, you need not wait until you can buy other furniture of the same period as the chair. I know a very successful living-room furnished with objects of widely different types. There is an oak Windsor chair of the old kitchen type, a reproduction of a Cromwellian chair with oak frame and leather seat and back, a perfectly new upright piano of absolutely simple lines, a small table of unpretentious design, and a graceful Stuart chair, all in perfect accord with the spirit of the oak paneling. One beauty of such simplicity is that a fine tapestry-covered chair might be introduced into this room, and the piano and kitchen chair would still be at home.

This room might have been spoiled in a dozen different ways. If the piano had been "ornamented" a bit with geometric devices, if a squashy leather chair of the tufted variety had been used instead of the simple oak-and-leather one, if a heavy "Mission" rocker had been used instead of the Windsor chair, if one of those elaborately carved

chairs miscalled "Early English" by the dealers had been used instead of the Stuart chair, the whole room would have been thrown out of key.

You must consider not only the harmony of line and color and design, but also harmony of mass, of proportion, when you mix furniture of different types.

It is not possible to tell you just the sort of furniture to buy: that is something every woman must decide for herself.

I am not one of those painstakingly careful people who would have you throw away good furniture just to keep each room "in period." I think very few of us need concern ourselves with the trying task of working out period rooms. Most rooms grow of themselves, if you give them half a chance. Even if they were begun in the wrong spirit, they may be made beautiful if you will weed out the ugly, mistaken things and give the good things a chance to assert their worth.

A woman I know started out, thinking she wanted to furnish a house with "Mission" furniture. Fortunately, she started in a very small way—in a three-room apartment—so her purchases were restricted. She bought a library table, a bookcase and several heavy oak chairs for the combined living-room and dining-room. In less than six months after this ambitious little home had begun, an old lady died and left my friend her beloved secretary, one of those dignified old desks with book shelves above, with doors of leaded diamond panes. The old secretary was so big it did not really belong, after it arrived at the flat, and it had to be done over, but it was so very much nicer than everything else that the rest of the furniture was pulled around to make room for it.

It was n't long before the clumsy chairs

were sold to a second-hand dealer, and a willow chair and a rush-bottom one and a chintz covered one were substituted, because they seemed more at home with the old secretary. The heavy round table soon gave place to a graceful old mahogany table with drop leaves. The bookcase was abolished, and plain white shelves were built in. This home grew of itself from the moment the secretary entered it.

I am not condemning Mission furniture! Certainly the plain oak models that have come to us along with the craze for the bungalow are very much better than the furniture we've suffered for so many years—the Victorian walnut, the awful golden oak, the imitation mahogany that is still flooding the cheaper shops. Mission furniture is very good in its place, but its place is necessarily an uncrowded, spacious room. Certainly massive oak chairs and tables, no matter how well made, have no place in small city rooms.

Nor is this chapter a brief for old furniture. We speak in the terms of old furniture because the best furniture offered us is made from the old models. There are new men who are making beautiful things, both in America and abroad, but the prices are prohibitive. So we will be wise to study the various styles and schools of furniture that are being reproduced by intelligent manu-

Wilson Eyre, Architect.

A strongly figured wall paper is possible if its colors be harmonious. But it is more limited in its possibilities than a simple flat tone paper, because the furniture and hangings must be chosen especially to match its character. This room is in Mrs. Goodnow's house at Forest Hills, Long Island.

facturers, and plan our rooms according to what we most like, what we most need, and what we can actually afford. In the bibliography at the end of this book you will find a list of books on furniture, books that will give you the arguments pro and con, the earmarks, the secrets of those passionate adventurers who spend their lives in collecting old furniture. Certainly it seems to me little short of foolhardiness for a woman to plunge into a furniture shop until she has read much, and thought more of her require-

ments. I have n't laid stress on it,—but mistakes are costly.

I should like to give a neat lot of rules, a list that might be followed as casually as your grocery list, but it can't be done. I can only beg you to accept my theory, that nothing is worth buying which does not offer you both pleasure and service. Pleasure should mean Comfort and Beauty, and Service means Economy and Utility. Put these principles in your pocket and go a-shopping, but go slowly—go slowly!

Charles Barton Keen, Architect.
Note the unusual arrangement of beams in this pergola porch.

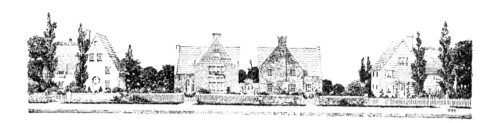

CHAPTER XXIV

A LIST OF USEFUL BOOKS

AND so we come to the end. A survey of the subject of home building such as is made in the foregoing chapters would be incomplete, however, if it did not include some suggestions for the further study of the subject.

The literature given over to the study and representation of architecture is extremely varied and in many respects satisfactory. Architectural histories and treatises are abundant. If you wish to study Greek or Roman or Italian architecture, there are many competent books which will give you plenty of information and inspiration. For the greater part this literature is occupied with monumental architecture:—the architecture of temples, palaces and public buildings generally. Domestic architecture of the formal and pretentious type is well represented, but, excepting the books devoted to English work, there is a very slight literature dealing with the more modest types of dwelling.

Of books treating of the American small house especially there are very few worthy of commendation. Of course one must remember that from the period of the later Georgian architecture until comparatively recent times,

there has been very little commendable architecture in this country to write about. The older Colonial or Georgian buildings have received much deserved attention, though the number of books at moderate prices is surprisingly small.

Our modern small-house architecture at its best is excellent; at its worst it is unbelievably bad,—and there is to-day much more bad architecture than good. Naturally enough, as a reflection of this fact, there is a paucity of books which present only the best examples of modern small-house design.

While books dealing adequately with the better aspects of domestic architecture are wanting, there is, unfortunately, no lack of books which advertise its worst aspects. Especially is this true of that type of commercial catalogue of house plans issued by certain "architectural firms" usually under such alluring titles as "One Hundred House Plans for One Dollar." They are filled for the most part with utterly reprehensible designs. The untrained person naturally enough cannot tell the difference between a bit of glass and a diamond, and while most of us know that there is a difference, we might be hard put to it to distinguish be-

Printed in Great Britain
by Amazon

30206993R00126

ESK VALLEY RAILWAY

RAILWAY

THROUGH TIME

Alan Whitworth

AMBERLEY PUBLISHING

Dedicated to all the loyal rail travellers, volunteers and rail staff on the Esk Valley Railway who keep the route going winter and summer

First published 2011

Amberley Publishing
The Hill, Stroud
Gloucestershire, GL5 4EP

www.amberley-books.com

Copyright © Alan Whitworth, 2011

The right of Alan Whitworth to be identified as the Author of this work has been asserted in accordance with the Copyrights, Designs and Patents Act 1988.

ISBN 978 1 4456 0645 3

British Library Cataloguing in Publication Data.
A catalogue record for this book is available from the British Library.

Typeset in 9.5pt on 12pt Celeste.
Typesetting by Amberley Publishing.
Printed in the UK.

Introduction

The River Esk rises in the Cleveland hills and flows east into the North Sea at Whitby. It drains a catchment area of 362 square kilometres. In length, from source to sea it is 42 kilometres, and is the only Salmon River on this side of England. From its mouth upstream, it is tidal for 5 kilometres from Whitby to Ruswarp Weir.

Today, most of the course of the river lies within the North Yorkshire Moors National Park, an outstanding area of countryside, which surrounds this ancient seaport. During the nineteenth century, this part of Yorkshire was mostly wild and inhospitable – high moorland intersected by deep, wooded valleys, with small hamlets scattered here and there. Even nowadays those who know and have visited Whitby realise only too well that the town is surrounded on the landward side by hills in every direction, and that all traffic to and from the interior has to be taken over these natural impediments, which in winter are made even more hazardous by the weather. In olden times, these natural barriers were, no doubt, even more of an obstacle, due to the type of vehicles and the state of the highways themselves.

As a consequence of this, at Whitby, most travellers to and from the town made journeys via the sea. However, by the early nineteenth century, it was becoming evident that, because of this means of transport, the town was lagging behind other places in many respects and failing to prosper as it ought.

Throughout the first two decades of the nineteenth century, the question of improvements by either railway or canal, and whether to Pickering or Stockton and Darlington, was hotly debated in the town. Eventually, a decision was made to construct a railway along part of the Esk Valley to Grosmont and then toward Pickering to join the rail network to York.

On 10 September 1833, work began and by 1835 the first six miles of track had been laid. The following year witnessed the opening of the Whitby & Pickering line as a horse-railway on Thursday 26 May 1836. However, it was not for another eleven years that the first steam locomotive would enter the town – on Friday 4 June 1847 – and from that date horse traction became a thing of the past, and the overland journey to Whitby could be made much more safely and comfortably.

Built by George Stephenson, and later extended by George Hudson, the course of the River Esk was diverted just upstream of Whitby. At other places, hills were breached with cuttings, and tunnels put through. Giant trees were felled and huge embankments built until, eventually, a railway link was formed between Whitby and Middlesbrough and the North East.

Popularly known as the Esk Valley line, the inland route from Whitby northwards began at Teesside as the North Yorkshire & Cleveland Railway. Authorised in 1854, the NY & CR was promoted jointly by the Leeds Northern Railway and the West Hartlepool Harbour & Railway Company. As with most other lines in Cleveland, the main attraction was the prospect of traffic in ironstone. The Leeds Northern was one of the constituent companies which amalgamated on 31 July 1854 to form the North Eastern Railway, which took over full control of the NY & CR in 1859.

The line from Picton to Stokesley opened on 3 May 1857 together with the two-mile branch from Potto to Swainby, which was soon carrying two trainloads of ironstone per day. The Swainby branch survived until 1892.

The railway was extended to Ingleby on 1 February 1858 and through Battersby to Kildale on 6 April. Castleton was reached on 1 April 1861 but it took until 2 October 1865 to complete the route to Grosmont on the Whitby & Pickering line. Meanwhile a branch had opened in 1864, initially only for goods, from Battersby to Nunthorpe Junction on the Middlesbrough–Guisborough line; the passenger service between Middlesbrough and Battersby commenced in 1868.

Today, a rail journey from Whitby to Middlesbrough is possibly the best way to see the glories of the Esk Valley with all its diversity of scenery. For myself, I love to catch the 9 a.m. train out of Whitby enjoy the journey, have a coffee and cake in the twenty-minute wait at Middlesbrough, and then return on the 10.38 a.m., which gets me home for noon; the best way to while away a morning.

A railway themed garden at the back of a new bungalow erected on the site of the West Cliff station, Whitby, which closed in 1963 and has now been converted to residential use. It forms the centre of a small estate of housing.

The Old Railway Station

One of the oldest surviving railway buildings in the world is the round weigh-house and booking hall of the horse-drawn railway of the 1830s, which was constructed by George Stephenson, and later taken over by George Hudson, the 'Railway King'. It was he who began the Whitby Stone Building Company and erected this small building, one of two matching that stood across from each other as part of his loading and unloading facilities near the waterside where he could transport heavy mountains of stone by sea around the country for building projects.

River Esk and Whitby
The River Esk empties out into the North Sea at Whitby. On the right bank are the Prussian Blue Dye works with its tall chimney, which made clothing of a distinctive 'denim' colour. This dye left its mark on the cliffs here well into the 1970s, long after it had gone. The railway can be seen snaking its way along the river bank and in the centre you can see the railway booking hall above the old gas works, which gives an appreciation of the distance it stood outside the town.

Whitby Harbour and Station

One of the oldest photographs of the rail complex at Whitby, taken from a lantern slide from above Bog Hall. The line from Pickering (which has already been joined by the lines from Scarborough and Loftus) enters from the left and passes the tall Bog Hall signal box. It then disappears behind the dockside works to emerge between the two-road engine shed and the goods warehouse. Above, a group photograph of railway staff in the goods yard shed at Whitby in 1888. Included are the stationmaster, seated, and the railway constable standing behind him.

Whitby Railway Station

At one time the harbour came up almost to the steps of the railway station. The station was opened on this site in 1847 by Robert Stephenson, son of George Stephenson, the 'father of railways', who was MP for Whitby between 1847 and 1859. The original station was about a mile out of the town, and it took almost ten years before the citizens believed it was here to stay. As consequence, they would not sanction a way over the shipyards, which were far more important then than this new craze!

Anne and *Endeavour*

The top photograph, taken on 19 September 1895 by Frank Meadow Sutcliffe, shows the vessel *Anne* in the upper harbour framed by the entrance to the North Eastern Railway Company's town station. Below, I can't remember the date I took this photograph of the Australian-built replica of Captain Cook's famous *Endeavour* from the same position, but as you can see, the importance of the harbour has shrunk in relationship to distance that dock end has been filled in and covered by the ubiquitous motor car. The station was opened before a large assembly of people with due pomp and ceremony; a band played, and a suitable poetic eulogy was prepared which read:

> When Whitby's wealth in yearly steps decay'd,
> By Stephenson's bold schemes her fall was stay'd;
> And now, behold! The works his labours won
> On wings of steam bring here his far fam'd son,
> Whose powerful genius and inventive mind
> Shall show us all how best our local wealth to find.

Hail! To the man whose well carried fame Through [all] the wide world is known; Happy the day! When Whitby's sons May claim him as their own.

The Angel Hotel, Whitby

In 1831, George Stephenson (1781–1848) (*right*), considered the 'father of railways', took an interest in Whitby and was invited to undertake any such survey and construct a rail link into the interior, following a meeting that took place in 1832 at the Angel Hotel (*below*), for the purpose of considering the practicability of forming a railroad from that place to either Stockton or Pickering and of raising funds for defraying the expense of a survey of the route. Later George Hudson (left) turned Stephenson's enterprise into a steam railway.

Whitby Engine Sheds and Sidings

On 10 September 1833, soon after work commenced, Robert Campion had the privilege and pleasure of turning the day's first spadeful of earth near Boghall. By 1835, the first six miles of track had been laid along the Esk Valley bottom. The earliest railway buildings were erected on the former shipyard of Fishburn & Broderick in which the ships that Captain Cook used were built. Of those early buildings, only one of two railway engine sheds survive, and the ruins of the original station built *c.* 1836 upstream on the banks of the River Esk.

The Railway Yard, Whitby

This photograph by Doran shows the aftermath of enemy bombing on Monday evening, 16 September 1940, when a German aircraft dropped eight bombs on Whitby. There were no serious casualties but considerable damage to property in Windsor Terrace, Bobby's Bank and the railway goods yard. The railway track in the yard was destroyed but the line was restored within forty-eight hours. Above can be seen an autocar combination that consisted of a coupled engine and carriage, which could be driven from either the footplate or coach, hence the porthole windows on the coach.

Railway Station Hotel, Whitby

At the beginning of the nineteenth century, Whitby fell almost overnight into a massive economic depression. Its wealth had been built on the sea and trades associated with it. As a consequence, unemployment rose, with just one in ten in employment. At that date it was not considered a holiday resort. It had but one or two coaching inns for accommodation, but no hotels or boarding houses for visitors. It needed to reinvent itself. George Hudson, as an influential and important person in Victorian society, after taking over the railway had a vision to turn Whitby into a resort to be visited by the elite. The Royal Hotel on the West Cliff was built and run by his brother Charles, and most of the early boarding houses and streets were constructed at Hudson's personal expense. In town, opposite the railway station, the Railway Station Hotel, then a warehouse and offices known as Albert Chambers, was converted into a first-class hotel around 1881 for J. J. Gutch of York, by the Whitby architect Edward H. Smailes. High above in the gable the original name can still be read; today it is the George Hotel.

Stationmaster's House, Whitby

Above, an early view of Station Square, today almost unrecognisable compared with the present scene. The large house was formerly the stationmaster's house opposite the railway station entrance. Later it became the Central Restaurant, as it is in this photograph. Eventually, the entire site was demolished and developed into the present bus station owned by Arriva. Behind in the lower view is the GPO telephone exchange building, and the pink-walled property is the side of the Temperance Hall, now the Coliseum, and in between a picture house and bingo hall.

The Men Behind the Machine

Staff of the Whitby Railway Station Sorting Office and Goods Depot, *c.* 1897, taken outside the goods depot along with other bowler-hatted dignitaries and the station dog, who was probably also the rat catcher. Below, the North Eastern Railway Brass Band in 1907 as inscribed on the drum – did they entertain the passengers during times of delay I wonder? Nothing is known about this group of musicians, except that on the middle row, third from the right is Walter Agar. However, crucial questions remain, such as whether they were in fact even employees of the railway company.

Larpool Viaduct

Larpool Viaduct was begun on 17 October 1882 and took almost two years to complete. It is 915 feet long and at its highest point is 125 feet from the river bed to parapet. It is supported on twelve piers with thirteen arches each with an average span of 60 feet. It is estimated to contain five million bricks and cost about £40,000. The viaduct was constructed to carry the Scarborough–Whitby coast railway, finally opened as a through route in 1898, which was operated by the North Eastern Railway Company owned by George Hudson.

Larpool Viaduct

It was the Scarborough–Whitby Railway that was carried over the river, the first locomotive crossing on 31 October 1844. The main station to serve this line was the West Cliff Station; this link was closed to traffic on 3 May 1961. It lay disused and trackless for many years, and was offered for sale at the price of one penny in recent years. Today the railway serves as a cycleway to Scarborough. The piers are set at an angle to the river flow to lessen the water pressure when the river is in flood.

Ruswarp Railway Station

Ruswarp railway station, erected in 1850 to a design by George T. Andrews, architect for the Yorkshire & North Midland Railway. He was friend of George Hudson and designed many of the bridges and stations for Hudson's great railway empire. It is constructed in the 'Tudor style' and the station house is now a private residence with the platform still in use. Notice the level crossing gates, now replaced by a modern rising barrier system and the absence of one of the platforms.

Ruswarp from the Air

From the air you can see the River Esk, and how both the road and rail bridges that span it interact. The church is evident as is the large Georgian house on the corner of The Carrs, which was demolished to make way for the open space and village green. The mill can be seen, and the cottages at the very bottom of the photograph stand on what was a staithe. Below is a photograph of the flooding, this time showing the lifeboat being brought through the village to rescue people trapped in the houses.

Ruswarp Railway Bridge

A scene showing the debris scattered over the railway line following the flooding of July 1930, including the pleasure row boats. The original road bridge adjacent had to be replaced after flood damage and the now familiar, curved iron girder bridge replaced it in 1933. An interesting feature of the new bridge can be seen in the stone wall leading up to it on the opposite side of the Esk, where, during the Second World War, the bridge name was carefully chiselled off as instructed in order to make life difficult for any invading Germans.

Ruswarp in Flood 1930

The Esk is prone to flooding hereabouts. The most spectacular flood has to be that which occurred on 23 July 1930. On this day, the waters reached a height of 5′ 2″ in the tap room of the Bridge Inn. Villagers in their homes had to be rescued by local men using the pleasure boats. In another flood not many years later, the lifeboat was brought overland by road hauled by hand from Whitby to rescue those trapped in their cottages and this can be seen on the previous page.

Ruswarp High Street
The High Street at Ruswarp at this point has changed very little from the eighteenth century, which most of the buildings seen here date from, except there is no ivy on the Georgian building. The church of St Bartholomew, with its distinctive spire, is a nineteenth-century edifice opened on 30 September 1869. Sadly, in 2011 the village post office closed after over a century of service. Nevertheless, the village still boasts a general store and a local butcher's, which ironically, now sells the local newspaper.

Boating on the Esk

The famous artist George du Maurier and his equally famous children Daphne and Gerald, often enjoyed picnics and rowing at Ruswarp – featured in this *Punch* cartoon of 1882. Below, the weir is tidal. The upper photograph shows the boats passing the Chainbridge Tea Gardens (*page 25*) sometime in the 1950s. A favourite spot until the late 1960s was the Chainbridge Café on the banks of the River Esk at Ruswarp. It took its name from one of the first iron suspension bridges erected in England, which spanned the river here in the early nineteenth century.

Ruswarp Mill

Ruswarp Mill was mentioned in the Domesday Book, and belonged to the monks of Whitby Abbey. A water-powered corn mill, it was later rebuilt and became a bolting mill and carries the inscription, 'Erected at the Expense of Nathaniel Cholmley by Philip Williams, Engineer, 1752.' The mill suffered a disastrous fire on 25 September 1911, when it was totally gutted. Rebuilt, it ended its life as a provender mill producing animal feed. It ceased production in 1962. In 1990 the mill and site were converted into luxury apartments and a small housing complex.

Sleights Railway Station

The next village along the railway is Sleights, although technically the station lies in the hamlet of Briggswath; another of Andrew's 'Tudor style' stationhouses, again a private residence. In the bottom photograph the new road bridge of 1937 can be seen. This replaced the 'ancient stone bridge of three arches which crossed the river eighty yards downstream destroyed by flood in July 1930', as recorded on a plaque fixed to the new road bridge, which can be seen in the bottom photograph.

Sleights Railway Goods Yard

Sleights railway station was closed under the 'Beeching Axe' of the 1960s. However, before then it was a busy station with railway sidings and a coal yard. After closure, gradually things began to slide as the station went into decline. The wooden platform waiting room was dismantled and re-erected at Grosmont station. Years later, the railway tracks were lifted making it only a single track line from Whitby to Middlesbrough, and the final nail in the coffin was when the coal man left to set up elsewhere.

New Ways, New Days

When the Esk Valley railway line was threatened with closure in the 1960s, public pressure prevailed and it received a stay of execution. This rail link is sometimes the only communication with the rural villages up the Esk Valley in the deep winter when the roads are impassable. Sadly, they ran very few trains – only three a day out and three back. However, in very recent years, the NYM Railway, after helping to strengthen and repair the track, has got permission to run steam engines and diesel locomotives into Whitby town.

Sleights Bridge washed away by Floods
28-7-...
No. 15

The Floods of 1930

It was during the 1930 floods that the 'ancient stone bridge' was washed away, causing a great deal of inconvenience. It was here that the main road from the moors into Whitby crossed beside the station and was guarded by a level-crossing. It also carried the main water and sewage pipes for the village. As a consequence services were severely disrupted. All this was eventually tidied up and now it is hardly possible to tell a level-crossing ever existed here at all, and only the signal box remains from this scene, standing derelict.

Sleights

Sleights Level Crossing and Signal Box

From my home on the Carrs, it is only a few minutes' walk to Sleights station over the Esk by way of the footbridge clearly visible before the tree growth. I often walk this way and, on Friday 24 August, I decided to take the train. As usual I followed the footpath beside the disused signal box, and prepared to wait for my train's arrival. It was then that I realised what was different about the view across the track – a new information board had sprung beside the gate up where none had stood before.

River Gardens Tea Rooms, Sleights

Like Ruswarp at the other end of 'The Carrs', the river was a big attraction. The Edwardian tea gardens still ply their trade in cream teas, enlarged today by the addition of a garden centre –there is still a putting green but sadly, the rowing boats have gone on grounds of health and safety. This area was first populated in prehistoric times and the remains of Bronze Age man has been found here on this site. We also know the soil hereabouts was trodden on by Cavalier soldiers.

The Station Hotel, Sleights

Coach Road gave access to the railway station at the very bottom and was also the main vehicular highway before 1930. Now it is almost a rural country lane, though the houses on the right are the same, as indeed is the public house to the left. Today, the hostelry has changed its name from the Station Hotel to the Salmon Leap Hotel. The new name reflects its proximity to the salmon leap on the River Esk. The stationhouse with its many tall chimneys is now obscured by mature trees.

Sleights Village Centre

Sleights village centre. The chap sitting on a local type of sledge, which was used to haul stone from the quarries around here, would be taking his life in his hands with today's traffic! The butcher's and local village store occupy these old buildings today, just as they did a century ago. The only difference is the insertion of dormer windows in the roofs – a modern phenomenon. The stone was taken down to the railway then shipped off to the port of Whitby for transportation around the world.

Eskdale Chapel, the Church of Sleights

The ancient chapel on Eskdaleside, shown above around 1774, when it had not long closed. Its origins lay in the thirteenth century. Locally known as 'The Hermitage', it is connected with the ancient Whitby custom of the 'Penny Hedge Ceremony', and the 'Legend of the Hermit of Eskdale'. This remote chapel was the main place of worship for Sleights and the surrounding hamlets until the eighteenth century. Today, its remains are a Grade II listed monument in the care of English Heritage. They still stand near to the railway though hidden in the trees.

Grove Hall and Salmon Leap

Leaving Sleights and passing under the high-rise road bridge, it is possible to see the Esk at close quarters. The River Esk is the longest Salmon River on the eastern side of England and a salmon leap has been here since the Middle Ages to assist the fish as they swim up the river to spawn. Grove Hall has its origins in the medieval period when the monks of Whitby had a watermill here and the building, dating from eighteenth century, is all that is left of the mill, which ceased operating in the 1920s.

Pond House, Aislaby

On the opposite side of the valley to Sleights, stands Aislaby overlooking the Esk and Briggswath, and this can be seen from the railway. There are many fine country house mansions hereabouts, and this is one. Pond House was reached over a small, decorative stone bridge that straddles a pond – hence its name. A gem of an eighteenth-century property, built for one of the Whitby ship owners around the year 1789. A great deal of industry took place here, and the tanning of hides for the leather was carried on at Aislaby.

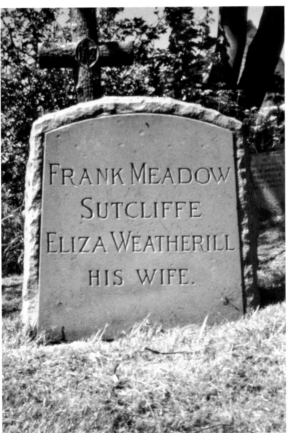

St Margaret's Church, Aislaby
Originally a Chapel of Ease to the
parish church at Whitby, Aislaby
is now a separate parish in its own
right. In 1732, after lying ruinous for
almost eighty years, it was rebuilt by
public subscription and fitted with
galleries. This church was replaced in
the nineteenth century. At first there
was no burial ground and parishioners
were generally buried in Sleights
churchyard. Eventually, a piece of
adjoining land was appropriated. It is
in the burial ground at Aislaby that the
Whitby photographer, Frank Meadow
Sutcliffe and his wife are interred.

Grosmont Station

Here at Grosmont Station, passengers can alight and join the Whitby & Pickering Railway, now known as the North Yorks Moors Railway. This was the original rail link George Stephenson completed out of Whitby and was, at first, a horse-drawn railway to which the present railway was coupled, giving access to York and the industrial West Riding of Yorkshire. Two stations exist here side-by-side, built in 1846 by G. T. Andrews in the 'Tudor style' of architecture with mullion windows filled with small leaded diamond panes and great heavy Tudor-arched doorways.

Grosmont Level Crossing and Co-operative Store

Grosmont, the junction where the Whitby–Pickering Railway, known as the North Yorks Moors Railway (NYMR), is a preserved line staffed by volunteers, and the Whitby–Middlesbrough Railway part company. The building here is the Co-operative store. In a small community the Co-op played a major role in village life. It was founded by local residents in May 1867. In 1900 the store was enlarged. Today it is still a truly run co-operative managed by the villagers.

Grosmont Ironworks

Today a peaceful tranquil village, only a century ago the scene was quite the opposite when Grosmont was overshadowed by the huge furnaces of its ironworks and coke ovens. All alongside the railway line was a hive of activity, noise and dirt as the furnaces spewed out clouds of smoke and dust from 1837 to 1915, just after this photograph was taken showing the station platform in foreground. Today, this small stump of masonry is all that remains of the numerous buildings seen above left as a reminder of former days.

The Station Tavern, Grosmont

The Station Hotel, Grosmont, now renamed the Station Tavern. Architecturally, one of the more interesting buildings in the village, it was erected about the year 1907, but with its old-fashioned ogee-headed downstairs windows it appears to date from almost a century earlier. Despite its sleepy appearance, it is still a popular haunt for locals and visitors alike and no doubt was the scene of many a labourer's dispute. Above, the horse ruled, today the car dominates the scene.

The North York Moors Preserved Railway

Negotiations involving the formation of the North Yorkshire Moors Railway were protracted, and almost four years elapsed after closure of the line and Grosmont Station before crowds assembled at Goathland on a wintry 2 February 1969, to see 0-4-0ST *Mirvale* making the preservation society's first train movement. The locomotive, photographed by Tindale's of Whitby, was *en route* from Pickering to Grosmont. Today the NYMNP can boast fifty years of existence and is a hugely popular asset to the district, now running steam locomotives from Pickering into Whitby town.

Grosmont Tunnel Entrance

Above, the entrance to the old railway tunnel at Grosmont as it originally was – an engraving that appeared in the earliest book on the subject written by Henry Belcher, solicitor to the Whitby & Pickering Railway, and published in 1836. Over the woo bridge and through this tunnel ran the horse-drawn Whitby–Pickering Railway. Today visitors can enjoy the novelty of walking through this tunnel to the Engine Repair Shed of the NYM Railway and view the workings. However, the old wooden bridge has been replaced by a sturdy stone structure.

Goathland Station – *Heartbeat* and *Harry Potter* County

Goathland of course, is best known for the setting to the TV series *Heartbeat*, based on the books of a retired policeman Nicholas Rhea. However, in more recent times, it is possibly more familiar to a younger generation as Hogsmead station, the stop for Hogswarts School of Witchcraft and Wizardry in *Harry Potter and the Philosopher's Stone*. Goathland station was built in 1865 and today forms part of the NYM Railway, a preserved line running from Grosmont to Pickering. Camping coaches could be found here, and this facility has now been reintroduced.

Egton [Bridge] Railway Station

Egton railway station was one of the last to open when the line final reached Grosmont in 1865, and once again the station buildings are by Thomas Prosser in his unmistakeable style. The countryside around here is agricultural and each year the Egton Bridge Old Gooseberry Show is held, the only one of its kind still surviving in Yorkshire. This has been held since 1800, and in August 1994 a new gooseberry named 'Goliath' broke all existing records when a single berry weighed in at 31 drams, 22 grains – almost two ounces!

Egton Bridge Station

Above, the approach to Egton Station, unchanged from the nineteenth century; how many feet must have trod these stone paving slabs? Below is the Postgate Inn, named after the Catholic martyr, Nicholas Postgate. The photograph was taken in August 2011 from the rail bridge that carries the railway over the road from Egton village to Grosmont and beyond. The figures looking toward the pub are Malcolm, proprietor of M&D Coaches, a local bus service that he and his wife operate, who are waiting for the early afternoon train and his son.

Egton Village
A busy crossroads – highways at Egton lead down the valley to Grosmont and Grosmont railway station, or another way leads to the villages of Lealholm and Castleton. This is the road running steeply downhill into Egton Bridge in the valley bottom from where you can travel over country roads to Goathland and other isolated communities. All the houses and the farm still survive, having hardly changed at all. Just behind the photographers' viewpoint on the right are some thatched cottages and beyond the bottom white houses on the right is the new doctor's surgery.

St Hilda's Church, Egton

Egton church, dedicated to St Hilda, is one of two churches at Egton. The older building stands isolated outside the village. As a consequence, when in the nineteenth century the church was expandings, another, more convenient site was picked for the Church of England church. Today the church is as active as it ever was, and here we see it being decorated by the villagers for the wedding of the Lord of the Manor's daughter in 2009. Lords of Egton have been descended from the Foster family, whose origins can be found at Bradford in the West Riding.

The Catholic Church of St Hedda, Egton Bridge

In the valley bottom is Egton Bridge, dominated by the huge Catholic church dedicated to St Hedda. Erected in 1860, its new 'white' stonework contrasts with the landscape. Egton Bridge has always been a Catholic stronghold, even in times of persecution, and one of a number of Catholic martyrs lived here – Father Nicholas Postgate, born 1592, who was executed publicly in a terrible fashion at York in 1679. Beside the Postgate Inn, the traveller by rail disembarks for Egton and climbs the steep hill to Egton village.

Glaisdale Railway Station

Glaisdale station was opened in 1865 and the buildings are typical of the architecture of this railway, having the distinct crow-stepped gables. The siting of ironworks at Glaisdale in 1868 prompted the promotion of the 10¼-mile Cleveland Extension Railway, which would have run across the moors starting at Lingdale Junction, south of Brotton, and joined the Esk Valley route about ¾ mile north-west of Glaisdale station. The route was incorporated in 1873 and some earthworks were completed before the premature closure of Glaisdale Ironworks in 1876 and the line was abandoned.

Damage by floods n'Glaisdale 23-7-30

Glaisdale Floods, 23 July 1930
On 23 July 1930, a stone railway bridge was destroyed by the swollen River Esk in Arncliffe Woods just east of Glaisdale. Traffic was suspended between Glaisdale and Egton until 25 May 1931 when a replacement girder bridge was opened using the old abutments. Unfortunately, after only three months this too collapsed during floods that swept away one of the abutments. In rebuilding, a new pier was sunk into the middle of the river to provide extra support. The route finally reopened for the second time on 27 August 1932.

Beggar's Bridge, Glaisdale

On the approach to Glaisdale station, the line crosses the Esk and below stands Beggar's Bridge, an old pack-horse bridge. The name Beggar's Bridge was given to it in memory of an ancient tale concerning its erection arising from a romantic tale of two local lovers from each side of the waters which met here, the man having to make the dangerous crossing to meet his girl. He made a promise to build a bridge here if he became rich – which he did and made good his promise in 1674.

Beggar's Bridge, Glaisdale

Careless driving or what! A bizarre accident while crossing Beggar's Bridge, when the horses suddenly took fright and fell over the low parapet. Here we see one still hanging by its harness. The other, already cut down, lies dead in the river below, waiting to be fished out. Leading down to Beggar's Bridge is a very steep and twisty narrow road called Limber Hill, which has caused many a motorcar accident. The lorry here around 1912 belonged to McVitie & Price and was delivering biscuits and cakes.

Underhill Cottages, Glaisdale

Glaisdale is a straggly village rising up from the river at Beggar's Bridge and then dipping down into a fold in the earth to climb up the other side. Like Grosmont, it had an industrial past of which only this terrace of miners' cottages known as Underhill, survives as testimony, and in the landscape can be found numerous spoil heaps that grew from the waste deposits. In front of the cottages a branch line once existed that allowed the wagons of iron ore to be taken direct to Grosmont and the furnaces.

Lealholm Railway Station

Lealholm station, around 1905, like a number of stations displays the distinctive crow-stepped gables to the design of Thomas Prosser. Lealholm station opened in October 1865 and in 1898 it was listed by the NER as a 'Preceding Place', which meant that a passenger train had the right of way and could overtake a goods train at this point. A great deal of goods traffic left Lealholm and consisted mostly of clay and ganister stone; goods traffic ceased on 2 August 1965. The engine shed today serves as the garage of John Cook.

Lealholm Village

The village centre; Lealholm was mentioned in the Domesday Book as *Lelum* and the placename is derived from the Old English *laela* meaning 'among the twigs' and the Old Norse *holmr*, and refers to a time when all this moorland was woodland. A clearing had to be first created to enable the villagers to build houses, and more importantly, a bridge to cross the waters at this point. Together, these two elements aptly describe the situation of Lealholm even today with its village green and bridge over the Esk waters.

Lealholm Floods 1930
The famous deluge of July 1930, when the River Esk caused enormous damage and distress along the Esk Valley. You can just spot the parapet of an old pack-horse bridge in the torrent of water. Despite the many inundations, in summer it is a pretty place to visit and has an annual 'show' in a field where the fun is to cross the stepping stones to the field in which it is held when the water is only inches deep, crystal clear and hardly dangerous.

Shepherd's Hall, Lealholm

In the days before Social Services, the NHS, the 'dole', National Insurance and sick benefits, welfare problems of the people were met by local Friendly Societies, often unions of like-minded members who paid weekly subscriptions into a common fund from which they could draw in hard times. In Lealholm these distinctive buildings are known as Shepherd's Hall erected by the 'Loyal Order of Ancient Shepherds Friendly Society No. 1343 built 1873' of which we see a group of member above posed for a group photograph.

Danby Castle

The situation of Danby Castle is exceedingly fine. It stands on a hillside with panoramic views and can be seen clearly from the railway. Built between 1296 and 1300 by an ancestor of the Brus family, from who are descended the kings of Scotland from Robert de Bruce. It came into the possession of the Neville family by marriage. Here also lived Catherine Parr, wife of Henry VIII. Danby also has the only remaining working watermill on the River Esk and the 350-year-old mill is often open to the public.

Danby Court Leet

One room within the castle is set aside for the use of the ancient Court Leet, which might be described as the People's Parliament and survives here at Danby with its power to this day. Danby Lodge below was a property of the Neville family, which was extended as an Edwardian hunting lodge by Lord Downe for weekend parties. Now it is owned by the North Yorkshire Moors National Park and is a visitor centre telling the story of the district. It offers some interesting interpretative exhibitions and puts on a range of demonstrations.

Duck Bridge, Danby

From Lealholm by one road the intrepid traveller soon reaches Danby. An ancient hamlet, it has a castle, which is reached via Duck Bridge built at the end of the fourteenth century and bearing on its keystone the heraldic arms of John, Lord Neville of Raby Castle. Duck Bridge is another old pack-horse bridge, which has survived various floods. The high arch saved many, as debris being carried down stream would pass under rather than piling up against lower arched bridges causing pressure on the stonework.

Danby Railway Station

Danby station became operational when the Castleton line united with the Whitby–Pickering service at Grosmont on 2 October 1865. In the photograph we can clearly see the stepped gable ends of the station house, a design much favoured by the North Eastern Railway, which took over the Esk Valley line from the North Yorkshire & Cleveland Railway in 1858. Here the station buildings are a plainer adaptation than those at Kildale, which were designed by John Bourne. The large metal water tank mounted on stone structure held 13,000 gallons of water.

Danby Railway Station

A Middlesbrough to Whitby locomotive DMU (diesel multiple unit) leaves Danby in 1966. By this date Danby station had lost some of its importance, and a number of its structures, in particular, the large water tank and stone building on which it stood had been removed along with the engine shed seen in the bottom photograph on the previous page, reached by sidings off the main line of which some rusted track is still visible. In later years a similar building was erected on the site for agricultural use.

Danby Wesleyan Chapel

An earlier chapel at Danby proved to be inadequate as the congregation grew and in 1887 a Sunday school was added to the building. By 1898, the Chapel Trust made a decision to rebuild on the site of the 1811 chapel that was to be a more conveniently arranged and handsome place of worship. On the 17 July 1901, seven memorial stones were laid for the foundation of the new chapel. The final cost of the chapel was £1,080 and it was opened in the August of the following year.

Castleton Railway Station

The first locomotive steamed into Castleton on April Fool's Day, 1861, and when the line from Castleton was extended to join the Grosmont section in 1865, access to Whitby and Pickering could then be enjoyed. One of the features at Castleton station was a wooden belfry. Inside the housing a bell was positioned for the use of passengers wishing to attract the rail staff, or traders requiring assistance with their goods. Castleton railway station today is officially known as 'Castleton Moor Station'; the station house was sold and is now a private residence.

Castleton Railway Station

In winter Castleton station was a remote halt. To improve communications between Whitby and Castleton a new omnibus service sprang up to enable passengers to connect with the government train that ran daily from Whitby to Middlesbrough in the nineteenth century. Below, a rare postcard of troops of the 1st Volunteer Battalion of the Northumberland Fusiliers disembarking from a train at Castleton station in 1904. The unusual headdress of a soft brimmed 'cowboy' hat was first worn by these troops in the Boer War, 1899–1901, and proved far more comfortable than the solar toupee.

Station Hotel, Castleton

The station at Castleton is situated outside the village on the road to Guisborough and over the bridge spanning the River Esk in the valley bottom – almost a mile from Castleton centre! Passengers using it have a hard climb to the main street. In times gone by, the local hunt met at the Station Hotel before fox hunting was banned. Later it changed its name to the Eskdale Inn and you could get your 'day fishing' license at this establishment. The bridge behind carries the railway over the road.

Castleton Market and Cheese Fair

Castleton was the ancient baronial capital of Upper Eskdale. It had an important Cheese Fair and regular cattle marts were held in the old market square. One of the best books on the history of Castleton was written by Joseph Ford, a resident, whose volume *Some Reminiscences of the Folk Lore of Danby Parish and District* was published posthumously in 1953. In this, he mentions the 'Hand of Glory', used by burglars to cast a spell over the inhabitants of the property they were about to rob and which is now in Whitby Museum.

Royal Wedding Celebrations, 2011

Castleton, the upper Main Street on which stood the Moorland Hotel that closed some years back. Castleton had numerous public houses at one period, but today there is only one. Below, the main street decked out for the wedding of HRH Prince William to Catherine 'Kate' Middleton on Friday 29 April 2011. This photograph is one of a series I took along the whole length of Castleton two days after the event. It was possibly the only village along the entire length of the Esk Valley which was so bedecked.

Westerdale Village

One of the highest and most remote places in the Esk Valley is Westerdale and Westerdale village. Here, on a bright clear day you feel you can touch the heavens. It is a wide dale and through the lower parts the tributary 'Tower Beck', as well as the 'Little Esk' itself, run down from the moorland heights. Westerdale village is served by the station at Castleton almost two miles away, yet nevertheless, in past times the residents made regular use of the railway travelling either to Guisborough market or Whitby market to buy and sell.

Westerdale Hall, Castleton

Westerdale Hall was built in the 'Baronial' style of architecture, which almost gives it the appearance of a Scottish castle. It was erected in the nineteenth century as a shooting lodge, and was later owned by the Youth Hostel Association (YHA). Now it is once more a private residence. By contrast, the rear of one of Westerdale's cottages, photographed in 2009! Neither buildings are any different from when first erected – both caught in a time warp.

Commondale Railway Station

Commondale, known as Commondale Sidings, ran for a mile long up to the Commondale Brick and Tile Works, north of the station. Commondale Sidings finally acquired the title 'Station' in 1894. Commondale became the first unstaffed station in the Esk Valley in 1954. Below, Trevor Goodall, volunteer inspector visits each station once a month to check on cleanliness, damage and to ensure all of the posters are current and up to date. Frank Elgee, archaeologist, author and curator of the Dorman Museum in Middlesbrough lived in the large bungalow behind the present station, called Shirley House from 1920–31.

Commondale Village

Having a brickworks onsite meant that a large number of the buildings here are made of the local brick. On the left, the brickwork site is now a Boy Scout camp. Ravensgill Beck, which runs down to the village through the old brickworks, has an interesting memorial stone to a George Watson, who drowned himself in a fit of depression in August 1876. Apparently he was employed at the brickworks and, after his suicide, the memorial stone was placed at the very spot along the beck where he drowned.

Commondale Brick & Pottery Company

A printer from Stokesley John Slater Pratt, who founded the Cleveland Fire Brick & Pottery Co. Ltd. He acquired an area of farmland south-west of Castleton, and had built Didderhowe Farm as his second residence. On his death in 1867, the brickworks ceased operations, but were taken over by John Crossley in 1872, becoming the Commondale Pottery. The works diversified their products, producing domestic pottery, pipes, bricks and garden vases. The industry gradually reduced its output until it suspended operations in 1947. Eventually all signs of the workings disappeared.

Kildale Railway Station

Built as an extension of the North Yorkshire & Cleveland branch line, opened in 1858, the station was adapted from earlier designs for that route by John Bourne, but given neatly emphasised quoins and keystones. Today, it is hard to believe that Kildale railway station was so well-appointed, with station house and passenger facilities that were all swept away in 1956, to be replaced by the present 'bus shelter'. Below, a modern DMU heads for Whitby. The man in uniform in the foreground is thought to be George Bindoff, who was stationmaster in 1906.

Kildale Church and Station

Adjacent to the station is the church of St Cuthbert, reached by the footbridge over the station. During restoration work and eventual rebuilding of the structure in 1868, Revd J. C. Atkinson discovered in the foundations several ancient tombstones that verified Danish occupation of the district. West of St Cuthbert's, the Percy family erected a castle in 1156 – a wooden structure initially, later replaced by a stone building. A local historian, Roland Close, during excavations of the castle site in 1970–72, unearthed a fragment of chainmail in the region of the kitchen fireplace.

New Row

Like so many villages, Kildale has a Methodist chapel. Prior to its erection services were held nearby in one of the 'New Row' cottages. New Row cottages can be seen from the railway as it passes between Kildale and Commondale. Standing isolated, they were erected during the late nineteenth century for habitation by railway workers and their families. To reach them, the line has to be crossed off the main road via a level crossing and then a long drive up a rough lane, even today.

Battersby Station

In the view below, one of the uniformed men could be John Dunn who was stationmaster at the time this photograph was taken in the early 1900s. A narrow-gauge railway had been built by the Ingleby Ironstone & Freestone Mining Company, from mines at Rudscar on the Cleveland Hills down to Battersby Junction (called Ingleby Junction in 1858). The line was absorbed by the North Yorkshire & Cleveland Railway, which constructed a single track standard-gauge railway from Battersby to West Rosedale, a distance of 14 miles in 1861.

Battersby Railway Station

Designed by Thomas Prosser, the station was called Battersby Junction by 1878, shortened in 1893 to Battersby. With the introduction of a passenger service in 1861, and the extension of the railway from Stokesley to Castleton, it became a busy junction. By 1865 the line had reached Grosmont, becoming part of the Whitby–Stockton service. The gradual loss of rail traffic in the 1950s left the station lacking its verandah. Unusually, it has first class ladies' and gentlemen's waiting rooms, which were possibly included as the station was often used by shooting guests of Lord de l'Isles and Dudley.

ROSEBERRY FROM NEWTON. №1584

Roseberry Topping

Known as the 'Yorkshire Matterhorn' because of its unusual shape, the 1,057-foot-high Roseberry Topping is a landmark of the northern moors. It lies on the Cleveland border and visitors have scaled its heights to enjoy the views from the sixteenth century according to the dates of the graffiti found carved on its rocks. There is a holy well near its foot, and a hermit once lived in a cave about halfway up. The discovery of ironstone led to extensive mining, which eventually caused the collapse of one side around 1910, resulting in its famous outline.

Great Ayton Railway Station
A busy station scene at Great Ayton, possibly taken in connection with Queen Victoria's Diamond Jubilee. Great Ayton station was constructed some way out of the town, and in 1928 it is known that Robert Minchin operated a 'taxi service' by horse and carriage to and from the station for the price of sixpence. Great Ayton has many connections with the famed explorer James Cook. Postgate School, rebuilt in 1785, which Cook attended, in 1928 became a museum, and on the Green is a statue of Cook as a youth by Nicholas Dimbleby.

Captain Cook's Monument

The 51-foot-high obelisk, raised to the memory of Captain James Cook on Easby Moor, overlooking Great Ayton, can easily be seen from the train. The foundation stone of the Cook monument was laid on the 12 July 1827 by Robert Campion of Whitby, then Lord of the Manor of Easby, who was a great admirer of Cook. The date chosen was highly significant as it was the date of Cook's last voyage, but also the birthday of Mr Campion. On 27 October in the same year, work on erecting this memorial stone to one of Yorkshire's best-known worthies was completed. In the photograph, taken by Frederick L. Stainsby of Middlesbrough, we see work-in-progress during the restoration of 1895. Interestingly, a doorway can be seen on the original monument (right-hand side). On Saturday 9 July 1960, the structure was split from top to bottom when it was struck by a bolt of lightning, and presumably the doorway of the damaged monument was blocked up during this second occasion of repair work following the thunderbolt incident. From Cook's Monument on a clear day you can see the familiar outline of Roseberry Topping.

Great Ayton Church and the Cook House
The explorer James Cook lived in the left-hand cottage above, seen here at Great Ayton, before the right-hand cottage was partially taken down during road widening in 1928. Later, the entire remaining property was removed and shipped to Australia where it was re-erected in 1934 and now forms part of a feature in a memorial park. In the churchyard of All Saints are buried the mother of James Cook and five of her children. It was in this building that the Cook family worshipped, although in their day it had a tower.

Nunthorpe Village and Post Office

Before the coming of the Middlesbrough to Guisborough Railway in 1854, Nunthorpe was a small village on the road from Stokesley to Ormesby. The name comes from the small nunnery that had been relocated here from Hutton near Guisborough. The main centre of population, now close to the station, appears to be ever-expanding with new housing springing up constantly. Unfortunately, the post office, photographed above by Ross, of Whitby, closed a long time ago and is now a private house, the post box remains in the wall.

Marton Village and Station 1907

Above, Marton looking toward the church, on the left is the old Rudds Arms inn. Up until the Second World War, Marton – the birthplace of Captain James Cook – was a rural community. Below, when the Middlesbrough to Guisborough railway was constructed in 1854, a station was constructed where the railway bridged the road from Ormesby to Yard (*below*). Marton station was then a much more substantial affair than its modern counterpart, which is nothing more than a halt today, as indeed are most of the stops from Battersby to Middlesbrough built to serve the new suburbs.

Awa' the Lads! Come on Boro!

As the train crawls into Middlesbrough through now semi-derelict industrial land awaiting development, it is possible to get a close-up view of the new Riverside football stadium, home of the 'Boro' opened in 1997. Above, one of the Boro's most famous players, Wilf Mannion (1918–2000) out on the streets with a group of local lads having a 'kick aboot'. He played 368 times for Middlesbrough scoring 110 goals and was so beloved by the town that they erected a statue to his memory outside the football ground.

Middlesbrough Docks and Dock Clock
Sailing vessels moored in front of
the original clock tower and row of
terraced houses which stood along
Dock Street, c. 1908. Middlesbrough
Dock was designed by Sir William
Cubitt, and opened on 12 May 1842.
When the dock opened the enclosed
water area was 3.6 hectares but further
extensions in 1869, 1886 and 1902
increased this to 10.1 hectares. The
original clock tower was replaced and
the new one was designed by Philip
Webb; however, it has a dual purpose
and contains a hydraulic water pump
to open and close the dock gates.

Middlesbrough, Transporter Bridge

A Transporter Bridge was originally proposed as early as 1872 and, if erected then, it would have been the first of its type in the world. A total of sixteen were built across the globe, of which only seven remain, five still in operation. The bridge was opened on 17 October 1911 by Prince Arthur of Connaught. It cost £87,000 and measures 850 feet long, 225 feet high with a clearance above the water of 177 feet. It is still in regular use today carrying passengers and cars in the manner seen above.

The Transporter Bridge, Middlesborough

Newport Bridge and Middlesbrough Port

Huge bridges to cross the port of Middlesbrough may seem strange today, but in the nineteenth century the river was teeming with industry as seen above. Below is the Newport Ironworks framed by the new Tees Bridge. It was the first vertical-lift bridge to be built in this country, and the heaviest of its type in the world. The lifting span and its counter balance weigh 5,400 tons. The bridge can be raised 99 feet, and the supporting towers are 200 feet high. The bridge, built by Dorman Long, cost £512,000.

NEW TEES BRIDGE
V. HAIG PARRY copyright.

Railway Station, Middlesbrough

Middlesbrough Railway Station

Middlesbrough station was conceived as one of a series of grand public buildings – the NER historian, Tomlinson, called it an 'architectural tribute to the greatness of Middlesbrough'. The new station drew on the example of St Pancras in a number of respects, and set the style for the town's grandest civic essay: the Municipal Buildings of the following decade. The need to cross two flanking roads placed the station well above street level, and the road approach was by a carriage ramp, with shops under the forecourt as at St Pancras.

Middlesbrough Railway Station

Even in this altered state, Middlesbrough station is still a powerful and evocative composition. It works especially well from Albert Road, where one sees the two-storey and attic range of refreshment rooms, with the taller block of the booking hall rising behind, enlivened by the dormer gables of its plate-traceried clerestory windows. From the forecourt one realises that most of the building is actually single storied with a concealed basement. The contract price for the station was £61,981 but the total cost came in at £69,382.40; builders, Shaftoe & Barry of York; ironwork Andrew Handyside, of Derby.

Middlesbrough Station Concourse

The British Railways concourse *c.* 1970 and in 2011; with its concrete vaults, the arch to the right connects with the booking hall. The need to cross two flanking roads placed the station well above street level, and the road approach is up a ramp, with shops under the forecourt as at St Pancras station in London. There were two through platforms, covered by a lofty arched train shed, only 76 feet in span but rising to 60 feet at the crown of the arch. The station was designed by William Peachey and William Cudworth.

Middlesbrough Railway Station

The main entrance to Middlesbrough railway station is approached on a higher level up a carriage ramp, this leads into the booking hall, which sadly is dark and claustrophobic as it is divided into three bays by dark wood partitions seen in the view below looking into the station shop. This is a great pity as the space is vast and open, revealing the hammer beam that supports the roof. The stairs descend into the subway, which takes passengers under the station to other platforms and an exit on the street below.

RAILWAY STATION & ZETLAND ROAD, MIDDLESBROUGH

Middlesbrough Railway Station
A small station was built on this site in 1847, which at that date was far from the town centre. Whilst the advantages of having the station were self-evident, the drawback was that the railway line gradually cut the developing town in two. This view is taken from the junction of Linthorpe Road and Zetland Road about 1904. The station as seen here cost £100,000 to build in 1877. Below, a tile map at Middlesbrough showing the NER rail network in its heyday. Another exists on Whitby station.

NORTH EASTERN RAILWAY.

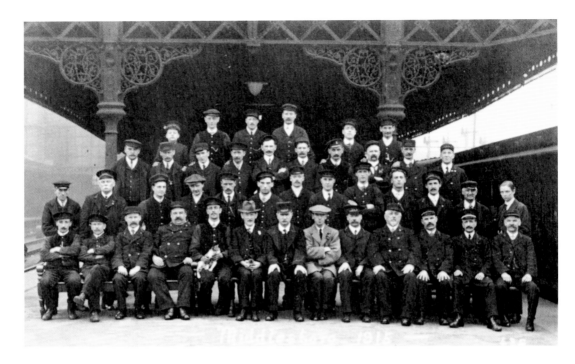

Middlesbrough Railway Station Staff

A group photograph of the Middlesbrough railway staff in 1915, possibly taken on the Up platform of Middlesbrough station, seen below in August 2011. Fifteen years earlier this Victorian cast metalwork was rusted and unkempt; however, it appears that the station in the first decade of the twenty-first century has had a major makeover and we can now admire the delicate and fine workmanship not apparent in the upper photograph. It can also be observed that the canopy has been replaced with one that lets in light.

Bomb Damage at Middlesbrough Station, 1940
The North East was heavily blitzed during both World Wars, but during the Second World War the station itself was severely damaged as a result of enemy action on Bank Holiday Monday, 3 August 1942, when a low-flying Dornier 217 bomber dropped four 500kg bombs. Rebuilding left a much-reduced station. Below, the damage inflicted highlights the construction of the two main roofs and shows the breach in the offices on the north side of the station; also observe that the facing of stone from Forcett and Gayles quarries is applied to a brick carcase.

Albert Bridge, Middlesbrough

The Albert Bridge, named after Prince Albert, husband of Queen Victoria, carries the railway tracks and station over the main Albert Road that links the two halves of Middlesbrough. This too, has had a major renovation and the ironwork is picked out in the patriotic colours of red, white and blue. It is possible to notice that the headroom beneath the bridge is 13 feet 3 inches, which just allows for a double-decker bus to pass safely through.